Tourists with Typewriters

D1550802

FLORIDA STATE
UNIVERSITY LIBRARIES

APR 8 2003

TALLAHASSEE, FLORIDA

Tourists with Typewriters

Critical Reflections on Contemporary Travel Writing

PATRICK HOLLAND AND GRAHAM HUGGAN

ANN ARBOR

The University of Michigan Press

PR
808
·T72
H65
1998

First paperback edition 2000
Copyright © by the University of Michigan 1998
All rights reserved
Published in the United States of America by
The University of Michigan Press
Manufactured in the United States of America
♾ Printed on acid-free paper

2003 2002 2001 2000   5 4 3 2

No part of this publication may be reproduced,
stored in a retrieval system, or transmitted in any form
or by any means, electronic, mechanical, or otherwise,
without the written permission of the publisher.

A CIP catalog record for this book is available from the British Library.

Library of Congress Cataloging-in-Publication Data

Holland, Patrick, 1943–
     Tourists with typewriters : critical reflections on
   contemporary travel writing / Patrick Holland and Graham Huggan.
     p.   cm.
   Includes bibliographical references and index.
   ISBN 0-472-10973-1 (acid-free paper)
   1. Travelers' writings, English—History and criticism. 2.
English prose literature—20th century—History and criticism. 3.
American prose literature—20th century—History and criticism. 4.
Travelers' writings, American—History and criticism. 5. Voyages
and travels—History—20th century—Historiography. 6. Travel in
literature. I. Huggan, Graham, 1958–   II. Title.
PR808.T72   H65   1999
820.9'355—ddc21   98-25512
                                                                        CIP

ISBN 0-472-08706-1 (pbk. : alk. paper)

3 1254 04006 7577

Contents

-- -- -- -- -- -- -- -- -- -- -- -- -- -- -- -- -- --

Preface

There is a moment in Swift's *Gulliver's Travels* (1726), already a satire on travel writing, when the exasperated Gulliver says he can no longer stand to look at another travel book. "I thought," he declares acidly, that

> we were already overstocked with books of travels; that nothing could now pass which was not extraordinary; wherein I doubted some authors less consulted truth than their own vanity, or interest, or the diversion of ignorant readers. (161–62)

Two centuries later, the situation can hardly be said—according to some—to have improved. Paul Fussell, for example, in his 1980 study of interwar British travel writing, *Abroad,* complains that the genre has become a haven for "second-rate [literary] talents" (212). In his 1955 classic *Tristes Tropiques,* the French structural anthropologist Claude Lévi-Strauss words it rather more strongly:

> Amazonia, Tibet, and Africa fill the bookshops in the form of travelogues, accounts of expeditions and collections of photographs, in all of which the desire to impress is so dominant as to make it impossible for the reader to assess the value of the evidence put before him. Instead of having his critical faculties stimulated, he asks for more of such pabulum and swallows prodigious quantities of it. (17)

These criticisms, while ironic (Swift) or open to question (Fussell, Lévi-Strauss), are by no means exceptional. Travel writing, as a genre, has always had a mixed reception, being seen by some as essentially frivolous or even morally dangerous. But the genre has proven remarkably immune to even the harshest criticisms, becoming one of the most popular and widely read forms of literature today. Travel writers have always had a knack, in any case, of capitalizing on negative publicity; sensation mongering might be anathema to their critics, but it is integral to their genre.

Nonetheless, suspicions persist as to the worthiness of travel writing as a serious subject. Academics have "discovered" it, only in most cases to move beyond it, preferring either to intellectualize it as so many discourses of displacement or to focus on the canonized writers, most of them from earlier periods. An in-depth study of contemporary travel writing as a *popular* phenomenon remains to be undertaken; this book does not aim to fill that gap so much as to show its continuing presence. The popularity of travel writing is itself a subject for discussion. The sales figures certainly indicate sometimes spectacular commercial success. Yet the most successful travel books are arguably those, like Mayle's or Bryson's or even Chatwin's, that identify a middle-class readership and then pander skillfully to its whims. With the global spread of tourism, travel writing—like travel itself—has been made available to a wider audience; but some of the best-known writers (and, as will be seen, many of the others) often seem to *react* against this democratizing process. The much-touted distinction between travelers and tourists is symptomatic—as if contemporary travel writers, always likely to pride themselves on being individualists, were still (ironically?) conscious of separating themselves from the vulgar herd. In this sense, to speak of the popularity of travel writing may be misleading; for while it is certainly true that travel narratives are being read by more people than ever, they remain to some extent a refuge for complacent, even nostalgically retrograde, middle-class values.

Travel writing calls out, then, for a sustained critical analysis: one that looks at travel writers as retailers of mostly white, male, middle-class, heterosexual myths and prejudices, and at their readers as eager consumers of exotic—culturally "othered"—goods. This book joins recent studies that adopt a critical approach to travel writing (Mary Louise Pratt's *Imperial Eyes,* Dennis Porter's *Haunted Journeys,* David Spurr's *The Rhetoric of Empire,* and several others), while focusing to a greater extent on contemporary "specialists" in the genre (Chatwin, Theroux, Naipaul, Morris, Bowles, etc.). Its thesis, unsurprisingly perhaps, is that travel writing frequently provides an effective alibi for the perpetuation or reinstallment of ethnocentrically superior attitudes to "other" cultures, peoples, and places. This thesis is complicated, though, by the defamiliarizing capacities of travel writing, and by its attempts, keeping pace with change, to adjust its sights to new perceptions—both of "other" cultures and places and of the writer's and reader's perceiving culture. Travel writing, as is now acknowledged, belongs to a wider structure of representation within which cultural affiliations and links—culture itself—can be analyzed, questioned, and reassessed. Travel has recently emerged as a crucial epistemological category for the displacement of normative values and homogenizing, essentialist views (Said, Clifford, C. Kaplan). The ubiquitousness of "traveling theory" is a sign no doubt that the world, as it opens up to physical movement, requires its citizens to account conceptually for migrating peoples, goods, and ideas. Yet this will to theorize also indicates a utopian impulse that is arguably the product, not of the world itself but of a "worldly" intellectual elite. Further, traveling theory risks once more eliding travel *writing,* emphasizing often highly intellectualized metaphors of movement at the expense of more prosaic but nonetheless powerful myths of place. This book seeks to turn the tables on the hypertheorization of travel-as-displacement without falling back on its opposite, the naively untheorized celebration of travel-as-freedom. It occupies a middle ground, then, between travel writing as a more or less elaborate textual performance (Butor) and as an economically sanctioned activity, a circumscribed material practice (Pratt). Emphasized here are the privileges that accrue to the (Western) traveler-writer: privileges due in part of course to sometimes crude economic advantage, but also in part to more sophisticated techniques of rhetorical control.

The traveler-writers scrutinized here do not all share the same degree of privilege; nor do they all share the same cultural background or similar (neo)imperialist views. It would be as foolish to claim of travel writing that it is uniformly imperialistic as it would be to defend travel writers as being harmless entertainers. Yet travel writing, however defined, is not an antidote to travel; it, too, is a form of—potentially positive, as well as conspicuously negative—*interference.* This book seeks to examine the "interfering" aspects of travel writing: its capacity both to fuel the expansionist ambitions of modern tourism and, at its best, to intervene in and challenge received ideas on cultural difference. There are obvious lacunae here. For one, what is the audience, or constituency, of travel writing? A detailed study of travel writing's by no means uniform readership needs to be written, taking its cue perhaps from Janice Radway's work on the reception of literary romance. A comprehensive industry analysis of the travel-writing business would also be useful, assessing to a greater extent than has been possible here the role of the "nonfictional" guidebook and of the various multimedia advertising vehicles that serve the global tourist trade. These and other projects lie outside this book's itinerary, although the ground it covers will hopefully open up further avenues of exploration.

This book offers instead an introductory critical survey, alerting the reader—both specialist and not—to contemporary modes of travel writing, as well as to staple elements that are continuous with earlier forms of textual practice. The field of travel writing is, of course, an impossibly large one—which might account for the book's self-consciously eclectic methods. Nonetheless, its selection principles, while tending toward encyclopedism, are likely to strike some readers as being worryingly random. Perhaps the book, in this sense, might be considered guilty of an imitative fallacy, insofar as it provides a guided tour of—a metacommentary on—its subject. Yet what surveys such as this one lack in a clearly focused argument, they gain in covering issues that, broad in themselves, are interlinked. Some of these overlapping issues might be briefly sketched as follows: What *is* travel writing, and can it be seen as a distinctive genre? How are definitions of travel and travel writing inflected by gender and influenced by particulars of cultural history and social class? What might a taxonomy of contemporary travel narratives look like, and how might it tally with travel writing's inventory of spatialized cultural myths? How has travel writing adjusted—or not—to contemporary realities, inserting itself into the late-twentieth-century discourses of postcolonialism and postmodernism, and addressing itself to new technologies and the global crises of the moment: overpopulation, scarcity, AIDS? Has the genre managed in the process to liberate itself and its practitioners from Empire, or is it still primarily a legacy of imperial modes of vision and thought? Is travel writing best seen as an agent of (Western) cultural domination, or might it rather be seen as transgressive, an instrument of self-critique? Where can travel writing go from here; what is in store for its future? Is it possible, in a genre much given to repetition, to come up with anything new?

All of these questions are essayed, if hardly answered, in this study. Introductory as it is, it makes no claim to be comprehensive. It might even seem at times to be as impressionistic as the impressionism it denounces—maybe that is an occupational hazard of all relatively unhistoricized books. Its aim, however, is to draw in most of the major contemporary writers in the field: a field constituted for its purposes as being predominantly Anglophone; and still primarily white, male, heterosexual, middle class. The book focuses on recent prose narratives (it has no place, alas, for drama or poetry) written after the Second World War—mainly after the sixties—by writers who see themselves for the most part as specialists in the genre. The genre itself, which is notoriously refractory to definition, is not widened out here into the novel (with a couple of defensible exceptions) or the putatively nonfictional guidebook. The narratives studied here are designed, by and large, as *literary* artifacts, mediating between fact and fiction, autobiography and ethnography, and combining—often with a whimsical self-consciousness and an awareness of the temptations of fraudulence—a number of academic disciplines, literary categories, and social codes. Close readings of texts selected, not so much for their "representativeness" as for their relevance to central arguments, are placed alongside discussions of the wider issues they raise: power and self-perception, cultural representation and imagination, as well as the changing role of travel and travel writing in the late twentieth century. Travel writing, in our view, deserves to develop as a genre; after all, it is a significant and, at its best, effective medium for the global circulation of (trans)cultural information. This book assesses the extent to which it *has* developed in the last few decades, and speculates as to the possibility of further developments in the future.

The introduction frames these developments by launching a preliminary inquiry into the status of travel writing as a literary/cultural form. Travel writing emerges as a practiced art of dissimulation, conscious of itself as at once generically elusive and empirically disingenuous, deliberately dissembling, unclear. Travel narratives, like their writers, tend to conceal as much as they reveal: their "factual" disclosures are screens for cannily structured fictions, and their personal confessions masks for motivational doubts and fears. One source of anxiety here is the awareness of complicity; for travel writers obviously participate in the tourist industry they claim to scorn. Another is the awareness of belatedness; for travel writers, equally obviously, hearken back to their precursors, seeking solace for a troubled present in nostalgic cultural myths.

The anxieties of traveler-writers, often linked to a sense of threatened cultural origins, vie with the pleasures of curiosity for new experiences of place. In chapter 1, these competing pulls are seen through the eyes of the "English gentleman": a rhetorical device used, mostly ironically, by several contemporary British travel writers as a means of reinstalling a mythicized imperial past. The second part of the chapter acts as a counterweight to this model, looking at travel writing's status in the age of "postcoloniality," and assessing its effectiveness as an instrument of imperial critique.

Chapter 2 furthers this argument through a detailed study of the myths of place through which current travel writers articulate their own, and reexpress other, staged (mis)encounters. "The Orient" and "the tropics"; "the South Seas" and "the Arctic": these are the topoi placed under scrutiny in this chapter. Each topos lends itself to prevalent modes of imperialist nostalgia and to atavistic stereotypes about originary cultural states; but the chapter also looks at how new mythologies have evolved, adjusting themselves to modern realities— emigration, media imperialism, transculturation, AIDS—and addressing themselves to an audience well attuned to (trans)national politics and to the complex global circuitry of the information age.

Chapter 3 is an inquiry into travel writing's transgressive potential, focusing on its capacity to analyze and transform gender perception and on the outlet it provides for sexual play and queer performativity. The first half of the chapter deals more specifically with women's travel writing, assessing the limits of its usefulness as a tool of feminist critique, and showing how the metaphor of travel itself is deeply gendered, shot through with presuppositions that potentially reinforce male privilege. The second half of the chapter examines the role of travel writing in reconstituting the gendered subject. It analyzes the discourses of gay liberation and queer performance, revising current perceptions of the (male) traveler's transgressive license and bringing these into line with the "queering" of (post)modern heterosexual culture.

Chapter 4, finally, brings the study right up to the present. It undertakes a further inquiry into the discourses of postcolonialism and postmodernism—arguably, the conceptual cornerstones of contemporary Western culture—and shows how travel writing in the late twentieth century has both responded to and reacted against its own condition of belatedness. The first half of the chapter deals in part with the impact of the electronic media on travel writing, and with the different modes of travel writing—virtual, hyperreal, and so on—that have evolved to meet the demands of an information-saturated society. The second half of the chapter also looks at new forms of travel writing: those that have affiliated themselves with the so-called New Age movement, and with the ecological principles on which certain strands of responsible tourism are currently seeking to remodel themselves in the interests of a "greener" future.

These chapters are followed by a brief reflective postscript. Balancing travel writing on the knife-edge of the new millennium, this postscript both looks back at the recent history of travel writing, gauging its dominant patterns, and looks forward to the directions that the genre might take in the future.

Tourists with Typewriters offers a series of reflections on its subject that, while largely unpolemical, are in the spirit of critique. It deviates, for example, from the commonly held view that travel writing upholds freedom, arguing instead that it can be seen—though not exclusively—as an imperialist discourse through which dominant cultures (white, male, Euro-American, middle-class) seek to ingratiate themselves, often at others' expense. Travel writing, though, has another side, and this too will be studied. For travel writers, as unreliable documenters of other people and cultures, have always had a say in the critical reassessment of their own. Travel writing, after all, is a valuable medium of estrangement, even if it operates all too frequently through familiar stereotypes and myths. This book examines the strategies by which contemporary travel writers attempt to persuade us that the worlds—often mythical ones—they describe are real. But it also explores the ways in which these writers address our own world, giving us access to cultural regions that, though "discovered," remain mysterious to us, or making strange those very territories, and the values and attitudes we ascribe to them, that we might imagine to be most familiar, the closest to our own experience. (It should be clear from this that the book is addressed primarily to a Western readership, although from a perspective that is often critical of the pretensions of "the West.") Travel writing, in this last sense, can be seen as a useful vehicle of cultural self-perception; as a barometer for changing views on other ("foreign," "non-Western") cultures; and as a trigger for the informational circuits that tap us in to the wider world. Travel writing, traditionally seen as affording a license for escapism, may yet show its readers the limits of their ambition and remind them of their responsibilities.

This book, then, makes a pitch for the ethical value of travel writing, even as it demonstrates that travel narratives are unreliable in the extreme. The book's title—deliberately glib—sets out to capture the contradictions that are inherent in this most hybrid and unassimilable of literary genres. As will be seen, many current travel writers like to see themselves as anachronistic, taking rhetorical advantage of their own imagined obsolescence. (Few, of course, are prepared to view themselves as being tourists, even though the advantages they reap here are all too palpable, all too real.) But "tourists with typewriters," while an appealing (self-)designation, is potentially misleading. Travel writers, as cultural commentators, are capable of trading places; by a rhetorical sleight of hand, they may appear as both behind the times and up to date. This book aims to negotiate some of these apparent contradictions, gauging the ironies of its attention-grabbing material—and its title.

Tourists with Typewriters, in keeping with its subject, has proven over the years to be something of a vexed itinerary. We would like to thank the many people along the way who have entered into the panic, but have also helped to heighten the pleasure, of this collaborative book. Among these are the following: Christine Bold, Diana Brydon, Larry Buell, Scott Couling, Vivienne Denton, Charitini Douvaldzi, Jonathon Eastcott, Tony Eprail, LeAnn Fields, Robert Fleet, Ian Goldring, Michael Gorra, Derek Gregory, James Harrison, Melissa Holcombe, Dorothy Holland, Michael Holland, Malcolm Imrie, Akash Kapur, Alja Kooistra, Suzy Lake, Camille Lizarribar, Shelley MacDonald, Patricia Merivale, Donna Pennee, Martin Roberts, Tim Youngs, and Gwen Wheeler. Our special thanks to our readers at the University of Michigan Press, who suggested changes that were essential to the current format of the book, and to Dorothy Hadfield who compiled its index. Thanks finally to all our students, of years past and present, at the University of Guelph and Harvard University, whose ideas and enthusiasm were crucial throughout the reading and writing process. Part of chapter I appears as Graham Huggan's "Travel Writing, (Post)colonialism, and the Production of Exotic Space," which was submitted in a different form to the collection *Colonialism, Postcolonialism and the Production of Space,* edited by Daniel Clayton and Derek Gregory for Blackwell (Oxford). Thanks to the editors and publisher for their permission to reprint material here.

Introduction

Travel Writing Today

"I do not expect to see many travel books in the near future," wrote Evelyn Waugh at the end of the Second World War: "Never again . . . shall we land on foreign soil with letter of credit and passport . . . and feel the world wide open to us" (*When the Going Was Good* 11). But Waugh, as it turned out, was seriously underestimating the resilience of travelers, and of the worldwide network—the business—that continues to support their enterprise. Travel and its literary by-product, the travel book, have a habit of justifying their continuation by anticipating their own decline; and if the postwar traveler lives, as Mark Cocker believes, "in fear of modernity's encroachment" (259), then that fear might well result in the publication of another book. Travel writing today is, like its subject, very much a going concern. Sales figures are good, with one or two best-sellers. Recent examples here include Peter Mayle's nostalgic memoir *A Year in Provence* (1989), which has sold over a million copies, been translated into seventeen languages, and been converted into a popular British TV serial; Paul Theroux's sardonic travel narratives, several of which have featured on the *New York Times* best-sellers' lists, making their author one of the best-known contemporary literary figures in America; and the highly successful Random House *Vintage Departures* series, which boasts about sixty current titles, and which has enjoyed a steady expansion since its inception in the mid-1980s. The shelves in the travel section of the big bookstores are well stocked; top newspapers in the United Kingdom, United States, and elsewhere feature thriving travel supplements; specialist magazines such as *Granta* (in Britain) and *Condé Nast Traveler* (in the United States) are reporting increased sales, while *National Geographic,* in a flurry of publicity, has celebrated its hundredth year;

travel vehicles (TV programs and commercials, films, videos, etc.) proliferate in the visual media; surrogate travel is available through the
Internet and what Martin Roberts calls the "global culture industries"
(world literature, world cinema, world music, etc.);[1] and academic
interest, too, is growing, with the publication of influential critical
studies such as Dennis Porter's *Haunted Journeys* (1991), Eric Leed's
The Mind of the Traveler (1991), and Mary Louise Pratt's *Imperial Eyes*
(1992), and the attempt to analyze the metaphorical implications of
travel as an analogue for different forms of intellectual and cultural
displacement in the age of globalization (Edward Said, "Traveling
Theory" [1983]; James Clifford, "Traveling Cultures" [1992]; Robertson et al., eds., *Travellers' Tales* [1994]).

Why the current boom in travel writing? One of the reasons is obvious: there is a greater degree of mobility in the world than ever before—
a greater movement of ideas, goods, peoples; and an increasing accessi-
bility to previously remote parts of the world owing to cheaper travel
and the unprecedented expansion of worldwide transportation net-
works. Another reason, however, is diametrically opposed to this one:
for those same globalizing processes that have helped make the world
more accessible have also arguably made it less exciting, less diverse.
The travel literature industry—and in this should be included both
literary-minded travel narratives and more information-oriented travelogues and guidebooks—has been quick to cash in on Westerners'
growing fears of homogenization, promoting its products as thrilling
alternatives to the sanitized spectacles of mass tourism; as evidence that
the world is still heterogeneous, unfathomable, bewildering; as proof
that the spirit of adventure can hold off the threat of exhaustion. In this
sense, the travel (literature) business has capitalized on, while contributing to, a new *exotic:* a celebration of the modern spectacle of
global cultural diversity that flies in the face of the very agency—the
universal market of mass tourism—that does most to make such a spectacle, and its literary representation, possible.[2]

It is no surprise to find, then, in a number of contemporary travel
narratives, a heated defense of the conventional traveler/tourist distinction.[3] The distinction is, of course, highly specious: travelers,
unlike tourists, are "nonexploitative" visitors, motivated not by the
lazy desire for instant entertainment but by the hard-won battle to satisfy their insatiable curiosity about other countries and peoples. As
Dean MacCannell and, more recently, James Buzard have demonstrated convincingly, this distinction has been manipulated by the

tourist industry to serve its own commercial ends. For MacCannell, travelers' seemingly plaintive need to dissociate themselves from "mere" tourists functions as a strategy of self-exemption, whereby they displace their guilt for interfering with, and adversely changing, the cultures through which they travel onto tourists; see themselves as contributing toward the well-being of those cultures rather than as exploiting them for their own benefit; and view themselves as open-minded inquirers rather than as pleasure-seeking guests. The tourist industry profits from this rhetoric of moral superiority (MacCannell), using it to lure the adventure-minded traveler onto an alternative beaten track (Buzard). To see travel as merely another form of tourism is to recognize the increasing commodification of place; what travel writers offer in this context is not an insight into the "real," but a countercommodified version of what they take to be reality.[4] The critical potential of travel writing—its capacity to expose and attack the invasive practices of mass tourism—is further diminished when it is recognized, not as an out-and-out opponent of tourism, but as a valuable adjunct to it. The armchair curiosity that Paul Fussell, among others, has seen as an inducement to read travel narratives should by no means be thought of as *replacing* the urge to travel; rather, travel writing sells while also helping to sell holidays. Nor are travel writers necessarily averse to taking their cut. Is it too cynical to suggest that many of today's travel writers are motivated less by the universal imperative of cultural inquiry than they are by the far more urgent need for another commission? Travel writing still remains lucrative only for a handful of recognized writers; many others ply a more moderate trade in largely part-time journalism. Nonetheless, contemporary travel writers, whatever their status or their institutional affiliation, are continuing to provide sterling service to tourism—about to become the world's largest industry—even when they might imagine themselves to be its most strident adversaries.

Clearly, not all travel writers are alike (nor, for that matter, are all tourists). To see contemporary travel writers *merely* as touristic scribes—as latter-day tourists with typewriters—is to fail to recognize their efforts to reexplore regions of the world that, although "discovered," remain unfamiliar, or to revive interest in familiar places, now seen from a fresh, informed perspective. It is also to underestimate the unsettling effects produced by travel writing: its ability to jolt its readers out of complacent beliefs and attitudes, and its challenge to prevailing stereotypes and cultural myths of place. Finally, it is to miss the crucial role played by travel narratives in interrogating the "stability" of the cultural subject—a role made more conspicuous, to be sure, in the age of postmodernity, but one that is evident throughout the history of travel writing, which shows a tendency to blur the lines between "true" and "false," documentation and fabrication, and to investigate forms of "otherness"—both biological and culturally coded—that alternately confirm and question the position of the investigating subject.

Travel writing can arguably be seen, then, as having transgressive potential: in allowing the writer to flout conventions that exist within his/her own society, it subjects those conventions—those often rigid codes of behavior—to close critical scrutiny. Examples here are the continuing usefulness of travel writing to women writers, who avail themselves of the freedoms of travel in order to celebrate their own independence, as well as to reassess the powerful myths surrounding a history of male exploration; and to postcolonial writers, whose travel narratives, charting changes in the geopolitical landscape of what is as much a *neo*imperial as a postimperial age, demonstrate at the same time the complicity between travel writing and the very (cultural) imperialist attitudes it often claims to resist. The patriarchal and imperialist undertones of travel writing—expertly analyzed by critics such as Mary Louise Pratt, Sara Mills, David Spurr, Tim Youngs, and, most recently, Inderpal Grewal—suggest that an uncritical view of travel writing as a celebration of human freedom needs to be adjusted to the modern realities of class, race, and gender privilege. In his recent study of modern British travel writing, Mark Cocker remarks, "In journeys we discover all over again the newness of the world. . . . travel is one of the greatest doors to human freedom, and the travel book is a medium through which humans celebrate this freedom" (260). This begs the question of who "we" are: who are such freedom's beneficiaries?[5] Clearly, the freedom of travel writers is not the freedom of all: it is the privilege of mobility that allows them to travel, and to write. Indeed, travel writing, like travel itself, is apt to claim its freedom at others' expense; in so doing, it sometimes betrays an attitude of cultural suprematism that has led critics less charitable than Cocker to see it as an agent of imperial dominance. In the nineteenth century, says Martin Green, travel narratives were among a plethora of adventure tales that energized the myth of Empire: they reinforced prevailing notions that the world was ripe to conquer. Their twentieth-century counterparts might be, by and large, more sensitive to their privilege, but as Charles Sugnet, among others, has argued, many twentieth-century travel writers still arrogate the rights of mobility and representation that once accrued to Empire. In a postcolonial world, they thus fight a rearguard action, concealing beneath their patronizing language and their persistent cultural nostalgia a thinly disguised desire to resurrect the imperial past. Sugnet, in his diatribe against the British magazine *Granta,* pulls no punches: its travel articles are designed to "restore the lost dream of empire in a way that allows young-fogy readers to pretend that they're still living in the nineteenth century. . . . A curious fusion of the 1880s and the 1980s is what keeps all those *Granta* travel writers up in the air, afloat over various parts of the globe, their luggage filled with portable shards of colonialist discourse" (85).

Sugnet's argument, in the nature of polemics, is boisterously hyperbolic; its effect is reduced by his failure to account for contemporary travel writing's ubiquitous self-irony: its awareness of its own belatedness (a point to which we shall return). Nonetheless, Sugnet's frontal attack reminds us that travel narratives have proved remarkably effective over time in (re)producing the "foreign" world as an object of Western knowledge (Pratt 5). At best, says Dennis Porter, travel narratives "[have] been an effort to overcome cultural distance through a protracted act of understanding. At worst, [they have] been a vehicle for the expression of Eurocentric conceit or racist intolerance" (3). In either case, travel writing tends to reinforce the authority of its predominantly metropolitan readership; its world of wonders is, in one sense, a world already known—one made available to readers "back home" through the comforting reiteration of familiar exotic myths. (Exoticism is precisely the mechanism for this process of retrieval, a means by which the "otherness" of the foreign world can be assimilated, and its threatening difference defused by taking on a familiar cast.) It is here that travel writing, for all its transgressive potential and vaunted claims to see the world anew, looks suspiciously conformist. "Home," after all, is the frame of reference for most contemporary travel writers (even when it is precisely the category of "home" that their writing calls in question).[6] Their experiences of travel are predicated on the possibility of return; their adventure trips are round trips. And their vocabulary frequently reflects the security of a shared culture; in this sense many travel writers, in spite of their cultivated eccentricities and assertive individualism, operate within a readily identifiable semantic field. Travel writing in the late twentieth century continues to be haunted by the specter of cliché: its catalogs of anomalies are often recorded in remarkably similar terms. The same words and phrases crop up again and again, the same myths and stereotypes, the same literary analogies. One begins after a while even to recognize the same faces. Indeed, there is a genteel clubbability about many contemporary travel writers—particularly British ones—that belies their apparent commitment to iconoclasm and adventure. Nor is the mutual backslapping confined to cross-quotation: among the writers under scrutiny here, Newby encounters Thesiger "in the flesh" in the wilds of Nuristan; Morris bumps into Raban in Cairo; Chatwin collaborates with Theroux on Patagonia (and also borrows Leigh Fermor's house in Greece); even the chronically displaced Trinidadian Naipaul seems to wish to reincarnate himself as a post-Edwardian Englishman.

The anachronistic ideals of (English) gentlemanliness are at work behind many of the writers whose work is featured in this book: ideals that, though often parodied, are still likely to attest to the traveler's honesty and courage, his sense of fair play. (This might account for the outrage some of the writers express when they are confronted with others' deceptions.) But it is the capacity for self-deprecation that most marks the gentleman's progress: an indication not only that he doesn't take himself too seriously, but that we shouldn't take him too seriously either. The impulse to trivialize is behind much contemporary travel writing, from the camp affectations of Chatwin and Barthes to the buffoonery of Cahill and O'Hanlon. The foppishness of some of these writers, who tend to make light of their misadventures, provides a useful alibi for their cultural gaffes and, at times, their arrogance; it also affords a reminder that their often dubious pronouncements about people and cultures are only the opinions of an enthusiastic amateur. The traveler-writer, in this context, contrives to masquerade as a faux naïf; his/her narrative is content to bask in an atmosphere of cheerful superficiality. (The reality is, of course, more complex; and it is no surprise to find that several of these writers—O'Hanlon, for example—are bona fide scientists.)

Obviously, not all travel narratives are given to such indulgence: the gentleman traveler is only one of many possible personas. Nonetheless, this figure, and the irony with which it is treated, is instructive. For the cult of gentlemanliness in contemporary Anglophone travel writing is both a throwback to another era and an ironic recognition that this era, and the values for which it stands, are now long gone. Self-parody, in this context, demonstrates the awareness of belatedness—an awareness that inevitably reminds contemporary travel writers of their own limitations.[7] It is an axiom of recent travel writing that writers offer tribute to their predecessors, homage often paid in adulatory terms. Contemporary travel writers thus consciously place themselves in a tradition—a tradition as much literary as historically based. Nor need these predecessors, literary or historical, have actually traveled; for travel writers are fascinated, rather, by the imaginative texture of place—the process by which places and their inhabitants are shaped and reshaped by (literary) myth. In paying their statutory respects to previous writers and travelers, contemporary travel writers realize that their own endeavors have come too late; it rests for them to emulate what others before them have achieved. Hence their weakness for self-parody: their tendency to view themselves as pale imitations of their distinguished forebears. However, the consideration of their own insufficiencies is less likely to cause them anxiety than it is to cause amusement. Self-irony also affords a useful strategy of self-protection—as if the writer, in revealing his/her faults, might be relieved of social responsibilities. Some travel writers, hiding behind the mask of escapist explorer-adventurers, or lurching from one disaster to the next for the delectation of their readers, are reluctant to be held accountable for their gauche but "inoffensive" actions. Others, quick to moralize about the ills of other cultures, exempt themselves from complicity in the cultural processes they describe. One strategy of self-exemption is to claim a cool detachment—as if travel writers were neutral observers of the places they visit. Another strategy is for the writer to designate himself or herself as an eccentric—as if eccentricity excused mistakes usually based on cultural ignorance. The most frequent strategy, however, is to assume a variety of disguises. In their self-presentation, travel writers are often extremely elusive, shifting roles with the same facility as they move from place to place. Now the pedagogue, now the clown; now the traveler, now (even) the tourist. They manage, thus, to benefit from alternative temporary privileges, one moment taking advantage of an honorary insider's knowledge, the next taking refuge in a foreigner's convenient incomprehension.

This manipulation of roles is one of the skills of travel writing; to condemn the travel writer for one form or other of artful dodgery is to forget that the genre has a long history a license—of entertaining fraud. The ambiguity surrounding travel narratives—the uncertainty, at given moments, of whether the writer is telling us the truth—is part of their appeal; the stories they tell are no less compelling if they happen to be mendacious. It is worth remembering, though, that travel writing, however entertaining, is hardly harmless, and that behind its apparent innocuousness and its charmingly anecdotal observations lies a series of powerfully distorting myths about other (often, "non-Western") cultures. To see travel writing in its current format as merely a vehicle for cultural prejudice is to overlook the genre's significant impact as an instrument of cultural critique. (Travel *is,* after all, at least potentially a learning experience: a means of testing, and then revising, the traveler's cultural expectations.) Nonetheless, travel writing shares some of the problems of its poor relation, tourism. Travelers *are* tourists, although of an independent breed, and the thrills and spills described in travel narratives, if different in kind and spirit from the organized pleasures of the much-derided "package trip," still provide their readers with the manufactured wonders, not to mention the scandals, of surrogate tourism. Travel writing, like tourism, generates nostalgia for other times and places, even as it recognizes that they may by now have "lost" their romantic aura.[8] Contemporary travel writing tends to be self-conscious—self-ironic—about such losses: it is both nostalgic and, at its best, aware of the deceptiveness of nostalgia. Yet if the tourist industry cynically dresses its expansionist designs in a rhetoric of lost innocence—as "other" places are destroyed, other "others" duly emerge to take their place—the travel writer is more than a shocked witness to this self-perpetuating process. Travel writers, and their readers, participate in global tourism: they contribute, if indirectly, to both its benefits and its worst excesses. So Waugh is right, after all, in believing that a certain approach to travel and the travel book is no longer possible: the one that cries foul at tourism and expects, in turn, to go unpunished.

FACTUAL FICTIONS

But what, exactly, *is* a travel book? By which criteria should it be judged? Who qualifies as a travel writer? And more specifically, who merits inclusion in a study of this kind? Travel writing, it need hardly be said, is hard to define, not least because it is a hybrid genre that straddles categories and disciplines. Travel narratives run from picaresque adventure to philosophical treatise, political commentary, ecological parable, and spiritual quest. They borrow freely from history, geography, anthropology, and social science, often demonstrating great erudition, but without seeing fit to respect the rules that govern conventional scholarship. Irredeemably opinionated, travel writers avail themselves of the several licenses that are granted to a form that freely mixes fact and fable, anecdote and analysis. Not least of these is the license to exaggerate, or even to invent: as Percy Adams says in his entertaining survey, travel writers are under no obligation to tell their readers the truth; instead, they are often practiced liars "infested with the itch to tell wonderful stories" or, in some cases, "inflicted with the desire to tell lies 'of a darker complexion'" (5). Not all travel writers, of course, are liars; among the contemporary figures, Peter Matthiessen and Barry Lopez would be upset at the allegation, and even tricksters, such as (the late) Bruce Chatwin, would defend their selective use of facts. Travel writing is best seen, then, as a "mediation between fact and fiction" (Fussell), referring to actual people, places, and events as the writer encounters them, but freely interspersing these with stories that are often of dubious provenance or derive from mythical or fictitious sources.

But what, again, is a travel book? Perhaps it is better to begin by defining what it is not. Travel books, says Paul Fussell, referring to the fully fashioned literary works that are the objects of his study, are to be distinguished initially from guidebooks, which

> are not autobiographical and are not sustained by a narrative exploiting the devices of fiction. A guide book is addressed to those who plan to follow the traveler, doing what he has done, but more selectively. A travel book, at its purest, is addressed to those who do not plan to follow the traveler at all, but who require the exotic anomalies, wonders, and scandals of the literary form *romance* which their own place or time cannot entirely supply. (203)

Fussell's distinction is a useful one, although it begs important questions. For example, cannot certain travel books be used, precisely, as guidebooks—is it not possible to combine the aesthetic and ideological functions of the "travel book" with the pragmatic function of the "guide"? (On a recent visit to Patagonia, one of the present authors noticed several fellow travelers using Chatwin's *In Patagonia* as a guide. Clearly, the "exotic anomalies" provided in plenty by Chatwin's narrative had not prevented its readers from checking out the terrain for themselves.) As argued earlier, travel books do not necessarily act as substitutes for actual travel; on the contrary, they may often function as its catalyzing agents.

Fussell's next distinction proves to be equally problematic: Travel books, he claims in a valiant attempt to reach a provisional definition,

> are a sub-species of memoir in which the autobiographical narrative arises from the speaker's encounter with distant or unfamiliar data, and in which the narrative—unlike that in a novel or a romance—claims literal validity by constant reference to actuality. (203)

Fussell's formulation is admirably neat, but it suffers again from simplification. Both novels and romances can make frequent, detailed "reference to actuality" without necessarily seeming less fictive or claiming "literal validity." The rise of the novel, indeed—if Ian Watt's influential thesis is to be accepted—depended on the rearrangement and embellishment of "authentic" information: on the attempt both to (re)present and to satirize "recorded facts."[9]

Fussell comes closer when he refers, via Frye, to travel narratives as displaced romances, distinguishing here between the picaresque mode of comic misadventure and the pastoral mode of contemplation and elegiac reverie (206, 209–10). These modes are certainly relevant to many (contemporary) travel narratives, as is their displacement, less through a reworking of the "original" literary forms than through an ironic juxtaposition of their usual components. In a contemporary travel narrative like, for instance, Chatwin's aforementioned *In Patagonia,* the reader is continually shuttled between alternative modes and registers, so that the hybrid work that accumulates from these various stylistic fragments starts to resemble, oxymoronically, a contemplative picaresque elegy or a rollicking pastoral adventure.

The formal approach to travel writing risks running aground on these definitional inconsistencies, and on the seeming determination of the genre to fly in the face of traditional boundaries. A more fruitful approach, perhaps, is that which sees travel writing as occupying a space of discursive conflict. Travel narratives, in this context, are examples of what Hayden White calls "fictions of factual representation": they claim validity—or make as if to claim it—by referring to actual events and places, but then assimilate those events and places to a highly personal vision.[10] Travel writing thus charts the tension between the writers' compulsion to report the world they see and their often repressed desire to make the world conform to their preconception of it. (Take the observations, discussed in this book, of Naipaul in India or Iyer in Japan, observations that miraculously conform to a cultural "essence" each writer believes he has discovered. In this sense, there is something Socratic about the inquiries made by many travel writers: they seek after "truths" they imagine they already have in their possession.)

The subjectivity of travel writing might be seen, in this sense, as a form of willful interference: it is not that travel writers try to veil their personal interpretation but, on the contrary, that they impose it on their putative reportage. Like certain forms of investigative journalism—another member of the genre's extended family—travel writing enjoys an intermediary status between subjective inquiry and objective documentation. In his book on Naipaul's travel writing, Rob Nixon similarly identifies travel literature as a polyvalent genre that alternates between "a semi-ethnographic, distanced, analytic mode" and "an autobiographical, emotionally tangled mode" (15). What is most characteristic about Naipaul's travel writing, according to Nixon, is the way it negotiates the slippage between these two modes in order to maximize the writer's discursive authority. Hence the paradox, previously mentioned, of travel writers' amateur expertise: they may back up their opinions by appealing in some manner or other to the rigors of science, but they usually fall short of allowing science to cramp their personal style.

Nixon's observation raises the more specific question of the indebtedness of travel writing to ethnography. As Valerie Wheeler, among others, has noted, travelers and anthropologists have more in common than is usually supposed:

> Both traveler and anthropologist are strangers who deliver the exotic to an audience unlikely to follow them to the place they have visited, but likely perhaps to follow their explorations of them. In neither case is the account written for the people or places experienced, but for person and profession. (52)[11]

In this context, travel writing and ethnography differ primarily in emphasis. Travel writing is self-consciously autobiographical, intentionally anecdotal, and (in some cases) deliberately ethnocentric, whereas ethnography has tended until recently to play down the personality of its author, to substitute scientific for anecdotal information, and to critique ethnocentric assumptions behind the study and description of "foreign cultures" while remaining aware at the same time of its own prejudices and biases. But distinctions between travel writing and ethnography remain, at best, problematic; and while anthropologists have sometimes made concerted attempts to dissociate themselves from travelers—Lévi-Strauss is a famous example—travelers may be equally keen to see, or even bill, themselves as anthropologists.[12] As with the tenuous distinctions made by Fussell between the travel book and the guidebook, or between travel writing and (romance) fiction, there is no prescriptive basis for differentiating between travel writing and ethnography, although there are a number of generally identifiable differences in *method* (travel writers are bricoleurs, unashamed dilettantes; ethnographers are research scholars) and *audience* (travel writing is written for a lay readership; ethnography aims at a more specialized audience). The central issue here, however, appears to be one of power. Again, no easy distinctions can be made: travel writers and anthropologists both occupy positions of power—granted largely by the economic differences between their own societies and the societies they visit—that allow them to establish an often unwarranted authority over their subjects. While travel writing tends to advertise the "special status" of the traveler as a privileged outsider—privileges that are merely confirmed when the outsider attempts to "move in," to "go native"—ethnography tends to downplay these privileges and to obviate the cult of personality, claiming instead to rely on a different kind of authority, conferred by the proven truths of science.

These generalizations can of course be questioned; for travel writing, to repeat, is generically elusive, as unwilling to give up its claims to documentary veracity as it is to waive its license to rhetorical excess. Perhaps it is best to see travel writing as *pseudo*ethnographic, insofar as it purports to provide a document of, or report on, other peoples and cultures while using them as a backdrop for the author's personal quest. Not all travel narratives, obviously, are of the questing variety; not all of them assimilate their encounters to the dictates of personal experience. Nonetheless, in travel narratives, as in other forms of autobiographical writing, the self is writ large in its alien surroundings. The attempt to find underlying rules and principles is secondary to the desire, or the mockery of the desire, to achieve self-understanding. Mockery is perhaps the key word here, for even the most earnest travel writers are usually aware of the discrepancy between their philosophical observations and the haphazardness of the experience from which those observations are derived. Travel writers, in this respect, flirt—quite literally—with charlatanism, claiming certain "truths" even when they know these to be dubious. The history of travel writing, unsurprisingly, reveals a propensity for hoaxes: either pseudointellectual "insights" that are embarrassingly believed in, or tall tales that masquerade as miraculous events. Many contemporary travel narratives follow in this profitable vein, exhibiting picayune "mentors" whose wisdom is dispensed like so much snake oil (Chatwin, Naipaul), or declaring "momentous" happenings that taper off into sheepish anticlimax (Newby, O'Hanlon). Some hoaxes are revealed; others, left uncertain, become the focus of suspicion. (The Mylodon skin in *In Patagonia* provides an object lesson. Allegedly discovered by Chatwin's cousin in South America, it now proudly ornaments his grandmother's dining room in southern England. The subject of innumerable tall tales, the Mylodon skin is of doubtful authenticity; it seems much more than likely that it is an utter fake. Its value as a collector's item remains, however, undiminished, its dubious origins merely serving as a catalyst for Chatwin's already vivid imagination [1–3, 188–92].)

The value of the Mylodon skin to a storyteller like Chatwin increases exponentially with the number of anecdotes that surround it. In collecting and recounting such anecdotes, writers like Chatwin reveal themselves to be skillful raconteurs. Often, one anecdote or story will tend to generate another: the more uncertain the origin of a word, or place, or object, the greater the number of possible contenders—and possible stories. Like opportunistic journalists, travel writers are often less concerned with ascertaining the details of a particular story than with judging whether it will make good copy. The less precise the story, the better copy it might make; for travel writing generates much of its revenue from rumor: it trades in the speculations that are attendant on uncertainty. In this last context, travel narratives mediate between the written and the oral. One of the minimum requirements of the travel writer is that he or she be a good listener: Raban, Theroux, and Chatwin, for example, spend less time recounting their own experiences than garnering the apocryphal stories of their colorful "informants." While, once again, similarities can be detected here with journalism and/or ethnography, another connection is with the folktale: the anecdote that aspires to legend. Travel writing, for all its trickery, remains a disseminator of folk wisdom; the travel writer, a raconteur among raconteurs, often cherishes this wisdom and is perfectly prepared to wander the globe to seek it.

Travel narratives articulate a poetics of the wandering subject. In most cases, this roving subject remains the focus of inquiry; in a few, the autobiographical persona of the traveler (or traveling writer) is subsumed by what Michael Ignatieff calls a "metaphysics of restlessness"— a philosophy of life based on the apparent need for movement.[13] Travel writing, in this sense, is a distinctive autobiographical form; like other autobiographies, it seeks to make retrospective sense out of discrete experiences: to convert a mishmash of impressions into a coherent narrative. But unlike most autobiographies—at least those seen from a traditional perspective—travel narratives are less concerned with recuperating, or reinventing, a single self than with following the trajectory of a series of selves in transit. This distinction fails to account, of course, for revisionist studies of autobiography, which stress the instability of both writing and written subject, and the multiplicity of personas that traverse the autobiographical text-in-process. It remains true, however, that in many travel narratives this instability is exacerbated, and that the self-inquiries conducted by travel writers, even the most apparently unsophisticated, are often likely to reveal a conflicted sense of belonging and allegiance. Perhaps, in this sense, travel writing is more closely affiliated with memoir. For Lee Quinby, among others, the subjectivity of autobiography, which is "presumed to be unitary and continuous over time," is at odds with the subjectivity of memoir, which is "multiple and discontinuous" (299). The subjectivity of memoir not only differs from that of autobiography, it also resists the very notion of autobiography's "individualized selfhood" (299).

It seems worth returning here for a moment to Fussell's definition of travel writing as "a sub-species of memoir in which the autobiographical narrative arises from the speaker's encounter with distant or unfamiliar data" (203). Fussell is presumably referring to memoir in its dictionary sense, as a "written record set down as material for history or biography."[14] His definition makes more sense, though, when memoir is seen, as Quinby sees it, as a discontinuous narrative revolving around a plural subject. The subjectivity of memoir is fragmented, or at the very least incomplete; in *travel* memoir, this sense of fragmentation—of psychic dislocation—is reinforced by physical distance and the experience of estrangement. This view of travel writing suggests a return to the earlier proposition that it disrupts conventional oppositions between the self and its others, the domestic and the foreign; and that it provides a vehicle for the revision of expectations concerning both individual subjecthood and the position of the home country with respect to the outside world. But while such a view certainly applies to many (contemporary) travel writers, it fails to account for others who use their travel writing, precisely, as a means of confirming their identity and consolidating their status as imperial national subjects. Into such a category arguably fall Eric Newby, Peter Mayle, and Patrick Leigh Fermor, and several others whose works capitalize on what Renato Rosaldo calls "imperialist nostalgia."[15] Clearly, there is a danger in claiming travel writing—and the metaphor of "travel" in general—for the purposes of subverting metropolitan ties to race, class, and country. Indeed, one of the characteristics of contemporary travel writing is its reversion to earlier forms—its cultivated anachronism—and, in more extreme cases, its studied reluctance to see the world as having irrevocably changed. A study of this kind needs to account for these retrograde, but hardly vitiated, forms of travel writing, as well as for those (post)modern forms that interrogate cultural identity and that provide a means for their writers and readers to learn, while also unlearning, modes of cultural self-imagination and exchange.

The "imperial I/eye" of the travel writer, in Mary Louise Pratt's conflation, is still operational in an age that, after Empire, has yet to settle imperialism's scores.[16] The connection between travel writing and imperial conquest is a long-standing one; as Stephen Greenblatt argues persuasively, the travel narratives of Columbus and other early European "discoverers" helped produce a "discourse of wonder" that both forestalled the act of conquest and paradoxically legitimized it by stimulating greed (79–80, 132–34). And Mary Campbell, delving back further into the premodern history of travel writing, shows in detail how the "wondrous" beings embodied in medieval geographic fantasies were behind some of the stereotypical images that the Spanish (among other) conquerors used to perceive their "monstrous" adversaries and put them to the sword.[17] Both Campbell and Greenblatt stress the dangers attendant upon the supposed eyewitness: the traveler whose "factual report" on far-flung lands enhanced the lure of difference while preparing the ground for plunder. For what had been witnessed really existed; it was empirically "proven" and thus available for those with the will and power to acquire it. The "eyewitness" reports of early travelers—even the obviously mendacious—thus acted as a means, not only of documenting the foreign culture for a domestic audience, but of adding to the body of knowledge, often falsely acquired or imperfectly transmitted, that led to that culture being seen as an opportunity for material gain.[18]

Contemporary travel narratives also rely upon the authority of the witness, even if they are less likely to be taken at face value or to expect their myths, passing as facts, to be (mis)read with an eye for profit. As Greenblatt reminds us, the eyewitness, real or not, functions as a rhetorical strategy to persuade the reader of the "authenticity" of what is reported (129). Contemporary travel writing, in postmodern vein, often plays on such notions of authenticity, either showing how the traveler imposes subjectivity on the narrative or laying bare the power structures underlying claims to truth. Needless to say, however, not all contemporary travel narratives do this; several remain more closely tied to documentary modes of presentation in which the traveler, recording scattered observations—usually by way of a diary or journal—then rearranges them into a more or less plausible narrative. Jan Morris and Colin Thubron are among those in this latter category, reminding us that a historically unreliable mode can still induce readers to suspend disbelief.

Probably the majority of contemporary travel writers, though—and the lion's share of those who feature in this book—play self-consciously on the conventions of an already self-conscious genre. One form this playfulness takes is the presentation of multiple personas; for the figure of the traveler, literally mobile, continually shuttles between different roles. This heightened consciousness of role-play and its performative dimensions suggests that travel writing, already a crossbreed between the essay and the novel, is also—and equally closely—affiliated with the drama. With its capacity for rapid role-play and the staging of misfortune, travel writing draws obvious inspiration from the history of comic theater. Not all travelers share a sense of the fun—some of the more serious-minded insist on their journeys being seen as spiritual quests, as surrogate pilgrimages—but even in the most earnest of travel narratives, there is an underlying hint of farce. In some cases, the traveler himself or herself cuts a farcical figure; in others, farce is displaced onto the places or cultures traveled through. Like farce, travel writing builds momentum from the accumulation of incongruities; philosophically relativistic, it enjoys no greater pleasure than in verifying the improbable.

The various comic techniques of contemporary travel writing run a gamut from understated urbane wit (Chatwin) to the crudest forms of slapstick (O'Hanlon). These two writers' work also illustrates the autobiographical range of travel writing: in Chatwin's narratives the traveler is primarily an observer, hiding behind the eccentricities of the characters he observes; in O'Hanlon's, the traveler himself is the greatest eccentric, making a virtue of his madcap antics and his wayward sexual fantasies, posing as a grown-up schoolboy in a bawdy summer-camp romp. O'Hanlon appears to be self-obsessed, Chatwin self-effacing. But this distinction proves to be misleading; for Chatwin, although less obviously egotistic than O'Hanlon, nonetheless fills his books with characters who partly resemble himself. Chatwin's narratives are also similar to O'Hanlon's in presenting not so much a self-inquiry as a self-mocking skit on the possibilities inherent in the figure of the traveler-writer. For the former, the traveler-writer emerges as a cross between a nomad, an inveterate wanderer and seeker in far-off, awe-inspiring places, and a collector, a patient gatherer of other people's stories and connoisseur of distant places, remote cultures, exotic things. For the latter, the traveler-writer is part teacher, part fall guy: a scientist eager to pursue, obtain, and record new forms of knowledge, but also a clown performing one (intentional?) blunder after another, and taking a perverse delight both in his own contrived misfortunes and in the equally contrived outrage that his words and actions arouse in others. O'Hanlon is the epitome of the self-indulgent traveler, even when his humor, as it often is, is directed squarely against himself; Chatwin, more urbane, is the dandy conscious of his coolness, but also conscious of his place among a gallery of itinerant wits and frauds. What is apparent in each case is the relative lack of introspection, and the tendency to present the self through an array of stock caricatural motifs. (Even more confessional or "questing" travel writers, like Dervla Murphy or Peter Matthiessen, tend to use these tropes as a means of identifying themselves as travelers, and of avoiding the excessive introspection that might immobilize their quests.) Travel writing, in this last sense, might even be seen as having an *anti*autobiographical aspect; or perhaps better, it might be considered as a disingenuous form of *pseudo*autobiography: one that, while purporting to examine the "real-life" (traveling) writer's personality, ends up instead by emphasizing the facticity of the (traveling) written subject.

By swapping masks and shifting roles, preventing easy identification, travel writers such as Chatwin and O'Hanlon distance themselves from their own, highly personal, narratives. A further role both writers play is that of the anthropological participant-observer: O'Hanlon's narratives, in particular, owe much to anthropological models; for example, *In Trouble Again* (1988), his raucous account of a field trip to the South American rain forest, is a parody of the work of Lévi-Strauss. Here the notion of the "roving I" takes on a different connotation; for like anthropologists fascinated to the point of prurience by their objects of study, travel writers eroticize their work through the act of cultural voyeurism.[19] Voyeurism takes many forms: at times, as in the narratives of Morley and Busi, sex itself is the subject; at others, the "exotic" people or places described are assessed for their seductiveness (Iyer, Chatwin); at still others, the very strangeness of the culture is compelling (Newby, Bowles). O'Hanlon, for example, confronting the spectacle of (Brazilian) Yanomami ritual, turns the privilege of the visiting foreigner into the license of the voyeur:

> Maybe I had simply been travelling in the jungle too long, but I just sat and stared at the young women, too absorbed even to clap. The sunlight threw long caressing flickers of light over them through the moving fronds, their unclotted skin was extraordinarily smooth. The woman with the mirror, who was last in line, danced with more passion than the rest: she had drawn squiggly lines down her cheeks and two more ran down the centre of her forehead, between her eyebrows, to either side of her nose beneath the long white stick in her septum, and then bent outwards to the corners of her bottom lip where two fresh sticks projected. She had covered her body with large, irregularly spaced round blotches like the spots on the coat of a jaguar; those on her breasts were as big as the aureoles around her erect nipples; they stretched vertically into ovals as she raised her arms above her head and her breasts tautened and flattened, and then became circular again as her breasts fell forward and rounded in the shuffling dance. (*In Trouble Again* 225)

In passages like this one, O'Hanlon combines a naturalist's eye for detail with a fetishist's delight for forbidden flesh; one is inevitably reminded here of the "soft primitivist" photographs of *National Geographic,* which so often focus on the erogenous zones of the female (native) body.[20]

In the work of Naipaul, meanwhile, a different kind of voyeurism can be detected, as India's squalor is reduced to a show, with himself cast in the role of horrified spectator:

You might think of taking an early morning walk along the balustraded avenue that runs beside the Mandoui River. Six feet below, on the water's edge, and as far as you can see, there is a line, like a wavering tidewrack, of squatters. For the people of Goa, as for those of imperial Rome, defecating is a social activity; they squat close to one another; they chatter. When they are done they advance, trousers still down, backsides bare, into the water, to wash themselves. They climb back on to the avenue, jump on their cycles or get into their cars, and go away. The strand is littered with excrement; amid this excrement fish is being haggled over as it is landed from the boats; and every hundred yards or so there is a blue-and-white enamelled notice in Portuguese threatening punishment for soiling the river. But no one notices. (*An Area of Darkness* 74)

The voyeuristic fervor with which Naipaul documents this activity is matched by the moralism with which he denounces it—a combination often found in travel narratives, which are quick to register distaste for the "degenerate" practices of other cultures, but are less inclined to recognize their enjoyment of the tawdriness those cultures display. For travel writing, although it freely avails itself of the license of the exotic— a mode that, as G. S. Rousseau and Roy Porter describe it, "afford[s] a moral 'time out,' a local habitation and a name for a fantasy world where all the normal rules—of decorum, taste, narrative, plausibility, and cause-and-effect—[can] legitimately be suspended" (13)—has the tendency, paradoxically, to see itself as an ethical commentary: as a critique of "declining standards," corruption, physical and spiritual decay. While it would be easy here to lambaste travel writers for their obvious double standards, what they are doing in effect is exploiting the doubleness already inscribed within the exotic. For if exoticists valorize difference, they are as eager to impugn it; exoticism functions as a dialectic of attraction and repulsion through which (cultural) difference can be acknowledged but also, if need be, held at bay (Todorov).[21] Travel writing tends to function this way, expressing itself through exotic registers that allow for often voyeuristic appreciation of "different" places, cultures, and peoples while reserving the right to judge them according to narrowly ethnocentric tastes. The roving "I"s of travel narratives, like those of ethnographies, seek out difference; but they are less likely than their ethnographic counterparts to relativize their findings, to analyze the local systems through which cultures shape and reshape meaning. Instead, they are often drawn to surfaces—more particularly, to bodies—onto which they project their fears and fantasies of the ethnicized cultural "other."

The voyeuristic tendencies of travel writing sketched above suggest a highly patriarchal model that indulges male fantasies surrounding the objectified—"othered"—female body. Such a model fails to account for the large, and growing, number of travel narratives written by women, both from the West and, increasingly, from "non-Western" backgrounds. While a male-dominated genre, travel writing has had its female practitioners—never more so than now. Dervla Murphy, Jan and Mary Morris, and Robyn Davidson are among the most popular and acclaimed of contemporary travel writers; Jamaica Kincaid, Sara Suleri, and Anita Desai are among those writers from formerly colonized countries who, in "writing back" to the imperial centers, are mounting a challenge to their complacent, sometimes racially jaundiced, views; and publishers, like Virago, which specialize in women's writing are recovering an increasing number of narratives that were previously "lost" or forgotten. The considerable interest in women's travel writing now evident in academic circles is a further sign, not only that travel writing has become a viable academic subject, but that it is being taken account of in current research on gender construction and on the changing place of the gendered subject in today's transnational world.

Women's travel writing is not insulated from the criticisms leveled at its male counterpart; more specifically, it is not immune from imperialist and ethnocentric nostalgia. However, its interrogation of the identity of the traveling subject—a subject recognized as being constituted by the complex interactions of gender, race, and class—marks contemporary women's travel writing as a vehicle for the displacement of patriarchal and imperial identitary norms. The ironic role-play of some women writers, such as Dervla Murphy or Mary Morris, is often designed to challenge masculinist myths. In the spirit of Isabelle Eberhardt, both traveler-writers "imitate," or disguise themselves as, men; while this cross-dressing serves at one level to facilitate their journeys, at another it flies in the face of conventional gender distinctions.[22] Murphy and Morris, among others, poke fun at the male bravado associated with the figure of the explorer, defying the restrictions (of dress, of speech and, above all of course, of movement) that are traditionally associated with their sex.

If travel, for women like these, is a medium of emancipation, it is also a vehicle for the "queering" of a heterosexual culture. An increasing number of gays and lesbians have turned to travel writing, drawing on models in part derived from earlier homoerotic fantasy, but also from current theories of queer performativity, which lay emphasis on the expressive potential of the (gendered) body as well as on the discursive power of language in performance. Several of these works posit a playful—often energetic—alternative to the geographies they associate with heterosexual (both male and female) thought and action. Aldo Busi, Roland Barthes, and, to some extent, Bruce Chatwin are among those writers for whom the experience of travel unlocks conceptual doors: Busi is the unrestrained libertine, moving from country (and partner) to country; Barthes and Chatwin are the aesthetes, connoisseurs of food and fashion, alert to the ritualized spectacles they make of foreign cultures, and producing travel narratives that, self-consciously seductive, dramatize their theories in a joyous "philosophy-in-performance." Pleasure is the principle that guides these different writers; as Chatwin's later writing shows, it is a pleasure that may exact its price. For travel, in the age of AIDS, has presented new frontiers of danger—dangers that are alluded to in Chatwin's final, poignant essays but that also feature more robustly in the work of Morley and Iyer, traveling in Thailand, and of Shoumatoff in Africa, investigating the virus's possible sources.

While providing another outlet for a staple of travel writing, the cautionary tale, AIDS culture has inevitably impacted the behavior of modern-day travelers, bringing with it a heightened awareness of the risks—an understanding not just that travel's apparent freedoms may be misleading, but that the pursuit of freedom itself may be at one's own, and others', expense. Traveler-writers who come from areas previously colonized by Europe were always likely to see such freedom from a critical perspective. Jamaica Kincaid's *A Small Place* (1988) and Caryl Phillips's *The European Tribe* (1987), both by writers born in the Caribbean but currently living in the diaspora, are two good examples of highly politicized forms of travel writing, which interrogate both the history of the genre they are employing and the underlying attitudes—often downright xenophobic—that have led to its becoming over time a fertile ground for misconception and for the unobstructed play of Euro-American (mostly white middle-class) fantasy.[23] Kincaid's and Phillips's work might be described as a kind of *counter*travel writing insofar as it pits itself against the dominant Eurocentric model. But how long will this dominance last? Certainly, travel writing today is beginning to take on a multicultural ethos. It is becoming increasingly difficult to justify the traveler's "one-way" vision—his or her perception, regulated from the imagined safety of the metropolis, of people, places, and cultures seen as alien or remote. For one thing, the metropolis itself is clearly a multiethnic entity, a place where different, often contradictory, realities mix and mingle. And for another, the older anthropological conception of a distinctive (separate) culture has been largely replaced by a longer view that sees all cultural forms, interacting in a transnational context, as strands in a global, hybridized pattern of dis- and relocation.[24] Roger Rouse states this view succinctly:

> We live in a confusing world, a world of crisscrossed economies, intersecting systems of meaning, and fragmented identities. Suddenly, the comforting modern imagery of nation-states and national languages, of coherent communities and consistent subjectivities, of dominant centers and distant margins, no longer seems adequate. (8)

What happens to travel writing in an age of what Homi Bhabha calls "transnational dissemination," at a time when the idea of a national culture, or even "culture," is under threat?[25] At least two, more or less diametrically opposed, sets of responses are possible. First, travel writing can recognize the conflictedness of cultural origins, focusing not so much on encounters between the traveler and the target culture (or cultures) as on the process of transculturation—of mutual exchange and modification—that takes place when different cultural forms collide and intersect.[26] Pico Iyer's *Video Night in Kathmandu* (1988) is a good example of this kind of travel narrative. And Iyer himself, a British subject, living in the United States, of Indian background, is an embodiment of what happens when travel writing adjusts its gauges to a postcolonial world. Iyer is not alone; indeed, several of the most accomplished of contemporary Anglophone travel writers are South Asian diasporics living in Britain or the United States. Vikram Seth, Amitav Ghosh, and Firdaus Kanga are just three of these. *From Heaven Lake* (1983), Seth's ebullient account of his visit to Tibet and mainland China, is a case study of the difficulty of ascertaining origins. Seth, who speaks fluent Chinese, wore the traditional Maoist blue trousers, jacket, and cap during his travels, and was duly taken by several of the people he encountered for a Chinese (100–108).

The second set of responses involves the recognition of belatedness. It is no longer possible to tout a view of, say, "the English gentleman abroad" as if this gentleman—naturally, white—existed other than in myth. Yet this myth, precisely, matters and is adhered to with a vengeance, even though its effect is largely comic and its power obviously in decline. This is the stance taken by Eric Newby and, to a lesser extent, Redmond O'Hanlon; it even lurks in the background of Chatwin's work and that of the Anglophile Theroux. Travel writing, for these writers, dramatizes the unwieldy paradox of reconfirming a national identity that is already recognized as being out of step with the times. This regressive cultural nationalism has more sinister implications, yet these are sidestepped by recourse to parody and preemptive self-critique.

These two responses are symptomatic of a "postimperial" era that has yet to deliver itself from the recrudescence of its beliefs. The discourse of "post" implies, of course, an ambivalent relationship with what precedes it, and a sense of temporal flux that argues against decisive break. Contemporary travel writers are arguably caught in this hiatus, aware of their temporal, as well as their geographical, displacement. Part of this dilemma has to do with the phenomenon of speed. Departing late, they find that they are arriving all too early: changes in the technology of transportation, while making travel more efficient and easier, potentially rob such traveler-writers of the leisure time they need.[27] Speed is antithetical to the physical and verbal meandering of conventional travel writing, which relies on modes of transportation (walking, cycling, rail travel) that require the passage of time. Speed also opposes the myth of labor on which travel writing so often depends. The idea of hardship is intrinsic to more traditional forms of travel writing—it is no surprise to find a popular anthology entitled, simply enough, *Bad Trips* (1991). As the editor of the volume, Keath Fraser, colorfully puts it, "Travel will still suggest 'travail' to those who know that by leaving home they risk wire-walking without a net" (xiv). And, even more colorfully: "A bad journey mirrors its exotic circumference, throwing back an image of the writer in extremis, who is willing to be tested, mocked, and remain remarkably undaunted when it begins to rain on his parade . . . when the rim of the troddened world degenerates into a *via dolorosa*" (xvii–xviii).[28] Fraser apparently knows the value of glibness in travel writing; the reality, however, especially for contemporary travelers, is that their journeys are rarely as traumatic or as heroic as they would have us believe. Fraser's anthology, published in 1991 with pieces collected mostly from the eighties, wryly illustrates how some traveler-writers, in eager pursuit of trouble, will find it when they least expect it—and often not deal with it very well. What happens, though, when the space of travel threatens to disappear altogether—when travel goes "virtual," and reality itself becomes confused with the hyperreal?

Needless to say, such a scenario does not spell the end of travel writing; what it does instead is to usher in some new, unusual forms. Umberto Eco's *Travels in Hyperreality* (1986) and Jean Baudrillard's *America* (1988) are two examples of contemporary travel narratives that, playing ironically on the perceptions of the "virtual" or "hyper" traveler, use those perceptions as a means toward rejuvenating the form. Eco and Baudrillard both present variants on what might be called the "theoretical traveler": their actual journeys are only the pretext for their theories and beliefs.[29] Both writers are perhaps best seen as "post-touristic" in sensibility, aware of tourism as a game.[30] "Post-tourists" (unlike self-designated "travelers") are not at all interested in accumulating authentic experience; they are much more likely to be taken with the obviously inauthentic: with the kitsch display of simulated places and copies of "genuine" native artifacts, or with the ludicrous attempt to reconstruct historical sites or objects that seek to improve on the original. Baudrillard's and Eco's fascination with the possibility of Absolute Fakery—with the construction of perfect models that then supplant what they once copied—is in part a response to the latest mediated forms of surrogate travel; but it also restates a perennial preoccupation of travel writing with the manufacture of illusions that test the boundaries of the "real." Travel writing, after all, is a pseudoscience of observation; inhabiting the indeterminate area between fact and fable, history and myth, it has thrived on a diet of half-truths, rumors, mysteries, illusions—the trappings of a world whose geography is only partly covered, and whose multiple possible histories are only partly understood.

Travel narratives strive to express the unfamiliar, but also to contain it; in scanning the past, they compile an inventory of domesticated mysteries, and yet they are made to confront the unexpected strangeness of the present. This book maintains that balance between adjustment and reversion: between travel writing's desire to come to terms with a complex world in transformation and its nostalgic need to restore the imaginary site of a "simpler" past. These competing drives are apparent among contemporary British travel writers, adept exponents of a labile, but somehow still parochial, genre. This parochialism is embodied in the mythic figure—already introduced—of the gentleman traveler, forever on the move but always missing home, and defiantly out of date. By showing how several travel writers manipulate the trope of the gentleman traveler, the next chapter examines the view that British travel writing, in the nominally postimperial era, continues to trade successfully in ironically recycled imperial myths.

Chapter one

After Empire

"As travelers and travel writers, the English are special," says Paul Fussell in his study of British literary traveling between the wars (73). For Fussell, the English traveler-writer is singled out from others by a particular brand of eccentric individualism. Fussell's (perhaps excessively) affectionate study is dedicated accordingly to the memory of such notorious "originals" as the irrepressible art historian Robert Byron and the more curmudgeonly, but scarcely less flamboyant, novelist Evelyn Waugh: larger-than-life figures both, but not untypical of English traveler-writers of the interwar period, who were frequently "outrageous, conducting [their] libertarian gesture against the predictable conformity, the dull 'internationalism,' of post-war social and political arrangements" (78). Romantically, Fussell sees Byron and Waugh as representatives of the "final age of travel," which has since given way to modern commercial tourism. In pronouncing the age of travel dead, Fussell echoes the sentiments of Waugh himself, who believed that the end of the war also signaled the end of the golden age of travel writing; gone were the halcyon days when "Mr. Peter Fleming went to the Gobi desert, Mr. Graham Greene to the Liberian hinterland . . . [and] Mr. Robert Byron . . . to the ruins of Persia" (*When the Going Was Good* 11). But Waugh's threnody turned out to have been premature; for a decade later, we find him again—and in characteristically ebullient mood—writing a preface for the book of a newly discovered literary traveler: Eric Newby. Newby, for Waugh, is "the latest, but, I pray, not the last of a whimsical tradition." Waugh celebrates Newby's understatement,

27

self-ridicule, delight in the foreignness of foreigners, complete denial of any attempt to enlist the sympathies of his readers in the hardships he has capriciously invited . . . [and] formal self-effacement in the presence of the specialist (with the essential reserve of unexpressed self-respect).

All of these qualities delight the heart of a man "whose travelling days are done and who sees, all too often, his countrymen represented abroad by other, new and (dammit) lower types" (Preface 12). It is precisely because he is *not* new that Newby is to be welcomed; for as the upholder of a tradition that is resolutely antimodern, Newby embodies in his work an antiquated, but still perfectly serviceable myth—that of the English gentleman abroad who "shuns the celebrated spectacles of the tourist and without any concern with science or politics or commerce . . . ventures to set feet where few civilized feet have trod" (Preface 12).

Waugh is partly right in his judgment of Newby; and Newby himself, in the opening pages of his autobiography *A Traveller's Life* (1982), is certainly quick to agree with him.[1] But it is important, at the same time, to see Newby's writing—like that of several of his old-school contemporaries (Thesiger, Lewis, Leigh Fermor)—as being situated both within and *against* the tradition of the English gentleman abroad. Newby associates this tradition more closely with the figure of the Victorian gentleman scholar: an avid student and consumer of other, mostly non-European cultures whose impressive erudition affords another reminder of the imagined superiority of his own imperial national culture. Waugh and, particularly, Byron retain some of these characteristics: self-consciously anachronistic figures both, they are—or perhaps better, they pose as—gentleman scholars out of their time. But for Newby, the sense of belatedness is that much more urgent. He has been born, he laments on more than one occasion in his travel writings, one hundred years too late; and not only in the sense that the forces of modern technology have conspired to spoil the pleasures of the ruin-seeking traveler—to ruin his ruins—but also because the myth of the English gentleman has lost its moral force. David Castronovo, in his historical study of the English gentleman, expresses the dilemma well. The English gentleman is no longer an ideal or model, but instead a popular entertainment; like the landed estate with which he is often associated, the gentleman can no longer be seen as "a force for social cohesion, but rather [as] a delightful aesthetic object" (131). Newby's persistent nostalgia is a throwback to the lost glories of Empire—an age of unparalleled success for the idea of the gentleman—but Newby rarely loses sight of the fact that the English gentleman abroad, and the code of conduct for which he stands, do not cut much ice in the rapidly changing world of the late twentieth century. Simon Raven sums it up: "Gentlemen can only now behave as such, or be tolerated as such, in circumstances that are manifestly contrived or unreal" (144). Perhaps Marx got it right after all: to replay the history of the English gentleman abroad, in an age no longer conducive to the ideals of gentlemanliness, is to play it out as farce.

Certainly, farce plays a role in several contemporary British travel narratives that self-consciously manipulate the imperialist myth of the gentleman abroad. Newby's *A Short Walk in the Hindu Kush* (1958), Thesiger's *Arabian Sands* (1959), and, more recently, O'Hanlon's *Into the Heart of Borneo* (1984) are all postwar travel narratives by quintessentially English writers that trade on, but also play on, what the anthropologist Renato Rosaldo calls "imperialist nostalgia." Imperialist nostalgia, according to Rosaldo, describes a prevalent, commodified mode of elegiac perception through which Western people are given to sentimentalize the former relationship between the Empire and its colonies. Such people, and the culture industries (film, TV, etc.) that foster their perceptions, contrive to mourn the passing of a world that they themselves have irrevocably altered. As Rosaldo puts it bluntly:

> Imperialist nostalgia revolves around a paradox: A person kills somebody, and then mourns the victim. In more attenuated form, someone deliberately alters a form of life, and then regrets that things have not remained as they were prior to the intervention. At one more remove, people destroy their environment, and then they worship nature. In any of its versions, imperialist nostalgia uses a pose of "innocent yearning" both to capture people's imaginations and to conceal its complicity with often brutal domination. (69–70)[2]

Imperialist nostalgia comes in handy for contemporary travel writers, who can deploy it to mystify their own economic motives, as well as to yearn for the "simpler" ways of life—often rural, premodern, preindustrial—that they, and their metropolitan readers, persuade themselves they need. Imperialist nostalgia, as Rosaldo sees it, does not have to depend on a vision of Empire; it describes a more generalized, pastoral mode of wistful reminiscence that seeks control over, but not responsibility for, a mythicized version of the past. In the work of several contemporary travel writers, however, this mythicized past actually pertains to Empire: it attempts the restoration of Empire's former (imagined) glories, and the resuscitation of Empire's erstwhile (imaginary) "subordinate" subjects.

Writers like these are aware, though, that their gestures are belated, and the result in their narratives is a turn to comedy—particularly farce. In O'Hanlon's *Into the Heart of Borneo,* the author and his sidekick, the poet James Fenton, embark on a madcap foray into the jungle that is also a journey back into a fondly reimagined past. (It is not surprising that one of O'Hanlon's favorite writers is Joseph Conrad, for his own travel narratives succumb all too easily to what Rob Nixon calls "Conradian atavism": the mechanism, displayed most clearly in the novella *Heart of Darkness,* by which a journey forward through space simultaneously moves backward through time.)[3] As in Conrad's work, there is an evolutionary thread to O'Hanlon's jungle narrative; but he is equally interested in re-creating and imaginatively inhabiting the colonial atmosphere of Sarawak in the nineteenth century, at least a hundred years before his own visit. One of his models appears to be the "gentleman-adventurer" James Brooke, who arrived, like his literary namesake Lord Jim, in Sarawak in the mid-nineteenth century, promptly became embroiled in a local war, and ended up with his own private kingdom.[4] Brooke was later succeeded by his nephew Charles, a forceful leader who "governed Sarawak for fifty years like a country gentleman managing his estates" (*Borneo* 14). And the line of Brookes was to continue until after the Second World War, when Vyner Brooke, under pressure to rebuild, finally ceded his estate to the British Crown (Moses). O'Hanlon sees the Brookes' history as having been one, by and large, of benevolent paternalism, an attitude he seeks to revive in his own much later expedition. But as he discovers, Sarawak is a much changed place since the days of Brooke and company. For one thing, the country—now a member of the Malaysian Federation—has only the slenderest of links to its colorful colonial history; and for another, O'Hanlon and Fenton, far from inspiring respect among the local people, are figures of fun, eccentric blunderers, the butt of many a private joke. O'Hanlon's pathetic efforts to remind some local children of his origins are rewarded unexpectedly:

> I dislodged [a] sealed bag of picture-postcards of the Queen on horse-back, Trooping the Colour. . . . "Look," I said, "this is for you. Here is our Tuai Rumah, our chief in England." "Inglang!" said the children. The cards were sheeny and metallic, the kind that change the

position of their subjects as their own position is changed against the light. . . . I gave one to a little boy. He looked at it with amazed delight: he turned it this way and that; he scratched it and waited to see what would happen; he whipped it over, to catch a glimpse of Her Majesty from the back. Small hands thrust up like a clump of bamboo; the old woman, annoyed, wanted a pile for herself. If the children had one each, the men wanted more than one each. In five minutes, four hundred mementoes of the Empire disappeared. (62–63)

In registering the unmitigated farce of such "cross-cultural" encounters, O'Hanlon deflates his self-appointed role as Great Conciliator, as well as showing the gap between his personal vision of the Empire and the realities of a present fashioned by the more impersonal forces of commercial tourism. O'Hanlon, as the locals know well, is a tourist and, as such, can be exploited; his mementos vanish, not so much because the Empire itself has ended, but because the trappings of an imperial past, now converted into touristic items, become the symbolic markers of a process of exploitative exchange.

O'Hanlon, it could be argued, is well acquainted with this process, well aware of his complicity with the tourist system he affects to despise. Yet it could also be argued that his propensity for self-deprecation and self-parody provide an *alibi* for his excesses: excesses arising both from his privileged status as a traveler and from his métier as travel writer, a métier that has brought him considerable financial success. It is no surprise, of course, that most travel writers are reluctant to discuss their own financial motives, and to reveal the means by which they can afford their lives of relative leisure. Travel narratives, in mystifying their own conditions of production, are not alone among literary works in hiding their face from their reading public. But this situation is made conspicuous by the "favored status" enjoyed by many traveler-writers, whose journeys may well be financed by rich corporate sponsors—or steady private income—but who are still given, like O'Hanlon, to capitalize on the manufactured "hardships" they experience without accounting for the genuine penury of some of the peoples they encounter.

Seen in this light, the figure of the gentleman abroad starts to look rather less endearing, and rather more like a strategy designed to protect the traveler writer from further harm. The gentleman abroad, in a postimperial context, might well appear ridiculous; but ridicule, precisely, becomes his license to perform. Nowhere is this clearer than in the narratives of Eric Newby: a writer, like O'Hanlon, who seems to cater to an (upper) middle-class English reading public. Also like O'Hanlon, Newby is the product of England's elitist private-school system and is quite prepared to publicize the entitlements the system affords. One of these entitlements is an idealized, thoroughly class-bound idea of Englishness: "As British as a Bath bun," he wryly declares himself at the outset of one of his journeys, a ride on the Trans-Siberian Express—and who can quibble with a man who, only a day into his journey, is already dreaming of "crumpets and buttered toast, Gentleman's Relish in a jumbo-sized pot, buckets of common sweet, orange-coloured English tea and a paperback copy of P. G. Wodehouse?" (*Big Red Train Ride* 10, 89). Newby's popularity among British readers—he has published more than a dozen commercially successful travel narratives—owes to his skill as a writer working within the genre's accepted clichés. More particularly, it owes to his reversion via Waugh and Byron, his obvious models, to an ideal of the eccentric gentleman traveler that is mocked for being dated but that is ironically celebrated, for the same reason, precisely *because* it is out of date. The early work *A Short Walk in the Hindu Kush* (1958), for example—a minor classic in postwar Anglophone travel writing—chronicles the exploits of Newby and his companion, the pukka diplomat Hugh Carless, in the remote mountain country of Nuristan in Central Asia. It is probably Newby's best book; it also represents his most sustained examination of the (English) gentleman traveler. Three aspects of this figure, and the mythology that surrounds it, are worth exploring in more detail here: amateurism, anachronism, and imposture.

The French explorer Raymond Furon provides the epigraph for *A Short Walk:* "Il faudrait une expédition bien organisée et pourvue de moyens matériels puissants pour tenter l'étude de cette région de haute montagne," warns Furon in his book on the Hindu Kush and Kaboulistan (7). Newby's expedition, unfortunately, fulfills neither requirement. For one thing, Newby and Carless are both novices to mountain climbing: a truth brought painfully home to them during a brief but hilariously eventful "training session" in Wales, where their bumbling efforts are presided over by "a flock of mountain sheep . . . making sounds suspiciously like laughter" (33). Nor do they appear to know a great deal about the place they plan to visit: a lack of knowledge exacerbated by their reliance on outdated guidebooks, their uncertain command of the local languages, and their singular reluctance to take advice. Not that Newby sees any of this as a disadvantage; on the contrary, he seems to exult in his own and Carless's amateurism, taking the opportunity to set—and send—himself up as the latest in a long line of colorful European explorers, each equipped with grandiose imperial visions of adventure and conquest, but little else besides. Of course, Newby and Carless are better prepared than they would have us believe; but rather than lend his expedition an aura of gravitas or expertise, Newby chooses to depict it, along with himself, as foolishly, even dangerously, amateurish.

The amateurism of the English gentleman abroad—the man lacking in expertise, but schooled for all eventualities—is a fitting subject for parody; but it also confers a paradoxical authority on the tweedy traveler, allowing him to see his egregious errors and violations of local custom as signs of his own wayward munificence. Amateurism also provides a spurious form of self-protection; for unlike professional ethnographers, whose participant-observation cannot help but create a certain complicity between themselves and the culture they are describing, adventure-seeking travelers may persuade themselves that they are free to indulge in an "innocent" enthusiasm for the wonders they behold.[5] These wonders are often held up as the objects of a naive or untutored curiosity; but in another sense, it is a paradoxical lack of curiosity that governs such travelers' endeavors. Gaping at the marvels of "foreign" peoples and cultures, they are apt nonetheless to assimilate them to a European frame of reference, thereby reinstating Europe—or, in the case of the gentleman, England—as the ultimate arbiter of cultural value. Newby's travel narrative consciously places itself within this self-privileging tradition. Discovery—itself a powerful European myth—takes second place to nostalgic reminiscence; and as a self-styled "literary traveler," what Newby is reminded of most often is books. Kipling looms large, as does Buchan; avoiding the dull precision of technical jargon, Newby directs his attention instead to the vivid images of heroic myth. As Philip Mason and David Castronovo, among others, have argued, the myth of the English gentleman has not only been sustained by literature; it has also been actively produced by it. By surrounding himself with images of previous gentlemen-explorers, mostly from nineteenth-century literature, Newby works toward conferring mythic status on himself. The pratfalls of the amateur correspond to a kind of definitional gaucherie; like its mountain-climbing protagonists, the narrative itself frequently slips: most often between categories of fact (Newby as professional travel writer) and categories of fiction (Newby as "legendary adventurer"). In the process, Nuristan takes on the configurations of an invented country—a playground, like

Lord Jim's island retreat or Carnehan and Dravot's mountain kingdom, for the acting out of self-aggrandizing but ultimately self-defeating imperial fantasies.

In keeping with most of Newby's travel narratives (as, for that matter, with O'Hanlon's), *A Short Walk* is peppered with references to the nineteenth century. In *A Traveller's Life,* during a visit to the "new" Istanbul in the fifties, Newby finds himself echoing the sentiments of an obscure Victorian traveler, the Reverend Walsh, who had visited the "old" Constantinople over a century before him. Rev. Walsh had feared that the beauties of Constantinople would prove to be transitory. For Newby, these fears are confirmed; casting a sorrowful eye on the rapidly modernizing city of Istanbul, he can only mourn the fact that he has been born "a hundred years too late" (161–62). *A Short Walk* is marked throughout by a similar tone of plangent reminiscence. Reading at times almost like an inventory of Orientalist myths, the narrative is suffused with affectionate memories of Britain's civilizing mission in the East. The heady days of the Raj, alas, are over. At Meshed, in northeast Persia, the opulent consulate building was

> lost and forgotten; arcades of Corinthian columns supported an upper balcony, itself collapsing. The house was shaded by great trees, planted perhaps a century ago, now at their most magnificent. Behind barred windows were the big green safes with combination locks in the confidential registry. (57)

Newby asks Carless how on earth the consulate's former occupants had managed to get the safes into the building. Carless's reply: "In the days of the Raj you could do anything" (57).

This half-parodic tribute to the past, straight out of Kipling juvenilia, typifies the tone of self-mocking anachronism maintained throughout Newby's travel narratives. Self-mockery is counterbalanced, however, by self-exoneration. By turning his travels into the stuff of legend and myth—into a series of gentleman's adventures—Newby attempts to convince himself and his readers that his experiences have little social consequence. This determination to trivialize is reminiscent of the sentiments of *camp.* "The whole point of camp," says Susan Sontag in a well-known essay, "is to dethrone the serious" (116). Camp is playful, antiserious, vigorously apolitical; but as Sontag points out, it also functions as a "solvent of morality [that] neutralizes moral indignation" (118). Camp may be disruptive, but it is always excusable: the "outrageous" behavior it spawns is primarily cosmetic and should be judged—or rather, should not be judged—accordingly. Camp, finally, proposes "a comic vision of the world . . . but not a bitter or polemical comedy. If tragedy is an experience of hyper-involvement, comedy is an experience of under-involvement, of detachment" (116). (It is interesting to speculate here how much twentieth-century British travel writing has its roots in camp: the work of Newby's two most obvious precursors, Waugh and Byron, is camp, as is the work of his two closest contemporaries, Chatwin and O'Hanlon.)

In Newby's travel narratives, camp provides the medium for a vision of the world—more specifically, a vision of the foreign world—that seeks to promote harmless entertainment while claiming a spurious disengagement. The gentleman abroad, always a good subject for parody, turns into an even better one for the "uncommitted" melodramatics of camp. Is the gentleman himself unreal, or does he confer unreality on his surroundings? Short of breath in the mountains of Nuristan, Newby and Carless find it easier to breathe in the rarefied air of High Romance. Yet even the most theatrical of circumstances cannot always match the gentleman's expectations of deference. In one memorable scene, for example, the fraudulent heroics of Newby and Carless are mercilessly exposed by the local Nuristanis, who converge on the two hapless adventurers as they prepare to set up camp:

> As the news of our arrival spread, the smart young men of town began to arrive. Half a dozen of the most elegant seated themselves on a large rock and watched us languidly. Like members of the Eton Society, they were dressed rather foppishly—big flat caps, embroidered waistcoats, silver medals and lucky charms. One of them was armed with a double stringed stone bow. From time to time he discharged a pebble at the lizards that crawled over the face of the cliff. Before these aloof dandies and an audience of at least fifty lesser men we hobbled backwards and forwards, performing our mundane household chores, like actors in some interminable drama in an experimental theatre. (208)

But even in scenes such as this one, where the tables are apparently turned on Newby and Carless, and they are made to confront the ludicrousness of their own affectations, the stage is set in such a way as to discourage serious judgment. The bravura of the gentleman abroad may be neatly deflated, and the "evidence" of his superiority revealed as flagrant imposture, but we are not asked to—are asked not to—carry the criticism too far. Self-parody offers self-protection: in a narrative that seems to take every opportunity to parade its own frivolity,

Newby hides his responsibilities as traveler and travel writer behind a facade of wry humor and knowing aestheticism. In this sense, Newby's work is following in a tradition of English travel writing in which posturing and self-inflicted wit mask a residual feeling of moral superiority. Camp is the primary medium for these humorous dissimulations; and what could be more camp than the late-twentieth-century English gentleman abroad—a man born a hundred years too late, still prey to fitful delusions of imperial grandeur?

The work of Bruce Chatwin, arguably the finest of Britain's postwar travel writers, is similarly indebted to the mischievous spirit of camp. But whereas Newby and O'Hanlon conscript camp aesthetics into the service of imperialist nostalgia, Chatwin is much more consciously concerned with camp as a form of art. Hence the conflation in his work between the gentleman and the *dandy:* the worldly aesthete who, wandering the globe in search of stimulation, converts his impressions into a Wildean treatise on the pleasures of luxuriant decay. Dandies are abundant throughout Chatwin's fiction: the itinerant art-collector Utz (*Utz,* 1988); the decadent slave-trader Francisco Manoel da Silva (*The Viceroy of Oiudah,* 1980); the Etonian bachelor Reggie Bickerton (*On the Black Hill,* 1982); and, above all, himself in his two most obviously autobiographical travel narratives, *In Patagonia* (1977) and *The Songlines* (1987). (Chatwin's work shows, as clearly as anyone's, the difficulty of defining travel writing. He always disliked the term *travel writer,* and of all his works perhaps only the first, *In Patagonia,* falls readily into the category of a travel book. Travel, nonetheless, was the greatest passion in Chatwin's life, and it remains the dominant metaphor throughout his diverse body of work.) Whether he is recording his observations in his immaculate moleskin notebooks *(In Patagonia)* or trying out dilettantish theories on the nomadic origins of the human species *(The Songlines),* Chatwin cuts a witty, almost languidly elegant figure even as he careens from place to place with an energy unrivaled among his peers. This combination of wit and elegance is reminiscent of the dandy, as is the apparent interchangeability between art and life throughout his work. Finally, the Wildean insistence on the aesthetic value of lying is appropriate to a writer working closely within the tradition of the traveler's tale.[6]

To see Chatwin as a traveling dandy—or to recognize his work as a dandified travel aesthetics—raises the question of the difference between the dandy and the gentleman, and between the social codes embodied by these two heavily mythicized figures. One account of the distinction is provided by James Eli Adams in his study of conflicting styles of Victorian masculinity. Adams's book sets out to explore a "contradiction within Victorian patriarchy, by which the same gender system that underwrote male dominance also called into question the 'manliness' of intellectual labor" (1). Several writers of the period, alert to this contradiction, sought to resolve it by appealing to models of masculine identity, including the gentleman and the dandy. These two latter models were widely understood as representing an "ascetic regimen" that laid emphasis on self-discipline as a distinctly masculine attribute (2). But whereas the gentleman was regarded by some—notably Carlyle—as a paragon of sincerity, the dandy emerged as a figure too theatrical for his own good. The dandy thus became a figure for the very contradictions he was intended to resolve: a reminder of the decadence threatening Victorian codes of ethics, but also a challenge to the honor of the "true" gentleman as a man of moral substance. As Adams explains,

> As the ideal of the gentleman broadened [during the nineteenth century], . . . it also gave new moral urgency to the . . . task of distinguishing between sincerity and performance. If the status of the gentleman is not secured by inherited distinctions of family and rank, but is realized instead through behavior, how does one distinguish the "true" gentleman from the aspirant who is merely acting the part? (53)

This anxiety is reflected, as we have seen, in the work of Newby and O'Hanlon, both of whom hark back to a model—of sincerity, authenticity, masculine prowess—that they recognize as no longer possible, and who turn the gentleman-adventurer, the paragon of masculine virtue, into his "fallen" modern counterpart, the traveling dandy as performing clown. In Chatwin's work, however, this formula is given another twist. For the dandy, far from being seen as "fallen," is *recuperated* as an admirable figure: his performative qualities are a virtue, as is his foppishness, as are his lies. Take Louis Rougemont (aka Henri Green), the peripatetic "French savant" in *In Patagonia:* author of a learned treatise on virginity; perpetrator of a scandalous, and therefore best-selling, autobiography; and later star in his one-man road show, "The Greatest Liar on Earth" (*In Patagonia* 167–69). Chatwin's narratives are densely populated with lovable rogues like this one: men and, sometimes, women who manipulate other people's credulity, and whose performances, drawing on the best tradition of the traveler as travel liar, remain unencumbered by the banal obligation to tell their audience the truth.

For Chatwin, the itinerant storyteller is both a nomad and a collector. Nomadism in Chatwin's work is both a creed and an aesthetic: it describes the pleasures of movement beyond the bounds of "settled" society—Chatwin tends to sympathize, somewhat romantically, with anarchists, exiles, and outlaws—but it also gives a name to the digressions, the flights of fancy and improvisational forays, that characterize the restlessness of much of his written work.[7] If the traveler/storyteller is a type of nomad, ceaselessly in search of stories, then he is also a collector, an accumulator of the world's (tall) tales. In this sense, Chatwin's work dramatizes a tension between the centrifugal forces of escape—the nomadic impulse—and the centripetal forces of retrieval—the passion to acquire, exhibit, collect. And that passion is registered in writings that display a connoisseur's appreciation for foreign cultures; to adapt a phrase from a man he much admired, the French novelist and art historian André Malraux, Chatwin's work comes to resemble a "museum without walls": an open exhibition in which foreign peoples and cultures, and the stories they offer, deliver themselves up as aesthetic objects for the delectation of a delighted, but conveniently detached, spectator.[8]

There is of course a certain disingenuousness about Chatwin's literary enterprise; for in pursuing the illusion of detachment, retreating behind his own and other people's stories, he seeks to protect himself from closer involvement in the societies and cultures with which he comes in contact. The dandy's hyperconscious posturing is a useful rhetorical strategy: it grants him performative license and a dilettante's range of ideas and options; it also gives him a freedom to assimilate his personal experience to aesthetic whim. Most of all, it liberates him from the burden of moral judgment; for the dandy—at least in the Wildean sense of the connoisseur of aesthetic objects—is neither to judge nor be judged for his own, or others', ethical standards. Instead, his task is to appreciate beautiful things wherever he sees them; and the result, for the traveling dandy, is a proclivity to convert the places through which he travels into a clutch of exoticized objects for his own voyeuristic consumption. Chatwin is well aware, though, of his own exoticist leanings, and his blatantly aestheticized portrayal of, say, the Central Australian Aborigines in *The Songlines* is less a homage to the Noble Savage than it is an exercise in wry self-parody.[9] Parody notwithstanding, Chatwin's work is unashamedly romantic; and with that romanticism comes a certain tendency to cultivated naïveté: a propensity to homogenize different peoples and cultures; to discover psychic or instinctual similarities rather than accounting for social or historical differences; and, at worst, to reduce an infinitely complex world into a random display of beautiful collector's items. These vices, however, are a dandy's virtues; for Chatwin's work is the product, above all else, of a dandy's will to *style.* And of a dandy's sense of *humor:* how else to account for stories like "A Coup" (in *What Am I Doing Here,* 1989), in which Chatwin and his colleagues, swept up in a vicious civil war in a heavily fictionalized Benin, take refuge in a luxury restaurant, where they quaff champagne (while loudly lamenting the lack of oysters); or descriptions such as this one, from an African interlude in *The Songlines,* where two Bororo youths parade themselves in a bizarre rite of passage?

> The "tough" one had a pink cupid's bow around his lips; his fingernails were scarlet and his eyelids green. His strapless bouffant dress had lavender panels over a rose-coloured underskirt. The effect was ruined by a pair of fluorescent lime-green socks and gym-shoes. . . . His friend, the "beauty," wore a tight mauve turban, a sheath of green and white stripes, and had a more modern sense of fashion. He had been very careful with the lipstick, and on either cheek he had painted two neat rectangles in bands of pink and white. He had on a pair of reflecting sunglasses, and was admiring himself in a hand-mirror. (264)

The ceremony being described here—which in fact exists—goes unexplained; Chatwin is much more interested in exploiting its comic potential as camp spectacle. Chatwin's dandies, like Newby's, act as comic foils to his (masculine) adventurer persona. But whereas Newby, in the end, seems uneasy with this puncturing of male bravado, Chatwin is only too happy to reverse conventional gender roles. His witty stories and observations—the products of an epicurean art-lover, an expert on food and fashion—offer a whimsical riposte to the more muscular exploits associated with the gentleman-adventurer. Like Newby and O'Hanlon, Chatwin recognizes that the myth of the gentleman has outlived its usefulness and, also like them, that the heroic code of conduct for which he stands is hopelessly out of date. Yet while Newby and O'Hanlon persist, nonetheless, in playing a role for which they are unsuited, Chatwin assimilates gentlemanly theatrics to a full-blown dandy's art. Newby and O'Hanlon, too, are dandies of a kind, but only Chatwin fully *accepts* himself as one; and realizes, at the same time, that the contemporary travel writer's (melo)dramatic aspirations—as itinerant aesthete, jackdaw sage, pseudo-explorer/reporter/

biographer—are ideally served by that most self-consciously theatrical of figures, the dandy.

If Chatwin's sybaritic tastes are best suited to the persona of the dandy, Peter Mayle's, in his hugely successful Provence books, are tailored to that of the *country gentleman* or *squire*.[10] *A Year in Provence* (1989) and its sequel, *Toujours Provence* (1991), sketch Mayle's experiences of moving from London to a quiet corner of the Luberon in southern France, where he and his wife, having bought a cottage, slowly adapt to the rhythms of "rural life." The two books—especially the first—are classic examples of pastoral travel narrative. Their accent is less on movement than on a nostalgic appreciation for a regional way of life that, though imperiled, remains recalcitrant to change. This way of life, affectionately rendered by Mayle with the rose-tinted glasses of the "permanent visitor," revolves around the rituals of growing and, particularly, consuming food. The Luberon, for Mayle and a string of fortunate (mostly English) visitors, is a gourmet's paradise: a place where food, in plentiful supply, is rightly treasured—especially by those who are relieved of the burden of producing it. Mayle, a professional writer, places unashamed emphasis on leisure: on what the sociologist Thorstein Veblen famously called "conspicuous consumption."[11] This life of leisure might be hard work (at least for the epicurean's digestive tracts) but it requires little hard labor, since the latter is taken care of by a willing local workforce. Much of *A Year in Provence* is taken up with Mayle watching other people working, mostly on his house and vineyard and in the surrounding farmers' fields. Here is a typical passage:

> The fields around the house were inhabited every day by figures moving slowly and methodically across the landscape, weeding the vineyards, treating the cherry trees, hoeing the sandy earth. Nothing was hurried. Work stopped at noon for lunch in the shade of a tree, and the only sounds for two hours were snatches of distant conversation that carried hundreds of yards on the still air. (43)

As in the best tradition of pastoral, Mayle's narrative sets up what William Empson calls a "beautiful relation between the rich and the poor": a relationship characterized by the apparent absence of class conflict, by the happy coexistence of the local peasantry with the landowning bourgeoisie. This neofeudal fiction is maintained by recourse to old-fashioned—English—"good manners": Mayle clearly prides himself on his honesty toward his faithful workers, and he gives short shrift to those who take their services in vain.

Mayle, like Newby, takes refuge in another English "national asset," self-deprecation: the Provence books make a virtue of his relative incompetence as a country gentleman, his slow adaptation to a foreign culture, and the eccentricities of his English peers. *Toujours Provence* even finds him mocking his own gestures toward "going native," recognizing that the casual lifestyle he and his wife have adopted in France owes less to the carefree attitudes he tends to ascribe to the local Provenceaux than to the privileges that accrue to a foreigner's choice of comfortable expatriation. Comfort, indeed, is a word that resonates throughout Mayle's two Provence narratives. Tensions are rare, and when these do appear, they are usually caused by guests. Mayle's narratives acquire momentum from the mutual exchange of hospitalities, the unhurried give-and-take that he associates sentimentally with the country life. Abuses of hospitality, invariably by foreign visitors, are guaranteed to raise Mayle's hackles, and to bring him "closer" to the locals whose trust he works so hard to win. In this sense, Mayle's books are travelogues that work to *erase* their "travel" status, both by establishing a foreign base that assumes the properties of home and by reversing the conventional traveler's distinction between the temporary guest and the permanent host.

Mayle's work fights free of affectation by stressing the affordability of luxury. While he is reluctant, like most travel writers, to confess to or discuss the reasons for his own affluence, he is more than willing to reveal the cost of a meal—which is, most often, "very reasonable." This, in turn, is one of the reasons for the staggering popularity of his books: for in showing that gourmet meals are within the range of the average citizen—or, by extension, that it does not take fabulous wealth to enjoy a life of leisure in the South of France—Mayle goes some way toward converting an aristocracy of refinement into a democracy of bourgeois comfort, bourgeois values, bourgeois taste. Mayle's fiftieth birthday, celebrated in style in *Toujours Provence,* epitomizes such affordable hedonism, as well as indicating the ideal age-range of his target (British middle-class) readership. (The phenomenal international success of the Provence books also indicates something else: the durability, for city dwellers throughout the world, of romantic myths of "quaint" village existence.) After being conveyed on a horse and carriage to a picnic site outside the village of Buoux, Mayle and company sit under the oaks sipping his favorite peach champagne.

There is nothing like a comfortable adventure to put people in a good humor, and Maurice [the host] could hardly have hoped for a more appreciative audience. He deserved it. He had thought of everything, from an abundance of ice to toothpicks, and, as he had said, there was no danger of us going hungry. He called us to sit down and gave us a guided tour of the first course: melon, quails' eggs, creamy *brandade* of cod, game pâté, stuffed tomatoes, marinated mushrooms— on and on it went, stretching from one end of the table to the other, looking, under the filtered sunlight, like an implausibly perfect still life from the pages of one of those art cookbooks that never sees the kitchen. (43)

Toujours Provence and its precursor similarly give us mouthwatering guided tours of their writer's favorite meals; we, like him, get to sample the menu, be it at a neighborhood cafe, a *routier* canteen, a private wine-cellar, or a country restaurant.[12] Travel narrative, for Mayle, tends paradoxically toward the immobility of still-life painting; or rather toward the festive representations of the frieze or *tableau vivant:* the rural event, the feast, the fair, the joyous spectacle of consumption. These are not, however, the vicarious pleasures of observing the rich and famous; for Mayle's books assume, in an age where "quality" tourism is no longer prohibitive, that the dreams he and his wife live out—the fantasies of the country gentleman—are available to those of average means, as well as to the wealthy: to all those in fact who, working to live, know how to profit from their enjoyment.

For Mayle, as in their various ways for Chatwin, Newby, and O'Hanlon, travel, despite its trials, remains a source of pleasure and enrichment. For their contemporary, V. S. Naipaul, travel—and the writing that springs from it—is something quite different. To be in transit, in Naipaul's work, is to be in a continual state of crisis. As Dennis Porter has noted, Naipaul's travel writings invoke a sense of originary displacement: a perception that all places are the wrong place.[13] And that all times are the wrong time; for as in Newby's and O'Hanlon's travel narratives, the traveler cuts a conspicuously, almost comically belated figure. (Some of the most searing invective in Naipaul's African and Indian books is directed, precisely, against the futility of imperialist nostalgia—not that Naipaul himself is necessarily immune.)[14] Naipaul's anachronism, however, is of a different kind to Newby's. It reflects the fear of abandonment, not the wish for revival; a colonial in spite of himself (raised in Trinidad, of Indian ancestry), Naipaul stands poised between a past he cannot accept and a future he cannot bring himself to countenance—a future that holds no place for him. Sara Suleri expresses the dilemma well: "[Naipaul's] writings lend expression to a dying generation. . . . In an arena of frantic change, Naipaul records a perspective that knows its time is done even before it has had the chance to be fully articulated" (*English India* 150). Hence the rage and, above all, the self-contempt of Naipaul's writings, as they struggle in vain to contain their own incurably melancholic impulses. The viciousness of Naipaul's attacks on romantic nostalgia for "home" and "cultural origins" is the viciousness of a man, and a writer, who knows the condition all too well. So much is clear from Naipaul's notoriously splenetic pronouncements on "Third World" cultures—particularly India's, which often reviles him but to which he feels irresistibly that he belongs. (Naipaul's Indian "trilogy," *An Area of Darkness* (1964), *India: A Wounded Civilization* (1977), and *India: A Million Mutinies Now* (1990), is remarkable for its sudden shifts in subject position from outsider to insider, and for the intensity of the pain that comes from the writer's memory of loss.) It is clear enough, too, from the alternating strains of patrician disdain and lingering affection that he expresses for Trinidad, where he spent his formative years. And it is clear, finally, from the ambivalence he demonstrates toward Great Britain—more particularly, England—where he has resided for most of his life as a fully entitled British subject but where, more than ever, he feels ill at ease, socially marginalized, displaced.[15]

Naipaul's travel writings straddle the gap between an unwanted colonial inheritance and an ambiguous postcolonial present that is neither fully accepted nor understood. Some episodes in Naipaul's work seem almost worthy of Eric Newby, so indebted are they to "gentlemanly" codes and modes of imperialist representation (Eurocentric pastoral, atavistic views on "primitive" cultures, and so on). At times, the persona he projects is willfully distant and elitist—as if he were trying to wed the rigorous asceticism of Brahminical culture to the class-consciousness and refinement of the gentlemen travelers' club. Naipaul might seem to aspire, perversely, to be one of the "mimic men" he despises: taking on the trappings of another imperial culture, emulating others' values and attitudes, consenting to his own subordination.[16] Yet this view is much too simple: for one, it fails to recognize Naipaul's divided cultural allegiances and his undercutting of *all* expressions of originary identity; and for another, it allows no place for Naipaul's critique of imperialist thinking—a critique that is pursued, if indirectly, throughout his work. Like Newby and O'Hanlon, Naipaul aspires jealously to the part of the "English gentleman traveler" while also distancing himself from that very role. But whereas self-irony, for the former two writers, is a strategy of self-protection, an alibi that permits them to reinstate outmoded imperial myths, for Naipaul it is a weapon turned on his own colonial upbringing. And that weapon is aimed at the institutions (in particular, the education system) that have shaped him, not as a member of the nation's ruling elite, but as one of its marginalized colonial and, more recently, immigrant subjects.

Naipaul's ambivalence toward the figure of the English gentleman traveler is perhaps best demonstrated in his autobiographical novel *The Enigma of Arrival* (1987). Strictly speaking, *The Enigma of Arrival* is not a travel narrative at all, but rather a fictionalized memoir of the writer's (Naipaul's) sojourn in western England. However, as in Chatwin's work, travel remains the dominant metaphor—more particularly in this case, as the title implies, the metaphor of "arrival." At the center of the text is Naipaul's reading of de Chirico's eponymous painting, which he construes as an ironic meditation on the deferral of "arrival": on life as a cyclical pattern of inevitably unfinished quests (97–104). The painting illustrates Naipaul's idea of travel as a Sisyphean task of enduring frustration. Shuttling between an irretrievable point of origin and an unassailable point of destination, Naipaul's world-weary traveler occupies an intermediary space between return and arrival. Travel writing—perhaps all writing—is a charting of that space: it delineates the unfinished chronicle of a self in constant transit. Naipaul's cottage, on the outskirts of a manorial estate in rural Wiltshire, is merely the latest temporary resting-place for the exhausted traveler-writer. The novel describes arcing movements away from this already peripheral "center"; it moves, like Naipaul himself, laboriously around its subject, following the rhythms of the seasonal cycle as they spiral downward to decay. Naipaul's is, as Rob Nixon says, a curious form of "postcolonial pastoral" whereby, having "deferred confronting, in autobiographical terms, his own presence in England . . . [he] ultimately faces a garden county suffused by an ambience of Constable, Ruskin, Goldsmith, Gray's *Elegy,* and Hardy" (161–62). This is not a pastoral, as it is for Mayle, of smug cultural nostalgia, but rather a pastoral of regret: a meditative site for dreams of loss. Naipaul's itineraries take him repeatedly to a series of ruins and remnants: reminders of an ancient past, unappreciated by its descendants, but fascinating for an "outsider" to whom "history" has been denied.[17] These gentleman's rambles, all tweeds and walking sticks and elegant self-mockery, reenact a narrative of decline epitomized by the crumbling estate; and by its landlord, a faded aristocrat, now well into his dotage, who survives on a dwindling legacy and vapid fantasies of a "glorious" past. *The Enigma of Arrival,* in this sense, both allegorizes and monumentalizes the work of Empire, reducing its latter-day products to a worn-out landlord, pitifully out of touch with the present, and to his gentleman-manqué tenant, mesmerized by another's past. Naipaul's role as a country gentleman is conducted from the wings; it is significant that his cottage is on the margins of the estate. But it is Naipaul, the "marginal," who gradually takes over the "center," revealing the emptiness and faded grandeur at its core. Naipaul is a "mimic gentleman," an obvious impostor; but no true gentleman presents himself—he is one impostor among the others. Gentlemanliness itself is a pose that mystifies declining power; and in resuscitating it, ironically, in a post-colonial context, Naipaul has produced an antitravel text that both disables forward movement and debilitates the nostalgic energies that sustain regressive myths.

Naipaul's work reminds us that gentlemanliness, in a late-twentieth-century context, has become a mythical act of office—an act in the literal sense that it performs a dramatic role. Naipaul's role as a mimic gentleman in *The Enigma of Arrival* merely accentuates this performance, assimilating it to a broader drama of imperial imposture. Newby's and O'Hanlon's gentleman-adventurers are, likewise, simulacral copies for a mythical figure whose authenticity is placed, like theirs, in doubt. Mayle's country gentleman is a bourgeois expatriate whose only duty is enjoyment; and Chatwin's dandy is an aesthete and a connoisseur of the social graces that make the gentleman, like the dandy himself, into another artistic object. Gentlemanliness, if it were ever genuine, is now almost certainly fake—and, as such, a fitting subject for contemporary travel narrative, which narrows the gap between reported facts, embroidered tales, and out-and-out fables, and which acts as a useful vehicle for the recycling of imperial simulacra in an age that, after Empire, is well attuned to Empire's myths. The English gentleman abroad, however contrived, appears nonetheless as an imperial remnant in narratives that, like Eric Newby's, play to a nostalgic middle-class audience. The popularity of Newby's and, particularly, Mayle's work owes much to a bourgeois conception of (English) cultural nostalgia—a nostalgia in which travel writing, from England and elsewhere, successfully trades. Such nostalgia is reflected in the recourse to comforting forms of pastoral that re-create the conditions for an idealized, mostly indolent, way of "country life." It is also reflected in the attempt, in countries or regions formerly under British authority, to rehearse the gestures that once contributed to the making and sustaining of the British Empire. The role of the "gentleman abroad" here, however ridiculous, is enabling: it springs from the ironic awareness that the Empire has collapsed, but that the traveler is free—or, better, can *pretend* to be free—to act as if it never had. The decline of Empire has further uses: for by taking on the role of the gentleman abroad, the traveler-writer not only transports himself back into another time, but also attempts to disabuse himself of the consequences of the present. As Charles Sugnet suggests acerbically: "The demise of the Empire is particularly convenient, making it easier for [travel writers] to suppress the sense that [they] or [their] readers are connected by lines of responsibility to the events they report" (85). Sugnet's case is overstated: most travel writers are only too aware of their escapist sensibilities. Nor need reportage be the only, or even primary, object of their exercise: for Newby and O'Hanlon, for example, reportage—the recent past recalled in the present—takes second place to the ironic but nevertheless concerted attempt to reinstall a romanticized version of nineteenth-century imperial history. Sugnet is perhaps too keen to discuss the seriousness of a genre that often does its best to persuade its readers not to take it seriously. But this, as Sugnet reminds us, may also be the genre's last line of defense. And also that of the English gentleman; for the gentleman today may be a figure of fun, a subject for camp performance, but he also represents a legacy that is still very much with us. And that legacy may contribute inadvertently to the furthering of the cultural prejudice that travel writers profess to critique but, in spite of themselves, also display. Sugnet again: "Though the traveler no longer represents a literal imperial power and may specifically disclaim such complicity, he still arrogates to himself the rights of representation, judgement, and mobility that were effects of empire" (85). An incident from Newby's *A Short Walk* seems to support the point. Newby and Carless are in trouble with the law after accidentally running down and killing a local peasant on the road to Tehran. Initially charged with murder, they are eventually acquitted. What made the prosecutor change his mind? "The Prosecutor asks me to say," says Carless's friend and interpreter Niki, "that it is because Mr Carless was gentlemanly in this [affair], because you were all gentlemanly . . . that he has decided not to proceed with it" (86). So Newby and Carless are saved, after all, by the myth of gentlemanliness. Should we, their readers, allow them, in turn, to get away with it?

COUNTERTRAVEL WRITING
AND POSTCOLONIALITY

Travel writing has been identified by many of its more discerning critics as a mode of colonialist discourse that reinforces European norms. In her study *Imperial Eyes* (1992), Mary Louise Pratt demonstrates that travel narratives have helped, directly or indirectly, to produce "'the rest of the world' for European readerships at different points in Europe's expansionist trajectory" (5). Pratt's work has been supported more recently by David Spurr (*The Rhetoric of Empire,* 1993), who identifies travel writing as one of those "discourses of colonialism" by which "one culture comes to interpret, to represent, and finally to dominate another" (4); by Ali Behdad (*Belated Travelers,* 1994), who sees his study of nineteenth-century European travel writing as contributing to what Homi Bhabha calls a "meditation on the myths of western power and knowledge which confine the colonized and dispossessed to a half-life of misrepresentation and migration" (qtd. in Behdad 138); and by Inderpal Grewal (*Home and Harem,* 1996), who traces the multiple discourses of travel in "Euroimperial" visions of "home" and "harem"—"spatial constructions," as she calls them, that "metaphorically and metonymically construct home and away or empire and nation at various sites in the colonial period through gendered bodies" (4). All of these writers, to a greater or lesser extent, adopt a "postcolonial" methodology: one defined by Spurr as an attempt both to analyze "the historical situation marked by the dismantling of traditional institutions of colonial power" and to "search for alternatives to the discourses of the colonial era" (6). Aware of the perils of the prefix "post," Spurr wisely resists the temptation to speak of a period "after" colonialism—as if colonialism, in a variety of new and virulent forms, were not still very much with us today. Nonetheless, his definition fails to explain the *pre*-twentieth-century focus of much postcolonial criticism, which directs its attention not so much to the cultural production of the former colonies as to those of the self-designated imperial metropolitan "centers." Postcolonial criticism, some might argue, founders on these definitional inconsistencies, and on the totalizing, ironically dehistoricized vocabulary it often deploys in order to talk about irreconcilably different cultures and cultural issues.[18] With the increasing—mostly academic—commodification of the postcolonial, a further discrepancy has arisen between the oppositional discourses invested in postcolonialism and the marketable exoticism of so-called postcolonial products. *Postcoloniality*—not postcolonialism—best describes the present climate within which such strategically "othered" products circulate within the global market. The postcolonial, in this context, is both an index of *anti*colonial resistance and a code word for the *neo*colonial process by which cultural "otherness" is assimilated, reproduced, and consumed.[19]

What is the status of travel writing in the age of postcoloniality? Historically, travel writing has capitalized on exoticist perceptions of cultural difference: it has made a virtue of, and a profit from, the strangeness of foreign places and cultures, delivering up to its mostly white metropolitan reading public what Paul Fussell calls "the exotic anomalies, wonders, and scandals . . . which their own place or time cannot entirely supply" (203). Clearly, travel writing at its worst has helped support an imperialist perception by which the exciting "otherness" of foreign, for the most part non-European, peoples and places is pressed into the service of rejuvenating a humdrum domestic culture. However, travel writing has also served as a useful medium of estrangement and as a relativist vehicle for the reassessment and potential critique of domestic culture. Both of these registers can be seen in contemporary travel writing, which acts alternately as a repository for exoticist forms of cultural nostalgia and as a barometer for the recording and calibration of cultural change. A postcolonial approach to contemporary travel writing—such as that loosely adopted in this section—might therefore seek to examine the continuing complicity between travel writing and cultural imperialism; to analyze new forms of travel narrative that resist these earlier models and that explore the possibilities inherent in travel writing as cultural critique; and, finally, to assess the extent to which these various revisionist or counternarratives are themselves bound up in an ideology of exoticist consumption.

Caryl Phillips's *The European Tribe* (1987) and Jamaica Kincaid's *A Small Place* (1988) are two recent examples of travel narratives set up in opposition to European norms. Both are extended diatribes against European cultural prejudice and, more particularly, against the destructive value-systems enshrined in hierarchies of race. Racism is the subject of Phillips's often caustic commentary, which draws on sev-

eral of the tacitly accepted conventions of European travel writing—
the assertion of race and class privilege, the traveler's license to com-
plaint, the use of a nonspecialist genre to pass off personal opinions as
sociological observations—but then, twisting those conventions to
meet their own unspoken biases, "wrestle[s] Europe's face around so
that she might at least be forced to stare in the mirror" (xiii). And
racism is the subject, too, of Kincaid's jeremiad on her birthplace,
Antigua, a tiny Caribbean island caught in the drifts of a larger history,
its people exploited playthings in the hands of foreign companies, cor-
rupt officials, and the tourist trade. Both narratives are based on the
authority of their own bitter experience: Phillips's recalls a year-long
trip as a black man in a white-dominated Europe; Kincaid's returns to
an island home distorted out of recognition by the neocolonial forces
of tourism and despotic governments.

What is most striking about these narratives, though, is not the
general quality of their anger but the specific hostilities that they direct
against their readers. These readers are identified, in each case, as being
white Euro-Americans, of the kind that might read travel writing for
the consolations it brings. The consolations, for example, of a temporary escape from a work-obsessed society: an escape, however, that
confirms rather than threatens the dominant (white) culture. Here, for
instance, from Phillips:

> In your churches, education, government systems, architecture,
> music, arts, you belong to a group which exports a culture to every
> corner of the world. . . . Wherever you go in the world, you can carry
> with you evidence of your visible achievements, and they will be uni-
> versally recognized. . . . [But] your eyesight is defective. Europe is
> blinded by her past, and does not understand the high prices of her
> churches, art galleries, and architecture. My presence in Europe is
> part of that price. (127–28)

Or, here, from Kincaid:

> As your plane descends to land, you might say, What a beautiful
> island Antigua is—more beautiful than any of the other islands you
> have seen, and they were very beautiful, in their way, but they were
> much too green, much too lush with vegetation, which indicated to
> you, the tourist, that they got quite a bit of rainfall, and rain is the
> very thing that you, just now, do not want, for you are thinking of the
> hard and cold and dark and long days you spent working in North
> America (or, worse, Europe), earning some money so that you could
> stay in this place (Antigua) where the sun always shines and where

the sun is deliciously hot for the four to ten days you are going to be staying there; and since you are on your holiday, since you are a tourist, the thought of what it might be like for someone who had to live day in, day out in a place that suffers constantly from drought, and so has to watch carefully every drop of fresh water used (while at the same time surrounded by a sea and an ocean—the Caribbean Sea on one side, the Atlantic Ocean on the other), must never cross your mind. (3–4)

The two passages indicate the difference in tone between Phillips's and Kincaid's narratives—the former dryly sardonic, the latter venomously provocative—but in both cases, the writer directs a sustained assault against the reader, designed not merely to jolt him or her out of a familiar sense of complacency, but to associate that complacency with the process of travel and the genre of travel writing. In this sense, both works might best be described as forms of *counter*travel writing that interrogate the privileges that accrue historically to the genre.

In Phillips's case, these privileges are also loosely connected to a specific itinerary: the gentleman's educative circuit otherwise known as the Grand Tour. The Grand Tour, which came to prominence in the eighteenth century as a formative journey for young Englishmen of means—a kind of peripatetic finishing-school for the comparative study of social graces—was treated from the outset with suspicion, if not scorn, by many of the nation's best-known writers. James Buzard quotes from (among others in an amusing selection) Adam Smith, for whom the typical Grand Tourist "returns home more conceited, more unprincipled, more dissipated, and more incapable of any serious application, either to study or to business, than he could well have become in so short a time had he lived at home" (qtd. in Buzard 66). Needless to say, such men of leisure, by definition, were white; their later variants—ironically deflating the pretensions of the tradition—include the American travel writers Bill Bryson and Paul Theroux.[20] In Phillips's case, however, the wry reexamination of the "educational" tour is taken a stage further, becoming the backdrop for a commentary, not so much on class (or gender) benefits, as on the privileges that fall to, and crimes committed in the name of, a "superior" race. Phillips's own European tour takes him from Casablanca, beyond the boundaries of southern Europe, to Moscow on its eastern edge, and back again to his hometown, London. Everywhere he goes, his original thesis is confirmed: that Europe is a tribal society, closing ranks against outsiders—especially those considered as belonging to a different race.

The gloom of Phillips's narrative, although alleviated by a lively sense of humor, is as oppressive as the heat in Morocco, the cold in Russia, and the rain in London. Casablanca, for all its glamour, is under the neocolonial jackboot; the Spanish coasts suffer from the thuggery of an army of British tourists; France, Italy, and Germany are openly racist in their attitudes toward immigrant labor; Scandinavia, too, is hostile, and Russia ideologically opportunistic. Phillips no sooner arrives in many of these countries than he wants to leave; and overall, we get the impression of a disaffected, often fractious traveler, more anxious to prove his point than to broaden his range of experience, and more anxious still to affiliate himself with other, mostly marginalized, blacks in Europe, only to discover that he and they have little to communicate, little in common.

Phillips learns little from his tour, it seems, other than what he knew so well already: that racism is ingrained in Europe's sense of self-identity; and that he, as a black Briton, culturally a part of Europe, can "find little empathy with the cultural bravado of a Eurocentric past" (128). Like Naipaul—with whom, ideologically, he has next to nothing in common—Phillips uses travel writing to examine his nagging feelings of displacement, and to attempt in vain to reconcile "the contradiction of feeling British while being constantly told in many subtle and unsubtle ways that I did not belong" (9). Phillips positions himself, like Naipaul, as a consciously liminal figure, wandering the margins of a continent that locks its doors against "his kind"; unlike Naipaul, however, Phillips has no wish to capitalize on his marginality, but rather to combat it—to make others recognize and accept his presence:

> Black people have always been present in a Europe that has chosen either not to see us, or to judge us as an insignificant minority, or as a temporary, but dismissible, mistake. I looked down at the Grand Canal and realized that our permanence in Europe no longer relied upon white European tolerance, but made a much more radical demand. Europe must begin to restructure the tissue of lies that continues to be taught and digested at school and at home for we, black people, are an inextricable part of this small continent. And Europeans must learn to understand this for themselves, for there are among us few who are here as missionaries. (128–29)

Like *The European Tribe, A Small Place* is tantamount to a moral crusade against white racism. Unlike Phillips, though, whose position as a black Briton remains equivocal, Kincaid immediately takes up the cudgels on behalf of the dispossessed. Or so it appears at first from the stinging rhetoric of accusation that Kincaid, as a native Antiguan, flings in the faces of her "touristic" readers. The battle lines are clearly drawn, and there can be no doubt as to Kincaid's side:

> That the native does not like the tourist is not hard to explain. For every native of every place is a potential tourist, and every tourist is a native of somewhere. Every native everywhere lives a life of overwhelming and crushing banality and boredom and desperation and depression, and every deed, good and bad, is an attempt to forget this. Every native would like to find a way out, every native would like to take a tour. But some natives—most natives in the world— cannot go anywhere. They are too poor. (18)

So much for romantic myths of the (Caribbean) Noble Savage, which, as Kincaid rightly points out, are part of the racism they deny. But the strength of Kincaid's position—vehemently antiwhite, vehemently antitourist—is compromised by her own status as a returning, if intimate, visitor. (Kincaid currently lives in the United States, where, like Phillips, she makes a living teaching creative writing.) Thus, we find her at times lapsing into nostalgia for the "old Antigua," or viewing her fellow Antiguans with what looks suspiciously like condescension:

> I look at this place (Antigua), I look at these people (Antiguans), and I cannot tell whether I was brought up by, and so come from, children, eternal innocents, or artists who have not yet found eminence in a world too stupid to understand, or lunatics who have made their own lunatic asylum, or an exquisite combination of all three. (57)

Like Phillips, Kincaid is occasionally trapped within the same romantic conventions of a genre she otherwise deromanticizes, strips of its triumphal myths. Phillips's and Kincaid's travel writing opposes narratives such as Newby's or O'Hanlon's, which are arguably less concerned with documenting the actual places their writers visit than with setting up a playground for the acting out of their own, and their readers', private fantasies. *The European Tribe* and *A Small Place* are sociological in their orientation, highly politicized in their impact, and, above all, deeply committed to the drive for social change. Yet they are also travel narratives, if postcolonial in their persuasion, and as such they remain complicit with the tourism they denounce. Kincaid's essay, for example, is itself arguably the product of a touristic sensibility; its rhetoric of blame has an antiracist motivation, but it also derives from a genre that traditionally sees itself as antitouristic. Phillips and Kincaid both show the advantages of a certain kind of travel writing—

one that resists, rather than panders to, the escapist fantasies of its readers, and that interrogates, rather than asserts, the privileges that accrue to the traveler-writer—while hinting, once again, at the contradictions inscribed within a genre that sets itself in opposition to the very economic forces that make it possible.

The limits of resistance are also amply demonstrated in a travel narrative that seeks to *document* resistance: Salman Rushdie's *The Jaguar Smile* (1987). The book is the result of Rushdie's three-week trip to Nicaragua in 1986 as a guest of the Sandinista Association of Cultural Workers, an umbrella organization "that brought writers, artists, musicians, craftspeople, dancers and so on, under the same roof" (12). As in Phillips's and Kincaid's narratives, Rushdie's sympathies lie clearly with the underdog: the book is a tribute to the spirit of endurance in which an oppressed and marginalized people continue to resist their stronger foe. The enemy is within, in the shape of the lurking Contra forces, but it is supported from without by a neurotically anti-Communist United States. The scene is a familiar one of U.S. neo-colonialism, and it is sketched by Rushdie with a travel writer's eye for—often comic—detail and a political journalist's ear for controversy and sensationalist debate. This mixture of comic travelogue and hyperbolic political commentary runs the risk of trivializing the object of its ostensibly "serious" study. Rushdie clearly sides with the Sandinistas, affiliating himself with their struggle:

> When the Reagan administration began its war against Nicaragua, I recognized a deeper affinity with that small country in a continent (Central America) upon which I had never set foot. I grew daily more interested in its affairs, because, after all, I was myself the child of a successful revolt against a great power, my consciousness the product of the triumph of the Indian revolution. It was perhaps also true that those of us who did not have our origins in the countries of the mighty West, or North, had something in common—not, certainly, anything as simplistic as a unified "third world" outlook, but at least some knowledge of what weakness was like, some awareness of the view from underneath, and of how it felt to be there, on the bottom, looking up at the descending heel. I became a sponsor of the Nicaragua Solidarity Campaign in London. I mention this to declare an interest; when I finally visited Nicaragua . . . I did not go as a wholly neutral observer. I was not a blank slate. (12)

Rushdie's ties to Nicaragua turn out, however, to be more complex. For one thing, he is a guest and is treated as such with grace and courtesy, mixing (mostly) with celebrities and the cosmopolitan literary set. And for another, his narrative, more traveler's tale than social commentary, is content to remain for the most part (as traveler's tales will) at the level of surfaces: hence the surfeit of anecdotes, joking asides, and folksy aphorisms—his comment, for instance, that the "beauty" of Nicaragua also contains "the beast" (90). Alongside interviews with political leaders (including Daniel Ortega and his foreign minister) are a clutch of jocular references to popular European and American cartoons: the poet Ernesto Cardenal is described as a "Garry Trudeau cartoon of himself: the radical priest according to 'Doonesbury'" (43); and at one point Rushdie, comparing Nicaragua's struggle to "that of the ancient Gauls in the famous French comic-books by Goscinny and Uderzo," likens Ortega to "a new Gaul: Sandinix" (163). (*The Jaguar Smile,* which takes its title appropriately from an anonymous limerick, can itself be compared to the genre that it incorporates: the political cartoon. As in Rushdie's novels, there is a strategic infantilism behind the narrative—a child's-eye view intended for adults, but mocking adult claims to truth.)

Rushdie's book illustrates the effectiveness of travel writing as a political vehicle—its capacity to undercut all forms of public discourse, thereby robbing political speech of its pretensions to high moral seriousness—but it also raises doubts, endemic to the genre, as to the writer's own position. Rushdie is seemingly caught between the critical enthusiasm of the part-time investigative journalist and the chummy complacency of the "invited writer": the honored literary guest. He clearly likes to see himself, as do Phillips and Kincaid, as a "writer in opposition," a writer whose role includes "the function of antagonist to the state" (70). Yet this role is modified, as he readily admits, in Nicaragua, where he is not only "on the same side as the people in charge," but is surrounded by other writers who, almost without exception, support the existing government (70). The writer's capacity to resist as a free-thinking "dissident" intellectual is contained in Nicaragua within a larger history of resistance. Resistance is embodied *in* the state to an oppressive outside power: this upsets Rushdie's largely romantic view of the oppositional writer—a view apparently based on the rights, not of the collective but of the individual. Understandably, Rushdie shies away from the idea of the writer as a party ideologue; yet his own idea of the writer as a "literary migrant" is also suspect, not least because it seems to allow him the best of both, or many, worlds.[21] Thus, in the epilogue to *The Jaguar Smile,* we find him swapping stories with another affluent migrant, a Nicaraguan woman returning home to France after attending her mother's funeral. Both of them sympathize with the Sandinistas, with a few pertinent reservations. (Prophetically perhaps, press censorship is the highest on Rushdie's list.) After talking on the plane,

> We parted in Madrid, and returned to our separate lives, two
> migrants making our way in this West stuffed with money, power and
> things, this North that taught us how to see from its privileged point
> of view. But maybe we were the lucky ones; we knew that other per-
> spectives existed. We had seen the view from elsewhere. (170)

Unlike Naipaul—or, in a different context, Phillips—Rushdie sees none of the disadvantages of migration (although to be fair, in his other work, these disadvantages are shown in abundance).[22] Instead, he co-opts migration into his own hybrid aesthetics, which, as he explains three years later in a response to the fated publication of *The Satanic Verses,* "rejoices in mongrelization and fears the absolutism of the Pure. *Mélange,* hotchpotch, a bit of this and a bit of that is how *newness enters the world.* It is the great possibility that mass migration gives to the world, and I have tried to embrace it" (*Imaginary Homelands* 394). Migration affords the privilege of a multiple perspective— but then so too does travel in its most generous, cross-cultural sense. Migrants, of course, are always likely to gain a deeper understanding of two (or more) cultures than is attainable for vacationing travelers, however much information these latter might glean from their temporary sojourns or trips. Yet the discourse of migration, like the wider discourse of travel of which it forms a part, is riven by its own—frequently unacknowledged—internal contradictions.[23] For Rushdie, migration seems to presuppose a luxury of perspective and a freedom of movement available to the cosmopolitan elite. (Obviously, such luxuries and freedoms—however hard-won—are in short supply. More obviously still, migration is driven above all else by economic need.) A connection apparently exists between Rushdie's migrant-oriented aesthetics and his ambivalent status as an "oppositional" traveler-writer in Nicaragua. And this connection resides in the writer's utopian rhetoric of displacement—a rhetoric that allows him to resist the state that continues to give him service, and to move about the world in search of a solidarity of the oppressed.

A less obviously "oppositional," but nonetheless unorthodox, stance is taken up by two contemporary travel writers, also of Indian background: Amitav Ghosh and Vikram Seth. Ghosh's *In an Antique Land* (1992) is, as its subtitle explains, "history in the guise of a traveler's tale": it uses travel as a bridging metaphor to interweave the contemporary narrative of Ghosh's anthropological research in rural Egypt with his historical reconstruction of the life story of a medieval Middle Eastern trader, Abraham Ben Yiju. Seth's *From Heaven Lake* (1983) is, in appearance at least, a more conventional travel narrative, relating the story of Seth's troubled passage, while on leave from his studies at Nanjing University in China, through northwest China, Tibet, and Nepal on his way back home to Delhi. Seth, like Ghosh, is clearly an adaptable and enterprising traveler: both men are gifted scholars from accomplished Indian families, well versed in the languages of the countries through which they travel and well informed about those countries' respective social customs, religious practices, and cultural history. What separates Seth and Ghosh, though, from the majority of contemporary traveler-writers is the perspective that they bring from a historically subjugated culture. Thus, Ghosh is introduced to a family in the village of Nashawy by his fellow scholar Ustaz Sabry as

> a student from India . . . a guest who had come to Egypt to do research. It was their duty to welcome me [Ghosh] into their midst and make me feel at home because of the long traditions of friendship between India and Egypt. Our countries were very similar, for India, like Egypt, was largely an agricultural nation, and the majority of its people lived in villages, like the Egyptian fellaheen, and ploughed their land with cattle. Our countries were poor, for they had been ransacked by imperialists, and now they were both trying, in very similar ways, to cope with poverty and all the other problems that had been bequeathed to them by their troubled histories. (134)

Seth, in contrast, must negotiate a history of mutual ignorance and conflict:

> If India and China were amicable towards each other, almost half the world would be at peace. Yet friendship rests on understanding; and the two countries, despite their contiguity, have had almost no contact in the course of history. . . . [N]either strong economic interest nor the natural affinities of a common culture tie India and China together. (177–78)

Conceding that time and patience will be needed to solve the two nations' border problems, Seth concludes that to learn [on a personal level] about another great culture is to enrich one's life, to understand one's own country better, to feel more at home in the world, and indirectly to add to that reservoir of individual goodwill that may, generations from now, temper the cynical use of national power. (178)

Goodwill is clearly a quality that Ghosh, as well, would like to believe in; but unlike Seth, he relates it further to two once rich but now impoverished countries (India and Egypt), whose cultures of "accommodation and compromise"—based on mutual trust and respect—have historically made them vulnerable to the aggression of the European imperial powers. In this context, Ghosh's finely crafted reconstruction of the medieval history of the Indian Ocean region—a region linked by commerce and the cross-fertilization of ancient religious cultures—emerges as a counternarrative to the European historical record: a record marked by violent conquest, the will to control land and resources, and a use of military force in the service of personal and collective greed.

Ghosh, however, like Seth, takes care not to present India as a mere historical victim. In *From Heaven Lake,* this entails the careful comparison of modern-day India and China—a comparison that, while weighed in favor of the more "democratic" nation, nonetheless shows the advantages brought about by state control. (Significantly, Seth takes on his travels a copy of Naipaul's *India: A Wounded Civilization:* a coruscating attack on the "degeneration" of Indian culture with whose thesis he cannot agree, but a book that still impresses him with its great passion and rhetorical force.) Meanwhile, in *In an Antique Land,* Ghosh—an inexperienced anthropologist, more at home in the archive than in the field—is made to take a dose of his own (culturally) relativist medicine. In a kind of reverse ethnography, Ghosh himself becomes informant: a respondent to others' annoyingly persistent questions about his Hindu culture and, more particularly, about its—to Egyptian Muslim eyes—"barbaric" religious practices. In a tetchy, characteristically self-deprecating exchange with the village Imam, Ghosh fends off the latter's attack on India as a "backward" civilization by appealing ironically to India's superior military technology:

"In my country . . . we have guns and tanks and bombs. And they're better than anything you've got in Egypt—we're a long way ahead of you." . . . "I tell you, he's lying," cried the Imam, his voice rising in fury. "Our guns and bombs are much better than theirs. Ours are sec-

ond only to the West's." . . . The Imam and I [were] delegates from
two superseded civilizations, vying with each other to establish a
prior claim to the technology of modern violence. . . . [D]espite the
vast gap that lay between us, we understood each other perfectly. We
were both travelling, he and I: we were travelling in the West. The
only difference was that I had been there in person: I could have told
him a great deal about it, seen at first hand, its libraries, its museums,
its theatres, but it wouldn't have mattered. We would have known,
both of us, that all that was mere fluff: in the end, for millions and
millions of people on the landmasses around us, the West meant only
this—science and tanks and guns and bombs. (235–36)

Ghosh's book attempts with some success to set up an alternative—
based on a history of friendship and nonalignment—to this master dialogue of destruction and international realpolitik. It also mounts a
challenge to the familiar kind of neoimperialist travel writing that, taking the West as its frame of reference, tacitly supports an ideology of
physical and mental conquest. Yet Ghosh is well aware that the
rhetoric of rapprochement surrounding his own, essentially humanis-
tic, idea of travel tends to occlude the workings of power and the interests of those who have or want it. And this applies both to travel as a
means of effecting trade between different regions and as a metaphor
for the process by which knowledge can be relocated in time and space.
Hence Ghosh's emphasis on archival research as a corollary to his
anthropology: a study not only of the ways in which documents can be
used to (re)define cultural history but of the manner in which knowledge moves and, through that movement, is transformed. Edward
Said's account of the ways in which "theory" travels is useful here.

Like people and schools of criticism, ideas and theories travel—from
person to person, from situation to situation, from one period to
another. . . . Such movement into a new environment is never unimpeded. It necessarily involves processes of representation and institutionalization different from those at the point of origin. ("Traveling
Theory" 226)[24]

One recognizes the basis here for Said's influential "Orientalism" thesis: that the "Orient," as it emerged as a body of knowledge about
other (Eastern) regions and cultures, involved techniques of representation that were designed to assert or reconfirm the intellectual authority of the West.[25] Orientalism goes hand in hand with what Said calls
imperial "imaginative geography": it redistributes knowledge in space
to serve the needs of a dominant culture.[26] Ghosh's narrative, in this

sense, fulfills a "counter-Orientalist" function: the travels of which it tells—including the circulation of information about and within the Middle Eastern/Indian Ocean region—are framed within the context of a recuperative historical narrative: one that, although supported in part by research done in Western libraries, brings that research back to its point of origin at the confluence between interrelated *Eastern* cultures. Travel writing, in *In an Antique Land,* mediates between the temporal reach of historiography and the spatial range of an anthropology that links two formerly colonized countries. The result is both a meditation on the power politics of History (Ghosh's capitalized master narrative) and a tribute to a "legacy of transience" epitomized by precolonial trade (173). In the process, Ghosh sketches a history of travel that predates European intervention: a history peopled by pilgrims, scholars, and, above all, itinerant merchants; and one that traces the knowledge they acquired back to a non-European source.

If Ghosh, in *In an Antique Land,* waxes nostalgic for a time when people, goods, and ideas could move relatively freely, unimpeded by the demands of war and the intricacies of foreign policy, Seth, in *From Heaven Lake,* recognizes that such heady days (if they ever existed) are now over, and that modern-day travelers, like it or not, must learn how best to negotiate borders that are the products of often invisible lines of geopolitical force. Seth is drawn in his Chinese journey to precisely such contested or marginal areas: Xinjiang, a northwestern province known ambiguously as "The New Borderland," and the partly "autonomous" but still closely guarded and supervised country of Tibet. Predictably, Seth finds himself fighting a running battle with the authorities, arguing endlessly over entry visas, exit permits, and travelers' rights. Travel, for Seth, seems to be less a celebration of human freedom than a confrontation of the political obstacles that are placed in freedom's path. The disputed India-China border is one such insurmountable obstacle—the reminder of a fraught history of international relations that has kept "these two great culture zones" irreconcilably apart (178). Seth realizes that his journey home (an uphill struggle in more ways than one) is only a small personal victory in the face of continuing cultural ignorance and political distrust. As in Ghosh's narrative, particularly its modern sections, the reciprocities of individual friendship are overshadowed by the collective forces that break up nations or wrench them apart. *In an Antique Land* ends on a plaintive note, with the attempted exodus of Egyptian workers from an Iraq caught in the hysteria of Saddam's "holy" war. *From Heaven Lake* ends with the traveler's successful negotiation of a final "border": the customs barrier at the international airport of New Delhi. The juxtaposition of these two endings affords an instructive lesson in the politics of displacement: Seth, the "foreign guest," is able after much difficulty to arrive safely home, while as war breaks out in the Gulf, Ghosh watches anxiously in Egypt, as the television screen reveals

> thousands and thousands of men [itinerant Egyptian workers in Iraq] . . . some in trousers, some in jallabeyyas, some carrying their TV sets on their backs, some crying out for a drink of water, stretching all the way from the horizon to the Red Sea, standing on the beach as though waiting for the water to part. (153)

Goodwill, for all its benefits, cannot alleviate economic scarcity; nor can it repair the historical schisms between nations and peoples. Worlds of time and difference separate the traveling merchant, Abraham Ben Yiju, from his descendants, economic migrants desperately seeking a passage home. Ghosh, like Seth, recognizes the privilege behind his own impulse to travel, and the changing tides of fortune that will allow him—others may not be so lucky—to cross the final border that divides him from his home.

Ghosh and Seth produce, in their different ways, counter-Orientalist travel narratives that challenge ethnocentric Western views of a mythicized East. For Ghosh, the Middle East—itself a Western geopolitical configuration—has discernible links with another Eastern conglomerate: the Indian subcontinent. Ghosh's narrative demythologizes (or, better, de-Westernizes) these connections, relocating them in an Asian trade bloc whose lines of communication are retraced with the aid of careful historical research. Seth is much less sanguine about the possibilities of pan-Asian union. After all, there are neither strong economic nor cultural links between India and China: "The fact," says Seth, "that they are both part of the same landmass means next to nothing. There is no such thing as an Asian ethos or mode of thinking" (178). "Asia," like "the East," is of course a mythicized construct, more a product of imported fantasy than of indigenous cultural contact. Yet as Pico Iyer shows in his cleverly observed travel narrative *Video Night in Kathmandu* (1988), Asian countries have come increasingly to see themselves through Western eyes. More particularly, Asia, insofar as it can be understood as a composite cultural entity, represents an amalgam of responses to and adaptations of Western commercial products. Through a series of arresting examples drawn from the different Asian regions—Rambo in China, fast food in Nepal, Hank Williams in the Philippines, baseball in Japan—Iyer demonstrates that the East's exposure to American popular culture has resulted in the emergence of new, exotically hybrid cultural forms. These products arise, not so much out of an imperialist imposition as out of a process of symbolic exchange involving the reindigenization of imported forms. Another way to account for this process is through *transculturation,* a term borrowed by Mary Louise Pratt from cultural anthropology to describe "how subordinated or marginal groups select and invent from materials transmitted to them by a dominant or metropolitan culture" (*Imperial Eyes* 6). "While subjugated peoples," according to Pratt, "cannot readily control what emanates from the dominant culture, they do determine to varying extents what they absorb into their own, and what they use it for" (6). Iyer's book lists numerous examples of this transculturative process: Hollywood films, fed into to the giant machine of the Indian movie industry, produce profitable East-West hybrids; American pop songs, imitated by note-perfect Filipino bands, "express a material optimism that defies [the country's] economic plight" (n.p.); baseball, another cultural import, is reinvented as the Japanese national sport. Clearly, not all of these Asian cultures are strictly "subordinate" to the United States; nor are all of them subject, in similar ways or degrees, to American pop-cultural imperialism. Iyer's task, however, is not so much to indicate the imperialist influence of America as to show how American imperialist myths can be adapted to local ends. And to show, as well, that East-West contact is very much a two-way process:

> A decade ago . . . lines of communication were so crossed that the East looked to the West to bring it the wisdom of the East; now, the process was reversed. For what the Asians brought over to the West were often not so much fragments of the East as new and improved versions of the West: the Japanese provided Tokyo-made Plymouths; the Thais filled L.A. with Bangkok-style American bars; the Chinese served up sweet-and-sour pork (a dish created expressly for Western palates). Japanese country-and-western bars, Korean grocery stores, Vietnamese French restaurants, Indian-run motels—all suggested that the Asians had absorbed the West, and mastered it, more fully and more subtly than anything that could be imagined in reverse. (360)

Iyer concludes from this, very loosely, that the Asian Empire will be much greater in the future than the American Empire is at present:

"the twentieth century [has been] American, the twenty-first century [will] surely be . . . Asian" (363).[27] Yet this conclusion is arguably the result of a Western—more specifically, Western capitalist—view of "global culture" that reduces cultural relations and the products that spring from them to their commodity value on the world market. It is no surprise to find, then, alongside Iyer's fashionable commentary on the ascendancy of Asia, an equally glib rehearsal of McLuhan's theories on that media chimera, the "global village": "Communications had sent the world spinning around so fast that every wheel came around full circle. Travel far enough East and you'd quickly end up in the West; go across the globe and you'd find that you had never left home at all" (102). Media simulations and instant information transfer create the illusion that cultural distance can conveniently be removed; meanwhile, cultural products from both East and West circulate in the global marketplace, creating the further illusion that cultural difference, once consumed, is understood. Iyer's "global culture," spearheaded by Asia, is the culture of the global shopping mall, where cultural artifacts from both East and West are made available for consumption. And *tourism,* as Iyer recognizes, is not just one of the world's largest and fastest growing industries but the most conspicuous manifestation of cultural consumerism on a global scale. Hence the irony, never far beneath the surface of Iyer's narrative, that his travels—and their literary by-product, his travel writing—are complicit with the very processes of commodification they seek to document and explore. The most obvious characteristic of Iyer's writing is its cultivated glibness: its awareness of itself and of its subject as a commodity. In Bali, for instance, which provides the opening sequence for Iyer's narrative, the writing tends to mimic the superficiality of that which it describes:

> Bali, for all the variety of its charms, was relentless in its charm, and it meant the same to everyone who came here. It offered paradise, and provided it. It was pretty as a postcard, and just about as deep. Only a special kind of person can remain for long in Paradise, making his peace with tranquillity. Most people, I suspected, took taking it easy pretty hard. Humankind, to invert Eliot, cannot stand too little reality. (51)

Here again one notices, as in Rushdie's work, the anecdotal tone and phoney aphoristic quality that are the effects of travel writing reflecting ironically back on itself. Bali, Tibet, and China, reduced to their own advertising jingles, are likened to a giant video screen of consumable touristic images. Video, as Iyer's title implies, is a primary weapon in the American pop-cultural arsenal:

[A]s the world grew smaller and ever smaller, so too did its props: not only had distances in time and space been shrunk, but the latest weapons of cultural warfare—videos, cassettes and computer disks—were far more portable than the big screens and heavy instruments of a decade before. They could be smuggled through border checkpoints, under barbed-wire fences and into distant homes as easily, almost, as a whim. (5–6)

Iyer's project is to demonstrate Asia's counterthrust to American cultural imperialism, to show its capacity to absorb, adapt, and reinvent Western cultural products while providing a mirror that reflects the West back on itself at new angles and in new forms. But this project is undermined by Iyer's reluctance to come to terms with his own technologies of representation, and to admit their investment in the ideology of consumerism he sets out to critique. He is certainly ready to confess his relative ignorance as a tourist:

I make no claim to be authoritative about the places I visited. Quite the opposite, in fact. I spent no more than a few weeks in each country, I speak not a word of any of their languages and I have never formally studied any Asian culture. . . . Instead, I let myself be led by circumstance. Serendipity was my tour guide, assisted by caprice. . . . What results is just a casual traveler's casual observations, a series of first impressions and second thoughts loosely arranged around a few broad ideas. (24)

The only special qualification he claims, in fact, is his own "hybrid" cultural heritage: "As a British subject, an American resident and an Indian citizen, I quickly became accustomed to cross-cultural anomalies and the mixed feelings of exile. Nowhere was home, and everywhere" (24). Yet despite his apparent honesty (which belongs to a long tradition in travel writing, the author's opening disclaimer), Iyer's narrative arguably conceals the economic motives and the consumerist ideology on which it is based. Iyer's writing, in this sense, provides another reminder of the ambivalence of postcolonial travel narrative. On the one hand, it demonstrates clearly that travelers, in a late-twentieth-century context, must confront a world of shifting allegiances, changing borders, and densely patterned transnational flows. In such a world, traveler-writers such as Iyer, cosmopolitans from mixed cultural backgrounds, are no longer the exceptions they once were; on the contrary, they might yet in time become the general rule. Thus, while their travel books might be seen in a sense as *counter*narratives, insofar as they pit themselves against the various forms of Western cultural imperialism still dominant within the genre, they also reflect on a world that increasingly *accords* with their own experience—a diasporic world, as the anthropologist Arjun Appadurai describes it, of global differences and disjunctures, in which "the United States [and, by extension the West] is no longer the puppeteer of a world system of images, but is only one node of a complex transnational construction of imaginary landscapes" ("Disjuncture and Difference" 327). Travel writing, such as Iyer's, which sifts the complex codes of what Martin Roberts calls the "global imaginary," serves a useful purpose in adjusting and complicating its readers' perception of the wider world.[28] Nonetheless, one wonders whether Iyer's work might be seen less accurately as a gauge than as a *symptom* of the commodified "global culture" on which it reports and in whose interests it inadvertently serves. While *Video Night in Kathmandu* ostensibly opposes the "Coca-colonization" of Asia, analyzing the various "counter-strategies" that are planned in its resistance, it might also be seen paradoxically as exemplifying what Simon During calls "the global popular": a celebration, rather than a critique, of the interconnectedness of consumer culture, and a tribute to the transnational humanism that such a culture strategically conjures.[29] It seems, says During, that

> almost everyone, almost everywhere, loves the global popular and sometimes consumes it: it produces a mood in which exoticism, normality and transworld sharedness combine, and in which consumption warmly glows. The global popular's humanism cannot be dismissed, precisely because it is so openly commercial. Its "general magic" relies on the trick by which global markets, technologies and information flows fuse into a humanism transcending national boundaries at the same time as, in its clear dependence on marketing, it leaves in tatters the idealism and naive appeal to human nature so integral to older humanisms. (343)

"Postcolonialism," says During, relies on a localized rhetoric of emancipation that tends to obscure the larger "rhythms of globalization" that determine our cultural futures. Postcoloniality, as has been argued here, is a better term to describe the conditions under which "oppositional" cultural products—especially those products, like travel writing, that are invested in the politics of (cross-)cultural representation—

are subject to global market forces that undermine or mystify their potential for resistance. "Antiracist" travel narratives such as Phillip's or Kincaid's; "resistance" narratives such as Rushdie's; "counter-Orientalist" narratives such as Ghosh's or Seth's; "anti-imperialist" narratives such as Iyer's: all of these are the products of writers seeking alternatives to European models, different ways of seeing the world that combat centuries of European prejudice, and that enjoin their readers in turn to adjust their attitudes and perceptions to a contemporary cultural climate in which "difference" is increasingly visible but not necessarily better understood. Yet these writers must contend, as well, with a perceptual legacy of exoticism: a mode of vision in which travel writing, fueling European fantasy, has acted as a primary vehicle for the production and consumption of cultural "otherness." In a postcolonial era, "otherness" is a profitable business, even if the exotica it throws up might look very different in kind from those of earlier times and places. Postcolonial travel writers, in this context, are necessarily embattled: they must struggle to match their political views with a genre that is in many ways antithetical to them—a genre that manufactures "otherness" even as it claims to demystify it, and that is reliant even as it estranges on the most familiar of Western myths. Not least among these mythologies are the ones attached to particular places. Some of these myths of place, and their ideological underpinnings, form the subject for the following—necessarily selective—chapter.[30] And here, too, travel narratives reveal their double nature, providing both an inventory of familiar spatial images and a means toward those images' revision and critique.

Chapter two

Zones

The desire to travel to, and account for, particular regions of the world often figures in the fraught motivations of contemporary travel writers. In fact, contemporary travel writing—at least when it is not about Europe—has arguably evolved from the identification and crystallization of regions that are specified through the processes of Western imperialism, tracing back to the fifteenth century. Later, these regions were to accrue ever denser layers of textuality as European travelers conducted visits in the wake of earlier "discovering" and exploring pioneers. In turn, these travelers' now classic books have spawned narratives that, stripped of immediate pioneering thrill, attempt to recapture it through recollection, parody, revision, or, in some cases, refutation. Thus, even when it strives to communicate change or fresh perception, the contemporary traveler's account will at best supplement earlier versions. Travel writing, for all its sensationalism, is inherently conservative, its narratives serving to repeat and consolidate tropological myths. This chapter examines (mainly) postwar travel writing as it relates to selected geographical/tropological regions: the Congo and the Amazon ("tropical"); Japan ("Oriental"); the South Seas ("exotic"); and the Arctic ("liminal"). Such regions, as travel writing and fiction construct and deploy them, are at best incidentally geographical; built up out of several different kinds of knowledge—historical, political, anthropological, cultural, mythical, and experiential—they become complex textual *zones*.[1] In *Postmodernist Fiction* (1987), Brian McHale uses "zones" to denote the ontological scrambling that he sees as characteristic of postmodernism. In postmodernist fictions, according to McHale, geographical space is continually reconstructed. The space produced by such fictions is inevitably overdetermined: it needs to be seen, that is, in ideological and mythical, rather than merely geographical, terms. Travel narratives tend to produce similarly overdetermined spaces—even if, by and large, postmodernist play is not on their agenda (see, however, chap. 4). "Zone" is more telling than "myth" for these narratives' geographical/textual spaces because it suggests that "[t]raditional catalogues of places and their attributes . . . in effect transcribe the unwritten encyclopedia of conventional wisdom and common knowledge" (McHale 47). Yet as far as travel writing is concerned, this encyclopedia is already written: composed of accounts that endlessly redeploy the topoi of "conventional wisdom and common knowledge," embedding them in the overdetermined cultural discourse of travel.

Reading travel narratives from the perspective of the zone, rather than from that of the traveler as experiencing subject, necessarily inhibits perception of the modern traveler as pioneer/discoverer or cultural discloser. Nor is it just that a "last frontier" no longer exists; for even the most conscientious of modern travelers must also labor to extract novelty and excitement from the frontiers that once existed. Furthermore, the traveler's experience, figured in relation to the zone, generally takes its coloring from previous accounts; if the South Seas, for instance, can still appeal to prospective visitors as an unspoiled hedonistic paradise, the "dreams and wish-fulfilments" (McHale 55) it awakens are likely to repeat those of, say, Herman Melville or Robert Louis Stevenson.

Travel writers today, like most of their predecessors, tend to share with professional ethnographers the yearning to establish a reciprocity with the people and places they visit and about which they write. Yet in most cases, the traveler-writer mobilizes fantasies, as much collective as personal, that are always already entangled in the myths and experiential categories of the zone: in the Arctic, as will be seen, the desire for purgation seeks experience of the liminal; while in Japan, the desire for a poeticized eroticism seeks experience of the feminized Orient. Travel writing, from this perspective, seems trapped within quest rather than discovery, insofar as questers seek what they know more fully on departure than on return. Thus, while travel writing sustains the allure of exchange and acquisition, it often ends up by collapsing back onto the reserves of previous journeys.

The zones of travel writing, then, are zones of repetition, whether it is a case of Redmond O'Hanlon stepping easily into the role vacated by his predecessor Peter Fleming—to exceed it—in the Amazon, or

Roland Barthes assuming the stock metaphor of penetration—to contest it—in Japan. The (Western) mythologies that adhere to world sites seem unshakable and offer an economical, if fairly basic, way of getting to know the world. But can the travel book offer more? As "popular" compendiums of different kinds of disciplinarity—history, geography, politics, anthropology—travel books offer comprehensive and informed commentary, a route along which travelers, whether armchair or field, can become knowledgeable and open-minded about the contemporary world. A few of these books doubtless do provide such routes. Many more, however, either contain the travel zone within the cultural stereotypes they presuppose from the outset or cannot negotiate those boundaries, maintained by an economically and culturally powerful travel industry, within which the travel book cleaves to its preassigned generic path.

ZONE ONE: THE TROPICS

THE CONGO

Nearly every modern travel book that features the Congo[2] as travel zone at some level reinscribes Conrad's classic novella *Heart of Darkness* (1898). In *Heart of Darkness,* as is well known, Conrad set out to contest aspects of Belgian imperial practice in the late nineteenth century while expressing, at the same time, the imperialist paradigm in its starkest form. Nearly a century later Paul Hyland, in his Congo narrative *The Black Heart* (1988), certainly has Conrad in mind when he observes that "[i]n an age of optimistic materialism [white men] held up this barely mapped territory as a mirror to the dark side of their souls" (63). Since Conrad, the Congo has become the textual site of a febrile metaphysics:[3] an abject zone of extreme yet undifferentiated "otherness" in which every aspect of life—landscape, people, culture, politics—presents itself as always already wrapped in metaphor and myth.

The Congo traveler is first apt to locate undifferentiated "otherness" in the landscape. The celebrated Africanist Basil Davidson—not otherwise known for his travel writing—offers the following parody of Conrad and Gide in a formulaic view from a boat:

> The river steamer checks its dilatory pace once a day or sometimes more, and halts at small log quaysides, each with its handful of humanity. But these are figures in a brooding void. Days ahead there will be a riverside townlet belonging to the "modern world" of futile

busywork. But this will be a brief glimpse of urban dust and decay before the bush and the trees close in again, and everything is once again as it was before. Nothing changes; there is only the immemorial merging of one day into the next. (254)

At the beginning of his earlier journey, documented in *Travels in the Congo* (1927), Gide had pronounced himself depressed by "[t]he absence of individuality, of individualization." "Everything is uniform," complains Gide; "there can be no possible predilection for any particular site" (137). The Congo, that is, offers no point where the Western observer might frame, perspectivize, and impose spatial pattern. But the absence of spatial pattern also denotes a historical absence: Congo travelers like Gide become involved in a journey that obliterates history as Europeans conceive it, a journey in which, while "travelling back to the earliest beginnings of the world" (Conrad 66), they are simultaneously "sucked . . . into the continent's maw" (Hyland 13).

The temporal "otherness" of the Congo acts in tandem with its spatial "otherness," impressing itself upon the prospective traveler with a power greater than motivation—with nothing less, it appears, than the inexorable force of fate. Thus, the nine-year-old Conrad, poring over a map of "darkest" Africa, and "putting [his] finger on the blank space representing the unsolved mystery of that continent, . . . said to [him]self with absolute assurance and an amazing audacity . . . 'When I grow up I shall go *there*'" (qtd. in Hyland 21), just as Gide remarks of his journey, "I had not so much willed it . . . as had it imposed upon me by a sort of ineluctable fatality" (4). This atavistic call not only drains the power of those who hear it; it also burdens them with a *metaphysical* load.

Contemporary narratives by writers like Hyland, Naipaul, and Shoumatoff hark back to this pattern, reinscribing Conrad's zone in different ways. Within the zone, history disappears; the landscape becomes sinisterly primeval; human figures become either hypersensual or abject; politics becomes anarchy; noncontinuous phenomena are sucked into an "essential" stigmatized center. Travel into the Congo disfigures, becomes a form of dystopic transgression.

By foregrounding personal sensitivity, accounts such as Hyland's *The Black Heart* seek, however, to mitigate the sense of radical "otherness" that decades of travel narratives have stamped on the Congo. According to this formula, Hyland represents *himself* as altered: he is the alienated one, the "other"; modern man in search of a soul, in search of home. Although Hyland sees himself as the "inheritor of Stanley's self-glorifying vision of the Dark Continent, of Joseph Conrad's ambiguous and anachronistic chronicle" (22), his ultimate destination is a mission station, far upriver even from Conrad's Inner Station, founded by his great-uncle Dan Crawford on the shore of Lake Mweru at Luanza. When he arrives there, a villager greets him: "Eeh Bwana, Bibi, you have come home. This is your village" (243). Yet even while the narrative situates the Luanza mission as an alternative reality (an "other" heart) to Conrad's Inner Station and affirms Hyland's inheritance there, it is not quite "home." Self-conscious modern angst plays between the senses of provisionality and nostalgia:

> Can you run away from home? Escape can feel like homecoming, love and success like death. Travel is gloriously promiscuous: the shifting destination, arrival again and again, the unknown possessed, the quest for an illusory home. So I may have travelled light with a heavy heart. The quest for a cure. I'm in the air, unearthed like Antaeus, needing to make touch. (211)

The perplexing ambivalence of this passage suffuses *The Black Heart,* poising Hyland between the figures of doubtful quester and missionary-inheritor.

At Luanza, Hyland plays the latter role, participating in the work of building and repairing the mission station, while his wife Noelle shares in the lives of the women teachers, nurses, housekeepers, and children. Recounting the life of Dan Crawford, Crawford's wife, and the mission's history, Hyland adopts something of the authority of the heroic male missionary, producing a framed narrative that installs order, progress, and traditional Western paradigms in Africa. Describing a mission that his brother-in-law once administered, Hyland becomes proprietary. He walks past "the orange grove Peter had planned," where "Peter's water-tank still stood high," and notes that an African man "had served as a corporal in the Force Publique for six years before Peter, 'Petrus' he called him, took him on to work" (89). The link between missionary consecration and appropriation is comically posed when the Hylands, arriving in Zaire, "[lay] hands on the *surface* of Africa" (13; emphasis added).

Seen in this context, *The Black Heart* affirms the very mythology it wishes to reject. Hyland wishes that "all white myths and histories for which the people have no use should vanish, as if flushed away by the rains" (136). Yet his mission moves in the wake of Stanley, who

> arrived before the mouth of the river to ascend it, [to sow] along its banks civilised settlements, to peacefully conquer and subdue it, to remould it in harmony with modern ideas into National States, within whose limits the European merchant shall go hand in hand with the dark African trader, and justice and law and order shall prevail, and murder and lawlessness and the cruel barter of slaves shall forever cease. (28–29)

While Hyland glancingly critiques the ideal of the nation-state, he nevertheless casually draws from the stereotype reservoir that writers from Stanley to V. S. Naipaul have invoked—one in which, for example, the traveler can feel "at once, the depth of this soil, the depth of those eyes, the history in the blood" (124); can observe someone practicing "the African art of blankness" (50); and can attribute to a colonial building an "African soul" (54).

Likewise, Hyland essentializes the Africans he describes, portraying them as either mysteriously sensual or extremely abject. Three young women cavorting by the ocean, doing a "naive, self-conscious strip-tease," stir him favorably: one "danced a shapely dance to the waves in a white bra and green pants," a second "wriggled with plump breasts held high, . . . pink drawers clinging darkly to proud buttocks," while a third was "a budding twig of a girl in white pants" (39). On the other hand, a man who "haunts" him "fell about, raving, . . . wearing tatters of cloth, filthy multi-coloured bands on arms and legs, wide eyes staring through glassless welder's goggles, lost somewhere between initiation in the forest and twentieth-century Zaire" (194).[4] When Hyland finally arrives at the demonic center, the Inner Station where Kurtz once reigned supreme, he has a vision of Conrad's gorgeous phantasmal woman:

> I saw Kurtz's familiars and, with Marlow's eyes, the woman, "savage and superb, wild-eyed and magnificent," bedecked with fetishes, gleaming with ivory, aglow with brass, whose arms flung skywards, whose shadow moved on earth and river and gathered the tin-pot steamer into her embrace. (203)

But soon, he conjures a fallen descendant of that figure, another "essential" African woman who

> burst from the hospital gates with her arms flung high, walking in a trance, wailing an extraordinary tune, strong and plaintive, an

exalted dirge, her spirit straining after the spirit of the dead. Sometimes I can almost recall the fierce quality of that sound. Sometimes
it seems like the anthem of Africa. (227)

It is with portentous symbolism like this that traveler-writers in the
Congo offer glimpses into the heart of the deadly "African" zone.

If V. S. Naipaul's incursions into the Congo—"the hot zone"—are
both less fanciful and more literary-minded than Hyland's, they are
also without the latter's ambivalence. In the novel *A Bend in the River*
(1979), and in the "New Journalism" pieces republished as *The Return
of Eva Peron* (1980), Naipaul claims to write in the spirit of a Conrad
portraying the disintegration of the colonial world. Feeling that his
own inheritance is a "mixed," "second-hand," and "restricted" world,
Naipaul first accounts for the Caribbean ex-colonies in those terms,
then proceeds to invoke them again to analyze decolonization in other
parts of the Third World.[5] Thus it is, in Africa, that he feels the

> ground move beneath me. The new politics, the curious reliance on
> men and institutions they were yet working to undermine, the sim-
> plicity of beliefs, and the hideous simplicity of actions, the corrup-
> tions of causes, half-made societies that seemed to remain half-made:
> these were the things that began to preoccupy me. . . . I found that
> Conrad had been everywhere before me. (*Return* 207–8).

When he visits Zaire, then, Naipaul treads in the steps of Conrad, but
with a reversal in mind. Where corruption in *Heart of Darkness* is represented by a European, in Naipaul's "A New King for the Congo:
Mobutu and the Nihilism of Africa" it is manifested in black Africans,
crazed by civilization. Rob Nixon's comment, "When the word *primitive* occurs in [Naipaul's] travel writings, it does so, not in the context
of a last-gasp romantic desire to salvage a purer past, but as a straight-
forward term of abuse" (*London Calling* 54–55), is certainly appropriate for Naipaul's African essays and novel.

Naipaul replaces Conrad's characterization of the Congo as mysteriously savage with a simplistic analysis of neocolonial derangement.
Taught to mimic their civilized colonial masters, Naipaul's Africans
have become caricatures, figures of fun, yet strangely sinister. What
Conrad had once read as nebulous and inaccessible, Naipaul reads as
the confusion, bewilderment, and resentment of "primitive" people
who have been removed from the bush then offered the blandishments
of a civilization they are incapable of attaining. Their resentments "can
at any time be converted into a wish to wipe out and undo, an African

nihilism, the rage of primitive men" (*Return* 187). Naipaul proceeds to naturalize this "primitiveness" within a drastically simple historical frame: in "A New King," for example, history is construed as a brief interval between an "Africa of the ancestors" and a new "mimic" civilization (169). Between these two is a colonial world whose passing Naipaul now regrets, as he deplores how "the Belgian past recedes and is made to look as shabby as its defaced monuments." That "the statue of Stanley that overlooked the rapids has been replaced by the statue of a tall anonymous tribesman with a spear" is part, for him, of the silliness of new Zaire—the same silliness that led the decolonizing state to choose for itself a "nonsense" name, and its president to reject Joseph Mobutu for the ludicrously grandiose "Mobutu Seso Seke Kuku Ngbendu Wa Za Banga" (167). Naipaul's commentary on Zaire describes the same phenomena as a multitude of contemporary African accounts: impoverished, degraded cities; a changeless landscape; grotesque people; government ostentation and corruption. The list stretches on and on. What makes Naipaul's version striking is its *extreme* characterization of the Congo as an overheated zone, a Heart of Nothingness doomed to drag itself back into the vacancy of bush and ancestors:

> To arrive at this sense of a country trapped and static, eternally vulnerable, is to begin to have something of the African sense of the void. It is to begin to fall, in the African way, into a dream of the past—the vacancy of river and forest, the hut in the brown yard, the dugout—when the dead ancestors watched and protected, and the enemies were only men. (196)

In the passage, typically, Naipaul's chosen adjectives—"trapped," "static," "vulnerable"—denote a collective psychology immune to the Western rational mind.

In more recent Congo narratives, the dark fascination with the "hot zone" has escalated once again with the emerging scandal of AIDS. For David Wills, for instance, the AIDS crisis represents "the whole mythology all over again of a monkey on a hot continent" (91):

> It is in a neglected Africa once again that an obsolete technology means dead bodies by the thousands, the threat of millions that would likely have me as dead as you were I one of them, for some strange reason they just keep on dying there in wholesale quantities of causes as old as bad water and as new as AIDS, while the First World disingenuously searches for the software glitch that must be

causing it all, so Africa comes back to hang on our necks, the weight and movement of it has you dizzy, it is Africa you balance on your head (91).

In Wills's account, the association between Africa and AIDS has upped the ante beyond Conrad's dark imperial metaphysics, Hyland's mystery, guilt, and sentimentality, and Naipaul's essential atavism, to reach the all-encompassing hysteria of deathly "systemic dysfunction."

In *African Madness* (1988), Alex Shoumatoff also records a journey into the dark heart of AIDS.[6] Shoumatoff does not present himself in a glamorous light: he is a professional journalist with a liking for tropical regions, always on the scent for stories to be tracked down in Africa and South America. Shoumatoff writes a direct, conventional, and unpretentious prose, from an American liberal point of view, with some resistance to American hegemony and minimal animus toward the African countries he visits. Nevertheless, he does not really challenge the foundational myths about "darkest" Africa that have proved indispensable to generations of traveler-writers. Nor can he resist the temptation to transform a scientific investigative concern to locate the source of the AIDS virus into a process actively symbolizing it as "the African disease"; and he seems repeatedly surprised that professional researchers have not shared his mission of "tracking down the source."

"How curious it would be," muses Shoumatoff, "if the source of the Nile and the source of AIDS prove to be one and the same, the vast teeming lake deep in the dangerous heart of darkest Africa" (133). A more economical formulation joining the traveler's personal quest to the conventional romance and horror of Africa (searches for the source of the Nile, the Rider Haggard romances of the Mountains of the Moon, and so on) can hardly be imagined. And although Shoumatoff tends to question myths about Africa and AIDS, he still foregrounds the myth-laden impulse behind his trip: "despite there being evidence of AIDS as early as 1972 in northwestern Uganda, in the Nile province, Idi Amin's homeland, . . . at some level, perhaps only mythical, Kansewero is the font of AIDS" (132). In Shoumatoff's search for the source, Africa becomes a portent of apocalypse, a promise of horrors that will invade the West in a parody-reversal of the European colonial mission in Africa: "[Many scientists] claim that what is happening in Africa is a nightmare vision of the future of the West" (134–35). Several of Shoumatoff's interviewees, too, "believed that the curtain was falling, that the flood was coming. . . . AIDS was the last straw, the final flail. It played right into the gathering millenarian terror" (170).

Shoumatoff displays a skeptical irony that holds his account back from promoting wilder millenarianism. He is ready to acknowledge ignorance and doubt, to pass on quips that might easily undermine his project, and to report personal encounters without condescension. He asks, for example, "[I]s the clinical picture of AIDS really African?" (140), reports a colleague's comment, "It's funny how they always say it's us. . . . First it's the African killer bees. Now it's AIDS" (180), and quotes a medical officer who, when asked about an Africa-to-Haiti-to-America route," replied, "[W]hy couldn't it have been the other way around?" (163). Ultimately, though, Shoumatoff's account does little to shake up the established myths and symbolic patterns that have long since marked the Congo as a distinct discursive zone. Thus, he links African AIDS historically with the maelstrom of decolonization, in which populations "mushroom," "upheaval" occurs, and HIV "sweeps" from its "hiding place" (139). Morally, he locates the virus in "degenerate" scenes like the bar in Uganda where, a horrified specta-tor, he witnesses "the closest thing to Sodom" (195). And finally, as if to confirm that African phenomena always exist in a "natural," dehis-toricized zone rather than a cultural and political one, he evokes the specter of AIDS in an anodyne domestic allegory:

> A colony of magnificent . . . egrets had taken over a huge tree above [a bungalow] and the roof and yard were spattered with their gooey white droppings. The owner seemed to be living with the situation, to be making no effort to drive the birds away. *It was a case study in tropical acceptance.* (145; emphasis added)

In scenes such as this one, Shoumatoff confirms the mythicized Congo of Conrad, Naipaul, and Hyland. The Congo reemerges as the tropical zone of sad inevitability, the terminus—the *endzone*—of extreme, death-driven abjection.

THE AMAZON

The Amazon, like the Congo, has a mythicized history of abjection, a legacy of remorse—"tristes tropiques"—that anticipates its own destruction.[7] Before recent years, however, when it has become the pre-eminent zone of the sensitive environment and threatened indigenous cultures, the Amazon was also a ludic space—a happy hunting ground—for the "tropical traveler": the adventurer-hero or, perhaps better, the would-be hero of the gung ho type most popularly expressed in the Boy's Own adventure tale.

This tradition, primarily though by no means exclusively British (the leading "foreign pretender" is probably the American Tim Cahill),[8] has been kept alive most conspicuously by the traveler-naturalist Redmond O'Hanlon. The genre within which O'Hanlon writes, like the tradition he stubbornly upholds, has thrived on turning outdoor danger into armchair comedy. One of the genre's "old hands," Peter Fleming, neatly demonstrates its awareness of its own clichés:

> The whole technique of exploring [in the tropics] is overlaid with conventions so unmistakeable and so often mocked—has a jargon so impressive and so easily guyed—that the man who at his first essay adopts the conventions and employs the jargon must lack both shame and humour. (122)

Fleming, whose 1933 travel book *Brazilian Adventure* is a classic of its kind, apparently lacks neither: his own experiences in the jungle, he admits self-ironically, were "always perillously close to the pages of those books which publishers catalogue under the heading of 'Travel and Adventure'" (122)—precisely the books that that other well-known tropical traveler, Claude Lévi-Strauss, derides, in which "actual experience is replaced by stereotypes," and in which "platitudes and commonplaces [are] transmuted into revelations by the sole fact that their author, instead of doing his plagiarizing at home, has . . . sanctified it by covering twenty thousand miles" (*Tristes Tropiques* 39, 18). "I hate traveling and explorers," are the famous opening words of *Tristes Tropiques* (1955); "yet here I am proposing to tell the story of my expeditions" (17). "Adventure is obsolete," declaims Fleming, then proceeds to regale us with his adventures (31). It appears the tropical travelogue needs to disclaim itself in order to bring itself into being. Drawn in spite of itself to cliché, the genre is also irresistibly attracted to parody. More than just attracted; for in the danger-ridden jungles of Brazil, parody provides both the amateur explorer (Fleming) and the professional anthropologist (Lévi-Strauss) with nothing less than a strategy of survival. Parody functions as protective covering, as camouflage; it constitutes a necessary act of self-defense. Here, again, from *Brazilian Adventure:*

> If Indians approached us, we referred to them as the Oncoming Savages. We never said, "was that a shot?" but always, "was that the

well-known bark of a Mauser?" All insects of a harmless nature and ridiculous appearance we pointed out to each other as creatures "whose slightest glance spelt Death." Any bird larger than a thrush we credited with the ability to "break a man's arm with a single blow of its powerful wing." We spoke of water always as the "Precious Fluid." We referred to ourselves, not as eating meals, but as doing "Ample Justice to a Frugal Repast." (122)

And so the show continues. "To anyone who did not think it funny as we did," concedes Fleming, "it must have been an intolerably tiresome kind of joke" (122). But the joke also serves its purpose, becoming, for Fleming, "an important feature in that private code of nonsense which was our chief defence against hostile circumstance" (122).

Two options appear to be open here to aspiring tropical travelers: either they can strike up a pose of moral rectitude, thereby allowing themselves to interpret their experience as a parable of ecological devastation and/or civilizational decline (the Lévi-Strauss model); or they can play out parody to the full, transforming their experience into the stuff of high melodrama (the Fleming model). Several contemporary Amazon travel books—most notably those of Joe Kane (*Running with the Amazon, Savages*)—succeed in combining these two models. Others, such as Peter Matthiessen's *The Cloud Forest* (1961) or, more recently, Brian Alexander's *Green Cathedrals: A Wayward Traveler in the Rain Forest* (1995) are better seen as moralistic "ecotravelogues" in contemplative Lévi-Straussian vein. And still others are ethnographic studies, popularized for a wider audience: examples here might include Alan Campbell's *Getting to Know Waiwai* (1995) and Philippe Descola's recently reissued *The Spears of Twilight* (1996). These books, and many others like them, add themselves to the steady flow of "rain forest" products that have transformed the vivid colors of the Amazon into a swathe of political green. Yet works like O'Hanlon's indicate that the zone of tropical comedy is far from empty, and that it occupies a residual space beneath even the most serious accounts.

The popularity of O'Hanlon's books owes much to their use of knockabout farce and juvenile humor to offset their scientific rationale: the observation of local flora and fauna. In his tropical travelogues to date, *Into the Heart of Borneo* (1984) and *In Trouble Again* (1988) (the most recent, *Congo Journey* [1996], is rather different, being much more "serious" and introspective), O'Hanlon combines Darwinian science with a keen sense of the theatrical: his narratives, like his predecessor Fleming's, are exuberant burlesques, a diet of vaudeville antics served up in a "racy" language and spiced with "naughty" jokes. The Benny Hill of the tropics, O'Hanlon careens around the rain forests of Borneo and Brazil with an almost demented enthusiasm, taking as much pleasure in leering at the local (female) talent as he does in sighting the latest rare animal or bird. "I have decided," says O'Hanlon's sidekick in Borneo, the poet James Fenton (himself a travel writer), "that the hunt for ornithological rarities is essentially frivolous" (*Borneo* 143). So it proves, too, in Brazil; but the more O'Hanlon's companions rave and bluster about their uncomfortable living conditions, about the absurd risks they are taking, about the sheer stupidity of the exercise, the more O'Hanlon enjoys himself, comforted that the people around him are as unbearable as himself.

O'Hanlon's outrageousness is, of course, a classic travel writer's posture; by acting the buffoon, he protects himself from further harm (see chap. 1). While in one sense O'Hanlon is sui generis—the oddest species in the jungle—in another he is following in a time-honored tradition: that of the European naturalist-explorer. *In Trouble Again* begins with an almost obligatory invocation of Humboldt, Bates, and Wallace, O'Hanlon's heroes, and throughout his travel writing he does his utmost to keep their memory alive.[9] In so doing, he allows himself to be seen—invites others to see him—as out of date: "You live in the nineteenth century," Fenton admonishes him in Borneo. "Everything's changed around you, although you don't appear to notice" (*Borneo* 34). O'Hanlon does notice, but he pretends not to; for the willful anachronism that permeates his travel writing paradoxically ensures its (and his own) survival. By presenting himself as a living fossil, a survivor from another age, O'Hanlon duly grants himself the privileges of his forebears. For example, his description in *In Trouble Again* of his brief stay among the Yanomami Indians—another Amazonian icon—draws self-consciously on evolutionary anthropology to reinforce the sense of his own cultural superiority.[10] The observation of "native rituals" provides him, too, with a further opportunity for voyeurism as, homing in on the Yanomami women, he details the markings on their flesh. This fetishization of the "native body" is offensive on many levels, but O'Hanlon seeks refuge by turning the stereotypes back on himself. Thus, in a move characteristic of this type of picaresque travel narrative, he overturns the mores of his "civilized" society to recast himself as a barbarian: "a horrible naked savage" (*In Trouble Again* 194). Nonetheless, we find him recuperating the moral high ground by the end. In the final paragraph of *In*

Trouble Again, the unexpected discovery of a tiny bird's egg affords a wistful reminder of the comforts of home:

> Beneath the tropical sun on Toucan Hill, ignorant, momentarily, like a Yanomami, of the laws of science, gazing at that little egg, I might have been looking at one half of an empty eggshell, a message of browny-white, a present from a mistle thrush dropped at my feet on a Vicarage lawn. (258)

By appealing to the twin discourses of (positivist) science and (High Church) religion, O'Hanlon reclaims a temporarily mislaid authority over his "ignorant" indigenous subjects. Basking in the knowledge of that authority, he allows himself a moment of harmless distraction: to associate the egg with England may run counter to the rigorous laws of Western science—laws that the Yanomami, in their "primitive simplicity," cannot understand—but such instances of fanciful nostalgia are only temporary aberrations; they are permissible, that is, within the context of an expedition that reconfirms the tried-and-tested methods of the West.

In Trouble Again provides a sequence of such aberrations; as if in defiance of the incontrovertible logic of Western science, O'Hanlon's narrative highlights the ridiculous antics and wayward fantasies of its blundering naturalist-hero. But far from diminishing his authority, O'Hanlon's buffoonery merely increases it. Secure in the knowledge of his sophistication, O'Hanlon permits himself the luxury of playing the fool. Charging about the tropics with his gringo's medical kit and outdated European manuals, O'Hanlon sets himself up as a figure of fun; but the last laugh is on us, for he also knows himself to be a serious scientist. However eccentric his methods, however outrageous his behavior, O'Hanlon never loses sight of himself as a scientist; nor does he forget the privileges that accrue to the Western scientist in the field. The wonders of science provide O'Hanlon with a more than adequate compensation for the aggravations of living in the jungle, instilling in him a fighting spirit that allows him to bounce back off the insults of his "uncomprehending" colleagues and return, refreshed, for more. Using the pose of the "reckless adventurer in the tropics" as a cover, O'Hanlon proceeds to go unchastened about his scientific business.

O'Hanlon succeeds in turning the stereotypical "bad trip" (Fraser) into a multifaceted comedy of errors in which the Amazon features as a zone of bewilderment, but also one of scientific expertise.[11] Travel books like O'Hanlon's offer a reminder that the zone of the (Amazonian) tropics has provided a fertile soil for the flourishing of European romantic myths. Persuading themselves that the tropics lends itself "naturally" to hyperbole, self-styled "tropical travelers" have given free rein to their conquistadorial ambitions and exoticist fantasies. Yet if the tropics can be seen as a playground for the voyeuristic European imagination (in search of "wildness"), it is also a vast sanctuary for the naturalist (in search of wildlife).[12] Poised between the fiction writer's desire to invent new worlds and the scientist's need to verify the known world, tropical travelogues such as O'Hanlon's add the survival skills of the seasoned traveler—skills that may themselves be seen as part of a romantic myth—to the knowledge and expertise of the professional naturalist. O'Hanlon's travel writing thus makes use of the tropical zone to recollect exotic (mis)adventure, but also to reinstate authority in Western science's name.

ZONE TWO: THE ORIENT (JAPAN)

Whereas "the tropics," as travel zone, is an area fraught with virile danger, "the Orient's" mystique is one of feminized sexual allure. Nowhere more so than in Japan, figured in many male erotic fantasies after the fashion of the French naval officer Pierre Loti who, arriving in Nagasaki for a four-month visit, saw the country "opened to our view, through a fairy-tale rent, which thus allowed us to penetrate into her very heart" (13). Schoolbooks used to tell of another arrival, Commodore Perry's in Tokyo Bay, and of his "opening" of Japan to the American and European powers. In Loti's text, the verb is used intransitively, indicating the enchanting disclosure of something hitherto concealed, while the next verb, "penetrate," expands the metaphor with suggestions of possession and sexual conquest that are only implicit in the historians' transitive form of "opening." Together, these metaphors suggest a range of significations for Japan as zone: mysterious and enchanting, inviting yet resistant and, above all—like other "Oriental" zones—feminine. In Western representations, Japan has most often figured as an alluring yet elusive feminine "other." Writers have generally eroticized the rituals and artifacts of the containing culture, while focusing these through attempts to locate a specific other in fantasy and reality. But while "Japanese" icons like Loti's Madame Chrysanthème and Puccini's Madama Butterfly have undergone several incarnations, "Japan" itself (herself?) has proven stubbornly resistant to penetration. From the early writings of Loti to the later narratives of Pico Iyer, John David Morley, and Roland Barthes, the impression is one of observers who have barely scratched the surface.

From Loti on, travelers have seized upon what lies closest to the Western popular imaginary to construct Japan as a zone: namely, romance and eroticism.[13] Loti, whose *Madame Chrysanthème* presented an early and influential image of Japan, consistently exploited the erotic potential of professional travel; as a French naval officer he visited and wrote about Tahiti, Senegal, and Turkey, as well as Japan.[14] In Nagasaki, Loti claimed the institutionalized privilege of taking a temporary Japanese "wife," Chrysanthemum. It is common to read Loti's book retrospectively through the lens of the Puccini opera it indirectly inspired. But other motifs of *Madame Chrysanthème* overshadow the initial romantic premise. Loti's condescending friendship with his junior sidekick Yves is ultimately more significant than his arrogant mating with Chrysanthème (Kikou-San), which seems almost immediately irksome to him. Loti anticipates many later writers in constituting Japan as a feminine world, objectifying its women and reducing its men, who resemble "nothing so much as dancing monkeys" (83). He undercuts his surface celebration of Japan as a libidinal territory by a continuous process of miniaturization in which Japanese women become "little Nipponese dolls" (74). If, he concedes, "I really make a sad abuse of the adjective *little*,"

> I am quite aware of it, but how can I do otherwise? In describing this country, the temptation is too great to use it ten times in every written line. Little, finical, affected—all Japan is contained, both physically and morally, in these three words. (242)

Far from being an excellent guide to Japan today, as one recent editor characterizes him,[15] Loti shows through his constant belittling his inability to engage with Japan—a people and culture with which "we [Europeans] have absolutely nothing in common" (184).

While Loti is the literary precursor of many subsequent chroniclers of Japan,[16] he is by no means foundational in constructing it as an imaginative zone. A craze for things Japanese was flourishing in European capitals during the 1880s; what Loti observed was already familiar from "the paintings of lacquer and porcelain" he had seen at home (42). Loti's response to what he labels the Japanese "art of decoration" (327) and, on a larger scale, to European fin de siècle decadence, is ambivalent. While he anticipates Roland Barthes in judging some designs he sees to be "the revelation of an unknown art, the subversion of all acquired notions of form" (186), overall he finds the art to be "entirely conventional" (298), decorative but cheap, trivial precisely in its femininity.

Loti's simple story of Western sailor dallying with the dependent affections of Japanese maiden was to become the powerful archetype for a version of Western Orientalism. Later Puccini, via John Luther Long and David Belasco, raised it to an even higher pitch in his romantic opera *Madama Butterfly*.[17] Puccini's opera raises the stakes by transforming Loti's generic Western sailor into a successor to Commodore Perry, Lieutenant Pinkerton of the U.S. navy. Affairs take a tragic turn: the young naval officer takes an American wife after abandoning his Japanese mistress Cho-Cho San, whose son (by Pinkerton) bears the melodramatic name of Sorrow. More poignantly still, Cho-Cho San, all her romantic illusions dispelled, takes her own life. *Madama Butterfly* reinforces some of Loti's powerful stereotypes without invoking Loti's brutal misogyny and contempt for Japanese culture. But as far as cultural representation is concerned, the effect is pretty much the same: Western men travel East to "open up" a culture that is beguiling, elusive, "other"; they court its fragile women; and then they—often abruptly—leave. Japan as imaginative zone encourages temporary engagement, followed shortly by disentanglement and nostalgia in retreat.

Loti's Japan continues to haunt several contemporary travel narratives like, for example, Pico Iyer's *The Lady and the Monk* (1991), even allowing for the later work's greater subtlety and more nuanced tone. Iyer's book is informed by a perceptive outsider's analysis of Japanese cultural traditions; but it is dominated, for all that, by the writer's fervid romantic imaginary, producing layers of self-conscious fantasy in a multilevel narrative. Within this narrative, Iyer locates two Japans, the "solar" and the "lunar." Solar Japan is "a toyland gone berserk with an intensity that could not have been further from the lyrical land I imagined" (5), and a nation poised to control the global economy, a "collective rising sun of economic power" (7). Lunar Japan, on the other hand, is romantic and mystical. The traditions of Kyoto, Hokusai prints, and Kawabata novels are part of this Japan; so too are "the rainy-night lyrics of Japanese women, [and] the clearwater haiku of itinerant Zen monks" (5). Kyoto, a "templed city that had been the capital for a thousand years" (12), is where Iyer begins his quest to join himself to a fantasy that seems to stir something in his own past. He finds the Buddhist temple where he makes his first home situated in the district of what is variously called "the water trade," "the floating world," and "the pleasure quarters," and imagines he will live the link, celebrated in literature and confirmed in etymology, between the worlds of monk and geisha-concubine. He clinches this link by citing one of Basho's classic haikus: "At the same inn / Play women too were sleeping / Bush clover and the moon" (21). He thus sets up for a narrative that will indulge both a religious text (Buddhist monasteries, Zen monks) and a romantic-erotic one, and will bring the two into mutual play. But the temple belongs more to "solar" than to "lunar" Japan, and Iyer stays only briefly. Its two resident monks are a eunuch and an albino: the one clad in a Mickey Mouse T-shirt and scooting around on a tricycle; the other showing snapshots of himself in famous world cities; both of them TV addicts. Iyer quickly escapes from this feminized, infantilistic cloister, moving to an apartment on the other side of the city. Immersion in the world of the monk seems difficult; but then perhaps Iyer is less interested in mediating Japanese traditions and ancient Zen practices than he is in invoking the *idea* of the monk as a point of self-identification to facilitate the production of the romantic-erotic text.

Given Iyer's tendency to assimilate Japan to his own nostalgia for a lost home, it is not surprising that he refers the country he visits in the late twentieth century back to the celebrated Heian court culture of nearly a thousand years before. Hugh Cortazzi has defined the Heian period as elitist, "created by a small hereditary aristocracy, who were largely divorced from the agricultural economy which provided the economic basis for their existence," and cultist, producing "an aesthetic cult of beauty in nature and art" (40). Iyer uses the lyrical set pieces of his narrative, featuring the moon, water, lovers, giggling girls, and playful children, to textualize the "Heian vision I had sought since childhood" (338). This vision provides scope in turn for Orientalist feminizing, as Iyer, exploiting the binary opposition of monk versus lady, teases it into a play of seduction and resistance, "lady tempting monk, monk renouncing lady" (98). Iyer's Chrysanthemum is Sachiko, around thirty, mother of two children, married to a salaryman. From the moment Iyer meets Sachiko, she carries the burden of mediating the "riddle" of Heian Japan. Sachiko has more roles to play, of course, than that of Heian Lady to Iyer's Monk. But while Iyer concedes "a sense of the tightly drawn limits of a Japanese woman's life" (89), he probes these only in relation to his fantasy of "Japanese woman."

Housewife, mother, Sting fan, avid moviegoer, Sachiko embodies the enigma of "Japanese woman," of Japan itself/herself. Iyer represents this updated Chrysanthemum as a figure of comic pathos, in whom American culture is assimilated into miniaturized Japanese frames. Loti's condescension resurfaces in Iyer's pidgin ventriloquism; here, for example, is Sachiko recounting her visit to *The Sound of Music:* "I very scared. All dark. Many person there. But then, film begin, I soon forget. I much love. I dream I Julie Andrews" (89). When Iyer responds in a similar pidgin, he seems to acknowledge the asymmetry involved in this kind of literary romance: "'But dream world not so good,' I replied, reflecting her English back to her. . . . I realized that I must be sounding bizarrely like Richard Chamberlain addressing the aborigines in *The Last Wave*" (252).

Having ruled out any engagement with a Japan that might pose a threat to American economic hegemony, Iyer is free to construct it out of scraps of literary tradition and an urban culture pictured as vulgarized fairy tale. For Iyer, Sachiko personifies both the Heian and the Walt Disney Japans. Sachiko's "soft femininity" allows him to project Japan as an alluring realm that makes no significant purchase on him; he is free to come and go, and finally to leave, while this mythicized "Japan" continues to exist in the form it had already taken on the day of his arrival. No matter how sensitive, self-reflexive, and knowledgeable he is as traveler and cultural commentator, Iyer fails to challenge enduring Orientalist myths "of strong manliness and soft femininity and the doctrine of male supremacy . . . invented during the samurai-militarist periods" (Miyoshi 196). He does, however, succeed in evacuating the *Japanese* male from the (Oriental) zone.

While Sachiko is spared Chrysanthemum's fate, Iyer leaves her just as surely contained by Western romance. Step by step he leads her to recognize her subjection to the dream world of the media. At the end, she plans to divorce her—already invisible—husband, has trained to be a tour guide, and has even plucked up courage to take a tour abroad with her "savior" Pico. Iyer revealingly remarks that she has been "clearly captive to nothing but her situation, captive to Japan, in fact" (265). So Iyer has "rescued" Sachiko, but only from the zone of his own enchantment. He then goes on to cite two powerfully manipulative myths, commenting that classical novelists dwelt upon young women "mostly for the use they made of them, pygmalionizing them, treating them as flowers almost" (332), and fantasizing that Sachiko "was a kind of sleeping beauty awakened by romance" (122). Such analytic embroidery suggests that Iyer's construction of an "other" (Oriental) culture seeks those familiar satisfactions of travel writing—nostalgia, fantasy, power—that are dependent on conventional and selective modes of experience.

John David Morley's *Pictures from the Water Trade* (1985), in contrast, demonstrates that the travel book can draw familiar items from a collective image-reservoir of the exotic and mediate them through personal experience to produce a culturally richer document. Morley's book is technically a novel since its traveler-protagonist is the third-person Boon, but its provision of a persona for the traveler and of a motivation for travel, and its use of illustrative anecdotes for ethnographic reflection, are evidence of the travel narrative, delivered in an innovative form. By creating the character of Boon, Morley achieves a doubled distance from his narrative material: Boon experiences Japan, and Morley reports Boon's reflections. And unlike so many other travel writers, Morley presents a Japan of conceptual difference, of codes not immediately accessible to amateur Western ethnography.

Morley's narrative finds its place within an expanding subgenre of travel writing, the "visiting teacher-student" account:[18] he went to Japan originally on a cultural scholarship and spent part of his three-year stay teaching English. The implied premise of this subgenre is that the pedagogical visit is in itself heuristic, and problematic aspects of the process of acquiring insider knowledge of a different culture are duly foregrounded. Morley underlines the provisionality of his experiment in cultural investigation, consistently exposing Boon's incomplete knowledge and emphasizing how cultural understanding undergoes continuous revision. *Pictures from the Water Trade* thus constructs a liberating play between its protagonist's cool self-confidence and the dawning sense of a cultural zone that proves resistant to decoding.

As its title indicates, Morley's book shares a central trope with most Western travel books about Japan—a strongly eroticized zone. While Boon/Morley, unlike Loti and Iyer, does not excise other men from the zone, he still centers the text on Mariko, the target of his particular sexual quest, and on the "water trade" (also known as the "floating world") as an enveloping context for his erotic adventures. Even when Morley focuses on cultural practices like calligraphy *(shodo)*, these suggest erotic experience. His most insistent metonym for Japanese erotics is the nape of the neck ("Japanese women showed themselves most beautiful where they were also most vulnerable" [87]), but, as he demonstrates, a great many things—not just parts of the body—can index the erotic:

> Boon still had no inkling of the breadth and resonance of *shodo*. For him it was largely the sensual friction of contrasts, black and white, wet-dry, hard-soft. The dark illicit sexuality with which *shodo* was flush, the rampant brush spilling onto the page, all this had excited him from the very start, and by chance it clashed with a discovery he made at about the same time he took up *shodo*. After three or four inert months he had awoken to the attractiveness of Japanese women. (86)

Passages like this one draw a clear connection between the erotics of cultural practices and the potentially sexual nature of cross-cultural encounters. And, in contrast with Iyer, who overlays his relationship with Sachiko with obfuscating layers of romantic sentimentality, Morley describes the Boon-Mariko relationship with candor while using the possibilities it affords for interrogating romantic conventions in different cultures.

Morley moves easily from experiential narrative through analysis to contextualization of the particular phenomenon within broader cultural structures. The water trade, for instance, produces specific practices in relation to cultural ideology. In analyzing one particularly vivid episode, in which Boon/Morley visits a cabaret where the extent of the clients' "freedom" is to fondle the employees' breasts, Morley sees the cabaret as an anti-Oedipal institution of mothers and daughters where the phallic aspirations of male customers must be "kept under the counter." What Boon/Morley sees is

> a myth as old as humanity . . . The desire for mothers and sisters, real enough but afraid of censure, defied taboo under the veil of symbol. The partners of desire were mothers and sisters in no more than name; it was only play. In this watery mythological landscape there was no Laius, and hence no Oedipus. Sage *mamas* prevented sons from putting out their eyes by keeping fathers eternally out of sight. (214)

The discovery that "the androgynous word *chichi* . . . was a homonym, either breast or father but not both at the same time" (213) makes the analysis plausible.

The densest cultural and ideological construct for Morley is the insider/outsider opposition. The urge to understand this opposition as fully as possible presents a material challenge to him, since it bears upon his own quest—at once cultural and sexual—to become an insider. The book suggests that the quest is partly successful, but even so Morley recognizes that no visitor can "penetrate" another culture. That recognition, and the way in which it is presented as evolving, are further indications of the narrator's candor.

> Much of what [Boon] had learned and thought he had acquired from the Japanese character and way of life was only a precious veneer, something on the surface which in his heart he did not share. As if this insight had disqualified him in his own eyes Boon began to feel almost like an imposter among his Japanese friends. What were these things he could not share. Ruefully he had to admit that he did not know. His claims to familiarity with Japanese culture were unfounded. (186–87)

Roland Barthes, whose *Empire of Signs* (1970) has been described as "one of the most radically different travel books ever written" (Porter 228), would probably have approved of the agnosticism Morley attributes to Boon. For Barthes, Europe's engagement with "otherness," demonstrated in an array of scientific and nonscientific discourses, "manifest[s] the destiny of our [European] narcissism" (4): in other words, when Europe encounters difference, it inevitably sets in motion a process assimilating the unfamiliar to the European known. Asia is a case in point: "We" end up "always acclimating our incognizance of Asia by means of certain known languages (the Orient of Voltaire, of the *Revue Asiatique,* of Pierre Loti, of *Air France*)" (4). In his travel book, then, Barthes turns Loti's fantasy of penetrating to the very heart of Japan inside out. Morley recognizes that Japan, as zone, is defined in codes he cannot penetrate; Barthes's conceit is rather that these codes, far from stimulating penetrative desire, insist on surface and plane. Japan attracts precisely because it contests the Western drive for understanding and mastery, for penetrating to the cultural "heart." It challenges Western semiological systems, especially the one that seeks to contain difference by situating it within a rigid binary of (Western) masculine and (Oriental) feminine.

Empire of Signs is not a chronologically ordered narrative, but rather a collection of essays that proceeds through a series of apparently arbitrary topics: food, city plans and maps, packages, Bunraku theater, Zen and the haiku, faces and bodies, and so on. Tokyo, which Barthes characterizes as "in itself an amazing mass of ethnographic material" (*Grain of the Voice* 264)—a city "he enjoyed . . . without the bad faith of an ethnologist who goes to examine foreign countries" (230)—draws the material into the cohesiveness of the conventional travel book. But Barthes disavows any intention to actually represent Japan; he invites the reader instead to accept "Japan" as a semiotic system, a fantasy zone constructed from "a certain number of [distinguishing] features" (*Empire of Signs* 3). Nevertheless, Barthes's empire of signs *does* signify, and in contexts that are similar to those of more orthodox travel books. Take his assertion that "in that country I am calling Japan sexuality is in sex, not elsewhere," whereas in the United States, "sex is everywhere, except in sexuality" (28–29). But for Barthes, as for Morley, the "elsewhere" that does not exist in sex is in eroticism—an eroticism that infuses hosts of cultural practices and productions. Thus, he talks of "the pure . . . erotic project of the Japanese body" (10); chopsticks are "something maternal . . . the instrument never pierces, cuts, or slits, never wounds but only selects, turns, shifts" (16); vegetables are "garbed in an aesthetic nakedness" (19); a calligraphy brush "has the carnal, lubrified flexibility of the hand" (86); and, more startling, he gives us the "the image of a naked Japanese boy, tied up very neatly like a sausage: the sadistic intent . . . absorbed in the practice of an extreme art: that of the package, of *fastening*" (45). The cultural seduction registered here is not, after all, so very different from the one we find in Iyer's and Morley's accounts.

Barthes's "Japan" is not a country so much as it is a pretext for rejecting Western sign systems that encode "the rights of the 'father tongue'" (6). This West, phallic and patriarchal, "moistens everything with meaning . . . impos[ing] baptism on entire peoples" (70): its "ways of interpretation are intended to *pierce* meaning" (72). Allying himself with other French poststructuralists of the period (Derrida, Lacan, Kristeva), Barthes uses Japan to celebrate the kind of play with signifiers that produces what these theorists call *jouissance*—a play that rebels against the fixed signification they associate with cultural authority.[19] When Barthes describes a Japanese body, in fairly ordinary circumstances, as "sustain[ing] with you a sort of babble" (10), he is probably alluding to the form of pre-Oedipal babble (explicated by Lacan and Kristeva) that functions as a mode of intimate connection between infant and mother, and that is briefly available before the baby is forced into the phallic world that Lacan calls "the Symbolic order." Dennis Porter, in *Haunted Journeys,* explains Barthes's improbable rhapsody over chopsticks in terms of his celebration of a maternalized Japan:

Chopsticks reawaken in Barthes the pleasures of orality and of the mother's body from which we are separated at the moment of our weaning and our entry into paternal language or the symbolic order . . . [They represent a] fantasy . . . of dyadic plenitude and a breast that is always there. (298–99)

Orality thus becomes a privileged alternative to the overdetermined codes of Western writing; it is not surprising, in this context, that Barthes takes particular pleasure in *not* understanding a foreign language, and in intuiting its challenge—beyond the tyranny of "meaning"—to the "father tongue." While *Empire of Signs* can certainly be seen as a different kind of travel narrative, Porter's claim that "it marks an end of travel literature as we have known it in the West" is excessive (111). Although Barthes's romanticization of Japan is very different from, say, Iyer's indulgent sentimentalism, his book still bears within its empire the familiar signs of (exotic) romance. If the book is marked by the particular grace, playfulness, and intelligence that Barthes has at his disposal, it is not so unusual in subjecting Japanese cultural forms to sympathetic scrutiny. And it does after all— inevitably inaccurately—represent aspects of an actual culture while transforming the site of that culture into an imaginative zone. Barthes continually reminds his readers that the Japanese sign has no referent that he will claim for it. But of course the sign does refer: its referent is found within the context of Barthes's rejection of Western semiology, with its rage for "meaning," joining with a particular perspective on Japan as a culture saturated with nonsignifying codes. If a feature of travel writing is its propensity for escapism, then *Empire of Signs* takes up its place *within,* as well as against, the genre; and if a feature of Orientalist travel narratives is characterization of the Orient as feminine, then Barthes's book certainly occupies space as an Orientalizing text. As Lisa Lowe has concluded about such narratives,

An antitext to the West[,] . . . Japan is ultimately not an "atopia" but a "Utopia." . . . [Barthes's] desire to escape his own subjectivity, history, and language is quite evidently an oppositional desire, still caught with the binary logic he seeks to avoid. Japan is continually described with reference to the Occident, solely in terms of what the Occident is *not.* (159)

Barthes's move to bracket referentiality in this "Japan" ultimately leads him to a mode of essentializing that is no less complete than in other, more conventionally presented travel books.

The "otherworldliness" of Japan, as captured in a variety of (semi)utopian Euro-American travel narratives, is replicated in that most utopian of travel locations: the South Seas. Paul Theroux, for instance, beginning his paddle-borne tour of the region in *The Happy Isles of Oceania* (1992), muses that "the Pacific seemed like outer space, an immensity of emptiness, dotted with misshapen islands that twinkled like stars, archipelagoes like star clusters" (18). Theroux's terms are suggestive of a last frontier, childhood wonder, and a frisson of the grotesque—all of which we might expect in a traveler's response to zones as "enchanting" as the Pacific. But the simile as a whole is also historically apposite, echoing the poetic delight of Keats, who, in "On First Looking into Chapman's Homer" (1816), registers the naive wonder of a "watcher of the skies / When a new planet swims into his ken." Astronomical science had made the heavens accessible as a figure for the wonder of "discovery" not so long before, when Cook, sailing the Pacific, observed the transit of Venus and produced his maps (1768–71); thus it was that the Pacific entered into British consciousness, both as a mappable region and, no less, as a myth-generating zone.[20] At the same time, the South Seas became available as a site for the interrogation of relations between different discourses: on the one hand, those of geography and anthropology and, on the other, those of travel writing. Contemporary travel writing about the Pacific inevitably supplements its testimonies of experience and contact with a variety of other discourses, particularly those of ethnography, for whose development the region has been so instrumental.[21] Traveling/writing the Pacific testifies to ambivalence and undecidability: poised between the scientism of disciplinary treatises and the heightened impressionism of narratives of (experienced) contact, contemporary travels/travelogues in the Pacific mimic both the accumulated records of the past two and a half centuries and the region's geography itself as they move restlessly from island to "enchanted" island.

The cultural geographer Derek Gregory has recently underlined the "extraordinary significance of the South Pacific for the development of the natural sciences" and, by extension, the human sciences at a time when the contents and contexts of European knowledges were beginning to constitute a new (Foucauldian) episteme (20). Observation records and expedition reports, although "mediated by European conceptual categories and European ways of seeing" (Gregory 23), claimed authority deriving from on-the-spot witness. Some early investigators attempted a degree of self-reflexiveness, acknowledging some reciprocity in encounters between themselves and indigenous "others," but obviously they could not simply cancel their position as colonizers, their immense privilege in situations where their ultimate aim was to possess the culture of the "other." Travel writing came to join anthropology, geography, and the human sciences generally as one strand of a new regime of knowledges and as an encoding of the Pacific. Chronicles of travel and adventure, as Gregory puts it, added "affective response" and "emotional investment" to more "scientific" modes of informational dissemination (20). But while such chronicles—of both past and present—might seem to be less mediated, and more experientially based, than formalized discourses, they inevitably share the space and borrow the authority of the human sciences for which the eighteenth century was to prove so vital.[22]

Recent South Seas travel narratives certainly attest to, as well as invoke, anthropological authority. Bougainville and Cook ritually appear, next a cast of missionaries, traders, and beachcombers with their talk of cannibalism, gifts, and taboos, to be followed by the professional observers Margaret Mead, Bronislaw Malinowski, and Marshall Sahlins. Paul Theroux carts Malinowski's talismanic ethnography *The Sexual Life of Savages* (1929) around with him in his knapsack; Ronald Wright interviews Sahlins in a Fijian museum (1986, 182–84). South Sea travel books thus rehearse ethnographic lore, setting it alongside the "encounter" anecdotes that are characteristic of their genre. In so doing, they echo Malinowski's own Pacific-inspired anxieties, as articulated, particularly, in his posthumously published *Diary in the Strict Sense of the Term* (1967). In *Diary,* Malinowski yearns for a new, more emotionally involved anthropology. Malinowski's last work testifies to the inability of social scientific discourses to account fully for "exotic" cultures or to offer an "objective" portrait of them. Malinowski reveals how his own subjectivity—his loneliness, longings, and erotic fantasies—effectively deconstructs the potential for authoritative observation and accurate description: the activities conventionally considered as both means and ends for anthropological knowledge. He realizes that a "dispassionate" approach to his material is simply not possible and, more importantly, that anthropological work cannot be accomplished without precisely those personal and cultural transactions that cast the project's claims to scientific truth in doubt. Anthropologists, Malinowski implies, are travelers before they are scientists;

their self-effacement papers over the gap between the "objective" truths the discipline seeks to capture and the instability—the motivations, desires, and will-to-power—of scientists as (fallible) people. On the other hand, friendly and informal contact experience—of the kind that most travel books aim to record—can never impart certain knowledge about the culture being visited; nor can they, in the words of that South Seas "old hand," Robert Louis Stevenson, "describe the life . . . of many hundred thousand persons, some of our own blood and language, all our contemporaries, and yet as remote in thought and habit as Rob Roy or Barbarossa, the Apostles or the Caesars" (6).

Contemporary narratives such as Theroux's, or Julian Evans's (*Transit of Venus*, 1992), or Gavin Bell's (*In Search of Tusitala*, 1994), all seem chastened by the opacity of the islands and people of the Pacific zone—although Theroux, as might be expected, is more forceful than most in his attempts to part the mist.[23] In the Pacific—and more particularly, for the male traveler in the Pacific—the experience of travel has often been represented in the topos of Venus: on one level, the planet whose passage across the sun Cook had sailed south to observe, but on another a mythical body of ambivalence—that teasing figure of female allure, seemingly ubiquitous in male-authored narratives. Characteristically, as Julian Evans suggests in *The Transit of Venus,*

> The real Venus that Cook observed, in the reports that he brought back from his first confrontation with the Pacific, had nothing to do with the shade of another planet trickling across the face of the sun. The real Venus observed was in those mythical anecdotes, of freedom and desire, that men are always astonished to relate about women. (184)

It is this familiar trope of "freedom and desire" that Melville famously invoked in his fabrication of the maiden Fayaway in his part novel, part travelogue *Typee* (1846). In her most celebrated moment Fayaway, vacationing on a Marquesan lake with her lover Tommo, is epiphanically "struck with some happy idea": "With a wild exclamation of delight, she disengaged from her person the ample robe of tappa that was knotted over her shoulder . . . and spreading it out like a sail, stood erect with upraised arms in the head of the canoe" (132). Fayaway seems to offer innocent delight; frankness and transparency; an alternative but readily accessible order of experience. She also seems to exist, at least in the lightheaded visions of a great many male travelers, as a *fact* of Pacific culture. But Fayaway, like Venus, is a figure of fiction as well as an object of fantasy. As Theroux, musing about Fay-away's lake in *The Happy Isles of Oceania,* notes with trademark wry-ness,

> [The lake] was where the naked Fayaway had mischievously played at being Tommo's mast, and where Tommo had splashed among the dusky bathing beauties. . . . "What about the lake?" I asked. . . . "There is no lake," Victorine said, and another illusion was shattered. (395)

Theroux, never less than a knowing traveler, is playing the role of arch tease here, but it is a tease that makes a point about how travel narra-tives can generate a space for themselves between fact and myth. This in-between space is not simply fantasy, but a kind of illusionary *surmise* in which an element of anthropological fable—the beauty and freedom of Pacific island women, for example—appears as factitious, yet as something, for all that, that "men are always astonished to relate." The travel writer's irony hollows out time-worn illusions but also holds them in suspension—as if there might be something to them after all.

In seeking to fulfil their fantasy quests in faraway (Fayaway?) places, Pacific travelers paradoxically enter a temporal zone of "exotic memories."[24] For travel writers, as for anthropologists, the "primi-tive," pre-European South Seas island corresponds to the lost world of childhood; in that world, they glimpse the possibility of recuperating paradise, only to foreclose on it. When both past and future appear illusory, the exotic assumes the form of a frontier zone of despoliation and destruction; as Evans concludes of one island, it was "trash and overcrowding, boys getting pissed on a Saturday night, fighting and porn videos. It was just like England" (218).

The motivations of Bell, Evans, and Theroux for a spell in the South Seas turn out to have been quite similar. Theroux, his marriage in tatters, "wanted to see the extreme green isles of Oceania, unmod-ern, sunny, and slow"; he imagines the Pacific to be a place where he might be "purified by water and wilderness" (19–20).[25] The journalist Bell, exhausted by the experience of covering a sequence of vicious war zones, recalls an episode where, on "returning to Java after having been scared out of my wits by an ill-tempered volcano near Sumatra, [he had] found peace on [Stevenson's] *Beach of Falesá*" (4–5). Spurred on by this memory of recuperative reading, Bell embarks on a tour of the Pacific in a quest for Stevenson's "spirit." Evans's motivations are rather more complex. Newspaper photographs of Peacekeeper tests (the missiles' reentry vehicles splash down in an atoll of the Marshall Islands) evoke memories of childhood, of hot Queensland summers, and later, bizarrely, of an old woman in London dancing with him to the song "Yellow Polka Dot Bikini" (7). Given the apocalyptic violence of its photographic trigger, Evans's dream of a "return to the heliotropic sensations of childhood" seems somewhat fraught (9). Nevertheless, in company with legions of other white travelers, he hopes for "some sudden liberation from neurosis and desire" (149). Such motivations already distance the South Pacific, linking it with a zone of return to childhood, or a retreat to something like a rest home for recuperative therapy—"exotic memories."

The visitors, at their most fortunate, arrive before it is "too late." The Canadian traveler-writer George Woodcock, in his documentary-style *South Sea Journey* (1976), notes the transition from "traditional subsistence economies" to tourism and remarks: "It seemed that we had chosen a crucial time. A decade's delay, and we might easily arrive too late" (19). He might well be echoing Stevenson, who had missed "things and practices . . . to be seen in use" ten years previously, going on to note that "ten years more, and the old society will have entirely vanished": Woodcock's "crucial time" is Stevenson's "happy moment" (Stevenson 224). Bell, meanwhile, still in hot pursuit of Stevenson's ghostly presence, throws a shadow of a different kind over the fleeting appearance of "traditional" life in the camera's lens when he sees an islander "sitting motionlessly on a stone bench looking out to sea, framed by the dark outlines of palm fronds," and speculates about whether he is "dreaming of the past, or wondering about an uncertain future" (62). Bell, needless to say, decides to consign him to the past: "I left him to his reverie, a lonely relic of a forgotten race of warriors and cannibals" (62).[26] Bell is ambivalent, nonetheless, about the success of his questing mission, feeling on the one hand that he has "discovered that paradise exists in the South Seas, and that the essence of it is love among peoples who have little else to share," but on the other that what he has glimpsed is "a way of life which may soon be remembered only in old tales" (318).

The vast amount of ethnographic and travel writing over the last one and a half centuries has diffused the South Seas into white consciousness as a dwindling residue of happy primitivism and paradisal innocence; travelers can still experience intimations of these states in the 1990s. The trope of the belated arrival—one of the staples of modern travel writing—is simply a stronger form of the equally ubiquitous "just in time" motif.[27] Christopher Bongie, in *Exotic Memories,* traces the trope back to the artist Gauguin's lament over the death of King Pomare V in Tahiti, uncannily foreshadowing Victor Segalen's arrival in the Marquesas just too late for a meeting with Gauguin himself (the painter had died only a few months before). Bongie finds these parallel accounts "firmly grounded in both the dichotomies of nineteenth-century exoticism and the fatidic pessimism that . . . had become the prescribed way of speaking about matters exotic" (72). Contemporary travelers are still in the habit of arriving just too late. If Bell can still find an idyllic Samoa, "less spectacular than Tahiti, less forbidding than the Marquesas, but with an ethereal beauty only a poet could capture in words," it is only to have the illusion punctured as soon as entertained: "Then we turned a corner and found a fleet of excavating machines building a reservoir; and we passed out of yet another shrinking dream world" (293).

This "shrinking dream world" transforms easily into an expanding apocalypse, the strongest form of South Seas disillusionment—a counterillusion perhaps. Many travelers' tales include their authors' repulsed descriptions of polluted atolls, garbage-strewn strands, and tourist-induced vulgarities. Far stronger, however, are larger scenes of neoimperial violence like Mururoa, the notorious location of repeated French nuclear testing. Bell, Stevenson's pilgrim, reacts with characteristic outrage, describing the site as "a laboratory for mass destruction in an illusory paradise," submerged below a lagoon where "a red and white drilling rig rises like a fairground helter-skelter, and deeply tanned young men foster the illusion of a holiday resort by cavorting on gaily coloured sailboards" (97). For the English writer Evans, the latest heart of darkness is the Marshall Islands, the culmination of his journey, which he begins to see as "a penance I had imposed on myself" (241). For Evans, Kwajalein, an American base close to where the reentry vehicles of nuclear weapons splash down, is the Venus whose "transit" provides the quasi-novelistic basis for his travel book. Ultimately, Evans decides, the base resembles not so much Dante's *Inferno* as a more modern surreality, "a Fifties s.f. movie, something in the tradition of *Fire Maidens from Space* or *Robinson Crusoe on Mars*" (257). Dystopias marked by surreality or virtual reality are very much part of the repertoire of contemporary travel writing (see chap. 4); in this specific South Seas context, they enact a kind of recoil of the exotic, transforming it and thrusting it toward an apocalyptic future. Apocalypse marks the end point of what Alan Moorhead has called "the fatal impact": the title of his 1966 study of "the invasion of the South Pacific."

Over a century earlier, Melville had already provided a sharp characterization of "fatal impact" in *Typee*:

> When the inhabitants of some sequestered island first descry the "big canoe" of the European rolling down through the blue waters toward their shores, they rush down to the beach in crowds, and with open arms stand ready to embrace the strangers. Fatal embrace! They fold to their bosoms the vipers whose sting is destined to poison all their joys; and the instinctive feeling of love within their breasts is soon converted into the bitterest hate. (24)

Almost every travel book and ethnographic account since Melville has implicitly accepted or rehearsed "fatal impact," although there are several different versions of the thesis in circulation. Bell, for example, quotes (Captain) Cook's opinion that "it would have been far better for these poor people never to have known our superiority in the accommodations and arts that make life comfortable, then after once knowing it, to be abandoned in their original incapacity for improvement" (178). The conclusion to Cook's sentence is surprising in its regret, not for the invasion but for subsequent abandonment; and two centuries later, writing about the Gilberts (Kiribati), Woodcock seems to agree: the islands' "fragile balance . . . has already been destroyed, and now their remoteness is no longer a protection, but the threat of an isolation that can only be destructive" (182). Theroux, for his part, is well pleased with the Solomons, naively professing on the contrary "that if the people were not interfered with by tourists or bureaucrats, the island would remain intact and the people would be able to manage on their own" (180). If the trope of fateful encounter (often combined with that of fatal abandonment) seemed almost indispensable to earlier travel writers, it is just as motivating and empowering for Pacific chroniclers today. These writers' commentaries implicitly acknowledge the various societies' emplacement in a world that draws even the remotest islands into transnational webs of trade and communication (the so-called global village); but the plot of the travel book depends on the continued revival of a nostalgic exotic vision—a vision, as Bongie points out, that is always already in and of the past.[28]

The narratives of South Sea travelers commonly become pseudoanthropological as they, too, attempt to bridge gaps between the observing subject and its "others," and between a lived present and an irrecoverable past. Obviously these attempts, though generally informed, are haphazardly unscientific; recent South Seas travel writers typically accumulate anecdotes in praise of native hospitality, using these as evidence of the traversal of cultural difference. Yet these anecdotes may also attest to the trials (or defeats) of interpretation, pointing in some cases to a measure of resistance to the traveler's apparent cultural mastery. Theroux, for example, includes one such "resistance anecdote" in *The Happy Isles of Oceania.* After setting up base on one particular (Trobriand) island, Theroux paddles back and forth between them, bearing gifts that seem to help him establish a special rapport with his host villagers. However, when he returns to one of the villages for a farewell visit, his hosts are unresponsive, hostile even. Theroux leaves disappointed; later, although the villagers have not told him so, he speculates that a feud between his hosts and a neighboring village must have dampened the enthusiasm that had greeted previous visits. He finally admits to defeat—"I could now see the utter impossibility of my ever understanding the place" (150)—but not without offering one of his characteristic parting shots: islands with "traditional" culture, he concludes, "are riddled with magic, superstition, myths, dangers, rivalries, and [the culture's] old routines. . . . The key to [the culture's] survival was that it laughed at outsiders and kept them at arm's length" (150). Theroux's humiliation gauges the complex cultural asymmetry that often tends to go unnoticed in Western (Euro-American) travel narratives. The host-guest contract, after all, is never one of stasis or equilibrium: even the visitor who adopts gift rituals with what s/he believes is informed sensitivity cannot profit from them precisely because s/he is a cultural outsider; and privilege passes back and forth, in this way, between honored guests and culturally vigilant hosts.[29]

Even though the Pacific zone has failed to supply full edenic therapy to its white traveler-writers, it has certainly offered them recuperative moments that serve to justify their trips. No matter how pervasive their stoical disappointment at the islands' failure to fulfil the paradisal dream, these writers do manage to locate "magical" moments that keep at least something of the dream alive; and consequently, even those readers who identify the Pacific with marketable ("Club Med") illusions—happy, childlike natives ministering to visitors in an ambience of sanitized hedonism—know that a future still exists for the South Seas travel book. Thus despite his frustrations, Bell, ever anxious to experience the Marquesas through Stevenson (and through more than just Stevenson's eyes), finds happiness and purity in a village Mass, framed by "two palm trees . . . etched in perfect symmetry against a crimson sunset." The idyll is described as follows:

> [A] thin sliver of moon directly above a church created a circle of bright light suffused with all the colours of the rainbow; the windows of the church emanated a warm, rosy glow; the lilting melodies from within drifted on the evening breeze. A more exotic scene could not be imagined. (71–72)[30]

And to cap it, each worshiper accords Bell "a smile and a friendly *bonsoir*" on leaving the church (72). Even the more grudging Theroux experiences serenely uncomplicated moments of grace, as "on one of those moony nights at the pavilion by the lagoon when the bliss of the south seas dream was palpable" (31).

Nonetheless, those moments at which the exotic becomes palpable are by their nature evanescent, expunging consciousness of alienation only to reintroduce it as inevitable reaction. Earlier "discoverers," after all, had invented the South Seas in a self-reflexive gesture that constituted a category of rupture: the exotic as a zone defined by its destruction at the moment of contact. In travel writing, the South Seas exotic flickers in its evanescence under the sign of guilty alienation. The exotic zone awakens a sense of anomie, confronting travelers, appropriately perhaps, with their own feelings of intrusion, guilt, and boredom—even if those feelings are often projected onto "tourists," "traders," "bureaucrats," and the like. For Evans, echoing Lévi-Strauss, white settlers—be they planters, traders, or beachcombers—"wanted somewhere . . . to bring their psychological baggage and dump it. . . . [T]hey longed for some sudden paradise to flower there, some sudden liberation from neurosis and desire" (148–49). But as Theroux notes, "It is simply not possible . . . to lose yourself in an exotic place. Much more likely is an experience of intense nostalgia, a harking back to an earlier stage of your life, or seeing clearly a serious mistake" (31). Arriving at this perception, travelers experience a bitter recoil, realizing, like Theroux, that the "sadness was mine" (180); or, like Evans, that exotic surfaces only yield "flourishing states of boredom" (186); or, like Woodcock, that "nostalgia . . . is darkened by despair" (182). South Seas travel narratives culminate most often in unliberated withdrawal, suggesting that even the most astute travelers inevitably project psychological and cultural deficits onto the places they visit, only to take those deficits just as surely with them home.

The motif of return in another, dissimilar but still "exotic" travel zone—the Arctic—is tied in with that zone's most obvious temporal attribute: deferral. "To travel in the Arctic is to wait," says the American biologist Barry Lopez in *Arctic Dreams* (1986). The unpredictable climate and shifting terrain of the Arctic present travelers with a stern test of patience: they may have to wait for quite some time before reaching their destination; again before traveling in the area; still more before returning home. The Arctic's indigenous peoples, inured to their treacherous environment, know well how to adapt themselves to the subtly changing rhythms of Arctic life; not so Western travelers and explorers, whose impatience—or incompetence—can cost them dear. (One of the many ironies of the Arctic is that while it has recently become a dumping ground for the detritus of Western [military] technology, it is still littered with the bodies of Western travelers—men who thought, mistakenly, that their technology was good enough.) Given the tragic history of exploration in the Arctic—a history allied, of course, to the continuing exploitation of the Arctic—it is not surprising that contemporary Arctic travelogues should tend to be cautious, soul-searching affairs: narratives whose halting progress affords one reminder after another of the need to reeducate Western sensibilities—to record not only what one sees, but also how one learns to see.

Three recent North American travel books—Lopez's *Arctic Dreams,* Rudy Wiebe's *Playing Dead* (1989), and John Moss's *Enduring Dreams* (1994)—might best be described as Arctic *contemplations:* accounts in which description prevails over narration to the point where travel narrative, reducing its metabolic rate as if to adapt to its wintry surroundings, hypostatizes into lyric poem, into crafted meditation on the motionless. The similarities between the three accounts override their writers' different professions—Lopez is a research scientist, Wiebe a full-time writer, Moss a professor of English—to suggest the shared category of the "Arctic dreamer." These writers are all fascinated by the phenomenological links between people and the environments they explore or inhabit. Their own encounters with the Arctic landscape (four years' research in the Arctic circle for Lopez, numerous visits to the upper reaches of their Canadian homeland for Wiebe and Moss) in turn raise larger questions about the human relationship with the land. These questions are in part metaphysical: how do we distinguish between the world "out there" and the world(s) inside our heads? They are also epistemological: how are we to "understand" the land, through which modes of knowledge and perception? And, not least, they are ethical: how are we to "behave" toward the land, to use it without abusing it?

The issue is complicated further by the singular elusiveness of the Arctic, both as (physical) landscape and as (metaphysical) idea. Fretting about the Arctic's apparent resistance to verbal language, Moss converts his experience of Arctic travel into oneiric metaphor: he dreams the Arctic "in a language of which I can only grasp the roughest edges, edges that break off in fragments when I touch them" (32). For Wiebe, meanwhile, the Arctic is construed as a liminal environment: located at the edge of the world, suspended between water and land (with the capacity to change almost imperceptibly from one state to the other), the Arctic defies, sometimes destroys, those who are foolish enough to think it changeless. The Arctic occupies a vast space; and yet, like the polar traveler in Neruda's poem (cited by Wiebe), it is poised between "the shores and the ocean," its surface "so narrow [that] it is no more than a possible line for a possible balance" (115). The Inuit peoples who populate this hypothetical region know how to negotiate and maintain the precarious balance they need to ensure their own survival. For those who are reared on the discriminatory classifications of Western science, the task of understanding the Arctic—knowing how to live with it, as well as within it—is all the greater. For as all three writers show, the Arctic has historically scorned Western pretensions to control and contain it. Overspilling the boundaries that scientists have sought to impose on it, the Arctic is apt to confound even the most meticulous observers, reminding them of the gap that separates what they see from what they *wish* to see.

Looming particularly large in the symbolism of Lopez's, Wiebe's, and Moss's narratives are the cruciform masts of John Franklin's two ships, *Erebus* and *Terror,* which ran aground on the ice during his third (and final) expedition to the Arctic in 1845. As Lopez explains, Franklin's ill-fated expedition quickly took on mythic proportions. Its leader emerged as an almost messianic figure, a man whose heroic self-sacrifice was to deliver his countrymen from that fata morgana of Arctic navigation: a Northwest Passage that led out beyond the upper Arctic to the silks and spices of the East. Franklin's catastrophic expedition did not put an end, however, to Arctic exploration. On the contrary:

> Scores of expeditions set out from England and America to search the entire unexplored Canadian archipelago if necessary. . . . Where once the goal [of Arctic exploration] had been to get *through* en route to somewhere else, now expeditions were proposed . . . to make the region itself the focus of their attention. . . . From this [collective] enterprise came, ironically, the first extensive and accurate maps of the high Arctic. (363)

Long after the British and the Americans had pulled their ships out of the Arctic—ships that had gone there, in several cases, in search of the lucrative reward that awaited Franklin's "discovery"—expeditions such as Franklin's were to keep their hold on the popular imagination, "in the minds of scholars and poets, in the perceptions of travellers, the sensibility of every outsider who holds the Arctic landscape as an optional reality in imagination, and among the bibliographies of Arctic dreaming" (Moss 96–97). Franklin helped to provide what Lopez calls a "legacy of desire" in Arctic history: the desire of "individual men to achieve their goals," but also one "that transcends heroics and was privately known to many—the desire for a safe and honorable passage through the world" (309).

Lopez, Wiebe, and Moss thus all incorporate Franklin's expedition into a larger, spiritual quest: one in which Western travelers, reminded of the limitations of their knowledge, and chastened against the dangers of cultural arrogance, set out to (re)discover the primordial nature of their relationship with the world. This understanding requires a sense of reciprocity with the land, an appreciation that the various landscapes through which travelers move, or upon which they are moved to contemplate, are to be seen "not solely [as] areas of human invention" but as "crucibles of mystery" (Lopez 412). Instead of imposing themselves on the land, molding it to their expectations or altering its dimensions to fit the shape of their dreams, travelers must learn somehow to merge with the land, to surrender in silence to its immanent mysteries. For Moss, to "enter" the landscape in this spirit is to abolish its threat of alienation: "You may enter landscape, but in humility; if truly there, you cannot tell yourself apart from it" (5). Such moments of mystical convergence are rare, but invariably epiphanic: hence Lopez, walking one night on the tundra, trading inquisitive but respectful glances with the birds while the "serene Arctic light . . . came down over the land like breath, like breathing" (xx); or Wiebe, also on the tundra, seeking communion with the "primeval earth" in a landscape that reaches out to him "like the knobby palm of God's hand" (113).

According to Moss, too many writers on the Arctic have dispossessed the Inuit, "making them intruders" and denying "native kinship with the land" (75). Consequently, any search for reciprocity with the land also entails a quest for reconciliation with its indigenous inhabitants. Wiebe recognizes that if he is to understand the Arctic—if the Arctic is to reveal some of its secrets to him—then he must, like his predecessor Vihjalmur Stefansson, learn to "think like [the] Inuit" (107). Lopez, on the other hand, cannot separate thinking from seeing; he seeks to recapture the "native eye": the keen-sightedness of a people who, aware of the "vaguest flutter of life" in an environment that might otherwise seem "featureless and interminable," are gifted with "a predator's alertness for minutiae, for revealing detail" (96). The Arctic is an environment that not only rewards such "preternaturally heightened awareness" (202), it requires it. None of the writers is so ingenuous as to suggest that the Westernization of the Arctic has not brought with it certain material advantages to Inuit peoples' lives, but they warn against the atrophying of spatial awareness that a reliance on machines and mechanized modes of transportation may inadvertently produce. In their cautious efforts to rehabilitate Inuit culture—a culture that, as Hugh Brody has reminded us, still suffers from the subordinating practices of Western colonialism[31]—they point out the benefits provided by traditional Inuit technologies. Wiebe demonstrates, for example, how "Inuit travel technology and their two-dimensional understanding of space, both of which were taught them by the awesome landscape in which they have learned to live" (20), can be used to explain the success of Franklin's first expedition to the Arctic in 1819–22.

Inuit tracking techniques, says Wiebe, depend on the perceived distinction between "areal" and "linear" dimensions of space. In Inuktitut, says Wiebe (via the linguist Raymond Gagné),

> All visible phenomena . . . are viewed two-dimensionally. Moreover, all of them fall into two basic categories: first, those of roughly equal dimensions, such as a ball, an igloo . . . or an ice surface; and second, those that are or appear to be of unequal dimensions . . . such as a harpoon . . . a rope . . . or a river. (Qtd. in Wiebe 15)

An object classified as areal (a ball) may become linear when it is in motion (a rolling ball). When human beings move, they too change from being areal to linear (15).[32] Inuit tracking techniques are based on an understanding of these transformations, as well as on a calculation of the intersection of linear routes: these were the techniques that saved Franklin's (grounded) expedition. Franklin's third expedition, however, was not so lucky. As Wiebe explains:

> A ship frozen in the ice has moved out of the linear into another dimension altogether: in the vast Arctic it has achieved the dimension of areal stillness. . . . a dimension which sailors experienced only in the endless, unburdened motion of the sea, cannot understand. Stillness destroys them. (117)

And it did: not a single member of Franklin's expeditionary party survived.

In a sense, Lopez, Wiebe, and Moss write travel books that themselves become "icebound," metamorphosing from narratives of movement into meditations on immobility. But immobility, in the Arctic, can mean many different things. Wiebe, for example, distinguishes between the potential benefits of apparent motionlessness—the advantage gained, in confronting predators, of "playing dead"—and the disastrous consequence of enforced immobilization: the impotent awareness of one's own entrapment. A further distinction is made by Lopez, for whom (climatic) stillness is not to be confused with (biological) stasis. The romantic notion of a "timeless" Inuit culture, says Lopez, has less to do with geographical knowledge than with cultural prejudice; such prejudices were, and to some extent still are, nurtured by stereotypical Western views of the Arctic as a "primitive landscape, a painting inhabited by attenuated people" (352). Nineteenth-century explorers in the Arctic often "mistook the stillness and the cold for biological stasis. They thought nothing at all changed [in the Arctic]. They thought it was a desert, a wasteland" (382). Such attitudes, says Lopez, betrayed a colonial sensibility: a sensibility, needless to say, by no means restricted to the nineteenth century. By envisioning the Arctic as a tabula rasa, a blank white page, nineteenth-century explorers (and some of their twentieth-century counterparts) were able to inscribe upon it the expansionist imperatives of their own "enlightened" culture. Yet as Lopez shows, it is a wholly different kind of anticipation that the Arctic calls for; to contemplate the stillness of the Arctic is not to prefigure one's own impact upon it, nor yet to imagine one's movement through or beyond it, but rather to appreciate its *own* potential for movement. Far from being lifeless or monotonous, the ecosystem of the Arctic, like that of the desert, is complex and varied: it allows not only for change, but for significant change; not only for life, but for abundant life. Stillness in the Arctic, as in the desert, connotes not stasis but deferral—in the oscillating ecosystem, "long stillnesses [are] broken by sudden movement" (175–76). It is true, as Lopez concedes, that vast expanses of the Arctic are, to all intents and purposes, "empty"; but the Arctic also contains within it concentrated pockets of life—pockets that, once discovered, amply reward the patience of the traveler or (in Lopez's case) the visiting research biologist.

Arctic Dreams records these exciting discoveries: its structure, like its subject, enacts a series of "long stillnesses" punctuated by instances of "sudden movement." It is significant, however, that Lopez consistently downplays his own movements. We are given little information about how he gets from place to another, still less about the length of time it takes him to get there. In one sense, this makes for a fragmented, discontinuous narrative; in another, it creates the illusion of simultaneous experience. Moss also suggests as much when he reports—in one of his free-verse interludes—the words of his Inuk host, who "spoke of Arctic places / as if time were nothing passing / and anything that happened happens still" (91). This illusion might easily lend itself to romantic clichés about the timelessness of "primitive" cultures, but Lopez, in particular, manipulates it skillfully to suggest the perceived totality of the Arctic lifeworld.[33] Lopez casts himself as an observer of this phenomenal lifeworld, but hardly a neutral or detached one. Anxious not to overburden us with his own personality (as Moss sometimes seems to do), Lopez remains aware, nonetheless, that his personality inevitably impinges on the environment he is describing. But description, for Lopez as for Moss, is not an act of disinterested documentation; it is a gesture, rather, of (unfulfilled) *desire.* In Mexico, far removed from the Arctic, Moss makes notes that are "souvenirs of contemplation and desire" (24). Similarly, desire translates the distances that separate Lopez from the Arctic, and that divide Lopez's culture from the indigenous culture(s) of the Inuit, into imagined lines of communication. Lopez recognizes the paradox: the more he wishes to establish contact with the Arctic, the more he becomes aware of his own "foreignness." Wisely, he decides to stay behind the scenes, allowing the Arctic's wildlife to take center stage. That wildlife is prolific, but also prodigiously mobile: in Lopez's travel writing, it may not always be the animals who do the traveling, but it is the animals who invariably get the credit for doing it.[34]

It is not only the mobility of Arctic animals that Lopez admires, it is also their quality of innocence. The Arctic is a vulnerable ecosystem, an environment "marked by natural catastrophe" (33). Within this ecosystem, animals such as the musk ox and the polar bear are the very "image of vulnerability" (118). After an afternoon spent watching musk oxen on the plain, Lopez is moved to the following observation: "They were so intensely good at being precisely what they were. The longer you watched, the more intricately they seemed a part of where they were living, of what they were doing. Their color, the proportions against the contours of the land, were exquisite. . . . They were, in evolution's terms, innocent of us and of our plans" (75). The biologist doubles as moralist, as aesthete: the pages of *Arctic Dreams* are crowded with rhapsodic homages to an unself-conscious, threatened beauty—a beauty threatened, above all, by the invasive presence of people. Lopez cites the case of the bears at Churchill, Manitoba, "innocent" victims of a "parade of amateur and professional photographers, filmmakers and television personnel [who bait the] bears with jars of mayonnaise [while] importun[ing] Churchill people to assist them in staging various scenes" (115). The bears represent a sad example of "an animal in a comparatively accelerated rate of evolutionary development [that] has encountered another creature evolving at a very much higher rate of change" (116). The distinction makes sound scientific sense, but Lopez's point is above all an ethical one; the "innocence" of Arctic wildlife, and of the environment in which it continues to live—if not always thrive—provides him with a necessary counterpart to the (liberal) white man's guilt. The Arctic can be seen in this sense as a confessional site for the unburdening of a troubled conscience. Yet it is also the repository of a "transcendent" wisdom, a wisdom that brings with it the hope for both individual and collective redemption. The Arctic, says Lopez, has a "pervasive spiritual presence" (124); it is invested with a mystical power that is frequently diminished or compromised in Western industrialized societies. As a sanctified space, the Arctic provides a splendid opportunity for beatific contemplation: Lopez, birdwatching one day among the ice floes, and "half-aware of the biological mysteries in placid, depthless waters," permits himself, without apparent irony, to feel "blessed" (124). Elsewhere, musk oxen grazing on the Alaskan tundra are "like Buddhist monks" (54); and icebergs off Belle Isle present, like "Potala Palace at Lhasa in Tibet, a mountainous architecture of ascetic contemplation" (206). The Arctic is, indeed, a liminal environment, and the line separating inspired lyricism from earnest sententiousness is a thin one.

The Arctic, as a liminal zone, inspires both Wiebe and Moss in their turn to a somewhat ponderous oracularity about subordinating "speech" to "experience." For Moss, the "greatest Arctic narrative was silence" (56), more specifically the silence of explorer John Hornby, who perished in the Arctic in 1927. Unlike several other doomed explorers, Hornby left no words behind: "He [refused] to extricate his dreams from the landscape, to enter with words the continuum of history and geography, culture and kindred consciousness" (56). Moss reads Hornby's silence as indexing the Arctic itself as liminal territory: "it is the absence of voice that makes Hornby's vision the ineluctable limit for others, writing of their own adventures to the edges of the same territory" (56). In *Playing Dead,* too, Wiebe presents an Arctic that conducts to silence and stillness:

> What I encounter here in the North, where I have of necessity come to look, are secrets; enigmas; mysteries. . . . [W]alking alone in this enormous landscape . . . I am steadily rendered more and more wordless. One could so easily, one perhaps must of necessity become a motionless dot of stillness. Experience the day and night and noon and sun and the imperceptible turn of the stars. (113)

At moments like these, the Arctic is conscripted into the service of a redemptive allegory; emptying itself of speech—the Zen concept of satori comes to mind—Arctic travelogue pares down to humanist parable (Lopez), metaphysical meditation (Moss), or devotional poem (Wiebe).

Arctic Dreams, Playing Dead, and *Enduring Dreams* all operate within the tradition of travel writing as retrospective pilgrimage, although Moss's book—the most recent of the three—embeds records of pilgrimage in layers of self-conscious memoir, commonplace, journal, and criticism of previous Arctic travel narratives. Such records, according to Eric Leed, effect "changes in the character of the traveler that are . . . analogous to a cleansing, the reduction of the purified entity to its smallest, truest dimensions" (11). As Lopez suggests, many Western explorers and travelers have perceived the Arctic as a site of both threat and salvation, as an arena for the playing out of purgatorial myth. The journeys of Lopez, Wiebe, and Moss are not, of course, purgatorial in its literal sense; but in their descriptions of earlier Arctic expeditions, as in their attempts to come to terms with their own limitations and weaknesses, all three writers go some way toward locating the Arctic as an agonistic space—as a site of psychic conflict and metaphysical investigation that demands accountability for human error, and for "the darkness not only in one's own culture but within oneself" (Lopez 413). To place too much emphasis on the "dark side" of these books would be misleading, though, for all three are primarily celebratory of the lands and peoples they describe. In each case, the Arctic is presented as a treacherous, but not necessarily hostile, environment. The enthusiasm that energizes all of these narratives derives from their writers' determination to project onto the Arctic landscape their unshakable faith in life.

Clearly, Lopez, Wiebe, and Moss all feel a deep affiliation with the Arctic. They see it, in Yi-Fu Tuan's terms, as a "topophilic" space—one to which they are compulsively attracted, less out of a sense of affection, perhaps, than out of a sense of admiration that borders on awe.[35] The Arctic thus takes on the aura of the romantic sublime: as Lopez says, in the Arctic

> the land works its way into the man. . . . [It] becomes large, alive like an animal; it humbles him in a way he cannot pronounce. It is not that the land is simply beautiful but that it is powerful. Its power derives from the tension between its obvious beauty and its capacity to take life. Its power flows into the mind from a realization of how darkness and light are bound together within it, and the feeling that this is the floor of creation. (392–93)

On a level that is more affiliative but also more abstract, Moss declares that

> intimations of another world shape the dreamer dreaming, the writer writing; we separate from psychological realities, metaphysical desires; in metamorphosis or visionary conceit we see ourselves, infinite and eternal, shadows without people, belonging to the landscape. (128)

Both of these passages speak with eloquence and sincerity, and yet they invite a degree of doubt. Their respective writers clearly have experience and knowledge of the Arctic, but they are still, in the end, *visitors*—travelers whose actions and observations are based on the knowledge that their stays in the Arctic will be temporary. "For a relationship with the land to be lasting," says Lopez, "it must be reciprocal" (404). But while Lopez may gesture toward such reciprocity, he cannot achieve the lasting relationship with the Arctic he desires. While awarding Lopez generous praise, Moss concedes—somewhat grandiloquently—that "the Arctic becomes a flourish on the margin of the chart of the writer's contemplation of himself" (59). Granted, but to what degree does Moss's Arctic become more central, more fully a subject? Such problems inevitably arise from the contradictions embodied in travel writing as a genre; for while travel writing—of the sympathetic kind, at least, that Lopez, Wiebe, and Moss practice—attempts to bridge the gaps between different peoples, places, and cultures, these are gaps that the genre itself cannot help but create. Travel writing reinstalls difference even as it claims to dismantle it; the humanist desire for reconciliation, in keeping with the desire for a more permanent relationship with the land, tends to founder on the very (socioeconomic) conditions that make travel writing possible. Travelers' economic power enables them to mobilize resources—the same power allows them both to leave and, eventually, to return. And because travelers can "see home while distancing [themselves] from it" (Fraser xvii), the writing that they produce tends to be paradoxically ethnocentric. The humanist sympathies of travel writing disguise its interested motivations—its (re)production of the world for a Western metropolitan audience (Pratt 5).

Lopez, Wiebe, and Moss are well aware, of course, of travel writing's capacity for dissimulation, and they all attempt to distance themselves from the genre's accepted conventions. Their Arctic contemplations contain few of the elements we might usually associate with travel writing, although they still remain an identifiable subgenre of contemporary travel literature.[36] (If, as Paul Fussell suggests [see introduction], travel writing can be located at the interface between Western picaresque and pastoral traditions, then the Arctic contemplation falls squarely into the category of the latter: its motivations, like those of pastoral, are to restore an ideal relationship with the land.) All three writers are "Arctic dreamers," projecting their individual desires and the collective longings of their cultures onto the indigenous landscape. Their books bear testimony to the impossible aspiration to become indigenous to the Arctic: to its places, peoples, and cultures.[37] They use the "open, unobstructed spaces" (Lopez 200) to exercise reflection; to escape from "[g]eographers with wry map parodies of the earth" (Moss 9); and to work "the mind we know in dreaming, a nonrational, nonlinear comprehension of events in which slips in time and space are normal" (Lopez 200). Lopez, Wiebe, and Moss are among the most sympathetic, sensitive, and "open" of contemporary travel writers. Nonetheless, their readers might do well to take heed of Moss's observation that "Ultima Thule is a projection of private and collective aspirations, a paradox, just beyond the last place to be reached. Figuratively it exists; literally it is a fantasy" (134). Ultima Thule, the mythicized "Arctic," is a zone of silence, contemplation, and the patience with which its visitors negotiate their stay—and their passage home.

This chapter has shown how, at their best, travel narrative offer subjective portraits of *zones:* geographical-tropological regions, countries, or groups of countries. These zones are defined, not only by the observant movements of travelers through territory, but also by an accumulation of lore (geographical, historical, ethnographic, mythic). Such lore, as hybrid totality, gives a textual density to travelers' experiences, even if they do not end up turning these experiences into travel books. On this level, travel becomes a potentially rich way of "knowing" the world: it mediates knowledges that are all in some sense "disciplinary" through a special kind of lived experience; and these knowledges, equally, mediate the personal experience of travel. On another level, the cumulative processes involved in textualizing (travel) zones have achieved, despite their complexity, a certain condensation. These processes have been economized, that is, by being carefully allocated within specific Western imaginative and ideological boundaries: the "frontier," the "liminal," the "exotic," the "Oriental," and so on. Travel narratives are best seen, then, as revealing explorations, but also interrogations, of these ideologically bounded discourses. Even when travel writers inscribe their texts "unproblematically" within one or other of these discourses, the texts themselves offer sites where readers can undertake the work of interrogation. Travel writing, in other words, becomes available as an instrument with which we can begin to refine, revise, and deconstruct the clichés that have reduced zones of great historical range and cultural complexity to a clutch of "instant" images and one-dimensional stereotypes. The following chapter links these stereotypes to gender (mis)perceptions. It suggests that the imagery of travel has historically been a male one, but also that travel writing may act to estrange these phallic myths and male tropologies; to interrogate their clichés; and to transgress—to some extent—the gender codes of heroic male adventure, clearing a space in the process for the subjectivities of women travelers, and for the exploratory journeys and performances of gay men.

Chapter three

Gender and
Other Troubles

WOMEN'S TRAVEL WRITING AND/AS
FEMINIST CRITIQUE

Travel and travel writing are saturated with mythology, but more often than not the myths they invoke are predominantly male. Accounts of travel writing tend to suffer, likewise, from an acute gender imbalance: Eric Leed, in *The Mind of the Traveler,* clearly has the male traveler in *his* mind, while Paul Fussell *(Abroad)* and Dennis Porter *(Haunted Journeys)* mention hardly a single woman writer.[1] Accounts such as these neglect a history of women's travel and travel writing; they overlook the obvious differences in the conditions facing women travelers; and they also forget that travel itself is a thoroughly gendered category. The rhetoric of travel is shot through with metaphors that reinforce male prerogatives to wander and conquer as they please. "Travel" itself—a currently fashionable metaphor for the slippage or displacement of cultural knowledge—is usually defined by men according to the dictates of their experience. Thus, while Edward Said's influential essay "Traveling Theory" (1983) rightly asserts that theory has no universal vantage point, it then misses the opportunity to inquire further into the *gendered* politics of location.[2] And James Clifford's "Traveling Cultures" (1992), while outlining a flexible, "cutting-edge" model of ethnography—one that sees ethnographers and their subjects as traversing, rather than merely inhabiting, a cultural territory—then fails again to account for the implications of sexual difference: to see how such traversals are always already gendered.[3] Said and Clifford, among other leading contemporary social and cultural theorists, have been attacked for being inadvertently masculinist. These attacks have been most concerted, significantly, in the field of geography. Gillian Rose's *Feminism and Geography* (1993) exemplifies a hard-hitting approach that sees geography, and its appropriation in current social and cultural theory, as an academic haven for (mostly white) bourgeois masculinity. Geography, according to Rose, is based on a positivistic legacy whose claims to objectivity and detachment bolster the ideology of masculinist reason; in addition, the discipline has tended throughout the course of its history to set and define itself over and against an "embodied feminized Other" (6–7, 60–61). Rose's book is both a critique of existing geographical models and an attempt to establish first principles for a feminist geography. A feminist geography insists on what Teresa de Lauretis calls "the politics of everyday life" (12); it breaks down cherished divisions between the public and private spheres; and above all perhaps, it dismantles white male claims to a privileged territoriality, in part by stressing cultural differences and a multiplicity of possible perspectives.

What does feminist geography mean in practical terms for contemporary women travel writers? First, it asserts women's travel narratives as both exploratory and disruptive, breaking the chain that ties generations of male explorers to the land. And second, it allows for the possibility of alternative perspectives: the opening up, for example, of utopian zones or liberated spaces through which women's travel writing can emerge as an exploration of female desire.[4] This balance between critique and celebratory self-expression has been emphasized in several recent academic studies of women's travel writing. Karen Lawrence's *Penelope Voyages* (1994), for example, sees women travel writers (her focus is on Britain) as reinventing an Odyssean tradition that legitimates the male explorer. In Homer's *Odyssey,* Ulysses wanders while Penelope, his wife, must wait; Lawrence counteracts this orthodox view by stressing Penelope's role as a weaver who, in Michel Serres's words, both "makes and undoes the cloth that mimes the progress . . . of the navigator" (7). Penelope can thus be seen as fashioning her own clandestine itinerary: an itinerary that, rather than emulating the exploits of the male explorer, incorporates them into a pattern—a weave—that symbolically crosses gender boundaries (Lawrence 8–11).

Lawrence's paradigm is somewhat contrived, but it is useful insofar as it reminds us that women have historically used travel writing to cut across gender conventions. By "weaving" themselves in and out of established places and social roles, women traveler-writers have fashioned a space in which to explore their own identities. They have used travel writing to liberate themselves, at least temporarily, from the constraints placed upon them by their own societies, and to find the freedom to engage in an alternative way of life. Needless to say, serious disadvantages remain for women traveler-writers. Some of these are historical: as Mary Morris points out in her introduction to a recent anthology of women's travel writing, *Maiden Voyages* (1993), "Flights and evasion, the need to escape domestic constraints and routine, to get away and at the same time to conquer—this form of flight from the home [has been] more typical of the male experience" (xv). And others are biological; for women traveler-writers cannot help but be aware of their own physical vulnerability—"the fear of rape, for example, whether crossing the Sahara or . . . just crossing a city street at night, most dramatically affects the ways women move through the world" (xvii). Morris holds the consensus view among women traveler-writers that "the constraints and perils, the perceptions and complex emotions women journey with are different from those of men" (xvii). Anthologies such as Morris's reinforce this special status, serving to celebrate women's triumphs over conditions unfavorable to their sex. Here, for example, from the introduction to Lisa St. Aubin de Teran's collection *Indiscreet Journeys* (1990): "Because of social taboos and the physical vulnerability of women, it has always been harder for them to travel, particularly alone. Perhaps that is why their feats seem all the more admirable once achieved" (xvi). Or here, from the introduction to Sonia Melchett's *Passionate Quests* (1991): "Modern travel stretches women's imagination and power of physical endurance to the limit. . . . By risking hardship, sickness, boredom and even death, and then by surviving," women travelers validate life, "not just escaping from a humdrum existence, but . . . reaching for a kind of liberty" (3).

There are problems, of course, associated with this separatist view of women's travel writing. For one thing, anthologies in the spirit of, say, de Teran's or Morris's risk essentializing women's travel writing, seeing it as inevitably "feminist" or preoccupied with "the private sphere." And for another, the tendency to look for connections between different women's travel narratives—to see women's travel writing as a repository of shared female experience—is a function, at least in part, of contemporary market forces: of the commodification of women writers, women's writing, women's literature, and the institutionalization of women's studies at Western universities. (So much is clear from the plethora of anthologies currently available on the market, or from the wide range of recent critical studies that focus on women's travel writing. Interestingly, though, many of these latter emphasize the nineteenth century, tending to succumb in the process to the very nostalgia on which men's travel writing is often based.) Finally, a temptation exists to conscript women's travel writing into the service of an emancipatory politics, most often through a combination of women's liberation and anticolonialism. Sara Mills's *Discourses of Difference* (1991) is valuable here in showing how women's travel narratives may be "feminist" in some respects while remaining "imperialist" in others. Mills's study of nineteenth-century women traveler-writers examines, precisely, the interface between women's travel writing and imperialism, showing how women such as Isabella Bird, Nina Mazuchelli, and Mary Kingsley reached in their travels for freedom from the constraints placed upon them by a Victorian patriarchy while remaining bound within the dominant imperialist discourse of the day (27–66). These writers, according to Mills, occupied an intermediary position like that of the (Anglo-Indian) memsahib: while they were relatively emancipated and sometimes championed women's rights, they were also called upon to uphold and protect the collective interests of Empire (58–80; see also Barr).

A similar position is arguably occupied by some of their late-twentieth-century counterparts, who in an age after Empire are still apt, in spite of themselves, to exercise imperial rights. Two postwar works written in this vein are Dervla Murphy's *Full Tilt* (1965) and, more recently, Mary Morris's *Nothing to Declare* (1988). Both are confessional narratives that illustrate Morris's view that women's travel writing is more directly personal—more revealing of the writer's own emotions—than men's. Murphy, for example, favors an epistolary form—seldom used by male travel writers—to recount her experiences of traveling alone by bicycle to Afghanistan, Persia, and India. And Morris, practicing what she preaches, sees the narrative of her extended journey to Central America as an opportunity for inquiry and often agonized self-debate. Both of these narratives enact a dialogue between adventure and introspection: their external journeys are accompanied by an inner quest for self-understanding. At times, the confessional strain of the writing becomes unduly narcissistic, lapsing in Murphy's case into a breast-beating examination of her own inadequacies or, in Morris's, into trancelike reveries redolent of New Age psychobabble:

> At various times ghosts or gods run my life. The ghosts I find in my room at night, in the eyes of brujas [witches], in the bird nailed to the tree. While the past struggles to keep me back, the gods propel me forward. Into risk and sacrifice, choice and responsibility. The ghosts are in charge of memory, the gods' domain is destiny. . . . I listen to the ghosts and obey the gods. The ghosts whisper, the gods prod. I listen like a cat at an opening to a wall, and then when it is safe, I pass through. When the gods recede, the ghosts take over and when I let go of the ghosts, some of whom mean me no harm, the gods send me out on my missions. I return to find the infiltration of ghosts. (125–26)

More endearing than such indulgences are Morris's and, especially, Murphy's efforts to analyze their compromised status as white Western women travelers. Thus, despite her—entirely conventional—revulsion for "busloads of French and German tourists," Morris manages (unlike some of her male counterparts) to admit that she is a tourist too; Murphy, meanwhile, irritated at being taken for and deferred to as a memsahib during her travels, nonetheless recognizes that her bohemian demeanor cannot mask her Western privilege. Murphy and, in a different context, Morris emerge as variations on what, adapting Albert Memmi, we might call the "memsahib who refuses." For Memmi, "the colonizer who refuses" plays an impossible historical role:

> He may openly protest, or sign a petition, or join a group which is not automatically hostile toward the colonized. This already suffices for him to recognize that he has simply changed difficulties and discomfort. It is not easy to escape mentally from a concrete situation, to refuse its ideology while continuing to live with its actual relationships. From now on, he lives his life under the sign of a contradiction which looms at every step, depriving him of all coherence and all tranquillity. (20)

The colonizer, however much he dissents, is still part of the oppressing group and—at least as Memmi sees it—will be forced to share its destiny. Memmi's opposition is overdrawn, essentializing "the colonized" as a victim and "the colonizer" as an oppressor who knows how to use his greater force; nonetheless, his critical description has relevance for Euro-American traveler-writers—especially for those, like Murphy, who have leftist anticolonial views. Murphy is certainly genuine enough in her anticolonial sentiments, and *Full Tilt* includes several full-blooded tirades against the First World's depredations on the

Third. But she belongs, like it or not, to a privileged group of First World wanderers: her romanticization of Third World plight and her fierce critique of Western materialism are in part the product of a cultural background that allows her freedom of movement and expression, in part the result of a genre that tends to take such freedoms for granted. Murphy's intermediary status as a traveling "memsahib who refuses" scotches the binaries of the "colonized woman" and the "colonizing man." But the slippage between these categories creates its own historical anxieties; and in recognizing these, Murphy resists the traveler's stock temptation to (false) escape.

Murphy, an Irishwoman in India, and Morris, an American woman in Mexico, are conscious throughout their narratives of the ambivalence of their position. On the one hand, they are First World tourists in relatively impoverished Third World countries; on the other, they are women travelers laboring under the (heightened) disadvantages of their sex. Both women, traveling alone, are the objects of unwelcome male attention, and Morris, in particular, is constantly alert to the threat of rape. In Mexico, she rides into the jungle, accompanied by a taciturn guide:

> I looked at Abondio carefully. He was a silent, hardened man. I had entrusted myself to him through this jungle that had no trail. And he could do anything he wanted to me. But there was a softness to his eyes, a gentle curve to his lips, and I knew he would not harm me. When you travel alone, you learn to read those inner maps. You learn to trust a landscape that is familiar only inside your head. (79)

Later, danger reappears after she has taken a moonlit swim. Believing—imagining?—that she is being pursued by two men who appear suddenly on the horizon, she dives back into the water and swims slowly under the surface:

> I thought how easy it would be for them to pluck me from the sea. I kept swimming up the shore, away from the place in the moonlight I had found, oblivious of the urchins, the barracuda, the night eaters, the reaching fingers of jellyfish. I swam into the darkest water of all and stayed there, until they were gone. (102)

The fantasy of being chased recurs many times in Morris's narrative; continually surrounded by things and, especially, people—men—that frighten her, she converts her writing into a graph of her subliminal fears and desires. These fears and desires are centered on her own eroticized *body*. Morris's body has its own geography, its own itineraries and landscapes; it acts both as a sensor for her experience in the present and as a receptacle for collective memories of experiences in the past: "Women remember. Our bodies remember. Every part of us remembers everything that has ever happened. Every touch, every feel, everything is there in our skin, ready to be reawakened, revived" (101). For Morris, travel is a register for the experience of embodiment: it sets in motion a process that provides the stimulus for "revival." But travel is also a site of risk where the "reawakened" female body becomes the object of others' desire and threatens to turn into a trap. Morris compares her situation to that of other women travelers, some of whom she befriends; she feels, as she imagines they do, that her journey is a test of mettle, a trial not only of her own strength but of the collective strength of her sex. More apparent, however, are the moments of weakness with which she punctuates her narrative—moments that draw her nearer, perhaps, to her target female readership, but that also show the gap between her and her fellow women travelers' aspirations to greater freedom and the awareness of their movement between alternative forms of confinement.

If the freedom of travel turns out, in some respects, to be an empty promise, it may yet hold consolations, Pyrrhic victories for the dispossessed. Not least among these is the capacity to play with gender stereotypes. Morris and Murphy try to draw attention away from themselves as women travelers by pretending to imitate men, both in their attitudes and styles of dress. Both travelers favor men's clothing, and Murphy, in particular, takes on a persona "so beyond the imagining of everyone [in India and, especially, Afghanistan] that it's universally assumed I'm a man" (27). Eric Newby, who negotiates similar geographical territory in *A Short Walk in the Hindu Kush* (see chap. 1), is seemingly horrified of being found to be effeminate.[5] Murphy, in contrast, takes advantage of her ambiguous sexual status; in Afghanistan, for instance, she grows accustomed to being the only woman present, on more than one occasion being asked to share in the locals' macho jokes:

> It certainly is a curious experience to be a woman travelling alone in Muslim countries. Most of one's time is spent in the company of men only, being treated with the respect due to a woman, but being talked to man-to-man, so that in the end one begins to feel somewhat hermaphroditic. (213)

While neither Murphy nor Morris goes to the lengths of another contemporary woman traveler, Sarah Hobson, who, emulating Isabelle Eberhardt, follows a forbidden trail in Iran by posing as a man,[6] they both question the boundaries separating male from female travelers, counteracting the perceptions associated with their sexuality by deliberately manipulating stereotypical gender roles. In this sense, they provide oblique examples of what Marjorie Garber wittily calls "cross-dressing for success": their "hermaphroditic" status is, in Garber's words, "a mechanism of displacement," opening up a "category crisis," revolving around the figure of gender, that "destabilizes the comfortable binarity" of conventional sexual difference (16–17).

This destabilization is taken a stage further by the popular Welsh writer Jan Morris, whose earlier narratives were not only written as, but lived as, the *male* traveler-writer, James. One of the most prolific and highly rated of contemporary travel writers, with more than twenty books to her name, Jan Morris was born in 1926 as the male child James Morris. James's childhood, affectionately rendered in the autobiographical volume *Conundrum* (1974), resembles that of the Charles Ryder figure of Evelyn Waugh's *Brideshead Revisited:* sensitive, somewhat feminized, sexually unformed, and avidly aestheticizing. Also like Ryder, the young Morris proceeded into the army as the Second World War ended, joining the Ninth Queen's Royal Lancers after a formulaic high school education at Lancing, one of England's great private schools. As *Conundrum* presents them, the next fifteen years of Morris's life were "doubled": for while on the surface he followed an exemplary male career pattern, emerging from the army of Britain's last imperial decade to take up the profession of foreign correspondent, he also felt on a deeper level that he was a woman imprisoned in the body of a man. As these feelings increased, Morris began to prepare himself psychologically for the sex change—initiated a decade later and completed in 1972 after an operation in Casablanca—from which Morris, James (male correspondent) emerged as Morris, Jan (woman travel writer).

Given the associations in other women travel writers' work between travel and sexual transgression, one might expect the sex change to have had profound implications for Morris's travel writings. Yet, strangely perhaps, the potential for travel to be figured as a fraught crossing of sexual boundaries is underemphasized in, if not entirely absent from, Jan Morris's later work. On one level, Morris seems in her travel writing to disavow her sexuality: "Much of the emotional force . . . that men spend in sex, I sublimated in travel" (101). Morris appears to have seen the sex/gender split that motivated her sex change more as a practical problem s/he needed to solve than as a psychological complex; consequently, there seems little scope for reading her travel narratives as screens for fables of (gender) subversion. Issues of gender throughout Jan Morris's work take a distant second place to the attempt—particularly evident in the *Pax Britannica* trilogy—to recuperate and imaginatively repossess the British imperial world.[7] Such a view of Morris's work implies that she might be better seen, alongside Newby and O'Hanlon, as a tongue-in-cheek chronicler of Britain's former imperial "glories." But moments of sexual tension *do* exist in Morris's work, both before and after the operation, that suggest a more conflicted view than the one she wishes to present in her autobiography. For James Morris, ideally positioned as a foreign correspondent for the romantic observation of a male world in the service of Empire, gives this world an unmistakably Forsterian homoerotic twist.

A touchstone location here is Cairo, where Morris, in the fifties, was clearly responsive to the same Middle Eastern/Arabian mystique, with its resonances of aristocratic masculinity, alluringly veiled femininity, and ambivalent sexual impulse, that Western writers and image-makers have invested in icons like Lawrence of Arabia.[8] While Morris might not have had any long-term fascination with exploring the borderline territories of sex and gender, the Levantine sphere of his activities as a correspondent during the fifties provided a site—a "contact zone" (Pratt)—for the romancing of his personal "conundrum," and for the selection of the various images that he might call upon to symbolize it. Cairo, the place where "Islam . . . is translated into worldly terms, into the languages of art, politics, showmanship and economics, into the dialectics of thinkers and the formulas of science" (171) is the focal point of this Levantine world; it is a city that achieves an almost magnetic resonance in Morris's work, a city that lures him (and, later, her) in, and draws both of them back for more. Into this symbolic site Morris introduces several of the strands that Edward Said later unravels in *Orientalism* (1978)—the Westerners' Orient of sexual allure, religious fanaticism, and political/moral duplicity.[9] Cairo, and the Levant in general, although described above in material terms, gather up elsewhere the more predictable associations of despotism and espionage. Here, for example, is a brief passage from the novel *Last Letters from Hav* (1985):

> The longer I looked at the Governor the less he seemed like the
> benevolent figurehead of an idiosyncratic Mediterranean backwater,
> and the more like one of those spidery despots one reads about in old
> books of Oriental travel, crouching there at the heart of his web. (117)

Not, of course, that Cairo itself is an "idiosyncratic backwater," and in
Farewell the Trumpets (1978), the final volume of the *Pax Britannica*
trilogy, Morris goes so far as to declare, "For some years of the war
Cairo was the military capital of the British Empire" (438). Across the
range of passages, essays, and chapters in books where Cairo appears,
it does so in a number of guises: as the setting for a late colonial show-
down between British ambassador Sir Miles Lampson and Egyptian
King Farouk (a triumph, in Morris's view, of British integrity over
Levantine weakness); as a nostalgically memorialized base for Morris's
activities as a foreign correspondent; as an "archaic" and medieval
city, capital of the Arab artistic world; and, latterly, as a hedonistic and
volatile city during the last days of President Anwar Sadat. The "essential" Cairo, however (which, like so many other travel writers, Morris
imagines herself to have discovered), is a place of evocation and long-
ing, a vestige of the "mysterious East":

> Yet there remains for me still that sediment of the sinister, a sugges-
> tion of stealth, secrecy and subversion. I sense it always in that
> immensity of desert, so empty, so close and somehow so threatening.
> I feel it in the detestable folds of the Egyptian bank notes, with a
> smell of their own and evocations of slum and bordel; in the postures
> of the silent, long-robed watchmen, sleepless in the night streets; in
> the tall presences of the minarets, elegant but always watchful; and
> most palpably of all, in those terrible monuments of egoism and
> enigma, the pyramids of Giza. (*Destinations* 176–77)

If here the Egyptian banknotes are "offensively" folded, the folds
of the alert watchman's robes are not so conspicuously stigmatized;
and it seems, indeed, as if the foldings, drapings, and obscurings of traditional Levantine costumes are offering Morris the possibility of
intrigue of a different, sexual, kind. The veiled figure is in fact a recurrent metaphor of self-representation in Morris's work. In *Conundrum*,
Morris refers to her previous position as a self-consciously ambivalent
male among the British soldiery in the same terms she will later use to
describe more conventional forms of espionage. Thus, she likens herself at one point to "a spy in a courteous enemy camp" (33),
"camouflaged" and viewing the world "from some silent chamber of

[her] own" (56); the text then explicitly finds an image for these ideas of detachment and isolation in the figure of the Muslim woman, whose veil "protects her from so many nuisances, and allows her to be at her best or her worst inside" (113). Finally, she returns us to the North African Mediterranean, and to a series of images she might equally well have applied to Cairo. Here, for instance, is a vivid, phantasmic vision of Casablanca—the place where the transformation from male to female was eventually accomplished:

> The office blocks might not look much like castle walls, nor the taxis like camels or carriages, but still I sometimes heard the limpid Arab music, and smelt the pungent Arab smells, that had for so long pervaded my life, and I could suppose it to be some city of fable, of phoenix and fantasy, in which transubstantiations were regularly effected, when the omens were right and the moon in its proper phase. (136)

Reflecting back on a former life, Morris hints at its sexual reawakening—a transformation that might be effected if "the omens are right and the moon in its proper phase." Such hints are as far as Morris goes in "transgressing" sexual boundaries; her primary project lies elsewhere, in the restoration of imperial myths. Nonetheless, in using an Oriental mystique to veil her personal feelings, Morris suggests a tactic available to women (as well as to homosexual) traveler-writers: the mystification of their sexual preferences—the masking of their sexual being—that allows them to move more freely in a male-dominated world.[10]

For Morris, freedom of a kind can be found behind the veil, concealed. For other traveler-writers, however, such as the Australian Robyn Davidson, freedom is best learned in the open, in the sunlit glare of "desert places."[11] Like several of her male contemporaries—Bruce Chatwin and Paul Theroux are the best-known examples—Davidson is drawn to the desert as a site of both adventure and contemplation.[12] *Tracks* (1980), one of the canniest of contemporary women's travel narratives, is her account of a six-month trip across the Central Australian desert, accompanied (for the most part) only by her pack camels and her ever-faithful dog. *Tracks* contains the classic ingredients for a woman's survival narrative: the courageous solitary traveler, defying the restrictions placed on her sex; the fearless confrontation of total strangers and "hostile" surroundings; the gradual adaptation to and communion with the environment. Yet Davidson, to her credit, counteracts these easy clichés, resisting others' attempts to corral her experiences into profitable myth:

> It would seem that the combination of elements—woman, desert, camels, aloneness—hit some soft spot in this era's passionless, heartless, aching psyche. It fired the imagination of people who see themselves as alienated, powerless, unable to do anything about a world gone mad. And wouldn't it be just my luck to pick this combination. . . . I was now public property. I was now a feminist symbol. I was now an object of ridicule for small-minded sexists, and I was a crazy, irresponsible adventurer (although not as crazy as I would have been had I failed). But worse than all that, I was now a mythical being who had done something courageous and outside the possibilities that other people could hope for. And that was the antithesis of what I wanted to share. That anyone could do anything. If I could bumble my way across a desert, then anyone could do anything. And this was especially true for women, who have used cowardice for so long to protect themselves that it has become a habit. (237–38)

Instead of playing up the hardships of her journey—taking advantage, like many of her peers, of travel writing's propensity for self-congratulation—Davidson emphasizes its feasibility, even calling it, afterwards, "easy" (254). Her major difficulty consists, rather, in dealing with publicity: in coping with those image makers, such as her sponsors *National Geographic,* who seek to capitalize on her "adventures" by turning them into lucrative media spectacle. Davidson could be accused here of acting in bad faith; after all, she accepts the sponsorship of a magazine she seemingly despises, then proceeds to turn her journey into another commodity, a travel book. *Tracks* is better seen, though, as a self-consciously critical examination of the media sensationalism that continues to dog—and partly, to define—books of its genre. In this respect, it ranks alongside Catherine Lutz and Jane Collins's recent critique of *National Geographic,* which lambastes the popular magazine for its media imperialism and its voyeuristic appreciation of photogenic "primitive" peoples.[13] Here, for instance, is an exchange between Davidson and the trigger-happy *National Geographic* photographer Richard Smolan, who joins her periodically, not always happily, on her trip:

> Whatever justifications for photographing the Aborigines I had come up with before, now were totally shot. It was immediately apparent that they hated it. . . . I also realized that coverage in a conservative magazine like *Geographic* would do the people no good at all, no

matter how I wrote the article. They would remain quaint primitives to be gawked at by readers who couldn't really give a damn what was happening to them. I argued with Rick that he was involved in a form of parasitism. . . . He came up with all the old arguments, but was torn, I knew, because he recognized it was true. (49)

Davidson's narrative resists, by and large, such opportunities for cultural voyeurism: her support for the Aborigines is of an entirely different kind to, say, Chatwin's in *The Songlines:* it is based on an understanding of their material situation rather than on an aestheticized admiration of the "mythic" qualities of their culture. Davidson is equally resistant to the mythicization of her own persona: she makes it clear throughout that she is (or, perhaps better, would like to be) a woman who travels rather than a credentialed "woman traveler," a candidate for the anthologies and a commodified "tribute to her sex." Nonetheless, her narrative is written, to some extent, from a feminist viewpoint, berating her Australian fellowmen for their crudeness and "small-minded sexism" (237); finding consolation, somewhat romantically, in an older Aboriginal system in which, "while men and women have separate roles, these roles . . . are mutually respected" (174); and vigorously dismantling the myths that surround the supposedly "weaker sex," myths that support the view of her own "uniqueness" or "exceptionality":

[Girls] waste so much of [their] energy seeking . . . to push up the millions of tiny thumbs that have tried to quelch . . . creativity and strength and self-confidence; that have so effectively caused [them] to build fences against possibility; that have so effectively kept [them] imprisoned inside [their] notions of self-worthlessness. . . . And now a myth was being created where I would appear different, exceptional. Because society needed it to be so. Because if people started living out their fantasies, and refusing to accept the fruitless boredom that is offered them as normality, they would become hard to control. (238)

Tracks raises unanswered questions about Davidson's collaboration in the mythologies of "exceptionality" she seeks so urgently to disclaim. Nevertheless, her uneasiness with the genre in which she is working, and her readiness to expose that genre to internal critique, are valuable correctives to those travel narratives—and here both women and men are implicated—that draw attention to themselves (and their writers) as saleable commodities and that profit unashamedly from marketable romantic myths.

Two examples of this latter kind of travel writing are Lucy Irvine's

Castaway (1983) and Joana McIntyre Varawa's *Changes in Latitude* (1989). Irvine's and Varawa's travel narratives are perhaps best seen as exercises in controlled self-congratulation, aimed at a commercial market that knows how to retail Western "island paradise" myths. Both writers celebrate their own ability to survive in, and adapt themselves to, a wholly unfamiliar environment; scorning the noncommittal attitude of the leisured traveler or, still worse, the tourist, Irvine and Varawa take on demanding—self-consciously heroic—roles: Irvine as a "castaway" on the tiny Pacific island of Tuin, Varawa as an "initiate" into the Fijian way of life she has adopted by marrying a local fisherman.

In writing about their respective experiences, Irvine and Varawa confront the paradox of seeking independence through apparently dependent means. Irvine's one-year stay on Tuin results from her answering the call to join English eccentric and latter-day Crusoe Gerald Kingsland, not just as his Woman Friday but as his wife—a role that, as she discovers, brings with it the usual "conjugal obligations." Varawa, meanwhile, adopts another culture as her own, but in so doing loses much of the independence she had previously enjoyed, as a single woman in the individualistic—and supposedly "liberated"—society of her native United States. *Castaway* and *Changes in Latitude* can be seen, then, as semi-ironic contemplations on the nature of freedom: as explorations, mediated through the escapist conventions of travel writing, of the cultural relativities of independence.

Irvine and Varawa assert their independence, in part, by manipulating the male conventions of travel writing to serve their own ends. Irvine, on Tuin to play the part of Woman Friday to Kingsland's Crusoe, forgets to read the script, and becomes instead a kind of self-appointed island monarch: "Tuinlady." The "castaway" myth is feminized as Irvine, taking over from the woefully inadequate Kingsland, plays out proprietary fantasies on an otherwise uninhabited island, and regards that island as "a private space, remote from the rest of the world, in which anything could happen" (17). For Varawa, as for Irvine, "her" island (Galoa) is "romantically remote" (1); the opportunity for romance is then pushed further when Varawa meets a local fisherman and, after a whirlwind courtship, marries him and begins to learn "the psychic reality of another way" (219). Quite how Varawa proposes to learn "the Fijian way" without learning the Fijian language remains a mystery. We are given to understand, nonetheless, that through a combination of sensory experience and anthropological readings about "primitive" cultures, Varawa eventually arrives at an intuitive grasp of the "essence" of Fijian culture; and at an awareness that she and her new husband, colliding "like mute planets in the night, in a quiet explosion of dark and light" (55), are "bridging a gap deeper than difference in language, a deep sea-trench that lies between our cultures" (227). As the florid prose suggests, Varawa's narrative belongs to the rarefied world of exotic romance; yet, like Irvine, she manipulates a genre that has often been used to cater to male fantasies, turning it instead into an outlet for her own previously repressed emotional needs.[14]

What is most apparent in both narratives, though, is the flagrant exhibitionism of their writers—a flaunting of self, in Varawa's case, that belies her desire to narrow cultural divides. *Castaway* is constructed, in part, out of clippings from Irvine's "secret" diary: an effective means of "revealing" herself to a mildly stimulated readership. Less a sharing of intimacies, then, than a baring of them; and Irvine certainly wastes no time in literally shedding her clothes, declaring herself with excruciating candor to be an unregenerate sun-worshiper, ready (and can we doubt it?) to "commit adultery with a sunbeam" (125). Irvine's titillating gestures and soft-porn posturing (*Castaway* includes several photographs of the scantily clad author) mock the same (male?) readers they appear to be attracting, as do her playful reiteration of male pioneering clichés and her parodic capitulation to erotic male fantasies (as in her pledge of allegiance to a "phallic mushroom!" [166]). These ironic tributes to malehood are entertaining enough; less endearing is her superior attitude toward the neighboring (Torres Strait) Islanders who "invade" Tuin, daring to land on an island she thinks is hers—the site of "her survival project"—but that is by entitlement theirs and that, like the islands that surround it, constitutes their primary source of sustenance. Varawa is guilty, likewise, of putting her own desires and fantasies above the needs of the people whose guest she initially is, and on whose generosity she continues to rely. Thus, even after the novelty has worn off of being "a star attraction, object of speculation and desire" (9), she maintains her self-importance by switching roles to Great Conciliator—an emissary of the (white) civilization she recognizes as being flawed, but whose gift of "reason" she can still find it in herself to bestow on her younger, volatile husband.

What I will teach him is uncertain; a gentler sense, a kindliness, I hope. Mostly I want to teach him that there is no need for that darkness to enter his eyes, the darkness that blots out thought and reason, that makes him want to smash and hit and flow with blood, to wash clean with anger. (37)

What Irvine and, particularly, Varawa apparently fail to comprehend is that the differences they perceive between their own "developed" societies and the relatively "backward" island societies they encounter are differences they (and, indirectly, the books they have written) help produce. Irvine, at least, is aware of her own escapist proclivities; but despite her frequent self-irony, her mocking awareness of herself as "less of a Great British Adventurer than a Small International Escapist" (139), Irvine seems reluctant to take responsibility for contributing toward the discrepancy between First and Third Worlds—the same discrepancy on which her narrative of isolation and its commercial viability so obviously depend. After all, her stay on Tuin is a carefully orchestrated touristic event; and as John Frow points out, "the logic of tourism is that of a relentless extension of commodity relations and the consequent inequalities of power between center and periphery, First and Third Worlds, developed and underdeveloped regions" (151). The isolation of Tuin, and the apparent backwardness of Torres Strait Island culture, may be attractive to Irvine because they seem so different, so removed from the world she knows. Yet as Frow tersely concludes (via Susan Buck-Morss), it is "precisely the *lack* of development which makes an area attractive as a tourist goal" (qtd. in Frow 151).[15]

Varawa, for her part, seeks to absolve herself from the stigmas associated with Western tourism by "going native": by adopting another culture as if it were her own. While the gestures behind her attempt at cultural conversion are clearly heartfelt, the manner in which they are described is suspect in the extreme. Thus, while she repeatedly states her wish to dissociate herself from the "material West," she reinforces the Islanders' perception of her by playing the part of wealthy benefactor. Varawa buys her husband Malé clothes, a speargun, a boat: should she really expect him not to see her as an affluent Westerner? Varawa acknowledges the dilemma: "I realized that I knew nothing," she says after buying Malé medicine that he is unable to stomach, and "could only offer the coldness of money and the burden of guilt that accompanies it. . . . The useless medicine staining his face in the light of the flashlight seemed to say to me, you are wrong, Joana, you have no heart, only a wallet to trade for love" (82–83). Such instances of bleeding-heart liberalism only emphasize Varawa's dependence on the material culture of the West; behind her attempt to bridge the gap between two "vastly different" cultures lies an awareness, albeit repressed, of the economic supremacy of her own. Varawa's rhetoric of reconciliation—a rhetoric derived not so much from her university anthropology textbooks as from the archetypes of light and dark that permeate Jungian pop psychology—cannot disguise the unequal power relations between First and Third worlds, her country and Malé's; and in this sense, Varawa's love match, along with the narrative that presents it, only helps ironically to drive their respective societies further apart.

Changes in Latitude is perhaps best seen as an exercise in flagrant cultural voyeurism, an adaptation of anthropological tropes to self-ingratiating ends. The Fijian islands satisfy Varawa's childhood fascination with the "primitive," a fascination nurtured by the (limited) anthropological knowledge she has acquired about "exotic cultures." Varawa seems to use anthropology primarily as a means of legitimating her erotic fantasies; and insofar as the text can be seen at all as conveying ethnographic information, it does so through the filter of "soft primitivist" romance.[16] In a typical passage, Varawa, while sitting drinking *yaqona* (a local concoction) with Malé's friends and family, casts furtive glances at the men sitting with such comfort on the grass, noting

> strong bodies, muscular arms and chests, the seductive careless way they wrap their *sulu* when they get up, the pervasive courtesy of their talk and motion. A timeless grace drifts here, an eternal dream time of people comfortable with where they are and with each other. (90)

For all its pretensions to anthropological accuracy, its on-the-spot explanations of local customs and events to an unaccustomed audience, *Changes in Latitude* is best seen as romantic travelogue—and in its most melodramatic vein. In its determination to exoticize its Pacific island environment, to play self-consciously on European paradisal myths, *Changes in Latitude* probably owes as much to the lurid tales of Robert Louis Stevenson as it does to the meticulous observations of its more obvious model, Margaret Mead.[17] Like Irvine, Varawa manipulates European conventions of the tropical island paradise so as to cater to her own desires and fantasies. In this sense, at least, both writers provide alternatives to traditionally male-oriented myths: the resourceful castaway coming to terms with, and eventually conquering, "his" island; the irresistible hero seducing "his" dusky maiden; and so on. In another sense, however, books like *Castaway* and *Changes in Latitude* show the continuities between women's travel narratives and the masculinist paradigms of conquest they seemingly wish to disavow. Both narratives seek to make capital out of a kind of cultural voyeurism, and to market themselves as quests for "freedom" from their own (and their readers') societies. Both narratives contradict the antimaterialist pretensions of their writers, merely accentuating the affluence of the societies to which they belong. Both narratives, finally, place an emphasis on fantasies of individual achievement, advertising the exploits of their intrepid traveler-writers and exhibiting, however ironically, their independence, courage, strength. It is unfair, perhaps, to bracket the books of Irvine and Varawa with those of, say, Murphy or Davidson: writers who are more obviously aware of the broader implications of travel writing, and whose works arguably reach out to a more demanding, critical audience. *Castaway* and *Changes in Latitude* are, however, by no means untypical of a certain kind of middlebrow travel narrative, one that continues to enjoy considerable commercial success. This type of narrative unabashedly supplies escapist entertainment, delivering Third World exotica to its target First World readership, but either tempering its cultural voyeurism with a measure of self-irony or assimilating it to the writer's allegedly cathartic personal quest. In the end, narratives like these do not so much celebrate independence as reinforce their writers' (and readers') ties to the societies from which they wish to escape. And the writers themselves know this; for travel narratives often contain an element of *strategic* wish-fulfillment, and while it may be true that Irvine and Varawa, and others like them, are "reaching for a kind of liberty" (Melchett 3), it also seems that they end up converting potentially liberating narratives into self-admiring confessions and recycled versions of marketable romantic myths.

Irvine's and Varawa's travel narratives, focusing on the "othered" body, assimilate "primitive" experience to the dictates of Western commodity culture. Irvine's body, in "native" posture, turns into a vehicle for consumption, just as the Fijians' seductive bodies become commodified objects of desire. This "othering" of the Third World body, or of its simulacral representation, is characteristic of metropolitan travel narratives that aestheticize their marginal subjects.[18] Sara Suleri's poetical autobiography *Meatless Days* (1989) provides an alternative to this model: one in which the body remains a focal point—an instrument—for women's travel narrative, without being turned into and exploited as an "otherness machine" (105). *Meatless Days* arguably belongs to a category of postcolonial autobiography in which the autobiographical subject is grafted onto a wider ethnic or "creolized" community (Lionnet).[19] Suleri's work, however, is distinctive in that it utilizes travel as a metaphor for the dispersal of its subject in both time (history) and space.

Travel has many connotations in Suleri's intricately structured text. On one level, travel refers to the diasporic movements of Suleri's family: across various cities, countries, continents; across linguistic and cultural borders. (Suleri's Pakistani father and Welsh mother form the nodes around which a multicultural family organizes itself, is disassembled, partially coheres.) On another level, the text itself is a densely patterned geographic circuit, traversing a variety of physical and cultural bodies, mapping out arcane itineraries and complex structures of speech and thought. And on still another, the body itself constitutes its own private geography: it has its own distributing mechanisms, its own structured patterns of response; and in acting on other bodies, it also has its own communicative signals: its register of facial gestures, its semiology of touch. *Meatless Days,* as a travel text, traces the movements *within* the body as it acts upon, and is acted upon by, the various environments that surround it; but it also records the movements *between* separate, related bodies as they interact with one another at different times or in a different space.

These movements take place across cultural borders in what is clearly a transnational space; in this sense, *Meatless Days* interrogates the kind of national (travel) narrative that it associates with ethnocentric vision and a patriarchal view of place. Such a view is affectionately ironized through the treatment of Suleri's father, an itinerant journalist committed to the cause of the Pakistani nation but "in too many places at once, recounting different histories for each" (112). Above all, though, *Meatless Days* enacts a family romance between different women's bodies: Suleri's and her sisters'; her sisters' and her mother's; all of theirs and their maternal grandmother's. These intimate connections establish a bond of shared affection that persists despite the turbulence of a new nation's (Pakistan's) history and the pressures of a family in bereavement, often, and almost always displaced. Suleri's text mourns personal losses while seeking out new paths and connections; it refuses to succumb to wistfulness or the paralysis of nostalgia, tracing alternative histories—and geographies—to that of "return." So much is clear from the treatment of Suleri's school friend Mustakori, herself a resolute transient whose passport stamps rival Suleri's own (Tanzania, Kenya, Pakistan, Ireland, England, America, China). Mustakori makes the mistake of returning to the country of her ancestry: "Those who travel curiously imagine that returning is somehow sweeter, less dangerous than seeking out some novel history, and Mustakori evidently had such nostalgia encoded in her genes" (49). Inevitably, she is disappointed; return only brings further departure, but a life of dedicated travel leaves her "untainted by experience, as though her wisdom consisted in remaining pure of any knowledge that travel pretended to confer" (66). Suleri's irony, of course, is that much more caustic for being partly self-directed; she recognizes her own life of transience and the empty wisdom it brings. If return fosters illusions, so too does departure with its false promises; Suleri's narrative oscillates energetically between unacceptable alternatives, unable, like its narrator, to settle for one consistent code. The following exchange between Suleri and her sister Tillat, who has "settled" in Kuwait, is instructive:

> "Sara, you must learn how to settle now." She was talking about the stringent graces of monogamy. "Oh sister most monogamous," my brain groaned, "how can I tell you what it is to have a hand upon your head that shapes itself unwittingly to someone else's cranium, so that every nerve end of fidelity in you leaps up to exclaim, 'This is not the cup my skull requires?'" . . . [M]y time to stay was done. It wrenched me to leave her and her brood: talking creatures all of them, those settlers in the dust. (83)

Suleri's narrative, despite its focus on Pakistan, is characterized by a determined cosmopolitanism that worries fixed identitary categories, blurring the boundaries between "self" and "other." "I've lived many years as an otherness machine," she complains to her brother Shahid, "had more than my fair share of being other" (112). Suleri, who currently teaches Third World literature at Yale, is well positioned to comment on the ironies of the academic "alterity industry." In her critical study, *The Rhetoric of English India* (1992), these ironies are made explicit: "[A]lteritism begins as a critical and theoretical revision of a Eurocentric or Orientalist study of the literatures of colonialism, but its indiscriminate reliance on the centrality of otherness tends to replicate what in the context of imperialist discourse was the familiar category of the exotic" (12). Suleri is only too well aware that her own work, like the subject she teaches, risks being appreciated primarily for its exotic cachet. *Meatless Days,* in this context, reacts preemptively against its own reception; its narrative of postcolonial transience challenges the commodified distinction between "self" and "other," rejecting a wholesale view of difference that "pays no attention to the cultural nuances that differentiation implies," and relocating it instead at the site where a colonial/postcolonial history is played out and reenacted across the gendered (and/or ethnicized) body. For Suleri, as for Mary Morris, memories are channeled through the body: embodiment is not just an analogue for the incorporation of experience but a mnemonic device for the recuperation of a personal or collective past. In *Meatless Days,* embodiment functions as a kind of countermemory that sets itself over and against the politics of cultural nostalgia.[20] Suleri's text travels back in time, not to recover an imagined wholeness, but to construct alternative histories to the ones inscribed in official records—histories that were written over, and are now rewritten by, the female body.

These abstractions do not do justice to the sensual immediacy of Suleri's writing or to the intricacy of a prose that aspires to, and sometimes reaches, the height of lyric. They indicate, nonetheless, that a case can be made for seeing *Meatless Days,* not just as an idiosyncratic autobiography or memoir, but as a self-consciously gendered travel narrative that raises several important questions: about the positioning of the traveling subject within a rhetoric of displacement (tourism, migration, expatriation, etc.), and about the need to understand the past, both in its broader sweep or trajectory and in the multiple, embodied micronarratives that go to make up what we call history. *Meatless Days* provides a reminder, as well, not only that women travel differently, but that their journeys can be used to install "difference" into the modern culture of travel. And this is a culture, as Inderpal Grewal reminds us, that is in much need of reassessment:

> There is much in the culture of travel that needs examination. . . . Particularly in the area of sexuality, more texts that attempt to decolonize cultural and national forms are necessary, creating narratives of the travel of sexualities that would, once again, fracture disciplinary practices that were part of European modernity and colonial modernities. (232)

Suleri's is one such text, although, as her criticism warns us, "difference" should not become a catchall academic category that enlists vaguely related cultural products in the service of a self-congratulatory "transgressive" cultural critique. Indeed, Suleri's narrative, placed alongside others in this section, emphasizes the enormous differences *within* the field of women's travel writing. The view of women's travel writing as necessarily liberating clearly needs adjusting just as much as the patriarchal models of imperial travel it often claims to disavow. Women's travel writing is more different, but also *less* different, than it might seem: more different insofar as it comprises a large, distinctly heterogeneous body of texts, but less different because some of these texts are entirely complicit with the dominant mode. The imperialist exoticism that Suleri abjures is also one that, say, Varawa practices (even though the comparison is perhaps invidious insofar as their texts are addressed to different audiences).[21] Obviously, not all women's travel narratives are feminist—however we might want to define the term—and in those that are, or profess to be, there is no necessary link between feminist critique and anti-imperialist revisionism. (This is also true, of course, as was argued in an earlier chapter, for "postcolonial" travel narratives.) As Sara Mills has shown for nineteenth-century travel writing—and her argument is surely relevant to the twentieth century as well—it is quite possible to be disadvantaged, even oppressed, with respect to gender while remaining privileged, even oppressive, with respect to race, ethnicity, class.[22] The commodification of women's travel writing tends to obscure these crucial differences, even as it celebrates the writers themselves—often, precisely, for being "different." Many of the best women travel writers, however, are much more self-aware than the anthologies give them credit for; and several of these, unfortunately, have gone unrepresented in this section. Writers as different as Christina Dodwell, Barbara Grizzuti Harrison, Sara Wheeler, and, from an earlier period, Freya Stark, are well aware, like Murphy or Davidson or (at the fringes of the genre) Suleri, that the traveling subject—a composite of the variety of rhetorical positions available to traveler-writers—is irreducibly complex: that it is situated firmly but subtly within the race-class-gender nexus; that it shapes, but is also shaped by, wider social, historical, and ideological forces.[23] The traveling subject is always gendered, always embodied, and always active: recognizing this, many women travel writers—although by no means all—have turned their narratives into critical explorations of both the potential for and limitations of female agency in the contemporary world.

The agency of traveler-writers implies a set of privileges—privileges, though, that are almost invariably occluded in travel narratives. Most obviously, privilege consists in the possession of ready money, particularly for unplanned trips. Money allows the traveler to decide on, but also to diverge from, destinations and routes; it also bestows power on the traveler at various sites along the way, a power that the resident native often expects him or her to exercise by passing along a modicum of wealth. In many cases, the native's purchase in the situation of being traveled *upon* depends on the ability to wrest money from a temporary patron. This patronage relationship remains an unequal one. All the same, it assumes a certain symmetry: the traveler is prepared to dispense largesse if it will permit licenses not available at home; while the native reciprocates with goods and services, where the recompense is significant and cultural integrity is ultimately not at stake.

Although recent travel narratives and commentary are gradually adjusting the dominant paradigm, it is still true that most of the world's producers of travel narratives are white heterosexual males who enjoy considerable economic privilege and, even when they have responsibilities, the capacity to shuck these off, at least temporarily. If travel is commonly figured as the embrace of freedom, of liberating (or libertarian) forays into less constrained locales, it offers freedom under the sponsorship of financial resources and apparent cultural detachment. On both sides, "transgressive" liberties need to be negotiated. The (male) traveler deploys disposable income to obtain exotic sexual adventure, the (female) native offers services in order to procure otherwise unavailable assets: income, comfort perhaps, or security in living arrangements. Such transgressions, for white heterosexual males, are inevitably bounded: the line in the sand is often indicated through moments of homosexual panic, when the traveler reclaims cultural norms by detaching himself from a homosexually compromising situation. These moments of panic also serve to reclaim normative heterosexuality as a "higher" (white) cultural attribute, in contrast with the frequently feminized, potentially contaminating "other" culture.

Given these circumstances, it is not surprising that travel cannot be linked to sexual liberation or gender revision in any simple way. Writers making such claims have generally done so within a male heterosexual context because only that context—universal white heterosexuality—has been competent to figure the sexual license associated with travel as transgression, while shutting out more radical transgressions, projecting these beyond the thinkable. Conversely, now that homosexuality is no longer intrinsically transgressive in white cultures, gay travel has become a field in its own right, connected with guiding gay travelers to favorable locales rather than with recording trajectories of sexual play in more or less coded discourses. Such recorded trajectories do indeed exist but, unlike most other texts considered in this book, they are in the main either historically embedded in earlier discourses or appear in stories and novels rather than in travelogues. The two categories of earlier, contextually coded discourses and contemporary travel fictions provide the basis for the following discussion of travel narratives as gay and/or queer texts.

For the contemporary reader homosexuality, as figured in the first two-thirds of the twentieth century, is for the most part present only in implicit and markedly coded terms. The term *homoeroticism* has long since dominated this literary region; only determined retrospection can reclaim the incidents and their nuanced literary representation as "gay."[24] Moreover, the codes are most recognizable in connection with *English* culture, where sexuality and eroticism often make sense only when read in terms of class. The English public school, with the privilege it granted to limited forms of same-sex engagement at the same time as it promoted homophobic masculinity, witnesses to this phenomenon, as does the special attention in some English fiction to homosexual trysts across class lines.[25] In this historical phase travel—literally understood—proved liberating, enabling franker exploration of sexual identities and practices, even when it was a matter of exchanging one set of codes and closets for another. Yet even when travel (in its most specific sense) was not in question, English homosexuality often involved a crossing of boundaries: over into the enclosed world of the public school; across class lines; or into a different age group. In the travel narratives of this period, even the most tenuous of boundary crossings can seem erotically charged.

Denton Welch's autobiographical fiction *Maiden Voyage* (1943) is a good example. Welch ran away from school in 1932, returned late for his final term, and then sailed to visit his businessman father in Shanghai. Welch retrospectively stages his travels as a series of encounters within a dialectic of risk and fear. At first things happen to him; then increasingly he participates in, and sometimes instigates, encounters.

Welch's delicate, highly aestheticized sensibility unfolds these encounters to suggest voyaging as a medium of sexual awakening. His understated declarative style evokes erotic nuance rather than explores sexual affectivity. Recording a routine caning, for example, he feels "two bars of fire eating into ice"; the light becomes "thick like milk and . . . seem[s] to float cloudily about the room"; and he feels a "surge of admiration for [his aggressor] Newman," with his "powerful body and springy, uncoloured hair" (55–56). Welch renders this episode as part of a larger experiment in which the risk-seeking traveler complements the aesthete's search for perfect objets d'art with a homoerotic quest for rougher men—soldiers, sailors, boxers. *Maiden Voyage* culminates with the boy's tentative (nonsexual) liaison with an older British sailor, a figure he seduces into friendship, singling him out and inviting him to tea. The sailor hesitates to enter the boy's luxury apartment, aware that his officers "might wonder what I was up to in there" (202); once inside, however, he teaches Denton to smoke and drink whiskey, while his young seducer sits on the sofa's arm, "look[ing] down over his shoulder" (204). When the Derbyshire-born sailor discovers that Denton has gone to school in the same county, he wistfully suggests, "We could have some lovely times in Derbyshire" (260). Interestingly, meanwhile—and in contrast with other literary travelers of the period—Welch's attitudes to the native Chinese remains one of racial and class condescension, sometimes escalating to distaste.

Welch foregoes interpretation so that incidents and encounters, held in abeyance, enact a kind of liminality where elements of aesthetics, affectivity, and sexuality float in adolescent indeterminacy. Nowhere is this more clearly demonstrated than in an episode of crossdressing experimentation. Guest at a neighbor's house, Denton occupies the room of his married woman-friend Vesta. Surveying her jewelry ("silver hair-pins with kingfishers' feathers, rose quartz, bell-shaped drops with caps of gilt filigree; rings carved out of pieces of jade and agate; two thick little tassels of seed pearls" [242]), he wants to dress up, a desire connected with a schoolboy episode when, returning by train to school, he had hidden in the lavatory "wondering if I could disguise myself as a woman, to escape being caught and sent back to school" (242). Now, however, he wishes not to disguise but to remake himself, an occupation "as absorbing as redecorating a room" (243). But the adventure soon turns risky when a stranger on the street seeks directions from him, and he beats a hasty retreat to the safety of the house and Vesta's room. The cross-dressing gesture terminates almost as soon as it has begun. In such episodes Welch places the reader at a cusp where incidents of awakening defer, rather than impel, moments of disclosure; travel occurs in the gap between remembered incident and its later emergence as narrated moment.

At much the same time that the young Denton Welch was running away from school, J. R. Ackerley's classic *Hindoo Holiday: An Indian Journal* appeared—a very funny book that cast a whimsical retrospective glance at an earlier year, 1924, when Ackerley had served a five-month stint as private secretary to the Maharajah of a small Hindu native state. In 1924, also, E. M. Forster's literary monument to the late phase of the British Raj, *A Passage to India,* appeared: a novel that memorialized a British India that had, in the view of many, already disappeared. Forster's novel is explicitly about travel, about a woman venturing upon different cultural territory that she is determined to empathize with and understand. But it is, above all, in the relationship between the Englishman Fielding and the Muslim Aziz that Forster addresses his big theme of the testing of cultural barriers and boundaries (the same theme that, later, was to dominate the posthumously published *Maurice*). At the same time, the smoldering intensity of the affection between Fielding and Aziz draws attention to the centrality of India (along with Egypt) to Forster's attempts to find human—including sexual—satisfaction during the period, 1917–25, when he was away from England on colonial service. The fictional Fielding-Aziz relationship draws upon Forster's loyal but frustrating and unconsummated friendship with the Indian Muslim Syed Masood. In fact, virtually all of Forster's experiences in the Levantine world and in India were inflected by sexual pressures. When he went to India for a second time in 1921, as private secretary to the Maharajah of Dewas, the latter found him a young retainer to satisfy his sexual needs, even though he himself customarily did his utmost to eradicate same-sex intimacies at court (Furbank 2:81–86). It was Forster who then got Ackerley the post of private secretary at Chhatarpur (Chhokrapur in *Hindoo Holiday*).

Hindoo Holiday is presented in the form of a journal, one so elegantly written and structured that it bespeaks careful retrospective editing. It is essentially the story of Ackerley's quest to kiss Sharma, most beautiful of the Maharajah's young cup-bearers.[26] The text's erotics are set up early on: first, in comments on the sculptures in a Jain temple, whose "indecencies, Major Pombey [was] considerate enough to mention, [included] a long file of soldiers marching gaily along, and another smaller, more elaborate design . . . both sodomitic" (17–18);

and second, in an exchange with the Maharajah who, after asking Ackerley about a literary reference to "Nero marrying Pythagoras in public," receives the coy reply,

> "Well, . . . it may mean either that Nero, as a patron, gave Pythagoras in marriage to some young lady, or that he publicly embraced Pythagorean philosophy."
> "But, my good sir," said his Highness, "this was not *that* Pythagoras; this was another Pythagoras, a boy."
> "Oh," I said hastily. "Well, in that case perhaps it means exactly what it says."
> His Highness simpered into his sleeve. (21)

This arch exchange is a prelude to Ackerley's accounts of the Maharajah's "Gods'" entertainments in which comely male Hindu youths dance for the court, enacting stories from the myths. It is at one of these cross-dressed entertainments that the Maharajah singles out the barber's son Sharma for his guest's attention. Ackerley's desire to take Sharma for his valet is initially foiled, though, when he alarms the shy boy with a demand for a kiss.

Ackerley is eventually gratified with some degree of intimacy at court, a triangulated succession of exchanges between Ackerley, Sharma, and Sharma's friend, the guest house clerk Narayan, allowing for a measure of physical contact. The English-speaking Narayan reveals that he himself is the object of Sharma's affections; Ackerley, meanwhile, seems increasingly drawn to both, on one occasion admiring Narayan's gracefulness "in his white muslin clothes, the sleeves of his loose vest widening out at the wrist, the long streamers of his turban floating behind him" (217). The description continues in similar vein:

> The breeze puffed at his *dhoti* as he approached, moulding the soft stuff to the shape of his thigh; then as he turned a bend in the path another gentle gust took the garment from behind and blew it aside, momentarily baring a slim brown leg. I took his hand and led him into my tent. (217–18)

On this, the account's most charged occasion, Narayan draws the Englishman into the shadow of a tree and kisses him on the cheek; not about to lose an opportunity, Ackerley seizes Narayan and plants two kisses on his lips—a marked transgression, since the high caste Hindu neither eats nor deigns to dally with those who eat meat. Sharma, too, unbends on one occasion, holding hands with the amorous Englishman.

Forster declined Ackerley's invitation to write a preface for *Hindoo Holiday,* unwilling to endorse a book that exposed the sybaritic Maharajah's sexual tastes and practices.[27] Nonetheless, it was enthusiastically received, becoming the kind of book that finds its way into the "top ten" on the lists of widely different readers. Given its clarity about the sexual preferences of its author (males; *young* males; young *Hindu* males), this seems surprising. Candor presumably removed the book's potential threat to its earlier English readers. The Maharajah, described condescendingly, is little more than a figure of fun; the Hindu Ganymede figures are feminized and aestheticized; and the author does his best to present himself as a harmless eccentric, unthreateningly attracted to characters who turn out to be no more than mildly exotic thumbnail sketches. Basking in his English privilege, Ackerley suggests that his job as private secretary to the Maharajah was just an interlude, a trifle; nothing was at stake for India, for him, or for the Empire. But Forster's refusal to indulge a friend by writing a preface suggests that he, at least, thought differently.

The travels of the Auden-Isherwood-Spender group to Germany, especially Berlin, between 1928 and 1933 represented a more determined bid to enlist travel as escape toward greater experiential freedom, while linking in a more complex fashion with English ideologies of the period. Growing familiarity with the work of Freud enhanced the resistance to repression that constellated around D. H. Lawrence's notorious fictions, joining with the initiatives of young Oxbridge graduates to get away from their genteel upper-middle-class families. Berlin was a strong magnet, and it was relatively accessible. As Stephen Spender put it in his introduction to *The Temple,*

> For many of my friends and for myself, Germany seemed a paradise where there was no censorship and young Germans enjoyed extraordinary freedom in their lives. By contrast England was a country where James Joyce's *Ulysses* was banned, as was also Radclyffe Hall's *The Well of Loneliness*—a novel about a lesbian relationship. England was where the police, at the order of Mr Mead, a London magistrate, took down from the walls of the Warren Gallery pictures from an exhibition of D. H. Lawrence's paintings. (x)

Shortly after arriving there, W. H. Auden proclaimed Berlin as "the bugger's daydream. There are 170 male brothels under police control. I could say a lot about my boy, a cross between a rugger hearty and Josephine Baker" (qtd. in Carpenter 90). Auden, Christopher Isherwood, and Spender all negotiated their way around Germany in the late Weimar period, characteristically moving from bourgeois host families into the resources their own English-contemporary circles afforded, and from there either into the German intellectual/professional set or into a sort of underworld populated by "adolescent boys who hung about many of the Berlin bars and cafes, and were willing to have sex with English visitors in return for presents and money" (90).

In the earlier part of the period, the English affectionately exchanged news about their antibourgeois sexual experiments against a background of heady conversation about sex, class, and politics. Young German males brought out in them a sort of boastful hedonism, evoking an interesting vacillation as the rugged Berlin hustler competed for favors with the noble blond Teuton. Both types, far from the delicate Oriental favored by Forster and Ackerley, shared the advantage of seeming to move around publicly, offering their privileged English clients a way out of the genteel closet.

Unsurprisingly, the homosexuality of the English circle in pre-Nazi Germany does not declare itself openly in their writings from the period but is displaced, in Auden's case, onto enigmatic Freudian lyrics and, in Isherwood's, onto the iconic evocation that eventually emerged as *Goodbye to Berlin* in 1939, more than half a decade after Nazi successes had made it impossible to view Germany as a healthy homosexual haven. Spender's major contribution to the literature came only with the (somewhat embarrassed) publication of *The Temple* in 1988. The rapid collapse of Weimar Germany brought the homosexuality of reasonably affluent, well-educated, "liberated" English youths up against German Fascism, rendering their admiration for blond nobility and tough physicality extremely fraught.

Goodbye to Berlin refracts Isherwood's homosexuality through the febrile atmosphere of Berlin between 1930 and 1933, giving it unstable definition. The first-person narrator is an observer, a shadowy figure providing sharply realized portraits of others in a relationship with himself that remains equally elusive. Among these is the legendary Sally Bowles, but the male figures are also piquant and suggestive. The depressed Peter has escaped from his father and family home, passing through the hands of several psychiatrists before imagining that he can finally settle down with the blond young German Otto. Then there is Otto himself, "squatting . . . on the bed, . . . so animally alive, his naked brown body so sleek with health" (118), his youthful vigor and working-class vulgarity as seductive to the narrator as it is to the unfortunate Peter. And then there are the street boys, who hang out at the

Alexander Casino "while their girls were out working the Friedrich-strasse and the Linden for possible pickups" (123), and who index Ish-erwood's and Auden's participation in casual same-sex liaisons in Berlin.

The most intriguing portrait, perhaps, is that of Bernhard Lan-dauer, who, in recounting his history to the narrator, describes himself as having been "a queer sort of boy." Son of a wealthy Jewish depart-ment store owner, Bernhard invites the narrator to his apartment and, later, to his lakeside villa. The narrator registers his host's bid for attention (he answers the door "wearing a beautifully embroidered kimono" [156]) and gestures of intimacy (the hand on the shoulder), presenting him as fastidious, overly ironic, and evidently pleading for friendship. While Bernhard ostensibly distinguishes himself from the narrator in the words he uses to express his own alienation, these words tacitly suggest a deeper connection between the two men:

> Remember that I am a cross-breed. Perhaps, after all, there is one drop of pure Russian blood in my polluted veins. . . . You, Christo-pher, with your centuries of Anglo-Saxon freedom behind you, with your Magna Carta engraved upon your heart, cannot understand that we poor Barbarians need the stiffness of a uniform to keep us standing upright. (161–62)

Stiff uniforms, of course, will not suffice long to keep Bernhard upright; equally, Magna Carta is not the guarantee of absolute free-dom for Christopher that Bernhard thinks it to be. The brutal Nazi assaults on the streets of Berlin, escalating through the 1930s, eventu-ally force the visitor to confront a contradiction between youthful, blond male beauty and Nazi ideology, as well as a parallel between the marginality of Jews and homosexuals. The moment of disengagement comes during Christopher's visit to a meeting of pathfinders where, to his discomfort, he decodes a Nazi icon:

> Above the table with the candlesticks was a sort of icon—the framed drawing of a young pathfinder of unearthly beauty, gazing steadily into the far distance, a banner in his hand. *The whole place made me feel profoundly uncomfortable.* (198; emphasis added)

Stephen Spender's *The Temple* required a far greater time-lapse between experience, writing, and publication than the work of Auden and Isherwood. *The Temple* is an allegorical roman à clef in which Spender himself figures as narrator Paul, Auden as Simon Wilmot, and Isherwood as William Bradshaw.[28] *The Temple* is motivated by Paul's infatuation with fellow undergraduate Marston, an idealizing homo-sexual attraction that misfires, and that leads him to accept the invita-tion of Ernest Stockmann, a visiting student at Oxford (and a figure who recalls Bernhard Landauer in *Goodbye to Berlin*), to join him in Hamburg. In the first phase of the novel, Germany signifies beautiful—and beautifully photographed—male bodies, carefree, generous com-panionship, and the trappings of modernity: "Paul watched the young Germans. They had a style which he thought of as excitingly 'modern.' The fashions they wore were sun and air and their bronze skin. The boys gentle and soft, the girls sculptural, finely moulded" (42). Paul's visit to Germany, then, seems like a discovery of the body—particu-larly the young male body—and the potential for a quality and inten-sity of companionship, sex, and love. This synecdochic body consoli-dates itself aesthetically in photographic images, like the one that provides the novel's central emblem:

> It was of a bather standing naked at the reed-fringed edge of a lake. The picture was taken slightly from below so that the torso, rising above the thighs, receded, and the whole body was seen, layer on layer of hips and rib-cage and shoulders, up to the towering head, with dark hair helmeted against a dark sky. V-shaped shadows of wil-low leaves fell like showers of arrows on San Sebastian, on the youth's sunlit breast and thighs. "Oh, wonderful!" said Paul, "The temple of the body!" (69)

Later, Paul tries to replicate this photograph with one that stages his friend Lothar as the Sebastian figure.

Another scenario, in the novel that William is working on when Paul visits him prior to leaving for Hamburg, involves the "image of a German boy whom [Mr. S] has to seek out in the lowest bars and dives of Berlin. . . . There are some people who, to be redeemed, have to go into the lowest kennels of the gutter—like Ibsen's Wild Duck diving to the bottom of the pond among the mud and weeds" (21). These "low-est kennels," in *The Temple,* include not only the waterfront street-and-bar life of Hamburg, but also characters who exploit their moneyed English patrons, who become Nazis, and who fail to realize the dream of unrepressed comradeship and sexuality. In fact, the novel, in the form in which it was finally published, seems to go beyond signaling its author's critique of an earlier English homosexual ideology. Marking a break from the androgynized and feminized figures of the colonial Raj, the idealized masculinity and heroic physicality of Nazi Germany put homosexuality into a different kind of closet, proleptic of later urban gay bar scenes.[29] Spender's rewriting of the novel he had first composed several decades before evidently enlists the picaresque hedonism of the English Berlin circle to produce an allegory of the rise of fascism.

Such moral strictures are scarcely evident in the work of Aldo Busi, a practitioner of the Italian new novel who exploits the travel narrative's ability to scandalize. One of Busi's more cryptic observations is that "[a] heterosexual does not travel—he moves forward" (102). What distinction is Busi suggesting here? Perhaps it is the distinction between experiencing a place as *other* and *queer*—"traveling"—and experiencing it as a variation of the *same*—and thus "moving forward."[30] Comparison of Busi with Paul Bowles, celebrated doyen of the Tangier circle of expatriates and visitors, establishes this difference more clearly. Interviewing Bowles for *Rolling Stone* in 1974, Michael Rogers suggested that Morocco was "really a very bisexual culture" (Caponi 69)—to which Bowles assented, more or less. Rogers thus neatly eliminated the need to deal with Moroccan sexual codes and practices as different and culturally specific, assimilating them instead, as he and others have assimilated Arab drug use, to a "liberatory" American counterculture. Such elisions presumably facilitate the moving forward—and moving on—of Busi's "normal" (heterosexual) traveler. But if the queer subject is at the center of Busi's fictionalized travels, what constitutes that traveling? Does the queer subject articulate particular and differentiated ways of acting and reacting in the situations of travel? Does he engage differently with the places he visits? And to what degree can he claim to situate authoritatively—to know—the other culture? Some reflection on Paul Bowles and William Burroughs, along with Busi, will bring these questions into clearer focus.

Paul Bowles has made Morocco—more specifically, Tangier—his home since 1947. Unlike Busi, Bowles has never publicly defined his sexuality; and in the Morocco that emerges from his writings, homosexuality is above all an atmosphere: diffused largely through legend, passing increasingly into myth. The literary foundation, evoking homosexuality only by nuance, is his novel *The Sheltering Sky* (1949), filmed by Bernardo Bertolucci some decades later under the same title. Both novel and film loosely associated travel in North Africa with fraught marriage, a love triangle, and violence: all of which, in conjunction with the hallucinatory desert setting, mediated a generalized image of existential extremity, particularly for American readers. Subsequently, Bowles was to draw enough literary and pop-cultural figures to Tangier—among them Jack Kerouac, Allen Ginsberg with his lover Peter Orlovsky, Truman Capote, William Burroughs, Tennessee Williams, Byron Gysin, and Gregory Corso—to suggest the American experience of a cult phenomenon. Bowles's wife Jane, herself a lesbian writer, was vividly present, if not precisely at her husband's side. To be part of cult life was to indulge bohemian, sometimes expensive, tastes for chic parties, drugs, spectacles, sorcery, and a freewheeling approach to friendship and sexuality. Michelle Green's *The Dream at the End of the World* (1991), itself a breathless synthesis, indexes gossip as another key ingredient of cult life. In effect, the combination of these elements and their transmission through a variety of media has given Morocco a cultural mystique—a *domesticated* mystique—that might well preempt travel in Busi's sense.

But Bowles's authority as traveler-interpreter of Moroccan (homo)sexuality derives from more than the mix of chronicle, reminiscence, and gossip that make up Green's book. Around the time he was completing work on his novel *Up Above the World,* in 1963, Bowles initiated a project that has spanned several decades. He began taping Driss ben Hamed Charhardi's (Larbi Layachi's) autobiographical episodes, delivered in Moghrebi; the edited result was the translated "novel," *A Life Full of Holes,* published by Grove Press in 1964. According to Jay McInerny, Bowles had "virtually invent[ed] a new genre" (Caponi 192). Mohammed Mrabet's similarly produced *Love with a Few Hairs* followed in 1967, and Mohammed Choukri's more elaborate *For Bread Alone* in 1973. Of fifteen generically similar books, Choukri contributed three, including *Jean Genet in Tangier* (1974) and *Tennessee Williams in Tangier* (1979), but Mohammed Mrabet's titles constitute the bulk of the project. New York's Inanout Press published the latest Bowles-Mrabet collaboration, *Chocolate Creams and Dollars,* as recently as 1992 in an expensive art edition, garnished with photographic illustrations by Philip Taaffe. The project has undoubtedly succeeded in commodifying the cultural mystique of Morocco for post-Beat North America and, to a lesser extent, Britain. The translation theorist Richard Jacquemond has described a process that seems appropriate to Bowles's work:

> In translation from a dominated language-culture into a hegemonic one, the translator appears as the authoritative mediator through

whom the dominated language-culture is maintained outside the limits of the self and at the same time adapted to this self in order for it to be able to consume the dominated linguistic-cultural object. (Qtd. in Venuti 155)

Jacquemond's comment, however, suggests that gay travelers—like heterosexual ones—can produce alibis through cultural appropriation for their own motivations and performances.

Characteristically, the chronicles of Bowles's "new genre" are narratives of native improvement and advancement. Their main characters, versions of their Tangier authors, begin as street-smart victims of class poverty and parental abuse. Illiterate but resourceful, they ally themselves with fellow Moroccans who scavenge, steal, and, at the high end, run small cafes. They meet up with and befriend American and English visitors who, in return for sexual favors, support them. Mrabet's male hero in *Love with a Few Hairs* manages a double success, parlaying the economic resources afforded by his intimacy with an English patron into ownership of a fishing fleet and a parallel career as a successful fisherman and wholesaler. He weds a Muslim woman and has children, while remaining loyal to his patron, continuing to perform services for him and to receive his due reward.

Recurring patterns in several of these narratives indicate how Bowles, along with other Euro-American expatriates and visitors, succeeded in constructing a mythicized "Moroccan" culture. The (native) protagonist generally searches for and marries a Muslim wife, who remains largely invisible; his other (hetero)sexual encounters inject romantic fantasy into a misogynistic stance; he entertains sexual activity with other men, mostly white patrons, but only when such activity need not be construed as homosexual—that is, when the partner is an older European and the hero is not at risk of being feminized; there is much kif consumption; Muslim identification is retained through piety, abstinence from alcohol, and participation in dance cults such as *jilala;* and there is a constant threat of sorcery, usually involving poison *(tsoukil),* following the betrayal of sexual/marital contracts. Native Moroccan culture, then, is Islamic, sodomitical, drug friendly, sorcerous, and ecstatic. For the traveler-expatriate circle, it offers an expansive field for licensed, if tricky, play.

European and native encounter each other in the shiftingly asymmetrical patron-protégé contract. Mrabet's most explicit account of this encounter appears in the autobiographical *Look and Move On* (1989). Mrabet recounts how he first met two visitors, Reeves and

Maria, on a cafe terrace. He tells them that he is "glad to have met some Americans" (13), subsequently visits them at their hotel, and travels with them to Marrakesh. He understands very well their interest in him:

> I said to myself: Both of these people are vicious. They both want to sleep with me. And with all the kif and whiskey I had in my head, Maria looked very beautiful to me, and Reeves looked very handsome, and I felt like making love to both of them. (14)

His attentions later lead to his accompanying Maria on her return to New York. From there Maria, discovering she cannot control his quest for experience, packs him off to Reeves's family in Iowa, where he proceeds to offend Reeves's abstinent middle-American parents and to embarrass Reeves himself, with his defiant pursuit of alcohol and sex. For good measure, he informs Reeves's mother, "I love to stay up all night and look for girls to sleep with" (52), adding, provocatively, "What did he have on his mind, your son, when he asked me to come here?" (55). So he is dispatched to New York and from there back to Tangier, shaking the American dust off his feet. The Reeveses have financed Mrabet, providing him with resources and opportunities otherwise unavailable to the Moroccan dependent; he, in turn, has offered sexual services that seem to justify something more than dependent maintenance—but on his own terms. There will always be other patrons. Mrabet's (or is it Bowles's?) skill consists in the discretion with which he negotiates the rawer edges of such arrangements. But Mrabet, all the same, does not repeat the limit case that the Reeveses represent.

Look and Move On invites the reader to situate Mrabet's various narratives of patronage within the wider framework of his relationship with Bowles; the episode involving Reeves sets up for an account of Mrabet's meeting with Paul and Jane Bowles on the beach at Merkala, after which point the autobiography devotes equal attention to life at the Bowleses and to Mrabet's courtship of and eventual marriage to Zohra. Mrabet recounts how Jane Bowles hailed him on the beach—"You smoke a lot of kif for someone so young"—after he had already identified the couple, Paul walking in the company of "a tall American they call El Hombre Invisible [William Burroughs]" (90). And it was thus that Mrabet acquired, not only another patron, but incorporation into an insider group whose prestige he has done his part to promote.[31]

The Morocco translation project complicates the sexual contract by situating it within a colonial context in which sexual acts mediate shifting power gestures and relations. Typically, the native protégé will assume only the dominant role in the sodomitical act. He will also be quick to characterize the acts of sodomy he witnesses in terms of power, especially colonial power. The European sodomite, for the native community, displays the normative decadence of the West; Mrabet consistently "others" the group he likes to call "the Nazarenes," dissociating himself from their values. In the strongest moment of resistance, his rejection of Western decadence explicitly links sexual/sadistic performance with colonial domination. In *Look and Move On,* he accompanies a friend to a Tangier party at which the English host, Albert, presides with a whip, lashing two Spanish boys as they lie face down on a rug. Then, at Albert's behest, a large black man publicly sodomizes two other Spanish boys who are lying on the same rug. As a "man who hates Europeans" (17), Mrabet reports his comments to the black man who is "work[ing] on" one of the boys:

> Happy with any American or Jew or Englishman, or any filthy Frenchman, yes? They come here and you show them your backside and everything else you've got. And they take pictures of you doing your work, and sell them later in Europe. And you like that. (19)

Mrabet temporarily enters into the colonial contract, only to expose and repudiate it. In seducing Maria and sodomizing Reeves, before eventually spurning both, Mrabet uses their cultural assumptions and fantasies in order to dissolve the contract. Seducing and being seduced (at least figuratively) by Mrabet, Bowles assumes the authority of presenter and mediator, standing outside of the engagements between Western visitors and Moroccan natives, and containing them within the literary frame (the "new genre") he invents. The material, while it embodies some sort of critique of the colonial/sexual contract, remains at the same time dependent on and complicitous with it.

By this time, the Tangier experience had already assumed more generalized form in the cult classic *Naked Lunch* (1959) by "El Hombre Invisible" himself, William Burroughs. *Naked Lunch,* offering an exoticized, fantasized paradigm of encounter between the state and its dropouts, stands on the threshold of postmodernism. Living in Tangier continuously for about four years, Burroughs played a comprehensive role as part of the Bowles circle; in *Naked Lunch,* however, he distances himself from the city more decisively than Bowles had done. Tangier, in fact, does not itself appear, but becomes iconic as Interzone: a travel site that draws on, magnifies, and transfigures sex, drug, and power themes already present in Bowles's work. Interzone is a liminal, surreal territory where regimes of law enforcement and medicine jointly control a total culture of transgression, including heroin consumption, sodomy, and coprophagy. Burroughs's Arab boys characteristically disport themselves in a sexual athleticism charged with violence:

> Ali seize him by one ankle, tug the ankle under the arm pit, lock his arm around the calf. The boy kick desperately at Ali's face. Other ankle pinioned. Ali tilt the boy back on his shoulders. The boy's cock extends along his stomach, float free pulsing. Ali put his hands over his head. Spit on his cock. The other sighs deeply as Ali slide his cock in. The mouths grind together smearing blood. Sharp musty odor of penetrated rectum. Nimun drive in like a wedge, force jism out the other cock in long hot spurts. (The author has observed that Arab cocks tend to be wide and wedge shaped.) (71)

Passages such as this stripped-down, observational narrative—which also occur in Busi's *Sodomies in Elevenpoint*—are intercut with scenarios in a very different mode; one phantasmic sequence, for example, celebrates a Moroccan funeral: "The hog is dressed in a jellaba, a keif pipe juts from its mouth, one hoof holds a packet of feelthy pictures, a mezuzzoth hangs about its necks [*sic*]. . . . Inscribed on the coffin: 'This was the noblest Arab of all'" (95).

Several interviewers since the sixties have persistently pressed Bowles to perform the time-honored task of the travel writer and authoritatively summarize "Moroccan culture." Bowles's characteristic responses have been adroit and coy. His reply to one question, for instance, was,

> No Moroccan will ever tell you what he thinks, or does, or means. He'll tell you some of it and tell you other things that are completely false and then weave them together into a very believable core, which you swallow, and that's what's considered civilized. What's the purpose of telling the truth? (Caponi 66)

Bowles's apparent reticence gives the impression that he has cannily plumbed far beneath the cultural surface; in contrast, Busi—in line with contemporary conventions of "reading cultures"—regards the challenge as inherent in codes that the visitor must crack: "I know where I am unbeatable—in acquiring in five minutes what is essential in the ethical codes of any people or social class. . . . The important thing is not to hit the nail on the head right away but not commit howlers right away" (44). Busi offers a line of reasoning: Moroccan culture is sodomitical. But sodomy is imbricated in a tissue of ethical codes and practices; the visiting Westerner should assess these codes rather than indulge the illusion of a liberated hedonism—the canny sexual tourist is the one who "leaves [his] psychologizing at home" (39). Armed with this attitude, Busi envelopes frank reports of sexual episodes in witty discourses on the writer and writing, contemporary literary theory, and subjectivity. And, no less, on travel and travel writing: "This is a no-travel and no-sex book," he declares at one point, signaling his aversion to "travel journals and travel literature" (65). The aphorism that follows—"People who discover nothing usually discover geography" (65)—is characteristically ironic, demonstrating the extent of Busi's impatience for the travel writer's rhapsodies of nature. *Sodomies in Elevenpoint,* for all that, is a bona fide travel narrative, which disclaims its own status partly in order to clear a cant-free space for its own resistances and assertions. Busi most noticeably resists the sort of domestications that earlier American expatriates had performed. He foregrounds, for example, the colonial relations that enable his own sexual pleasure: "the white man . . . while he fills the bellies of three generations of mixed blood, lets himself be stuffed, comfortably served and revered. Colonial shudders!" (38). More forcefully, he reports the comment of an "educated Moroccan stallion," who tells him,

> The tourists don't grant us a glance that is not *sentimental*—that is to say erotic. . . . The public organizations and the Jewish shop-and hotel-owners tell them we are all thieves—thieves and rapists and murderers, and the tourists give us a wide berth or come up to us only sufficiently to take our measurements. (60)

For Busi, the sexual pleasure he takes (and gives) amounts to "maximum privilege" (217). A setting free from quotidian life, it does not need a travel narrative to justify it; and it is on this basis that Busi offers his own fiction as "non-heterosexual."

Busi's sharpest episode of travel/sex in Morocco, however, is far from the ironic hedonism that generally informs his work. The episode recalls the Bowles-Mrabet account of the doubly violated Spanish boys in *Look and Move On;* in it, Busi dramatizes the link between colonialism and the Moroccan sexual economy, in which the sexual assault is staged as the colonized's vindictive rage. A schoolteacher acquaintance of Busi's, Said, has taken him to a Berber village in the High Atlas. Said has invited two other boys along to the village where he teaches. The three of them subject Busi, virtually imprisoned in the house, to repeated rape. The least comprehensible, a thickset black, is the last to join the invitation to rape. Providing this latter with oral satisfaction, Busi realizes: "I have to make him come publicly if I want to have any further hope of saving myself, I must make him the equal of the other two" (84). In keeping with his candid—even brutal—unveiling of the colonial dynamic, Busi attaches his own aim of escape to the necessity of "robbing [the black's] hatred of me of its drama" (84).

Throughout his notably laconic accounts of sodomitical encounters in Morocco, Busi insists that such intercultural engagements have nothing essential about them. They are made possible by material features of cultural exchange and specific life-practices; generalizations along the lines of "Morocco is a bisexual culture" cannot universalize homosexual experience from the point of view of either individual desire or global geography and history. Nevertheless, the impulse to universalize—to erase specificities of time, place, and culture—remains strong. The assimilative tendencies of North African travel narratives like Bowles's and Busi's have recently been matched by ethnographic texts locating homosexual societies in the South Pacific, particularly (Papua) New Guinea. Gilbert Herdt (*Ritualized Homosexuality in Melanesia*, 1984) has pioneered this field, writing of tribal social custom and ritual in adoption practices; of wife exchange and the production of male potency through semen transmission. Tobias Schneebaum, following Herdt, has produced an inventory of these practices in his (pseudo)ethnographic travelogue *Where the Spirits Dwell* (1988):

> The people of the South Casuarina Coast did not have the great raids and headhunting ceremonies of the north and northwest. They had no known rites of passage that demanded heads for initiation, though this was true further south among the Marind Anim, where masculinity was stimulated in youngsters by the absorption of semen through sodomy with older males. The Asmat also believe that semen has magical qualities, although conception comes about from the spirit world. It is, however, only through repeated acts of sexual intercourse that the fetus will grow. Without a constant buildup of semen from a number of different males, including the husband, the child will not be born normal and healthy. In the same way . . . a boy becomes increasingly masculine and grows more quickly as he takes in more and more semen as the passive partner in sodomy. (181)

This sounds like the kind of summary that might issue from a more fully researched analysis by a professional such as Gilbert Herdt. Such summary accounts, however, are embedded in autobiography and experience, merely advertising the traveler's personal investments and anxieties. For Schneebaum, these concerns are centered on his quest for accommodating places where he might be able to live out his homosexuality unashamed. His travels, in effect, are a "going out" of America to places where he need not hide "a vital part" of himself:

> Why did I have to go out of my country, out of my family, to find the kind of assurance and companionship necessary to my inner peace? Why did no one tell me early on that I was not alone? Why was I always guilty? What can heterosexual men and women know of what it is like to be homosexual—the suffering and frustration of always hiding a vital part of one's being? (43)

With the Asmat of New Guinea, Schneebaum finds a functioning culture that answers to his own sexual needs, fostering intimate same-sex relationships and authorizing sodomitical connections. Although it seems at times as if Schneebaum is removing these practices from the Asmat as a specific cultural body (he "felt for the first time part of a universal clan" [43]), he generally takes care to link them to the imperatives of a group life.

Schneebaum finds a closer connection between his own need for homosexual exchange and Asmat cultural practice in the institution of *mbai* or "exchange friend," an aspect of the culture that a member of the tribe, Akatpitsjin, teaches him. Although he is already bound by a permanent *mbai* contract, Akatpitsjin still chooses Schneebaum as a temporary "exchange friend," consummating the relationship in the act of "balancing" (engaging in reciprocal sodomy) with his white guest. Subsequently, Schneebaum is able to formalize his practical knowledge in a seminar with Akatpitsjin and others of the tribe:

> It astounded me that everything was so open, that everyone knew what went on between Akatpitsjin and myself, that old men listened and talked and young boys, too. Akatpitsjin even called me *mbai* in front of his wife, startling me. Everyone knew what *mbai* did together and there appeared no reason not to discuss all aspects of the relationship. They obviously trusted me completely and even paired off to show me whose *mbai* was whose, allowing me to take photographs. (195)[32]

The subject's documented experience produces a moment of anthropological discovery—one that, however much it might invite the reader's skepticism, mediates the romantic white dream of incorporation with the culturally "other" body.

The amazing final sequence that acts as a coda to *Where the Spirits Dwell* projects Schneebaum's narrative into the more extreme fantasy realms of transgression, signaling the travel tale's trajectory toward and across limits: territorial, textual, cultural, and sexual. In the sequence, Schneebaum dreams that he is in the very different landscape of the artists' colony at Yaddo, running in a wintry New York landscape—lakes, ice, northern trees—on his way to join a luncheon feast. Abruptly, Akatpitsjin appears at the door and orders poached crocodile's eggs. Then Janet Frame, the eccentric New Zealand novelist, appears. All the guests, it transpires, are part of one family. Akatpitsjin, speaking "with a clipped British accent" (202), confirms that there is indeed sex between *three* people. Suddenly he shoots all the guests except for Frame and Schneebaum, and they proceed to eat the flesh of the slain. Schneebaum awakes to find himself lying with Akatpitsjin, who proceeds to inform his companion of the Asmat protocols for sex between three people (203).

Schneebaum's work locates the project of liberating the gendered subject in the space—physical, geographical, cultural—of a field-worked "other." In so doing, he draws attention to the close links between travel writing and ethnography. Both discursive categories are partly founded on liberatory premises, travel writing privileging a putatively free, mobile, transformative subject and ethnography a culturally defined, fixed, yet potentially transforming space. These categories join together in an unstable equation that the male traveler of same-sex orientation—homosexual, gay, or queer—must interrogate. Such is the project of Edmund White's exploration of pre-AIDS America in the period of gay liberation, *States of Desire: Travels in Gay America* (1980). The title itself references both sides of the equation, since the "state" corresponds both to the desiring, traveling subject and to the geopolitical terrain through which he travels. White is a reluctant traveler, anything but nomadically inclined, and his book vacillates between the informative mode of the guidebook and the personal, anecdotal style of the travelogue.[33] "Though traveling sounds glamorous," White observes, "I found it arduous and alienating. Listening to other people and seldom talking is frustrating for someone as opinionated as I am. Eating alone and sleeping in rented rooms can be depressing" (334). White, however alienated he may feel, focuses on the relation between gay desiring subjects and the various "states" in which they live, searching out how gay life organizes itself socially in a representative scattering of urban environments in the United States. He recognizes that gays construct individual and group identities, along with ways of acting, within a series of specific and historicized social settings. He thus converses with closeted gays, as well as participating in social encounters with gays who, though "out," form specialized, private communities. White's work highlights problems for the wider category of travel writing by complicating the relationship between an "out" world and a "closet." Isherwood's Berlin, Busi's Morocco, and Schneebaum's New Guinea all represent more or less liberated terrains for their respective visitors; but they are liberated precisely because, from a historicized global perspective, they are specialized areas—the "free zone" emerges in effect as merely another kind of closet.

White's work seems to position him within the gay liberationist discourse of post-Stonewall America, but he also prefigures an emergent queer discourse in his attraction toward a constructionist, performative model of self-definition. At one point he declares himself to be "an afficionado of the provisional" (154), acknowledging how gays invent and stage themselves differently in differing settings:

> Like Nietzsche . . . we could speak of the "gay science," that obligatory existentialism forced on people who must invent themselves. . . .
> Once one discovers that one is gay, one must choose everything, from how to walk, dress and talk to where to live, with whom and on what terms. (16)

Contesting Richard Sennett's assertion that modern man is "an actor without a stage," White finds New York to be a preeminent space for performing the self: on the streets of New York he is out "to *farmi vivo,* as the Italians say, to 'make myself alive' in a responsive and observing public" (286). Of course, New York is a special place. White realizes that he could not claim the same liberties in many other world cities; that the performance of sex and sexuality is always part of a larger cultural and site-specific production.[34]

White deploys both gay liberationist and queer performative models in his charting of gay America; he thus demonstrates the impossibility of producing any consistent account of how the traveler brings his (homo)sexuality to bear on his travels, or of providing any fixed model for the discourse of gay/queer travel. While gay/queer travelers locate spaces that promise to provide (or do provide) performative freedom, these selfsame spaces are beholden to specific codes that constrain performance. Every travelogue ultimately discloses a different relation between self and (cultural) space in which the latter is eroticized—and sexualized—through nuances of perception. One of the more distinctive travelogues in these terms is that of another White, Patrick, whose account of his travels in the Greek islands forms a section of his autobiography *Flaws in the Glass* (1981).

Although (Patrick) White pays statutory tribute to that darling of travel writers, Patrick Leigh Fermor,[35] his record of his travels in Greece and the Greek Islands could hardly be further from Leigh Fermor's, or Lawrence Durrell's. White sets out to show "how [the Greek islands] add to this self-portrait I have undertaken, and [to] the most important relationship of my life" (171). White is referring here to his companionship with Manoly Lascaris, whom he had first met in Alexandria during the Second World War, who later accompanied him back to Australia and a lifelong relationship, and with whom he traversed Greece and its offshore islands on several occasions. White, like Busi, is an acerbic traveler: tourists irritate; food disgusts; celebrated sights disappoint, disillusion even. Nothing could be further from the traveler's characteristic blend of scenery and society with romance than White's cantankerous chronicling of his journeys through Greece with Manoly. White's frankness and candid vulgarity do manage to produce the occasional illuminated moment of travel: "Any Grecophile will understand when I say that the unsinkable condom and the smell of shit which precede the moment of illumination [a first glimpse of Olympus] make it more rewarding when it happens" (157).

White peppers his narrative with vivid characterizations that suggest a camp, operatic perception: "Orthodox monks scream like enraged queens" (158), and "exquisite acolytes tittuped on some errand for an imperious superior" (160). Yet he stays away from familiar modes of sexual suggestiveness: no arch innuendos, no gentle homoeroticism, no bravura sexual exploits. White enlists the Greek islands, rather, as a space in and through which he can explore his relationship with Manoly. If they are on a pilgrimage, White suggests, it is one split between "my lusting spirit and Manoly's orthodox devotion" (177). White persistently pursues "the idea of" Greece (175), moving from deflation to the edge of disillusionment. The more patient Manoly accuses White of hating Greece, spurring him to reexamine his relationship with his lover:

> [Each of a disparate group of islands] plays a particular role in my
> relationship with Greece and Manoly. Over and over . . . when
> Manoly tells me I hate Greece, I cannot explain my love. . . . I cannot
> prove that what I believe in most deeply, the novels for which my
> conscious self can't take full responsibility, our discomforting but
> exhilarating travels through Greece, our life together, its eruptions
> and rewards, my own clumsy wrestling with what I see as a religious
> faith—that all of this is what keeps me going. (187–88)

"Travels through Greece" turn out to be travels with, and through,
Manoly; and these are, tautologically, "what keeps [the traveler]
going."

Such a disarmingly casual, yet startling, elaboration of the trian-
gulation between self, companion, and place twists the commonplace
"bad trip," queering it into an encounter between antitraveler and
overdetermined space. White, in interrogative mode, suggests as much
by wondering: "Lacerations ["Lascarations"?] alternating with visions:
is this what hooks the more perverse Grecophile?" (162).

Patrick White's journeys suggest the scope for associating gay
travel with memory and desire rather than free spaces, with personal
and phenomenal differences rather than with quests for gay-liberated
territories. Edmund White, meanwhile, writing at the end of the "gay
liberation" era, concedes that for women and gays (as for other minori-
ties) "the goal has always been a change in our society that would bring
equality of opportunity and restored dignity and autonomy to all"
(62). He makes clear, though, that there is a significant impediment to
this goal's achievement: "a steadfast denial of the real sources of power
in our society, i.e., money. Rich and middle-class gays are not likely to
identify with the poor; they retain a loyalty to members of their own
class, whether straight or gay" (62).[36] To theorize the writing of homo-
sexual/gay/queer travelers is to confront, once more, the problem of
the privilege of the traveler—the one whose "liberation" is likely to
take the form of exploitative license, or the one, pulled this way and
that, whose "tourist map [is continually] traversed by new trails"
(Hollinghurst 99). In both cases, what must clearly be resisted is the all-
too-easy impulse to celebrate travel either as *necessarily* perceptive or
as *essentially* liberating. The next chapter takes this argument in a
slightly different direction, looking at the supposedly liberatory discourse of postmodernism, and at the ground it opens up for
textual/generic play. In negotiating the tensions between playfulness

and responsibility, the chapter also suggests that travel writing's aesthetic features may be at odds with its ethical credos; and that its capacity to reflect on itself risks being accused of self-indulgence in a postmodern era characterized by destructive overconsumption, and by the split between material exhaustion and textual excess.

Chapter four

Postmodern Itineraries

VIRTUAL PLACES: TRAVEL AND
THE HYPERREAL

The celebratory rhetoric of travel—its perceived capacity to open up new epistemological, as well as geographical, horizons—has been associated in recent years with the "disruptive" discourses of postmodernism. At first blush, it certainly seems there *ought* to be an affinity between travel writing and postmodernism; for among its many, not infrequently contradictory features, postmodern theory foregrounds the instability of the human subject, shifting ontologies of space and place,[1] and the undermining of linear history, which characteristically assumes a fractured or palimpsestic structure. In short, the traditional narrative ground that modernist texts were already testing has collapsed—or such is the claim—into perspectivism and radical contingency. One might expect such relativizing features not just to occur in, but to be necessary to, travel narratives. Travelers tend to present themselves, after all, as unusually flexible people, who are more open than most to alienating experience, and who seek out places that defy quotidian expectation and preformed assessment. The traditional mistrust of travel narratives—as if truth-seeking readers had already anticipated and prefigured their unstable narrative ground—shows up in the popular disarming phrase "travelers' *tales*": tales that invite a healthy skepticism.

All the same, postmodernist devices have not so consistently infiltrated the travel book as they have the contemporary novel. Perhaps travel writing, as genre, has remained relatively immune precisely because of its practitioners' need to defend—and its readers' to inoculate—themselves against contamination by travelers' lies. At some point, it might be argued, both parties need to appeal to the "authenticity standard"—to envision the possibility of "new" and "genuine" experience, even if that novelty and that genuineness are simultaneously acknowledged as doomed. In fact, the bulk of works that currently appear on bookshelves as "travel books" adhere to one modernist paradigm or another. Equally, travelers continue by and large to assume stable experiential identities, and to present their destinations, guaranteed by geography and history, as ontologically secure. Paradoxically, it often seems that the potentially transgressive, destabilizing character of travel seeks a compensatory stability in both its subject and its destination. The typical travel book (insofar as it can ever be agreed upon that such a creature exists) continues to cleave to modern realist conventions.

When postmodernism impinges on travel writing, then, it usually does so obliquely, under the sign of "meta": metatravel, metahistory, metageography, metafiction. Postmodernist travel books are almost invariably metanarratives, reflecting on their own status as texts—as *theoretical* texts—on travel. This section examines some recent and notable instances of such metanarratives, from suggestive revisionings of space, site, and destination in Calvino, through the semiotics and hyperrealism of Barthes, Eco, and Baudrillard (linked, in Iyer, with a postcolonial perspective), to various, more or less self-reflexive constructions of the traveling subject in Chatwin, Dessaix, and Theroux. As a body, this writing insistently attends to that instability, in both terrain and subject, which tends to be elided in more traditional types of travel narrative. It also insists, through its employment of pervasive citation and intertextual inflection, on the inseparability of travel and writing—as if all travel, to bend Pater's aphorism, aspired to the condition of literature.

While such "literature" can recapitulate a (travel) site, it can never capture it. Italo Calvino's *Invisible Cities* (1974), a fantasy on Marco Polo's conversations with Kubla Khan, insists accordingly on the irreducibility of cities; as Polo warns the Khan, "the city must never be confused with the words that describe it" (61). In the case of Aglaura, one of the many cities canvassed,

> nothing said of [the city] is true, and yet these accounts create a solid and compact image of a city, whereas the haphazard opinions which might be inferred from living there have less substance. This is the result: the city that they speak of has much of what is needed to exist, whereas the city that exists on its site, exists less. (67)

Polo thus points to the ambivalent, shifting valences of words and things that are so germane to travel writing: the lived-in city irreducibly *is,* but its experiential discourses cannot describe it; the city, as described from the outside, is *not* ("nothing . . . is true"), and yet it represents "much of what is needed to exist." Polo's descriptions, however precise, ultimately conduct their interlocutor toward invisibility and immateriality.

Calvino's cities do exist in fact, but as formal, abstract entities. They are explicitly signal: synecdochic of every organized space, they are constellations of signs that reduplicate, rearrange, and even project their own mirror and shadow systems. Each stop on Polo's itinerary is a Saussurean demonstration; since a "city [is] made only of differences" (34), its description seems at once systematic and arbitrary, and "the passage from one [city] to another involved not a journey but a change of elements" (43). Calvino's reader might well recall here the effect of those travel accounts that lead from one locale to another, differentiating successive destinations through comparison and contrast, and often inducing a kind of exhaustion—exasperation, even—not unlike that brought on by the Khan's responses to Polo. The unknowable individual cities, in relation to "the city" as a systemic entity, are like Saussure's parole in relation to langue: "each man bears in his mind a city made up only of differences, a city without figures and without form, and the individual cities fill it up" (34). And just as Saussure's *langue* postulates a point from which the idiosyncrasies of *parole* take on meaning, so it is with Polo's city:

> All of Eudoxia's confusion, the mules' braying, the lampblack stains, the fish smell is what is evident in the incomplete perspective you grasp; but the carpet proves that there is a point from which the city shows its true proportions, the geometrical scheme implicit in its every, tiniest detail. (96)

Is there a space for the individual traveler within the overarching system? Calvino suggests, through the evocative spareness of Polo's speech, the indeterminate and evanescent movement of subjectivity: "It is more difficult to fix on the map the routes of the swallows, who cut the air over the roofs, dropping long invisible parabolas with their still wings" (89). No wonder the Khan upbraids him: "Confess what you are smuggling: moods, states of grace, elegies!" (98). "Cities, like dreams," we are told, "are made of desires and fears, even if the thread of their discourse is secret, their rules are absurd, their perspectives deceitful, and everything conceals something else" (44). Calvino's cities, then, bring two characteristic postmodernist vectors into alignment: that of the abstract, apparently static system (the arrangement); and that of—seemingly wavering—individual desire. These two vectors begin to conjoin, or more accurately to merge, in the Khan's garden, where the distinction between inner and outer worlds is momentarily elided:

> At the moment when I concentrate and reflect, I find myself again, always, in this garden, at this hour of the evening, in your august presence, though I continue, without a moment's pause, moving up a river green with crocodiles or counting the barrels of salted fish being lowered into the hold. (103)

Within the broader context of Calvino's poetics of travel, the Khan's frustrated attempt to link Polo's images with his own desires suggests the possibility of a personal, rather than collective, relation between desire and image. Interestingly, the failure of the two to fuse is a matter of things, not words: "Falsehood is never in words; it is in things" (62).

Calvino's preoccupation with images (Polo cites at one point the "special dignity of images" [53]) is shared by the semiotician Roland Barthes and his successors, Umberto Eco and Jean Baudrillard. These latter also recognize the "immanence of desire in the image" (Baudrillard 56) but explore that immanence in terms of public and cultural, rather than individual, investment. In Barthes's work (as, later, in Eco's and Baudrillard's) the images that arrest the traveler are certainly significant, but they do not signify outside of the frames of ideology and myth. As in the images surrounding the "new Citroen," they lay claim to a mythical world that exists above and beyond nature, a world in which "one can . . . see at once a perfection and an absence of origin, a closure and a brilliance, a transformation of life into matter . . . and in a word a *silence* which belongs to the realm of fairy-tales" (*Mythologies* 88). Later, in the work of Eco and Baudrillard, we enter the terrain of the simulacrum and hyperreality: a terrain in which image makers have discovered the magical art of subsuming nature, and where "[a]bsolute unreality is offered as real presence . . . [with the] sign aim[ing] to be the thing, to abolish the distinction of the reference, the mechanism of replacement" (Eco 7). In Eco's and Baudrillard's work, the cultural critic is a traveler, exploring the complex relations between history, nature, and culture at what has become the paradigmatic site of collision (and collusion) between the Real and the Mythical—America.

Eco's America, prefiguring Baudrillard's, is a terrain of "furious hyperreality" (7). America, for the deeply humanist Eco, is a country without a sense of history—indeed, without a sense of experience. Haunted by a *horror vacui* (8), the country seeks instances of plenitude in which it might materialize, realize, iconize *everything,* making experience itself palpable and consumable. This emptiness, the implicit result of a failure to harmonize history, culture, and nature, must be filled equally with icons of the past, present, and future—William Randolph Hearst's "castle," the White House, Cape Kennedy rockets. In Eco's America, "knowledge can only be iconic, and iconism can only be absolute" (53). Even collective fantasy demands to be made real and palpable. Disneyland, the product of an "obsessive determination not to leave a single space that doesn't suggest something" (23), is *the* American dream-factory: a factory that totalizes "fakery," creating monuments of instant nostalgia.

If Eco recognizes in America the universal shape of things to come—the preeminent signs of global postmodernity—he stops short of saying so; rather, in juxtaposing a hyperreal "America" with a Europe that honors the irrecoverable *pastness* of the past, and that retains the capacity to discriminate between reality and imitation, he situates his cultural critique within a set of privileged, traditionally Eurocentric parameters. Eco's presentation of an America that is ubiquitously sign, fake, and facsimile best serves, perhaps, as a polished gloss on a rash of more or less undistinguished travel books purveying adventures in America as infernal Disneyworld "descents."[2] Baudrillard's *America* (1988), in contrast, taking Eco's commentary as read, proceeds to engage more strenuously with American geography, society, and culture. Baudrillard's American journey induces a metaphorical frenzy, as the traveler-writer determinedly scans the landscape in search of some metaphysical essence. No matter that the profusion of metaphors entails the collapse of metaphor, or that the essence the writer seeks turns out to be the limit of evacuation; to the extent to which Baudrillard insists, like Eco's Americans, on reading signs to exhaustion, he assimilates terrain and culture to a symbolized state of desire.

Baudrillard's desired "other" recalls Calvino's famous travel apothegm: "Elsewhere is a negative mirror. The traveler recognizes the little that is his, discovering the much he has not had and will never have" (29). America is the negative mirror here, inducing a "[n]ostalgia born of the Texan hills and the sierras of New Mexico" (Baudrillard 1). Draining land- and cityscapes into abstractions of horizontality, verticality, and emptiness, Baudrillard celebrates his fantastic "America" as a "collapse of metaphor" (27), even as he so patently metaphorizes beyond the horizon of Barthes's earlier "empire of signs" (see chap. 2), which had insisted that "Japan" was a semiotics, without reference to any "real" place. Baudrillard's "non-referential desert" (10), located at the heart of America, becomes "an ecstatic critique of culture, and ecstatic form of disappearance" (9). This America is both pre- and postcultural, involving as it does the *virtual* abolition of Europe's discriminations, ironies, and subtleties. Its various sites call the visitor to an experience beyond that of the tourist or holiday traveler, to "pure" object-free itineraries into the gloriously "banal" zones of desert and metropolis, which are "not at any stage regarded as places of pleasure or culture, but [are] seen televisually as scenery, as scenarios" (9). Baudrillard's "extraterritorial" virtual scenarios, appealing to the fantasy screens of "sophisticated, nuclear, orbital, computer technology" (4), make Barthes's nonreferential signs seem curiously old-fashioned.

Baudrillard's text cannot help but recall Eco's earlier essay on hyperrealist America; but Baudrillard, unlike Eco, salutes the American processes of the simulacrum with all the heady enthusiasm of someone greeting a marvelous future:

> [Since the Americans] were not the first to be in on history, they will be the first to immortalize everything by reconstitution (by putting things in museums, they can match in an instant the fossilization process nature took millions of years to complete). But the conception the Americans have of the museum is much wider than our own. To them, everything is worthy of protection, embalming, restoration. Everything can have a second birth, the eternal birth of the simulacrum. (41)

And as for the past, so for the future: whereas, for Europeans, fiction is a means "to anticipate reality by imagining it," for Americans it "anticipates imagination by giving it a form of reality" (95). And this anticipatory "form of reality" is none other than the simulacrum.

Baudrillard endorses the transformation of dense materiality into the smooth surfaces of the simulacrum; and yet, at the same time, he *de*materializes the phenomena of travel into a series of abstractions, so that the desert "assumes the status of a primal scene" (28); Los Angeles becomes "merely an inhabited fragment of the desert" (53); speed is "simply the rite that initiates us into emptiness" (7); and change embodies "the aesthetic form of a mutation" (23). For the European traveler, the experience of travel through America becomes a glimpse in Calvino's "negative mirror":

> This is one of the advantages, one of the pleasures of travel. To see and feel America, you have to have had for at least one moment in some downtown jungle, in the Painted Desert, or on some bend in a freeway, the feeling that Europe has disappeared. (104–5)

Nonetheless, it is Europe (though less obviously than in Eco's essay) that continues to haunt the nexus of political, historical, cultural, and geographical affairs to which Baudrillard attaches the label "America." And what is more, the very commentator who had seemed to abolish metaphor and myth from the travel book has ended up smuggling it in—and not so surreptitiously—by the back door.

In Baudrillard's text, the experience of travel in America is converted into surface, or—to be willfully, if appropriately, paradoxical—into the essence of surface. Recalling "the immensity of the Texan hills and the sierras of New Mexico," Baudrillard insists that photographs cannot, will not, recreate the experience:

> We'd need the whole film of the trip in real time, including the unbearable heat and the music. We'd have to replay it all from end to end at home in a darkened room, rediscover the magic of the freeways and the distance and the ice-cold alcohol in the desert and the speed and live it all again on video at home in real time, not simply for the pleasure of remembering but because the fascination of senseless repetition is already present in the abstraction of the journey. (1)

"Real time" is, of course, reel time or, perhaps better, an approximation of it, since Baudrillard's virtual travel depends on the "futurist" technologies of the shallow surface: the video screen and the computer monitor. The drained landscapes of America find their mirror in the reduplicative surfaces of simulation technology. Virtual travel, as experienced on the video screen, promises an "interactive" experience that makes simulation more real than actuality. As Baudrillard implies, it is the very abstractness of the surface that enables such satisfying travel. In the viewer's "darkened room," the combination of visual and aural effects melds into a total but absolutely abstracted—and thus perhaps essential—experience, at the same time as the "futurist" technologies of fast-forwarding and hypertextuality evoke an instant nostalgia.

As with other aspects of a commodified contemporary metropolitan lifestyle—food and sex being two obvious commodities—virtual technologies hold out the promise of participatory, interactive experience. But such experience amounts, in Eco's terms, to another form of "fakery"; the interaction it produces is with a variety of surfaces—surfaces that overlay the subject in a uniform, abstract blanketing. This "travel of the future" precludes travel from the outset; ubiquitous instantaneity converts labored movement into abstract patterns of "senseless repetition."

Virtual travel is the latest link in a chain that runs from the travel book through the travel guide, film, and video. It is tempting, again, to invoke nostalgia: lament for the progressive evacuation of "real" experience from travel. But "travel," in whichever form it is mediated, is always textual and supplementary; it responds to personal and collective mandates that are necessarily overdetermined. Complex tracts, these mandates seek to superimpose one grid or another on an experience (of travel, of the world, etc.) that remains irreducible.

This study has already discussed Pico Iyer's "grid," in *Video Night in Kathmandu* (1988), as a postcolonial response to Asia's entry into a "global culture" (see chap. 1). But *Video Night* is, equally, an off-the-shelf postmodernist response: in its stretched comparisons, its startling parallels, and its self-consciously ingenious textual effects. Iyer sprinkles his essays with references to leading theoretical figures (Barthes, McLuhan, etc.), along with numerous pop-culture allusions, designed to assure his readers that he is moving around in the age of global culture with easy authority. Iyer's "video night" is hyperrealism at low temperature. We need to ask what specific commentary—about mobility, cultural representation, and myth—Iyer's supple tour provides.

Iyer's book offers something of a thesis about late-twentieth-century capitalism—a phase in which the older forms of imperial conquest have given way to a "new invasion" by tourists, the latter-day "terrorists of cultural expansionism" (13). But this thesis is really no more than an enabling framework: a space within which Iyer can operate relays of incongruities. This Asia, ironically *re*colonized in free-floating postmodernist fashion, is a land of surfaces that Iyer composes according to the "laws" of pastiche, collage, the crazy quilt. Kathmandu strikes Iyer, for example, as "exactly the kind of cross-cultural crossroads" he had hoped to find (94); yet although this situation invites definition and analysis, it is less compelling to Iyer than are its surface incongruities. These Iyer describes in a flippant tone of comic horror, as time and again he finds himself falling "like Alice through the looking glass" into "upside down worlds" (78). At one moment, he discovers that he has "traveled 8,000 miles only to end up . . . in a facsimile of the East village" (103); at another, Western visitors to Bali—"beefy men with sunglasses propped up in their hair" and "freshly turned blondes in halter tops and miniskirts"—have transformed Kuta Beach into "the poor man's Club Med" (47); at still another, Balinese sales assistants, "now sport[ing] tight jeans and sun-glasses . . . had scarlet headbands above their mascaraed eyes . . . [and] wore T-shirts that said 'proudly Australian' across their chests" (68).

Video Night is, to be sure, an attractive and superior travel book. Well informed (to the point of sometimes appearing too knowing, too up-to-the-minute) and stylishly written, it nevertheless begs several questions that readers might well want to ask about the "not-so-far East" as a conjunction of postcolonialism with postmodernism. The most obvious question here is: how do these two "posts" relate to one another? Iyer's response typically vacillates between wonderment and controlled nostalgia: he marvels, for example, at the Japanese appropriation of baseball but insists, at the same time, that Japan has not succeeded in making the sport fully its own, indicating a wistful preference for exhibitions of more "distinctive" Japanese social codes. A rather less obvious question (if the first one proves ultimately unanswerable) is: what kind of analysis might the travel book offer that would exempt author and reader from the charge of bad faith? Iyer seems at his most vulnerable when he targets "overlanders"—those ubiquitous hordes of global backpackers toting their Lonely Planet guidebooks—as a tribe of "counter-cultural imperialists that wanders the planet in search of cut-rate paradises" (78). In the Asian "outback," travelers like these have to "turn themselves into locals" to survive, eating cheaply and locally, washing clothes in streams, and adopting the locals' dress styles. And yet, simultaneously, these travelers "were forcing [places like] Lhasa to turn [themselves] into a rough version of the homes they had quit" (81). Iyer, it bears remembering, undertook his trip under the sponsorship of *Time:* a global magazine par excellence. Long-haul backpackers; short-term visitors on package tours; peripatetic English-language teachers; international business travelers; and, not least, Iyer and his readers: all of these groups are interested, not to mention implicated, in both the preservation of the

East as a site of cultural difference and its propulsion into a world theme-park, a global visitor-friendly arena. And ironically, it is this latter development that keeps the adrenaline of nostalgia flowing; Iyer, after all, is very much part of the process that produces regret that "the real Balinese smiles seemed to be fading" (68).

Iyer invokes techniques of identification and reduction that are related to those of, say, Baudrillard (likening exotic Kuta to "Duval Street in Key West on a Saturday night" [47]), but he stops just short of collapsing layered actuality into virtual representation by taking care to discriminate between surfaces and depths: "The whirling surfaces [of Kathmandu] existed, no doubt, but they seemed to be no more than surfaces" (105). His reproach seems less directed toward the Orient's "provision of all the latest in post-post-Modernist chic" to America than toward its conspicuous (and conspicuously late) consumption of its own electronic products (105).

On another level, Iyer's descriptions lead back to Calvino and his revisitation of Marco Polo's travels. So many of Calvino's cities split, engendering reflective or reversed doubles, that the city becomes a *mise en abyme,* that favorite among contemporary textual effects of destabilization. "[A]s each of the three tourist havens had grown more bloated," Iyer comments about Bali, "each of them had spawned a kind of shadow self, an annex-town that had materialized by its side to cater to the overflow" (53). Iyer's book, in fact, references postmodern writing practice much less in its descriptions of crazy-quilt surfaces than in those moments of abstract formulation when it reads like a parody of Calvino:

> Everything, in fact, approximated to its Platonic image: every Zen garden was a picture-perfect image of what a Zen garden should be; the Emperor disappeared within the idealized role of an Emperor; and every geisha corresponded exactly to the proto-typical model of a geisha (a Tokyo rose was a Tokyo rose was a Tokyo rose). (386)

Encountering this kind of distanced commentary, readers might well be drawn to reflect on those passages of actual travel where the unfamiliar village, town, or city awakens not so much a sense of material estrangement as one of metaphysical dis-ease.

For all its vivid celebration of paradox and hybridity in the encounter of East and West, *Video Night* communicates a strong sense of what Iain Chambers has called the "Eurocentric domestication of space" (31). Iyer's destinations feature as divisible "chapters" of travel and experience, as well as neatly separated sections in his book. Each is discursively contained and discriminated, either by a leading idea, a set of images, or an intertextual frame; there are few signs here that the traveler-writer has found himself—and his sense of self—unsettled by incongruities of place, culture, or situation. So far this section has discussed some of the ways in which travel writing configures space— cities, deserts, countries—while examining briefly a few more or less postmodernist effects of spatial representation. But postmodernist inflection is also relevant to the traveling and writing subject. For if travelers are dependent on a sense of stable identity from which to experience and interpret difference, they also tend to claim another, rather special identity as travelers: one that is experientially open and interpretively flexible, generous. Chambers has described postmodern, metropolitan travel as experience of

> the dislocation of the intellectual subject and his—the gender is deliberate—mastery of the word/world. The illusions of identity organised around the privileged voice and stable subjectivity of the "external" observer are swept up and broken down into a movement that no longer permits the obvious institution of self-identity between thought and reality. In this disjunctive moment, the object of the intellectual gaze—the cultures and habits of the "natives" of local, national and global "territories"—can no longer be confined to an obvious chart or map, and there freeze-dried as a fixed or essential component of knowledge. (95)

The traveler who can recognize and confront such a "disjunctive moment," while leaving the objects of his/her gaze "unconfined," may well be something of an ideal. It is at this point, where the need to construct a "good" traveler as against the "bad" tourist figure again comes to the forefront, that the *nomad* has proven to be a useful rhetorical device.

Bruce Chatwin, something of a cult figure in the travel-writing industry, has been instrumental in making the nomad available as an ideal version of the modern traveler. Chatwin's theories on nomadism are articulated most conspicuously in his celebrated *The Songlines* (1987), but they can also be found in some of his shorter essays in the posthumously published collections *What Am I Doing Here* (1990) and *Anatomy of Restlessness* (1996). Chatwin at one stage planned a book on nomadism, but the outline that he wrote for it (excerpted in *Anatomy*) is rather puzzling. Puzzling, because nomadism emerges both as a universalized yearning and as a number of specific ways of life that are constrained by time and place. "Evolution intended us to be travellers," claims Chatwin: "Our mad obsession with technological progress is a response to barriers in the way of geographical progress" (*Anatomy* 102). Whatever evolution may have intended, nomads first denote herdsmen, then later huntsmen, who "shift for economic reasons" (76). But nomads, according to Chatwin, are "intransigen[t] in face of settlement"; they are drawn to wander even when it makes economic sense to stay put, and as a result a "mutual antagonism" has gradually evolved between "citizen and nomad" (76). At a much looser remove, "the nomad" becomes a generalized figure of restlessness and escapism, or a semi-ironic metaphor for the itinerant storyteller—"a superfluous person such as myself"—for whom nomadic wandering is also an analogue for the "stringing together" of travelers' tales (14). Chatwin poses a link, then, between the modern nomadic romance and travel writing, in the "stringing together" of glittering kernels of travel experience into artful wholes. These assemblages are strategic; for Chatwin-as-nomad is a figure that is constructed retrospectively, providing an alibi for his particular travel-writing enterprise.

On the face of it, Chatwin's writing does not look particularly postmodern. His very formed and Eurocentric sense of style—of the sparkling object in the antique showroom or from some cabinet of curiosities—places him rather firmly within a tradition of English collection and connoisseurship.[3] He is aware of the early stirrings of postmodernist theory in the work of Marshall McLuhan, whom he sees as arguing that "literacy, the linch-pin of Civilisation is OUT; that electronic technology is by-passing the 'rational processes of learning' and that jobs and specialists are things of the past" (*Anatomy* 84). He has reservations, though, about McLuhan's endorsement of a "new Internationalism," in which "[m]uch of the world's population is on the move as never before" (84). Curiously, he associates McLuhan's "global village" with parochialism and separatism; certainly, he recognizes the dangers in espousing nomadism as a universal program—one of these being that "the nomad" is robbed of special motivation, and of effectiveness as a serviceable alibi for the travel writer.

Chatwin's stylistic and descriptive gifts are certainly very strong; and yet there is something in excess of these gifts that has produced the "special" appeal of Chatwin—and that something, as Veronica Horwell has suggested, has much to do with the allure of the nomad-individualist: "This is Chatwin the blond flirt. . . . tossing his boots by their laces over his shoulder and looking back, using travel as a come-on.

Do you want me? Or do you want to be me?" (28). This airy sketch of the unfettered, venturesome, and freewheeling individual suggests why there is always likely to be a gap between "cultural" theories of the nomad and envisionings of nomadism as a pretext for personal—romantic—flight.[4] In Chatwin's work, nomadism is different again from either of these theories; it is tantamount to a highly idiosyncratic personal mythology, relying on a potpourri of materials that Chatwin, as determined bricoleur, can seize upon and utilize at will.

It is in *The Songlines* that Chatwin deploys his talents as a bricoleur most ambitiously; for it is there that his gifts as a travel writer, combined with those of the amateur ethnologist and cultural historian, find their ideal subject in the Aborigines of Australia, an extant instance of nomadism. Iain Chambers, who in passing cites "[t]he Nietzschean vision of the world" suggested "in Bruce Chatwin's marvellous book *The Songlines*" (53), conflates nomads with contemporary "migrants." "Migrancy," in Chambers's theory, becomes a defining characteristic of social life in a "new," increasingly globalized, postmodern culture:

> It is the dispersal attendant on migrancy that disrupts and interrogates the overarching themes of modernity: the nation and its literature, language and sense of identity; the metropolis, the sense of centre, the sense of psychic and cultural homogeneity. In the recognition of the other, of radical alterity, lies the acknowledgment that we [Europeans] are no longer at the centre of the world. Our sense of centre and being is displaced. As historical, cultural and psychic subjects we, too, are uprooted, forced to reply to our existence in terms of movement and metamorphosis. (23–24)

For Chambers, the sense of migrancy, "of living between worlds, between a lost past and a non-integrated present, is perhaps the most fitting metaphor of this (post)modern condition" (27). The (post)modern sense of cities, in turn, is that they are "both real and invisible, to echo Italo Calvino: places whose symbolic and real alterity provide another chance, a further question, another opening" (28). Even in the metropolis, "we, too, become nomads, migrating across a system that is too vast to be our own, but in which we are fully involved—translating and transforming what we find and absorb into local instances of sense" (14).

Chambers's object is to open up the condition of migrant (post)modernity, to make it serve as an imaginary site for the exercise of greater cross-cultural understanding and freedom. Chambers acknowledges the danger in domesticating "poetic figures of travel and exile" (6), and he is well aware that contemporary migrancy is more often a matter of brute necessity than cosmopolitan privilege. It proves difficult, nonetheless, *not* to celebrate, in terms reminiscent of Chatwin's "Nietzschean vision of the world,"

> the human adventure in which the movements of peoples, and the rigours and rhythms of bodies, limbs and voice, set the patterns, the design, the nomination, of the land, our country, our home. The religious aura of this nomadism has clearly waned in the more secular networks of Western society. Perhaps it still continues to echo inside the miniaturised headphones of modern nomads as the barely remembered traces of a once sacred journey intent on celebrating its presence in a mark, voice, sign, symbol, signature, to be left along the track. (53)

In such heady evocations of Chatwin's general meditations on travel, as well as in more specific commentaries—obviously indebted to Jacques Derrida's account of the "trace"—on the songlines of the Australian Aborigines, Chambers veers away from theorizing a postmodern/postcolonial cultural condition, seeming intent instead on extrapolating a poetics—even a metaphysics—of travel.

In the process, Chambers quotes at length from the work of Paul Carter: an Australian theorist of space, place, and travel who has more cogently argued the implications of nomadism and migrancy. In *Living in a New Country* (1992), Carter speculates,

> An authentically migrant perspective would, perhaps, be based on an intuition that the opposition between here and there is itself a cultural construction, a consequence of thinking in terms of fixed entities and defining them oppositionally. It might begin by regarding movement, not as an awkward interval between fixed points of departure and arrival, but as a mode of being in the world. The question would be, then, not how to arrive, but how to move, how to identify convergent and divergent movements; and the challenge would be how to notate such events, how to give them a historical and social value. (101)

Nomadism, whether it takes the form of Chatwin's elite romance or of Chambers's uncritical theorizing, fails to give a satisfactory account of movement as a problematic. How to move, and why; how to identify movements; how to notate these movements, giving them historical and social value: all of these questions are broached in a remarkable recent travel book by another Australian writer, the *Night Letters* of Robert Dessaix (1996). *Night Letters* is an exercise in postmodernist metanarrative: the travel book posing as fiction, or fiction posing as the travel book. The anonymous first-person traveler-narrator of *Night Letters,* like several other "end of travel" writers already encountered in this study, regrets that "travel in the old sense [is] now out of the question—travelling to whet your appetite, to pique your hunger, not to satisfy it" (214). Modern travel, for Dessaix's narrator, is "[f]ull of movement but nothing actually *happens.* I'm beginning to hanker for travel of a different kind" (191). And it is travel "of a different kind" that Dessaix in fact produces throughout the thoughtful pages of his fiction/travel book.

The major postmodernist strategy on hand in the *Night Letters* is the destabilization of the work's textual/generic status. Subtitled "A Journey through Switzerland and Italy," the work is "by" Robert Dessaix; but it is "[e]dited by Igor Miazmov," who records in a prefatory note that "these letters (if that is indeed what the documents are) were written in a first-floor room in the Hotel Arcadia in Venice to a correspondent [who remains anonymous] in Melbourne." Although the "letters" were all originally composed in Venice, Miazmov has grouped them under the headings "Locarno," "Vicenza," and "Padua," since "the reflections contained in them appear to arise quite specifically from the author's brief sojourn in each of these three cities." Miazmov has heavily edited this correspondence; and in what looks like an ironic sideswipe at certain kinds of detail-conscious travel books, he reveals his editorial practice:

> Some passages of a deeply personal nature, as well as references to matters of no conceivable interest to anybody apart from close acquaintances (details of menus and railway timetables, complaints about the weather and the rates of exchange, amorous encounters and the like) have been omitted from this edited version. (Preface, n.p.)

Augmenting the already highly mediated character of the work, Miazmov goes on to provide a series of notes and references to the letters—notes that are often critical, directly or indirectly, of their writer.

It is hard to imagine a more mediated travel account: "letters" that are not necessarily letters; anonymous dispatcher and reviewer; a break between the sites where the discourse (of travel) is generated and where the "letters" were written; and the intervention of an editor—himself suspiciously fictional—who has removed a great deal of the raw material from the travel account, and who has also "[standardized] the English in the reported speech of certain Italians and Germans the author encountered" (preface, n.p.). This is clearly a book, then, that foregrounds its own textual packaging, insisting that the reader is at several removes from immediate, "authentic" travel—the possibility of which, nonetheless, animates much of the book's discussion.

"Illness is the night-side of life": Susan Sontag's poignant metaphor, which seems suggestive of Dessaix's title, obliquely raises the issue of motivation that occupies the book's opening pages. For the letter writer is impelled on his Italian journey by the doctor's revelation that his patient is HIV-positive and likely suffering with the AIDS virus.[5] The writer's ensuing quest is unconcerned, however, about searching for a cure or evading the disease; rather, what is at stake is experiential, traveling inquiry: finding out what living in the world entails, what makes for "genuine" travel. And the risk of a premature death merely raises the stakes, making the traveler-writer's inquiries that much more vital, that much more urgent.

At one moment, watching passersby on the street, the traveler is struck that "they all thought they were *going* somewhere, they were all *facing the front*" (10). Later, in Padua, he discovers "something suspiciously religious . . . about modern tourism":

> At least when you travel alone the temptation to tick things off is weakened. . . . You're less likely to give in to the narky little voice telling you you *should* see St Anthony's tomb, you *must* look at the "remarkable loggias of the Law Courts" (why?), you *ought* at least to look in on St George's Oratory. Why should I? you can say to yourself. In the infinitude of the cosmos what difference will it make whether I do or I don't? I like sitting here, just looking at the red-tiled roofs and the tinted, buttressed hair. I'll just sit. (215)

If this attitude seems to convey a modestly hedonistic yearning for freedom, it is distinct from the freedom associated with the contemporary nomad. It is the attitude, rather, of a certain state of desire, as exemplified in the traveler's memory of a man who recounted his practice of randomly choosing someone in a crowd to follow: "for hours, on and off trains, in and out of shops, in lifts, across parks" (14). When Dessaix has this man describe the process as productive of "unbearable bliss" (14), we might well suspect that it is Barthes's idea of bliss he is invoking. Like Casanova, introduced later in the book, the pursuer "wasn't hunting for happiness . . . , which is always episodic, he was trying to experience bliss" (254). And as with Barthes, bliss turns out to be the moment of an experiential "gap," a temporary loss of self-possession. This moment might be "like waking up without a self in an unknown country" (14), or like "step[ping] off a train at an unknown station far from anywhere [when] the train clatters round a bend into silence and you're left standing there, momentarily without a self" (25).

In Barthes's work, bliss is inextricably linked with textuality: "the pleasure of the text." This points to another feature of Dessaix's book, its allusiveness and intertextuality, which are contained within a large, markedly postmodern, field of reference. At one point, somewhat archly, the traveler notes, "I didn't care a scrap about whether or not I wrote another book, got the new bathroom cupboards built, ever really understood poststructuralism, ever really travelled again" (123). Yet the letters are full of references to modish contemporary authors: Patricia Highsmith gives the traveler an audience, and among the many names he drops are those of Vikram Seth, Paul Auster, George Steiner, and Mario Vargas Llosa (27). There are numerous, exaggeratedly self-conscious meditations on walled gardens and ghettos, while one of the traveler's interlocutors "favoured Barthes' theory of the city tower: it's the city-dweller's belvedere, turning the cityscape back into nature" (117). This same figure, a German academic vacationing in Venice named Professor Eschenbaum, seems to be a ludic amalgam of Thomas Mann's Gustav von Aschenbach and Michel Foucault. Eschenbaum observes, for instance, that "Casanova and Marco Polo have come to represent entire . . . 'mentalités' (241); the traveler expects him to give an answer to one of his questions that "would involve the Other, and possibly Transgression" (132); and when Eschenbaum expatiates on Casanova as "yet another subverter of paradigms," and as an exerciser of transgressive sexuality, the traveler is vindicated, for he had guessed that "the word 'transgressive' would come up eventually" (251). The invalid's travels are playful, here as elsewhere, in a knowing, redoubled manner.

The traveler's "stages"—Locarno, Vicenza, Padua (with the letters all written from Venice, and with Vicenza as a "hell," the journey's nadir)—lightly echo the stages of Dante's *Divina Commedia,* though in incorrect order, as the editor notes. The *Divina Commedia* acts as the leading intertext for the *Night Letters,* lending the contemporary book the aura of an "open" medieval allegory. But each stage of the Dantean itinerary also incorporates allegorical narratives that align the text more closely with contemporary (post)modern textual practices. Locarno presents the tale of the peregrinations of an erotic amulet of Indian origin through Oriental, Levantine, and northern Italian hands; Vicenza offers a frightening tale of the bizarre sexual codes of Venice around the time of Marco Polo; and Padua incorporates an extended conversation between traveler and professor that contrasts Marco Polo and Casanova as journeyer-adventurers, and that provides the Australian traveler with "blissful" moments, passing from Casanova to Dante, that eventually bring him to the decision to return "home." Professor Eschenbaum—never short of a theory—believes that Polo and Casanova, who turns out to be bisexual,[6] each represents "one important kind of journeying":

> Almost opposite kinds, in fact. And journeying, after all, is so funda-
> mental to the way we humans think of ourselves and assign our lives
> a meaning. Every second book you read is about some kind of jour-
> ney, really, isn't it? And we constantly talk about paths in life—ways,
> roads, progress, stages and so on—all travel metaphors, when you
> think about it. I would say that Marco Polo and Casanova have come
> to stand for completely different ways of travelling—and therefore of
> living out your life. (241–42)

Eschenbaum's disquisition seems as if it should accord well with the afflicted Australian's views on travel, especially when he presents Casanova as one who "zigzagged through time in search of timeless moments, blissful instants when the past and the future ceased to exist for him—the only kind of spiritual perfection he could conceive of" (254). Yet Dessaix's protagonist ultimately prefers a version of Dantean spiraling: traveling as "gradually suffusing mere human knowing with timeless seeing (until you are seen—which doesn't so much demolish as put to one side the long drawn-out modern arguments about subjectivity and objectivity . . .)" (262–63). Dessaix's traveler-writer, having completed his journey, sets off for home having apparently escaped the nets of choice and chance.

In Dessaix's book, evidently, readers can find ample material for a theoretics of the self, of illness, and of travel (and, by implication, travel writing). The book's richness can be gauged by its deployment of various postmodernist textual strategies, best summed up in its thoroughgoing self-reflexiveness, what we might call its "meta-activity." It is worth noting here that travel books—particularly those that declare themselves as generic—do not generally exploit opportunities for textual play and reflexivity. Such play might perhaps threaten the different kinds of authority the traveler claims, including that of truth telling, itself dependent on the fiction of a centered self. One contemporary writer, however, has increasingly found ways of (re)vivifying the travel account through the use of a variety of metanarrative techniques. This writer is Paul Theroux, whose cross-generic *My Other Life* (1996) mixes fiction, autobiography, and travel in a virtuoso, confessedly self-indulgent performance. *My Other Life*—like all of Theroux's travel narratives—raises a series of important questions about travel writing: about its status as a "truth" narrative, its relation to the performance of the self, and its right to claim the privileges of fiction.

It is the "self" that is most obviously "indulged" in travel writing, for as Theroux remarks in one of his blunt asides, "One of the delusions of travel is that you can be a new person in a new land" (432). Elsewhere, Theroux comments with characteristic self-irony on the travel book:

> There was something so artificial about a travel book: taking notes, and then lugging your notes back and making them into a book, as though in justification of all that self-indulgence. Yet what was more self-indulgent than writing such a book? As a writer, I felt somehow that I was forever having to account for my movements, and in so doing having to make them seem as though they mattered. (276)

But which self is being indulged here; and what does it mean, anyway, to *indulge* the self? Theroux continues to enjoy the somewhat dubious reputation of belonging to Sterne's category of the "Splenetic Traveller" (see, for example, Porter 57–59). This type of traveler, in the uncompromising words of one of Theroux's reviewers, "drags his emotional baggage along with him on excursions . . . merely injecting his fluctuating biorhythms into the heart of his tales" (Buhasz n.p.). But it is more complicated than that; for while Theroux has never explicitly joined postmodernist writers in theorizing the instability of the self or its constructed character, in his travel books he has increasingly presented himself and the people he encounters as characters in fictions or as actors on the stage. "Reality for me was the past, and it was elsewhere. This—London—was like a role I had been assigned to play, and I was as yet still unaware of my lines" (*My Other Life* 145). While Theroux's novels tend to read as workmanlike contemporary fictions in the political-existential tradition of, say, Conrad, Greene, or Burgess, his travel books foreground intertextuality and performance, and all the self-referential trappings we usually associate with metafiction.[7] By following the—increasingly favored—procedure of nominating *My Other Life* a novel,[8] Theroux also claims the authority that the writer of fiction exercises over the reader. (Anthony Burgess the novelist becomes "Anthony Burgess," a fictional character, and an episode presenting a dinner party at which "Burgess" is a guest becomes a fiction [*My Other Life*].) In this way, Theroux retains the freedom to compose a (fictive) autobiography, a travel account, and a commentary on the self as at once exhibitable entity and concealed identity. Theroux does not so much "inject his fluctuating biorhythms" into his travel tales as hide *and* disclose them in a series of (mock-)fantastic episodes. Theroux's fictive/autobiographical fantasies, however, do not emerge as part of a project to dissolve the self; quite the reverse, they reaffirm the authority of the self through the act of shaping the episode, inventing its details, characterizing its agents, and masking its fictionally fantastic producer by blurring the boundary between "fact" and "fiction." Theroux invites us to speculate about who he "really" is, but not *that* he really is: "We are better off knowing that we belong here, alone in our own world. No one is waiting for us somewhere else" (436).

The dedicatee of *My Other Life* is the British writer Jonathan Raban, the symmetry of whose writing life with his own must surely not have escaped Theroux. Both writers have divided their production between novels and travel books; both are much given to intertextual referencing and casual theorizing in their travel narratives; and, more specifically, Theroux's "British" travel book, *The Kingdom by the Sea* (1984) is neatly counterpointed by Raban's "American" one, *Hunting Mister Heartbreak* (1990). To cap this symmetry, whereas Theroux lived in Britain during the middle period of his career, Raban moved to America in the middle stage of his. Raban's work, like Theroux's, shows increasing tendencies toward metafictionality. In an episode in *Hunting Mister Heartbreak,* Raban (transformed here into the genial man of letters "Rainbird") finds himself pleasantly occupied in the city of Seattle. The city is just the right size; he finds an affordable apartment with a view; he has a novelist friend there he can meet for a drink and chat in the evenings; and there are several interesting people to interview—an ideal situation, all in all, for the itinerant novelist. Rainbird soon plans a novel, fictionalizing his situation, about a gay actor who has relocated from New York and a Korean woman who has "learned the astounding temerity that had at last enabled her to walk out of a Korean marriage" (312). But to finance his relocation, Raban—travel writer—needs first to complete his travelogue. Deciding that a final chapter, to be set in Florida, is needed, he flies off to the Keys for a little exploratory coasting. A twilight trip, perhaps, for this inveterate traveler-storyteller; at around the same time, Raban and Theroux discover the zone where autobiographical travelogue merges imperceptibly into the fantasy life of fiction.

Theroux ends *My Other Life* with an epilogue, reminiscent of Chatwin the collector, in which he compiles a list of objects assembled by various means and in differing circumstances on his travels. But the similarity between Theroux and Chatwin falls short of that between Theroux and Raban; for whereas Chatwin establishes the relation between travel and collection through "nomadically" associative narrative, Theroux neither collects (generally) nor travels as a "nomad," and his travel narratives tend to treat episodes as freighted confrontations rather than as elements in free collage. As a "nomad," Chatwin seems to insinuate himself into situations rather than impose himself on them; without necessarily removing himself from the scenes he describes, he extrapolates objects and stories from them or assembles theories from their scattered fragments. Theroux, very un-"nomadically," projects himself emphatically, indulging the anxieties of travel while defending his apparently vulnerable ego. But while the two writers produce distinctive versions of travel and travel writing, both suggest different postmodernist possibilities: Chatwin through the fluid narrativity of the "nomad," and Theroux through programmed travel as a self-reflexive narrative site. These writers, although in very different ways, demonstrate that considered travel cannot endorse any single model of movement, self, or writing.

"Postmodernist *possibilities*": this section has assumed that postmodernism cannot be defined as a unified field but must be understood, on the contrary, as a contested site in cultural discourse. Postmodernism does of course impinge on and overlap with travel writing; but as this discussion has suggested, it can only do so in differing aspects at different times. Calvino's cities index the abstracting and reduplicative tendencies of travel description; but the textual effects *Invisible Cities* makes possible would freeze in its tracks—would ironically immobilize—any travel book that deployed them beyond a certain point. Similarly, hyperrealism and virtuality prove useful in foregrounding incongruity and anomaly; but in insisting on the fake and the primacy of the perfect surface, they also subvert the travel book's project to provide a sense of experiential depth. The dissolution of the unitary subject—already threatened in the process of travel—also places at risk the layered, enigmatic transactions between self and place that some travel narratives provide. To position the traveler as an ideal nomad is to snatch at a metaphor one might not be too happy defending—to be a (European) nomad today, after all, is to enjoy a privilege, an availability of options, which is obviously quite different from that of the desert herdsman/huntsman. Chambers's attempt to conflate nomad with migrant calls, equally, for skeptical attention. And while the various techniques of metafiction provide scope for injecting a sense of play into travel narrative, by definition they also detract from the travel book as a more or less "authentic" autobiographical account. Nonetheless, if travel writers turn to these techniques more often, and use them more discriminately, they may well help to induce a much-needed critical reexamination of earlier Eurocentric theories and practices of travel writing.

ECOTOPIAS: TRAVELING IN THE NEW AGE

Yet how "visionary," how innovative, can travel writing ever really be? And how can it respond, in a different way, to the dangers of extinction: to the risk of "disappearing" cultures, and to global environmental threats? In Ernest Callenbach's futuristic novel, *Ecotopia* (1975), a large chunk of the American West Coast has seceded from the United States. "Ecotopia," the state thus formed, is a self-governing, survival-oriented community, committed to the environment in an age of increasing global scarcity. Such visionary communities—a throwback to the countercultural sixties—are much in vogue as the twentieth century draws inexorably toward its close. The millenarian revivalism of the New Age—also an outgrowth of sixties' optimism—is partly a response to the overdetermined postmodern rhetoric of exhaustion.[9] Yet it also belongs to the globalized commodity culture of postmodernity, one characterized by the saturation of media images of a global future and by the conversion of endangerment, a genuine threat at many levels, into the media-friendly spectacle of a world at mortal risk.

The New Age desire for "global consciousness" and the postmodern fascination with apocalypse converge in commodified expressions of environmental angst. One such expression is ecotourism: one of the fastest growing branches of the modern tourist industry. Ecotourism, as one of its critics, Joe Bandy, has recently pointed out, stands poised between the seemingly contradictory agendas of environmental sustainability and industrial development. Ostensibly it is an attempt to democratize leisure consumption, both by encouraging local participation in its environmental projects and by raising consciousness of global issues (poverty, scarcity, the protection of the lifeworld, and so on). Yet as Bandy suggests, ecotourism is as much a variant on as an alternative to the "mainstream" tourist industry, and, as such, it remains governed by tourism's neocolonial relations of power: "Ecotourism is a transformative policy of inclusion and democratization, as well as a product of a racialized justification for modernization, in which marginalized peoples are subject to a new dependency and a new colonialism" (541). Ecotourism, or nature tourism, as it is sometimes called, is "thinkable only in an era in which nature has become an unstable sphere of our panicked lifeworlds that is ever more at risk of total annihilation, and a spectacle of a postmodern commodity culture of deferred aesthetic pleasure, leisure consumption, and virtual adventure" (541).

This suggests in turn an alternative view of ecotourism's literary by-product, *nature writing:* one that stresses the postmodern commercialization of narratives of disappearance ("vanishing worlds," "endangered species," and so forth), and the incorporation of these narratives into a Lévi-Straussian redemptive allegory that combines (collective) environmental consciousness with (personal) spiritual quest.[10] This section collapses the distinction between nature writing, which focuses mainly on the phenomenal lifeworld, and more conventional forms of travel narrative that document the traveler-writer's adventures. In the process, several connections emerge that may be attributed in part to the cultural climate of postmodernity: first, the co-optation of primitivist aesthetics into a consumer-driven fascination with scarcity—symbolized in the traveler's examination of "vanishing species" (or, in some cases, exploration of "lost worlds"); second, the link between the spectacularization of environmental crisis and the marketing of New Age myths of spiritual regeneration or awakening; and third, the use of travel/nature writing as a vehicle for the popularization of "salvage ethnography" (Clifford),[11] and for the commodification of spiritual and ecological alternatives through the motif of the traveler's quest. Such conflations bring into alignment apparently disparate kinds of travel narrative: from the adventurer Laurens Van der Post's metaphysical memoir *The Lost World of the Kalahari* (1958) to the naturalist David Quammen's evolutionist parable *The Song of the Dodo* (1996) to the self-styled guru Marlo Morgan's New Age odyssey

Mutant Message Down Under (1994). These narratives attempt, in very different ways and with varying degrees of self-consciousness, to account for "disappearing" realities or perceptions of reality, and to articulate "caring" alternatives to the destructive material culture of the West. None of these texts is identifiably postmodern in its aesthetics, and Van der Post's and Morgan's are resolutely antimodern (if still arguably modern*ist*) in their primitivist nostalgia. What links them is their reverence for more or less threatened nature. This reaction is characteristic of the modernist desire for ecological reconnection; but it has been assimilated in an age of increasing environmental awareness to a postmodern commodity culture: one in which nature is presented as an edifying spectacle for consumption, and as a repository for spiritual wisdom available at market price.

Two postwar narratives of disappearance that present similar ecological dilemmas are Van der Post's previously mentioned *The Lost World of the Kalahari* and Peter Matthiessen's *The Cloud Forest: A Chronicle of the South American Wilderness* (1961). Both narratives follow the pattern of the spiritual quest into the interior, Van der Post's taking him into the South African Kalahari desert-region in search of the talismanic Bushman, Matthiessen's taking him on a more labyrinthine journey through South America that ends in another "lost world": the ancient rain forests of Peru. Both of these journeys, spiritually motivated, amount to a kind of surrogate pilgrimage: for Van der Post, the desert and its original—now endangered—inhabitants are spiritual entities, an antidote to the destructive material culture of the West; for Matthiessen, the wilderness is a site of personal (and collective) redemption: the place he goes to purge himself of the corrupted values of Western civilization. The tone in both works is Lévi-Straussian: serious, moralistic, lamenting the plight of "primitive" peoples whose authenticity has gone unrecognized, and whose way of life, irrevocably altered by their contact with (Western) modernity, is now "degenerating" (Matthiessen) or residual in the face of extinction (Van der Post). The following passage illustrates the melancholic awareness of deterioration that suffuses *The Cloud Forest:* "At present the Cashibo [Indians] are in a degenerate state and may soon disappear; unlike the river Chamus, they have failed to adapt to civilization. Not only is their culture disappearing, but they manifest such symptoms of decline as indiscriminate exchange of mates and two husbands for each wife" (257).[12] *The Lost World of the Kalahari,* meanwhile, is redolent of the nostalgia of Noble Savagery:

> [The River Bushman's] lean-to shelter of grass and reeds on his island
> . . . was surrounded with mounds of the bones of fish he had con-
> sumed over the years. No one knew where he came from or who his
> people had been. Whether he knew himself, no one could tell. I stood
> there stirred to the heart, watching him progress across the burning
> water into the papyrus standing so erect before the night. In that
> mythological light of the dying day he seemed to me the complete
> symbol of the silent fate of his race. (141)

Matthiessen's and, particularly, Van der Post's pathos for "disappearing" Aboriginal cultures is recorded with Rousseauesque nostalgic
fervor and an almost biblical intensity. Both writers turn, as if to seek
scientific support for their romantic myths, to anthropological models:
Matthiessen is most obviously indebted to *Tristes Tropiques* (1955),
that landmark text in which Lévi-Strauss converts anthropology (the
study of man) into "entropology" (the study of disintegration) by
expressing the conviction that native cultures are dying out, to be
replaced by a global "monoculture"; and Van der Post, for his part,
appears to be influenced by the work of earlier evolutionists, such as
Edward Tylor, who recuperate "primitive" cultures even as they consign them to the historical trashcan, and who disguise their cultural
arrogance by appealing to a mythicized indigenous wisdom. What is
evident, in each case, is that the conventions of travel writing are being
used to popularize *outdated* anthropological notions (hierarchies of
human "development," "disappearance," the idea of a "pristine"
native culture). Perhaps foremost among these notions is the idea of
anthropological rescue. As James Clifford points out, the idea of rescue, however vitiated within the contemporary discipline, has still
retained much of its earlier ideological force:

> The rationale for focusing one's attention on vanishing lore, for res-
> cuing in writing the knowledge of old people, may be strong. . . . I do
> not wish to deny specific cases of disappearing customs and lan-
> guages, or to challenge the value of recording such phenomena. I do,
> however, question, the assumption that with rapid change something
> essential ("culture"), a coherent differential identity, vanishes. . . .
> Such attitudes, though they persist, are diminishing. . . . But the alle-
> gory of salvage is deeply ingrained. ("On Ethnographic Allegory"
> 112–13)

In contemporary travel writing, which is less concerned than anthropology with the accuracy of its terminology, or with the rules and regulations that govern its disciplinary practice, one might go further: one

might go so far as to say that "the allegory of salvage"—the exoticist recuperation of the disappearing native "other" (Behdad)—remains an essential ingredient of what has always been a self-consciously mystificatory genre.[13] Travel narratives like Van der Post's and Matthiessen's have little interest in explaining native customs or in assimilating their writers' observations to a coherent intellectual system; instead, they aim to capitalize on the mystique of authenticity: an authenticity, loosely associated with ancient peoples and "primitive" nature, which is perceived as disappearing, or as having disappeared, from the modern world. Here is a sample passage from *The Lost World of the Kalahari:*

> With our twentieth-century selves we have forgotten the importance of being truly and openly primitive. We have forgotten the art of our legitimate beginnings. We no longer know how to close the gap between the far past and the immediate present in ourselves. We need primitive nature, the first man in ourselves, it seems, as the lungs need air and the body food and water; yet we can only achieve it by a slinking, often shameful back-door entrance. I thought finally that of all the nostalgias that haunt the human heart the greatest of them all, for me, is an everlasting longing to bring what is youngest home to what is oldest, in us all. (163)

The shamanic ring to Van der Post's statement is characteristic of certain kinds of spiritual travelogues that attempt, not only to quest after Aboriginal sources of knowledge, but to mimic Aboriginal leaders—the legendary "wise men" of their tribe.[14] Van der Post's hieratic rhetoric, invoking the mysteries of creation, helps set *himself* up as a kind of visionary, a divinatory Western seer. Matthiessen, to his credit, is well aware of the perils of such afflatus; and even though, like Van der Post, he is by no means immune from romantic flights of fancy, he tends to temper these with caution and a traveler's recourse to self-irony. (Like Lévi-Strauss, Matthiessen adopts a skeptical, even scornful attitude toward the rumors and legends that continue to surround the figure of the "tropical traveler" (see also chap. 2). "[Colonel] Fawcett has his disciples still," says Matthiessen at the outset of his jungle adventures in *The Cloud Forest,* adventures that culminate in a hazardous boat trip upriver in search of the fabled Picha ruins. "I attracted [these disciples] like flies all the way upriver. But since I am doing my best to remain hardheaded, I had better not report their stories here" (32). But the stories creep in, nonetheless, and Matthiessen cannot help basking in their reflected glory. Nor is he averse to a little bragging of his own: "Andreas and I are the first white men to travel the Pongo de Manique in what the Indians call 'the time of the water.' Since this feat was the one farthest from our minds we thus became the greatest heroes *malgré eux* since the voyage of Wrong-Way Corrigan" (213–14).

These slippages are not uncommon in a genre much given to self-congratulation, and Matthiessen remains, in many ways, an admirable example of a travel writer who refuses to allow his ego to overshadow his collective cause. This cause has less to do with the Indian peoples he encounters than with the environment in which they live: one that, like them, is under threat. Like the good naturalist he is, Matthiessen is sensitive to ecological issues and well informed on the fluctuations and fragilities of the world's different ecosystems. (Van der Post, in contrast, offers little by way of detailed nature description, and one is left with the impression that the Kalahari functions primarily as a psychic or moral landscape: an objective correlative to the "lost world" captured in the writer's memories of childhood.) Matthiessen is hard-headed enough, at least, to recognize his own fantasies of innocence, and to take care not to project these onto a prelapsarian wilderness. The wilderness, as a mythicized "zone," is thus as much a place of deceit and lawlessness as it is a locus of spirituality and a site for mystical trains of thought. It is a "contaminated" area, not only through its exposure to (Western) mercantile interests but through the abuse of its resources, which have become chronically depleted. The myth of eternal return that is joyously dramatized in *The Lost World of the Kalahari* is unavailable to a traveler, like Matthiessen, who has a clearer sense of environmental history. Thus, while Van der Post's and Matthiessen's texts are clearly derived from similar liberal-humanist agendas (despoliation of the environment, mistreatment of indigenous peoples, and so on), they fulfill, as narratives of disappearance, very different ideological functions: whereas *The Lost World of the Kalahari* recaptures a—largely imagined—world of the past to its cause of spiritual revival (making Van der Post an unlikely precursor of New Age gurus such as Morgan), *The Cloud Forest* records an elegy to an irrecoverable way of life. Both texts are "allegories of salvage," but only Van der Post's is successful—mainly because it obscures the history behind its own triumphal mythology. For in eventually conjuring the reappearance of the "authentic" Bushman, Van der Post's narrative inadvertently erases the circumstances that have led to his near extinction. As Mary Louise Pratt has observed, Van der Post's narrative advertises its own contradictions: on the one hand, it historicizes the Bushmen "as survivor-victims of European imperialism"; on the other it "naturalize[s] and objectif[ies] them as primal beings virtually untouched by history" ("Fieldwork" 48). Thus, while *The Cloud Forest* is disabused by the end of its previous "jungle hallucinations," *The Lost World of the Kalahari* succumbs in spite of itself to its illusion of Timeless Nature.[15] It is Van der Post, the proto–New Age seer, not the "magical" Bushman, who is sanctified in a narrative that ends up by reinstating the white man's proprietary myths:

> The desert looked as empty as it had ever been. Yet in that vast world behind the glitter of pointed leaves and in the miracle of sand made alive, and thorn of steel set alight with flower by the rain, the child in me had become reconciled to the man. The desert could never be empty again. For there my aboriginal heart now had living kinsmen and a home on which to turn. I got back into my Land-Rover. I drove over the crest and began the long, harsh journey back to our twentieth-century world beyond the timeless Kalahari blue. (279)

A different kind of narrative of disappearance is one that focuses on endangered species: into this category come two recent studies, Diane Ackerman's *The Rarest of the Rare: Vanishing Animals, Timeless Worlds* (1995) and David Quammen's *The Song of the Dodo: Island Biogeography in an Age of Extinction* (1996). Both of these books are popular accounts of the biological process of extinction, written by professional naturalists who, like Matthiessen, double as travel writers. *The Rarest of the Rare* and *The Song of the Dodo* are perhaps best classified as nature writing: they focus, that is, on description of the natural environment and its various lifeworlds, deemphasizing in the process the specific adventures—and the general self-absorption—of the traveler-observer. Nature writing is more likely than other kinds of travel narrative to moralize about its surroundings, less likely to psychologize the traveler-observer's personal experience. At times, as in Barry Lopez's work (see chap. 2), the traveler-observer is ironically immobilized: at a hidden vantage-point, recording the movements of other creatures (birds and animals); or at a lab desk, using biological data to develop theories of migration. Notwithstanding, biological fieldworkers are another kind of traveler, however much they might want to distinguish themselves from mere tourists or casual observers, and however much they might want to downplay their own subjective roles. (As was argued in an earlier chapter, the position of Lopez is somewhat anomalous: far from wishing to hide behind a set of more or less objective data, Lopez infuses his material with his own finely nuanced subjectivity.) As Mary Louise Pratt has argued for ethnographers, so might also be said of naturalists: there are continuities between their accounts and more orthodox forms of travel narrative—continuities that blur the boundaries, on one level, between amateurism and professionalism and, on another, between the dominant strategies of journalistic narration (travel writing) and informed description (scientific research) (see also Pratt, "Fieldwork"). Nature writing, which is clearly designed in most cases for a lay (if educated) audience, mediates between these modes: it can be seen simultaneously as a carefully researched, ethically saturated medium for the raising of global consciousness of environmental issues and as a popularized, thoroughly commodified vehicle for the recycling of journalistic clichés about endangerment on the planet.

Clearly, not all nature writing falls into the category of the cautionary tale. Yet it is equally clear that nature writing thrives, ironically, on the fear of natural cataclysm, and that its current boom can be attributed both to the threat of unprecedented extinction and to the need—as Ackerman's subtitle graphically illustrates—to reinstate the myth of a "timeless world" in an era when time, for so many who live in it, appears to be running out. Hence the paradox, whose anthropological equivalent can also be seen in works such as Van der Post's, that popular books on "rarity" have become almost a commonplace; and that "vanishing creatures" and "lost worlds" victoriously reemerge, in writing.

Books like Ackerman's and Quammen's are alert to these ironies, well attuned to their own commodified status. Of the two, it is Ackerman's that plays most obviously on the fears of its lay readership. Taking care to distinguish itself from dry academic studies of biodiversity, Ackerman's book bills itself as both a tribute to the Earth as a single, if multifarious, organism and a warning that it must be protected, or else it and its creatures (including ourselves) will surely perish. The tone, as might be expected, is consistently homiletic, as can be seen from a random sample taken from the introduction:

> The vanishing of so many other animals may indicate that we're not far from the brink ourselves. If we'd like our species to hang around for a while, we must be vigilant about what we're doing to other species, because evolution is a set of handshakes, not a list of winners. (xiv–xv)

We are among the rarest of the rare not because of our numbers, but because of the unlikeliness of our being here at all, the pace of our evolution, our powerful grip on the planet, and the precariousness of our future. We are evolutionary whizz kids who are better able to transform the world than to understand it. . . . Because vast herds of humans dwell on the planet, we assume we are invulnerable. . . . Because our cunning has allowed us to harness great rivers, to fly through the sky, although we were not born to, and even to add our artifacts to the sum of creation, we assume we are omnipotent. Because we have invented an arbitrary way to frame the doings of nature, which we call time, we assume we are immortal. (xviii–xix)

Humans could be among the fossils other life-forms speculate about one day (if they speculate), puzzling over our tragedy as we puzzle over the dinosaurs'. (xiii)

These dire injunctions remind us of Ackerman's view of biodiversity as "a sort of rigid morality play" (xvi), with herself cast in the role of principal moralist as well as mystical "naturalist/poet who patrol[s] the wilds of the world and the emotional jungle of ourselves with snares made of sentences and darts tipped with wonder" (xx). Ackerman's task, playing on "rarity," is to show the preciousness of existence while lamenting the dwindling numbers of some of the world's most precious creatures. And her own language, as if in sympathy, also lapses at times into the precious, most obviously in those overwritten sequences where she compares (rare) monk seals to "a dying race of monks, swimming through underwater caves in a cathedral of light" (28), or where she likens her search for rarity to "an arduous religious journey," a pilgrimage during which "we will take many unavoidable steps and endure many hardships" (60). "In ancient times," she continues, "people went on quests to behold a sacred relic or other artifact. The journey was as important as the goal, more important, in fact, because it was meant to anneal the soft metals of the soul" (60). Such bargain-basement mysticism undermines a book that is, in other respects, a well-observed and ecologically sensitive variation on the travelogue as spiritual quest.[16] What is most noticeable in the book, though, as in Van der Post's, is its tendency to ahistoricism: its ironic reversion to the very primal myths its subject—extinction—debunks. Thus, while Ackerman is at pains to point out that the Amazonian rain forest is not the original Garden of Eden, or that the romantic image of the fieldworker in a pristine environment is far from the truth, her impulse to lyricism precipitates her back into these selfsame clichés—making her sound, at times, like a voiceover for a *Discovery Channel* program, or like a female Attenborough uttering platitudes about "teeming life" on a "shrinking planet." To single out Ackerman for criticism is no doubt unfair and possibly smacks of self-righteousness; her work is better seen as an example of an identifiable genre. Nature writing, like travel writing at large, involves the negotiation of clichés—to call it platitudinous is, in this respect, surely to miss the point. At its best, nature/travel writing is able to redeploy its chosen clichés in the service of a thoroughgoing cultural critique. The problem, though, is that this critique may itself acquire commodity status—it may be appropriated by and remodeled for a materialistic culture. In this sense, books like Ackerman's are faced with an irresolvable contradiction: as "nature studies," they objectify—naturalize—the phenomena they investigate, turning their celebrations of life into collections of natural-history curios, and into exotic objects of consumption in the overdeveloped world.

David Quammen's *The Song of the Dodo* faces a similar dilemma, but the strategies it adopts to counteract it are very different from those of Ackerman. For one thing, Quammen is by no means averse to rehearsing academic arguments: a large part of his weighty book is given over to the intellectual sparring that has historically surrounded (and still surrounds) the evolution debate. For another, he has a thesis to present, evident from the first pages, where he sets out his theory of the partitioning of the planet into isolated island zones that place their resident flora and fauna increasingly at risk. And for a third, his work is clearly aimed at a different, more specialized audience; with its close attention to details, its precise definitions, its careful lists and copious bibliography, *The Song of the Dodo* is much less like *The Rarest of the Rare* than like Lopez's *Arctic Dreams* (see chap. 2): a well-written study, geared for a lay readership but hardly a mass audience, of the effects of environmental change on evolutionary patterns of habitat and migration. Unlike Lopez, though, Quammen is content to play the twin roles of scientist and adventurer; as he says, referring to pioneers of biogeography like Alfred Wallace (a hero, incidentally, to O'Hanlon, and much cited in O'Hanlon's books; see chap. 2): "Biogeography was always romantic, physically challenging, enlivened by adventurous field trips to exotic locales" (426). Quammen sees himself as a latter-day Wallace, following in the footsteps of his famous predecessor, venturing into areas that, although long since "discovered," remain relatively remote. (Examples here include the Aru Islands in the Malay archipelago, or the better-known but still isolated islands of Madagascar and Tasmania.) Quammen's book accordingly maintains a balance between scientific commentary and gung ho adventure, as its writer alternates between the nitpicking details of his treatise and his rambunctious expeditions, often led by equally flamboyant guides.

Like other nature writers operating at the fringe of the conventional picaresque travel narrative, Quammen uses interludes of adventure to offset, as well as to illustrate, his serious study. Thus, we find him at one point narrowly escaping from the clutches of a carnivorous Komodo dragon or, at others, in anxious nocturnal pursuit of the Guam tree-snake and the (probably extinct) Tasmanian tiger. Quammen's escapades are sensationalist enough to capture the interest of even the most distracted readers without compromising the intellectual rigor of his broader evolutionist argument. This argument sees "disappearance" as a possible prelude to extinction—the likely result of a series of biogeographical factors including population size and geographical distribution, as well as of a whole panoply of frequently avoidable man-made causes. Quammen is well aware of the shock appeal of disappearance: an appeal that, for example, has turned the obscure (Mauritian) dodo into an unforgettable subject of literary myth. He is also aware of the pitfalls surrounding the rhetoric of disappearance: in a brief excursus, for instance, on the reputedly vanished Tasmanian Aborigines, he makes the conventional but valid point that their descendants are still with us, and that their culture, although decimated by a history of European depredation, has adapted like any other to meet different environmental needs. By showing the susceptibility of myths of disappearance to ideological manipulation—by ironically exploring the authoritarian temptation to rescue "threatened" creatures and cultures, or to resuscitate "vanished" ones—Quammen is able to fend off the argument that seems to make *him,* and *his* work, vulnerable: that they are both exploiting the current vogue for cautionary parables of depletion at a time when rarity and extinction have themselves become consumer items.

Narratives of disappearance such as Quammen's and Ackerman's focus on a threatened planet whose diversity is dwindling and whose ecosystems are in decay. As is evident in Ackerman's book (if not in Quammen's), the mystical tenor of the writing counteracts the gloominess of its subject, turning what might potentially be an elegy for moribund nature into a eulogy of nature's capacity to regenerate itself, even at high risk. This optimism in the face of disaster is reminiscent of the

New Age: a smorgasbord of beliefs and philosophies, often drawn from mystical traditions, which aim to turn the apocalyptic fear of material cataclysm into the clarion call for a joyous spiritual renaissance at the millennium.[17] The New Age encompasses a dizzying variety of "therapeutic" media, from protective crystals, self-help manuals, and arcane treatises on angelic bodies to in-depth studies of holistic medicine and the complex structures of Native belief. Travel—on many levels—is integral to the New Age ethos, as is a concern for the environment, usually considered in "alternative" (i.e., non-Western) spiritual terms. New Age spiritual odysseys, with ecological ramifications, are among the most popular—and idiosyncratic—of contemporary travel narratives. Unsurprisingly, the sixties, with its developed counterculture, has been the "boom" decade so far for the production of such narratives. (Probably the best known among these are the cult "Don Juan" books of the anthropologist Carlos Castaneda, whose recycled primitivist wisdoms, inspired by an impressive array of hallucinogens, were to prove irresistible to their mostly youthful, often disaffected, Western readers.)[18] The nineties, however, with the millennium at hand, is not far behind; for New Age products proliferate—the merchandise of the Earth's salvation—in a postmodern age that "extends the power of the market over the whole range of cultural production" (Harvey 62).[19] Such products, it might be said uncharitably, provide a series of "quick fixes" for an alternative-seeking populace reacting against its own materialism in material ways. What is evident, at any rate, is that the New Age is more than just a "transformative" philosophy; it is a full-blown industry, catering to a growing number of consumers, which markets "alternative" spirituality in a variety of appealing forms.

Hence the staggering worldwide success of one of the more recent New Age vehicles, Marlo Morgan's controversial Australian-based travelogue *Mutant Message Down Under* (1994). Morgan's book, a massive best-seller in her home country, the United States, aroused a storm of protest after its much fanfared publication in 1994. At the eye of the storm was Morgan's contention, within the framework of a fictionalized account of her travels in Australia, that she was "let into" the tribal secrets of the Aborigines among whom she traveled, but that in order to protect these secrets she could not reveal the name of the tribe. Playing up to this transparent fiction-within-a-fiction, Morgan proceeded to regale American audiences with further stories of her "induction," and was astonishingly touted for a while as a genuine

New Age savior figure: the "messenger down under," chosen by her Aboriginal kinsmen, spreading spiritual enlightenment to the "Mutants"—the materially clouded folks back home. Here, in Morgan's narrative, is the culminating moment of her selection:

> You have been chosen [said the Elder] as our Mutant messenger to tell your kind we are going. We are leaving Mother Earth to you. We pray you will see what your way of life is doing to the water, the animals, the air, and to each other. We pray you will find a solution to your problems without destroying this world. There are Mutants on the edge of regaining their individual spirit of true beingness. With enough focus, there is time to reverse the destruction on the planet, but we can no longer help you. Our time is up. Already the rain pattern has been changed, the heat is increased, and we have seen years of plant and animal reproduction lessened. We can no longer provide human forms for spirits to inhabit because there will soon be no more water or food left here in the desert. (148)

While the oracular tone of the passage is laughable, the appropriation of Aboriginal spiritual wisdom—however mischievously intended—is not. Morgan risks being taken here for another of the New Age's fraudulent gurus, exhibiting disrespect for the people whose factitious "tribal wisdom" she retails so shamelessly, and exploiting the gullibility of her unsuspecting audience. Another reading is possible, though, which might help put *Mutant Message* in perspective. This reading, emphasizing the status of Morgan's text as a travel narrative, draws attention to a genre that historically juggles "fact" and myth. Travel writers are often hoaxers (although very few are mistaken for gurus); and in this sense, Morgan's sleight of hand might be seen in a less inquisitorial light. Notwithstanding, Morgan's text certainly rings bogus as a New Age narrative of spiritual awakening. Taking rhetorical advantage of the "disappearance" of the Australian Aborigines—needless to say, Morgan's critics have corrected her, less than kindly, on that point—Morgan uses their "inheritance" for a worldwide spiritual transformation: a revelation, nothing less, that the world exists in a state of Oneness, and that this Oneness must be intuited and protected for the sake of all. Morgan's mysticism is arguably more opportunistic, and certainly less informed than, say, Van der Post's or Ackerman's; but it is not wholly unrelated to these writers' recuperative projects, which either seek to make capital out of a "timeless" Native wisdom, even as they consign Native peoples to a premature extinction (Van der Post), or which take a romantic view of interdependence on the planet, using that view to lyricize—and reify—the "lost innocence" of endangered species (Ackerman). The connections between these otherwise highly disparate cultural products indicate the moral righteousness that is arguably common to their (sub)genre. They also suggest that New Age populism may underscore very different kinds of nature/travel writing, and that travel writing—at least of the more serious, environmentally conscious variety—has become a valuable source for the marketing of New Age myths (the healing of the Earth; the nostalgia for more authentic, nonmaterialistic ways of life; the recovery of wholeness in the face of global extinction). Finally, they hint, once again, at the contradictions in contemporary Western nature/travel writing, contradictions in part attributable to the belatedness of postmodernity: that in celebrating threatened nature, it observes the products of the West's destructiveness; and that in recuperating "timeless" peoples and cultures, it obscures the West's part in their decline.

These contradictions are also contained, of course, in the zeitgeist of the New Age, and some younger, knowing travel writers have already started exploiting them to satirical effect. One such satirical travelogue is Melanie McGrath's *Motel Nirvana: Dreaming of the New Age in the American Desert* (1995). *Motel Nirvana* takes its young author to the Arizona and New Mexico desert in search of New Age eccentricities—and she finds them in abundance. The charlatan gurus and crackpot psychics McGrath encounters on her travels are symptomatic of a New Age culture taken to its absurd limits. Whether she is describing tree-hugging hippies in latter-day communes in the forest or smarmy televangelists ministering to their flocks on their luxurious estates, McGrath has a keen eye and ear for pseudomystical entrepreneurship and spiritual fakery, and for the confused ideals and values that underlie New Agers' soulful quests. In a typically caustic sequence, McGrath recounts the days she spends at a New Age retreat—the Lama Foundation—high up in the Sangre de Christo mountains of New Mexico. A ritual event at the foundation is the "consensus" of its raggle-taggle members: an open meeting at which decisions concerning the running of the retreat are made. A man "in a T-shirt bearing the imperative 'Get Naked!' opens the meeting and everyone looks up and smiles oversized smiles, which makes me wonder if we all use the same muscles because every time I try to emulate them, it hurts" (177–78). The meeting soon turns into yet another opportunity for bonding:

> Get Naked announces that it is time for the consensus, so please to close our eyes and delve into our innermost selves. We join hands and close our eyes and so I imagine we look into our hearts. After a long pause Get Naked whispers "yesss" and the woman next to him whispers "yesss" and when it comes round to my turn I whisper "yesss" and so it goes on. The group resumes its mammoth smiling and I wonder if it's just me who hasn't the least idea what all the yessses are intended to add up to. (178)

In example after hilarious example, McGrath suggests that the New Agers' heartfelt confessions and passionate camaraderie only serve to reconfirm a creed of frantic selfishness:

> Turned in upon themselves, the outside world can seem uninteresting and profane, even irrelevant, to New Agers. Faith is no longer a matter of trust, something to which one must abandon oneself, but an exercise in introspection, whose outer expression is sincerity. Hence the New Age preoccupation with "authentic experience," and with sincerely-expressed emotion, for to New Agers these are both a protest against post-modern life and a visible manifestation of the sacredness within. The tear and the hug are the sacraments of New Age ritual. (179–80)

New Agers' spiritual quests are at once reactions against postmodern material lifestyles and effects of the postmodern commodification of spirituality.[20] McGrath recognizes this: the New Age, she concludes acerbically, is "the consumer culture's answer to spirituality. It takes what serves it and leaves the rest" (182). She is astute enough to recognize, also, that travel books about the New Age—including her own—risk subscribing to the same consumerist essentialism they debunk. Hence the link McGrath explores between travel writing, New Age soul-searching, and cultural voyeurism: deluded manifestations all of an essentialized cultural knowledge, or of the temptation to sift experience for the signs of an essential self. Travel books, as last-gasp guardians of the "authenticity" of lived experience, might seem ideally positioned against the postmodern technologies of a globalized capitalist culture. But as McGrath points out, "[e]ven as 'first world' travel books and magazines berate the global spread of KFCs and Coca-Cola and prophesy the death of cultural difference, their readership of cultural voyeurs keeps them in business" (224). Cultural voyeurism, she continues provocatively, is a "kind of essentialist pornography,"

> and we in the West are eager consumers of it. We sally forth, with the intention of buying up all experience, then retreat in the face of difference, like sullen hermit crabs. We are deflated by the popularity of Bart Simpson among the Thais, and yet we are secretly thrilled by the potency of our cultural exports. We invest in "third world" folk art, but never trouble ourselves greatly with their politics, expecting to send in our boys when the local population accidentally elects some devil-in-a-turban. The disease is so prevalent that Pornamerica [McGrath's ironically commodified code-word for the iconography of American consumer culture] . . . has come not only to represent the culture of the United States to Americans and foreigners alike, but also the idea of contemporaneity itself. This is as reductive and disregarding of American culture as it is of any other. Nonetheless we become daily more and more accepting of the notion that the essence of humanity lies in the consumption, aspirational or realized, of American iconography. Pornamerica is beginning to be our unifying spirit. . . . [And when] the Coca Cola company can print billboard posters with the legend "We taught the world to sing," then our spiritual alienation is complete. (224–25)

McGrath's is a more or less conventional attack on the material arrogance and spiritual impoverishment of postmodernity; it is enlivened, though, by her awareness that travel writing is not so much a desirable antidote as a *symptom* of the voyeuristic essentialism that characterizes the postmodern era. *Motel Nirvana,* in this context, is both an anti–New Age satire and an ironic confession of travel writing's investment in a self-centered New Age culture. In such a culture, alternatives collapse in an interplay of knowing paradoxes: spiritual guidance becomes dependent on the latest material products; global consciousness is intuited at isolated backwoods retreats; and travel itself, the very symbol of travelers' desire to reconnect with nature, transforms itself into an index of their alienated state.

In *Motel Nirvana,* as in other recent self-ironic explorations of New Age therapies, collective environmental awareness is assimilated to the individualistic quest for "harmony"—for an arrival at the dubious understanding that the self is balanced between contending psychic forces, and for a realization of the self's at-homeness with the wider natural world.[21] McGrath, for all her satirical intent, takes care to show that New Agers are by no means ecologically irresponsible— that, on the contrary, they are hypersensitive to the future of the planet. (Conservation, as McGrath shows, is very much a New Age issue: a battle between the desire to preserve the natural environment and to insure its availability for restorative trips and transcendent quests.) But McGrath also indicates the discrepancy between New Agers' search for global harmony and the excessive self-absorption that may lead them to neglect, or even ignore, the outside world. *Motel Nirvana* charts the contradictions in New Age attitudes to the environment even as it accepts, in principle, its greater ecological cause. But as an ecotravel book—as much a product of the New Age as a diatribe against it—*Motel Nirvana* is itself conflicted. It recognizes that ecotravel, however responsible, is after all a form of tourism; and that ecotravelers, like other tourists, are inevitably alienated from their environment—an alienation that only increases when they attempt to "reconnect." Environmentally conscious travel narratives tend to register this alienation in a variety of pastoral, elegiac, and romantically mythicized forms. Yet as McGrath suggests, the discourse of environmental consciousness is, or should be, as much a subject for critical analysis as the environment itself. To invoke the beauties of nature (the romantic travelogue) or to seek to express natural feelings (the New Age quest) begs the question as to how nature and the natural are ideologically constructed. As the late Alexander Wilson, a widely respected ecological theorist, reminds us,

> Nature is a part of culture. . . . Our experience of the natural world . . . is always mediated. It is always shaped by rhetorical constructs like photography, industry, advertising, and aesthetics, as well as by institutions like religion, tourism, and education. . . . Today nature is filmed, pictured, written, and talked about everywhere. As the millennium approaches, those images and discussions are increasingly phrased in terms of crisis and catastrophe. But the current crisis is not only out there in the environment; it is a crisis of culture. . . . To speak uncritically of the natural is to ignore these social questions. . . . Those who wish to speak on behalf of nature must be especially careful. (12)

While ecological theory has stepped up the pace in interrogating its own ideological biases, nature/travel writing has been slow to do so—partly because it remains a site of escape. In fact, as Mary Louise Pratt suggests, the invocation of nature in contemporary nature/travel writing might be traced back to the imperial practices of eighteenth-century European natural history. Natural history, according to Pratt, emerged as an all-encompassing classificatory system that, while designed to assert "an urban, lettered, male authority over . . . the planet," did so in a dissociative way that made this authority seem benign (*Imperial Eyes* 38). "Claiming no transformative potential whatsoever, [natural history] differed sharply from overtly imperial articulations of conquest, conversion, territorial appropriation, and enslavement. The system created . . . a utopian, innocent vision of European authority. . . . an *anti-conquest*" (38–39). While it would be excessive, churlish even, to see contemporary nature writing as surreptitiously imperialist—as merely another clandestine form of Euro-American domination—it is easy to see how some, certainly not all, environmentally conscious travel narratives run the risk of aestheticizing nature as an object of wonderment and control. While the best nature writers—Lopez, Matthiessen, Quammen—arguably function as both moralists and aesthetes (see chap. 2), they are also alert to the dangers of reifying the wonders of nature. Other self-conscious travel writers, like McGrath, enter in a similar caveat: that nature and the natural are not pristine essences but mediated concepts; and that these risk becoming the ideological pawns of a consumer-oriented culture that seeks belatedly to rescue, advertise, and sell the very resources that its own expansionist imperatives have helped to place at risk. Clearly, consumer culture in the age of postmodernity has much to gain from the retailing of endangered species and vanishing worlds. Yet consumers, including the readers of travel books, also have their part of the bargain; and while nature writing—travel writing as a whole—certainly needs careful critical sifting, it may yet teach its readers about the fragility and impermanence of our world. One certainly hopes so; for otherwise, traveler-writers in the not too distant future may really find themselves, like Lévi-Strauss's forlorn modern traveler, "chasing after the vestiges of a vanished reality" (43).

Postscript

- -

Travel Writing
at the Millennium

This study began with Evelyn Waugh's apocalyptic—if wry—1946 announcement that the end of travel writing, and of real travel itself, was drawing nigh. Waugh's announcement, echoed by Lévi-Strauss, later elegized by Fussell, was very much part of late—specifically postwar English—modernist anxiety. Bureaucratic impersonality; progressive means of transportation allied to a sophisticated travel infrastructure; the monstrous rise of tourism—all of these struck Waugh as symptoms of the modern (male) adventurer's decline. But as we have seen, Waugh's sense of crisis—of belatedness and approaching impotence—was a component of the traveler's anxiety rather than its baleful diagnosis. Travels multiplied exponentially; and travelogues also flourished, impelled like their guidebook counterparts by an ever-expanding tourist industry. Whatever losses the crisis of modernism precipitated, travel and its adjunct, the travel book, have hardly been among them. But why not? How is it that travel writing has continued to flourish, only gaining in prestige? This study has sought to reflect on these compelling questions. Summarizing those reflections, we have suggested that contemporary travel writing has answered Waugh's challenge by invoking a number of late-capitalist cultural possibilities. Three of these are notable, and can be briefly recapitulated here: commodification, specialization, and nostalgic parody.

The inexorable cultural mechanism of commodification works symbiotically with textuality: with writing, as with a whole host of other media forms (film, video, computer graphics, artistic and photographic images, and so forth). However strenuously the travel text might attempt to decommodify travel—to recuperate its "authenticity"—it presents itself to a world that the travel industry has played a

197

major role in referencing to the global. The global field emerges not so much as a two-dimensional, chartable surface but rather as a set of interlocking—specialized but also readily accessible—spaces: exotic zones, adventure terrains, hedonistic playgrounds, interactive museums, political mazes, "new" frontiers, and so on. The late-capitalist process of hypercommodification involves the production of commodities that are commodifying in their turn—such as travel and the travel book. Many travel books, of course, are little more than advertising vehicles, commodifying their respective terrains as a means of selling their second-level products. But even those books—and there are also many—that seek to disrupt the flow of the market invariably show their complicity with it (as might also be said, of course, of this particular study!). This is not a call for dismissal, but rather an invitation to analysis—an analysis that takes account of the resilience of travel texts. Such resilience can be seen, for example, in the appeal to specialized kinds of travelers. Among those we have identified in this book are (postcolonial) countertravelers, resisting the history and cultural myths of Eurocentrism; women travelers, subverting the male traveler's traditional values and privileges; gay male travelers, either seeking liberatory spaces or flouting heterosexual travel codes; and ecological travelers, reacting against the environmental damage that they most frequently associate with tourists. Such special-interest groups generally locate themselves in opposition to "conventional" modes of travel, particularly tourism; this oppositional stance provides a further alibi for travel writing while still depending on its traditions and its—not least, commercial—cachet. Together with the invention of new models for the traveler (the postmodern nomad, the virtual traveler) and the traveled world (the global village, hyperreality), these guises—or, more accurately, *dis*guises—have produced a spawn of recent travel narratives while conveying the illusion of all but endless travel/writing possibilities. In invoking a specialized mission, these writers often appeal to the reader's yearning for a kind of countertravel to assuage their heightened (Western, postmodern) guilt. Countertravel, of one sort or another, has certainly energized travel writing and, increasingly, travel theory in the decades since the war. Yet such oppositional narratives cannot escape being haunted by an array of hoary tropes and clichés (originary, primitivist, exotic, etc.), any more than they can hope to distill "authentic" encounters from their commodified sources.

Specialization, the several forms of countertravel, might have been expected to put Waugh's old-fashioned travel adventurism out of business. But it has not done so. On the contrary, English imperial questing—or more or less self-conscious parodies of it—continues to form the basis of many a recent traveler's tale. In such tales, as we have seen, a surface gesture to self-parody barely conceals a deep nostalgia for obsolete empires and manly discoverer-explorers. This, it seems, is a subgenre that lends itself to endless replication. Many readers continue to find exercises of even the most basic kind (say, Newby's) hilariously funny, as parodies of any developed genre can often prove to be; but even writers aiming for some more complex response than the belly laugh tend to produce moments of parody and self-indulgence, perhaps to disarm that shifting line known to all travelers who *tell:* the line where recounted episode sinks into repeated cliché. But then repeated cliché sometimes appears to be the stuff of travel writing, a commodity that cries out to be purchased and consumed and purchased again. It is as if this cycle of production, consumption, and reproduction were at the genre's core; and as if repetition were the paradoxical gesture that both marked and warded off the risk of its demise.

It is hardly surprising, then, that Waugh's postwar premonitions about travel and writing are currently being repeated on the edge of the third millennium. Countless writers—from erudite scholars to sensation-seeking journalists—seem to assume that the world is poised at a crucial, epoch-making moment. This moment is spatial, as well as temporal, the product of boundary marking; confusion over where exactly to place the millennial moment reflects the shifting borders of the contemporary political world. Similarly, the times through which we are moving, whether with hope or in despair, carry no essential dates, no definitively demarcating stages. The world's millennial moment cannot be revealed as if by magic; the world is less in progress (or in regress) than it is in process.

Millennial discourses usually invoke two registers. On the one hand, there is the register of decisive ends and beginnings: the "end of history" (Fukuyama); the beginning of "global culture." On the other, there is the register of process: of emergence and rise, of fall and exhaustion. Both registers, however much they reference postwar/postmodern intellectual trends (the paradigm shifts of Thomas Kuhn, for example, or the world-systems theory of Immanuel Wallerstein), seem to risk miring the traveler in the well-worn tracks of Western thought, with past matched against future, East against West, center against margins, atavistic tribalism against progressive globalism, apocalyptic dread against millennial optimism, and so on. And it is within these all-too-familiar, frequently stereotypical parameters that the current debates surrounding travel and travel writing are often placed.

A glance, for instance, at the relevant *Guardian Weekly* files from the midnineties reveals a startling unanimity among British travelers, travel writers, and reviewers on the subject of travel. It might seem inherently silly to ask a question like "where is travel/travel writing going?" But asked the question is and, increasingly, answered: "nowhere; don't move; just stay at home." While the general (postmodern) malaise of belatedness encourages inertia, the specific forms it takes—political resistance, postcolonial guilt, antitouristic distaste—can produce something stronger: a revulsion from travel. Catherine Bennett, for example, one of the contributors to the *Guardian Weekly* debate, seeks an explanation for "[w]hy the right people choose to stay at home" by excoriating the travel industry itself. For Bennett, the industry's glossy brochures strike all the right exotic chords, inviting clients, say, to indulge their postimperial fantasies in Burma (Myanmar) from the insulated space of the appropriately fabular cruise ship *The Road to Mandalay*. These brochures say nothing, of course, about child exploitation, forced labor, the torture of dissidents, and the persecution of opposition leaders in countries like Myanmar. And although some guidebooks (in trendy series like Lonely Planet) do refer to such unsavory features, they tend to do so in what Bennett calls inappropriately "jaunty" terms. The Lonely Planet "Myanmar," for instance, mentions "hav[ing] heard tell [there] of a smorgasbord of dictators, anti-government rebels, guerrillas, insurgents, and assorted malcontents"—an unruly hodgepodge of troublemakers that merely makes travel in that country more compelling. Bennett quotes tellingly from the guidebook: "[Myanmar] offers a glimpse of an incredibly Orwellian society. . . . We believe—now more than ever—that the positives of travel to Myanmar outweigh the negatives" (qtd. in Bennett 30).

Bennett avoids the usual classificatory markers—group/individual tourist, "alternative" backpacker, and so on—that might allow her to justify a superior kind of travel; instead, she blames the increasing thirst for travel in "difficult and bewildering territory" on the romantic travelogues of writers like Thubron, Chatwin, and Raban, correctly if uncharacteristically acknowledging the link between "high literary" travel narratives and their "lowly" counterparts, the guidebook and the tourist brochure. Rounding off her brief commentary, Bennett offers the caustic judgment that "most travelers bring back nothing more useful than tarnished jewellery from their expeditions into the lands of contrast. It seems like a small justification for . . . callous curiosity" (30). And, collapsing travel with travel writing, she goes on to quote from Robyn Davidson: "I think perhaps the whole genre needs to close. . . . We all carry a lot of cultural prejudices, and I just don't feel comfortable with it" (30). It seems to have escaped Bennett's attention, though, that Davidson is making a different point; for while the former is implying that travelers should embargo such territories as Myanmar and Iran as a form of political dissociation, the latter is caught up in something quite distinct, a version of liberal cultural guilt. Bennett's high-handed dismissal overlooks the fact that travel to "other" countries opens up, at least potentially, an opportunity for considered self-reflection—it offers a chance, that is, to interrogate and negotiate, if not eliminate, both the traveler's cultural prejudices and those of the peoples he or she encounters.

In her own contribution to the *Guardian Weekly* debate, Davidson, respected author of *Tracks* and *Desert Places* (see chap. 3), recounts how she came to see herself as a cultural "invader." Davidson's confession falls, however, into some of the usual traps. She endorses the myth that tourists are, by definition, people who "impose home environments on a foreign place"—as if, by implication, travelers do not—but she does express some sympathy, that rare commodity, for the tourist: "It's a bit much to ask people who have three weeks holiday a year to spend it struggling with the confusions of an alien place, or to put up with discomforts when what they have earned is rest" (27). Is Davidson, with perverse magnanimity, doing herself out of a job here? Apparently not, for the solution she offers to the tourist's quandary is the travel *book:*

> If literature was a compensation for the problems created by civilisation, then perhaps books provide us with a way out. Reading is like taking a journey. It's an entry into another world, another consciousness. It can satisfy curiosity, educate, excite imagination. There are too many of us: there are too many books. Ergo, stay home and read (27).

However frankly Davidson might disabuse herself of some of the recurrent myths of travel—the one, for instance, that leads the lonely, enterprising, hardship-enduring pioneer to wax self-righteous on encountering signs of others' invasions—she leaves herself at the end with the travel writer's standard escape clause: namely, she will continue to travel and to produce further literary journeys in order to satisfy that most insatiable (and most convenient) of consumers, the "armchair traveler."

Ian Sansom, another contributor to the *Guardian Weekly* symposium, produces a similarly double-edged review of a recent anthology of travel fictions. Such travel stories, Sansom suggests, might be taken along as holiday reading, but then again "the mass-market middle-brow paperback . . . is the modern *vade mecum* for a journey" (28). Sansom's skepticism about travel targets the figure of the traveler himself/herself, a figure who is always liable to return from trips arrogant and wasted. At best, according to Sansom, travel is futile, unduly bothersome:

> Travel, etymologically, is identical with "travail"; they share a common root in the Latin *trepaliare,* meaning "to torture with a *trepalium,* a three-staked instrument of torture." There's no denying it, travel is a pain—you're better off staying at home, reading. (28)

Tongue similarly in cheek, Veronica Horwell, also a reviewer for *Guardian Weekly,* acidly observes that "we lost an empire and gained The Traveller's Bookshop" (28).

Sansom, discounting the potential of travel to diffuse (and also defuse?) the traveling subject, underlines the "terrible truth that confronts any travel writer": "you can run but you can't hide; you can pretend to be someone else, but you can't escape yourself; you may be moving through a landscape, but it's still you who's moving through it" (28). An obvious but still interesting theorem, one that the travel books of Paul Theroux might confirm; and one that Sansom, as in his comments on travel as travail and pain, raises without inflection, with no apparent connection to issues of postcoloniality, postmodernity, or even "post-tourism" (Feifer). Sansom's theorem, nonetheless, usefully suggests the topos of *exhaustion.* There is literal exhaustion, of course, where the traveler runs out of steam or the destination is crowded out. But an end-of-century and, especially, an end-of-millennium view is more likely to indicate less literal forms of exhaustion, to point to the ways in which travel and travel writing participate in hypertextual exhaustions, where both subject and world are construed as postcolonial, postmodern, "posthistoric." Significantly, though, the *Guardian Weekly* writers cited above (with the possible exception of Catherine Bennett) take care to reserve a last place for travel writing—and thus for travel writers. Their collective advice is to stay home, because there is nowhere left to go, because travel is essentially futile, because "correct" people do not travel. But they then displace travel itself onto the travel book, which apparently—or so they see it—offers a "purer" form of journey. In this way they manage, in spite of themselves, to reinstate some threadbare distinctions: between the traveler and the tourist, between both of these and the travel writer. Travel writing's value as commodity rises as that of travel itself falls.

Sallie Tisdale, whose personal perspective on pornography, *Talk Dirty to Me: An Intimate Philosophy of Sex* (1994), gained her some notoriety, has recently recommended that even travel writers are best off staying home. Tisdale's long piece in *Harper's,* "Never Let the Locals See Your Map," purports to be a review article covering eight travel books, but the article soon turns into a wide-ranging discussion of travel writing that canvasses a number of issues currently under debate. The article exhibits ambivalent attitudes. On the one hand, Tisdale follows Evelyn Waugh, Paul Fussell, and others in lamenting the exhausted possibility for "genuine" travel and the sad decline of the travel book: whereas "[t]ravel books were [once] shiny with promise—informing and diverting in good measure," now, in contrast, although "travel literature is booming," "good travel writers are few and far between" (66). Since her travelers of promise turn out to include such household favorites as Robert Byron and Eric Newby, Tisdale alerts us to the link between the notion of exhaustion and the barely concealed motivation for a good deal of travel writing: nostalgia. Decrying a cult of personal idiosyncrasy in the travel writer, Tisdale decides that "[t]oday, true travel writing—the lyrical account of an adventure marked by curiosity and courage rather than showmanship—scarcely exists" (67). As if neither Byron nor Newby enlists idiosyncrasy or showmanship in his narratives! It is worth noting again (see the introduction) that this type of lament for "true" travel writing can be used to *promote,* rather than discourage, the circulation of contemporary travel narratives.

Tisdale falls short, however, of simply endorsing Fussell, whose second major thesis is the necessity of distinguishing the "true" traveler from the tourist. While she agrees that "a particular distinction between travel and tourism marks modern travel writing," it is a fine distinction, and "all travel writers think they know where it is—far from themselves" (67). One function the contemporary travel book serves, then, is to flatter readers who "wish to separate [themselves] from the rabble," to identify themselves as bona fide travelers, not vulgar tourists. In dismantling this distinction, Tisdale makes an ingenious move: she argues that the traveler's professed desire to "pass" is fundamentally dishonest, because he or she is also yearning to be noticed, to stand out: "Travelers dissociate themselves from tourists not because tourists are noticed but because they are *not*. . . . tourists are the least intrusive travelers of all" (72). For Tisdale, it is not tourists who give offense but contemporary travel writers, who strive (seemingly in panic) to purvey "authentic" experience. Travel narratives, Tisdale concludes, may well discourage not only tourists but also "purer" travelers. Marred though her essay is by its nostalgic appeal to a history of "true" travel, Tisdale's association of exhaustion with the commodification of the dream of "authentic experience" needs to be taken seriously. It is hardly surprising, in this context, that a number of recent travel books make their pitch to the "traveler [who] grows ever more desperate for pure experience, something *authentic*" (72); nor is it surprising that this ideal traveler is more likely to be a reader.[1]

This quest for "authenticity" is, as will be clear by now, curiously fraught. It seeks to engage further frontiers that are, by definition, exotic. These frontiers are at extremities: of the map; of the Western, metropolitan world; of historical regimes; of fully grounded worldly experience.[2] There is seldom any doubt, though, that the frontier is out there somewhere: as one writer puts it, "beyond the last tollbooth on the last scrap of potholed pavement at the very end of the turnpike" (Millman 239). The frontier exists in the future, beckoning, enticing, seducing. Yet it is also chimerical, vanishing, already extinguished as soon as reached (see discussion of the exotic travel zone in chapter 2). Tisdale formulates the conundrum neatly: the traveler "wanders the back roads, then writes his book so that everyone will know what matters most: not to be the first to see remote lands, but to be the last to see the land remote" (72). The traveler-writer attests to having been there last, and to having turned out the lights on leaving. All the lights but one: the bedside lamp that allows the reader to accompany the author into the always-receding territory of the exotic. While there is nothing intrinsically harmful in the transactions between traveler, writer, and reader that satisfy individual fantasies of discovery, exploration, and exotic experience, the relationship of such fantasies to collective geopolitical practices of control, exploitation, and subjugation is problematic at best.

The end-of-millennium commentary just examined illustrates the dilemma. This commentary, offered through a series of book reviews and articles, makes clear that it is the genre itself, rather than the work of any individual writer, that is at stake. For, as Tisdale says, travel writing has proliferated as "travel has burgeoned" within a global, media-driven economy (72); as the genre has "become . . . a way of life, a way of seeing the world" (67); and as it has begun to formulate its protocols, to shape a canon for itself. No doubt Paul Fussell's study *Abroad* has been instrumental in suggesting not only criteria for a serious canon but also individual "landmark" works. Evidence of a travel-writing canon, and of its importance to the marketing of travel books as both supplementary to and an alternative form of travel, can be seen in the recent establishment of the "Picador Travel Classics." This is a series that partly announces the classic status—the canonicity—of its volumes through their hardback covers, their introductions, and their numbering—they are intended to form a library.[3] This canonizing impulse is foreshadowed in Ian Pearson's article in *Destinations,* the travel section of the Toronto *Globe and Mail* (November 1992): "Around the World in 6,000 Pages. A Guide to the Ultimate in Arm-chair Journeys." Pearson is unsure whether classic travel writing is literary privilege or salvage mission, its primary function being to "pre-serve" the "truly great journeys" in books, even while the "serendipi-tous adventure is becoming harder and harder to achieve as the jugger-naut of massive tourism levels the planet" (15). But whether they are mandarins of a superior order or merely last-ditch rescuers, the mainly British, postwar "club" members all find themselves represented: Byron, Leigh Fermor, Lewis, Thesiger, Newby, O'Hanlon, Raban, Theroux, Chatwin—and one woman, Dervla Murphy.[4] Literary cre-dentials are strengthened by the inclusion of such older works as Kinglake's *Eothen* (1844), Twain's *The Innocents Abroad* (1869), and Stevenson's *Travels with a Donkey* (1879). Pearson leaves the reader in little doubt that travel writing is a consolidated genre, with its acknowledged classics—its founding monuments—and its rapidly expanding membership; and that it has achieved respectability as a (Western) cultural product by moving off the beaten paths of travel into the rarefied sphere of "high" literature. Henceforth—or so the for-mula runs—every ambitious travel narrative will have to situate itself in relation to its literary precusors even before it gets to the starting line. The tacit message here is that travel is a primarily textual activity; and that in an age of depletion and exhaustion, writing is "better" then experience.

To publish, or retrospectively place, an individual writer's book within a named series already gestures toward the canonical by proclaiming the work's affiliation with a supposedly identifiable, and already validated, group. (The Picador Classics imprint assumes both the patent existence of the "travel classic" and the purchaser's automatic assent to the volumes' "classic" status.) Some readers of travelogues might be predisposed to favor certain imprints or series, knowing, like seasoned travelers perhaps, what kind of thing they want. The dust jackets and back covers of travel books are also witness to the process and function of canon formation. You can see the "club" at work as established authors write blurbs congratulating one another, or signaling a probationary acceptance for lesser-known writers. One of these latter might be hailed as a "true successor" to Redmond O'Hanlon, another as a "stylish descendant" of Robert Byron, a third as an "eagle-eyed observer" of the absurd, like Paul Theroux.[5] The blurb industry, an indispensable agent in moving books off the store table and into consumers' hands, always risks discrediting itself; after all, some readers are more likely to see blurbs as revealing, not the candid opinions of experts, but the interested gestures, insider friendships, and mutual puffery of a handful of card-carrying club members.[6] At this point, prestigious literary prizes (like the Thomas Cook Award) become useful supports, supplying the travel-writing business with a regulated set of "impartial" endorsements. As with other elements in the travel-writing infrastructure, such prizes validate not only the single, notable instance but the genre as a whole, which emerges worthily as a stable yet expanding entity.

The expansion of travel writing as genre, particularly in the cities for urban audiences, arguably serves to counteract the discourse of exhaustion. The travel sections of major newspapers, as well as journals like *Granta* and *Condé Nast,* work continuously to recuperate and reinvigorate travel in a format that blurs the distinction between activity and text and (even when it seems to invoke it) between traveler and tourist. These travel sections offer practical instruction for those who seek to be "active"; responding to inquiries about equipment for "tramping" New Zealand wildernesses or about the cheapest way to Tibet, they rehearse the travelogue in personal profiles of particular places or, playing up the travel-as-literature angle, they include brief reviews of travel books. A quick survey of the substantial "Travel Books" column in the "Travel" section of the *Toronto Globe and Mail* over a period of some weeks in 1996 confirms that travel can be marketed as replenishment and innovation, whether in guidebooks, travel narratives, or anthologies of shorter travel accounts. Laszlo Buhasz, for example, recommends Jim Haynes's *People to People* "guides to eastern European countries," which are "directories of people . . . who speak English or another western European language, are from professions ranging from medicine to engineering, and who are willing to house, guide or help visitors to their countries"; Haynes, effuses Buhasz, "is trying to transform tourists into travellers. Good for him" (August 14, 1996). Buhasz also notes that *Arthur Frommer's New World of Travel* "deals with a rapidly growing demand for alternative ideas by spirited, intellectually curious travellers tired of mass-produced vacation packages," and quotes from Frommer's preface: "After 30 years of writing standard travel guide books, I began to see that most of the vacation journeys undertaken by Americans were trivial and bland, devoid of important content, cheaply commercial, and unworthy of our better instincts and ideals" (March 23, 1996). Anthologies, too, seek to recuperate and reinvigorate travel. Buhasz commends the *Travelers' Tales* series (edited by James O'Reilly and Larry Habegger) for their "articulate explanation of the difference between travel guides and travel literature," a difference apparently marked by the latter's emphasis on experience and story. According to O'Reilly and Habegger, travelers need to be prepared, "with feelings and fears, hopes and dreams, goals. . . . Nothing can replace listening to the experience of others, to the war stories that come out after a few drinks, to the memories that linger and beguile" (February 10, 1996). The *Travelers' Tales* editors clearly throw their pitch to those who plan to use travel texts as an overture to travel, as a preparation for the real thing.

As suggested throughout this study, neither travel itself nor the travel book exists in isolation; in the symbiosis between them, it is less a matter of seeing one as "superior" than of seeing each as a supplement to the other: the travel account as a companion to actual travel, the travel itinerary as supplementary to its texts. Eric Korn, in a recent *TLS* article, suggests that supplementarity can take positions of "before," "after," and "instead":

> I went to Marrakech because I read *The Alleys of Marrakech;* I went to Cannery Row because I read *Cannery Row.* . . . On the other hand I returned from Haiti late in Papa Doc's time, read *The Comedians* and discovered . . . just where I'd been, who had been sitting in my chair, sleeping in my bed, floating in my swimming-pool. In retrospect (the best way to enjoy abroad), a deeper tint of danger coloured my rather placid trip. . . . On the third hand, I didn't go to Borneo

. . . and have given the Yanomami a wide berth, because I read Red-mond O'Hanlon. (36)

Various mechanisms continue to enforce a distinction between actual, degraded, "post-touristic" travel and "purer" forms of travel, not of course as a means of actively discouraging travel, but rather of replenishing it by appealing to untainted motivations and higher ideals. The material continuity between higher and lower forms of travel is evident in most bookstores, where the shelves filled with travel guides are adjacent to those, almost as many, carrying travelogues. The Lonely Planet imprint, among others, has begun to exploit this overlap by establishing a sister series, Lonely Planet Journeys, which converts the raw material of travel guides into more "literary" travel accounts. This travelogue series, like its guidebook counterpart, is clearly aimed at the lifestyle and mindset of self-styled "offbeat" travelers and "irreverent" backpackers. The following summary, for instance, is taken from the cover of the first in the series, Sean Con-don's *Sean and David's Long Drive* (1996):

> Sean Condon is young, urban and a connoisseur of hair-wax. He can't drive, and he doesn't really travel well.
> So when Sean and his friend set out to explore Australia in a duck-egg blue 1966 Ford Falcon, the result is a decidedly offbeat look at life on the road. Over 14,000 death-defying kilometers, our heroes check out the re-runs on TV, get fabulously drunk, listen to Neil Young and wonder why they ever left home.
> *Sean and David's Long Drive* mixes sharp insights with deadpan humour and outright lies. Crank it up and read it out loud.

Another in the series, Annie Caulfield's *Kingdom of the Film Stars* (1997), takes the reader (according to a brief newspaper notice) "through a jolly romp through contemporary Jordan. As you'd expect from a long-time television comedy-script writer . . . , Caulfield always sees the funny side of things. And there's plenty to laugh at: struggling with her toilette in the middle of the Jordanian desert, dealing with the 'Marlboro Boys' and their horses at the foot of the ruins at Petra." Aficionados of the popular Lonely Planet "Travel Survival Kit" series will be familiar with the travelogues' jocular, wryly self-ingratiating tone. But the publishers also acknowledge a more significant point, namely that the transparent "fictions" of travelogues are closely inter-twined with the guidebook's hard "facts." Their spaces overlap; you can stay home with the Lonely Planet "Australia" kit or you can "overland" with Sean and David—both books serve as facilitators of the actual process of travel while locating the traveler fair and square within a set of (Western) travel myths.[7]

Clearly, the culture and media industries are continuing to mobilize travel in its widest sense, both activating and responding to mainstream, overwhelmingly metropolitan avidity to experience—or, rather, purchase—the greatest range of global commodities. Among those commodities are, of course, the ideologies and collective fantasies of the West, in particular America, Britain, the white diaspora in Canada, Australia, New Zealand, and South Africa, parts of Europe and, increasingly—though in a different form—the countries of the Pacific Rim. As the millennium approaches, the fetishizing of the moment in terms of "end of" and "dawn of," of (pessimistic) apocalypticism and (optimistic) global progress, is ubiquitous. Some travel writing, particularly the strand that crosses over into political journalism, seems well attuned to geopolitical hysteria, the obverse of global optimism. The work of the American writer Robert D. Kaplan— *Balkan Ghosts* (1993), "The Coming Anarchy" (1994), and, most recently, *The Ends of the Earth: A Journey at the Dawn of the 20th Century* (1996)—is worth considering at some length here because of the eagerness with which many readers have embraced his vision of the Balkans and the Third World. A blurb for the paperback edition acclaims *The Ends of the Earth* as "a terrifying journey around what is both the rim and the center of the world," a journey that "describes, in haunting detail, the abyss on which so much of the world teeters." Where Kaplan's Balkan chronicle had specified a local instance of breakdown, and his *Atlantic Monthly* article had generalized the terrain and deepened the despair, the last item in his trilogy fits in somewhere between, with the journey moving from Africa through Central Asia and ending up in the Indian subcontinent and Indochina, and with Kaplan attempting to balance a sense of the abyss with tentative hope. Overall though, Kaplan's work evokes "The Second Coming" in its remorseless apocalyptic gloom, and it seems likely that the title of his article "The Coming Anarchy" was intended to stir an echo of Yeats's famously doom-laden poem.

Kaplan himself labels *The Ends of the Earth* a "travel book," "a premodern generalist's book that mixes history and other subjects in with travel," and is written "in the style of John Gunther, not Paul Theroux" (preface, n.p.). Using Gunther and Theroux to represent opposing extremes of the travel book seems at first to be a useful move:

Gunther's "*Inside . . .*" series establishes these "insides" through an accumulation of facts and statistics, largely erasing any sense of a traveling, perceiving subject, whereas Theroux foregrounds a subject who constitutes place precisely through his unstable "outsider" presence. But the distinction is hardly that simple, and Kaplan's narrative, far from locking on factual details, floats between alternative means of recording and registering cultural difference. At one point, Kaplan claims that, to optimize knowledge of the "other," the traveler should go on foot:

> In an air-conditioned four-wheel-drive Toyota Land Cruiser—the medium through which senior diplomats and top Western relief officials often encounter Africa—suspended high above the road and looking out through closed windows, your forehead and underarms comfortably dry, you may learn something about Africa. Traveling in a crowded public bus, flesh pressed upon wet, sour flesh, you learn more; and in a "bush taxi," or "mammy wagon," where there are not even windows, you learn even more still. But it is on foot that you learn the most. You are on the ground, on the same level with Africans rather than looking down at them. You are no longer protected by speed or air-conditioning or thick glass. The sweat pours from you, and your shirt sticks to your body. This is how you learn. (25)

Kaplan's apparent aim is to move through Africa on the level, presenting a sequence of experiential encounters whose "authenticity" is guaranteed by the rejection of insulating media (speed, windows, air conditioning, etc.). Yet this smacks (as it so often does in this type of narrative) of disingenuousness; as a seasoned American journalist moving freely on the international circuit, Kaplan frequently capitalizes on reliable and expensive transport, on comfortable, protected lodging and, especially, on the kind of personal contacts only available to the privileged Westerner.

In spite of distancing himself from the kind of self-absorbed travel associated with Theroux, Kaplan, in his account, makes use of several similar materials and techniques. For example, like Theroux, Kaplan works up the personal encounter or interview. When a man approaches him on the road, inviting recognition, Kaplan has to think hard before he recalls having met him the previous day. Kaplan remembers that the man, seeing him without change, had offered to pay for his Coke: "Though I had thanked him profusely only yesterday, today he was at first glance just another black face, another of my statistics" (26). Here, however, a major difference between Theroux and Kaplan emerges, for where the former would likely disarm the episode of sentimental potential, the latter makes it stand, somewhat improbably, for universal prospects: "To see individuals, I realized, was to see possibilities and, thus, more hopeful scenarios" (26).

Kaplan also shares with Theroux—and with a great many other contemporary travel writers—an impulse to keep (inter)textual layers between himself and what he is reporting. Kaplan's citations range from C. P. Cavafy to the Lonely Planet series, from Thomas Malthus to Thomas Mann, from Joseph Conrad to Barry Lopez, from Richard Burton to Bruce Chatwin.[8] It seems as if Kaplan has less confidence in what observation and interaction can achieve than his comments about traveling on foot might suggest. He confesses, at any rate, that he "read a lot" in preparation for his various tours (95). And then, surprisingly, he enlists such reading to distance himself from tourists: "In an age of mass tourism, adventure becomes increasingly an inner matter, where reading can transport you to places that others only a few feet away will never see" (96). It also suggests the achievement of an existential authenticity: "The more I read about a place and about issues that affect it, the more I feel I am traveling alone" (95).

While Kaplan's dense allusiveness and cultivated sensitivity align his travel with Theroux's, his anxiety to assign causes to the various regional malaises he witnesses links his work more closely with Gunther's.[9] Here, encounter narrative yields to data and written history. But neither of these can satisfy Kaplan's relentless search for causes, and his narrative returns addictively to—largely undeveloped—general theories. Africa is trapped in atavism (Kaplan entitles the section, "Back to the Dawn?") and enervation. "Nature," Kaplan observes, "appeared far too prolific in this heat, and much of what she created spoiled quickly" (19). Africa is a place of "passivity, fatalistic and defeated" (24), racked by overpopulation and disease, and lost in a kind of "premodern formlessness" (45). Even climate and geography point to violence and atrophy: "When you read the history of Sierra Leone you cannot help but realize how much the past was decreed by geography and climate" (48). The travel account swerves into disaster journalism. "Causes" become too "natural" ("blood," "heat," "tribalism," "the forest") or too pseudoscientific (overpopulation, disease, boundary problems) to engage. Such "causes" work against the production of useful analysis. The constant deployment of vivid metaphor, in which such natural phenomena as seeds, eruptions, and conflagrations produce cultural effects, occludes both historical terms and the consideration of economics and politics: those of the states and territories themselves, and those of powerful international interests and institutions.

In "explaining" what he sees in the Third World, Kaplan returns obsessively to a key formula. "Geography is destiny" (130) is not only Kaplan's personal motto; it is also a kind of shorthand for Western traveler-observers whose accounts of the countries through which they move substitute easy myths for hard analysis. Kaplan's speculations about Iran in *The Ends of the Earth* are symptomatic:

> [W]ere more of Iran—rather than just its north and northwest border provinces—graced by the moist and moderating influences of the Caspian, then perhaps the history and character of the Iranian people would have been very different, and the transformation of an airplane cabin into a veritable mosque would never have occurred. (176)

But geography's edicts are complicated by other universalizing structures, which lead Kaplan in turn to a number of portentous statements and questions: "The story of man is the story of nomadism" (130); "rural poverty is age-old and consistent with an ever-turning planet" (107); and, most egregiously perhaps, "the condition of a country's public toilets—or the lack of them—says something about its progress toward civil society" (274)! On the other hand, as Kaplan admits, "No-one can foresee the precise direction of history, and no nation and people is safe from its wrath" (438). Harmonizing such a cacophony of explanation is no easy matter. What is the relation between the human "story of nomadism" and "progress toward civil society"? How can we protect "a country's public toilets" from the wrathful judgment of an implacable history? In Freetown, Kaplan says, "I wished I had been younger and more naive, and that I was not addicted to political analysis" (43). Yet it is precisely firm political analysis, from any perspective, that seems to be missing, as Kaplan's text repeatedly entraps itself in a kind of apocalyptic banality:

> The end was nigh in the failed battle, fought valiantly by the liberal West, to equalize cultures around the world. The differences between some cultures and others (regarding the ability to produce exportable material wealth) appeared to be growing rather than diminishing. (54)

Platitudes like these render statements such as "Africa . . . has to be confronted" (25) opaque to the point of futility.

Kaplan's title phrase, "the ends of the earth," is oddly anachronistic, belying the awareness he otherwise shows of global shrinkage; while the subtitle, "a journey at the dawn of the 21st century," hints at an exploration of newness that flies in the face of the text's tired stereotypes and despair at the possibility of prediction. Kaplan's stated aim is to "map the future, perhaps the 'deep future,' by ignoring what was legally and officially there and, instead, touching, feeling, and smelling what was really *there*" (6); but his conclusion is that "the effect of culture was more of a mystery to me near the end of my planetary journey than at the beginning" (425). Kaplan's journey of political travel ends in all kinds of exhaustion: the exhaustion of the traveler, of the terrains and cultures he has traversed, of the textual effects of travel—and, perhaps, of the reader. Such a journey might perhaps more accurately be described as a "midnight" (of the twentieth century) than as a "dawn" (of the twenty-first).[10]

The programmed travel account, insofar as it fulfills a documentary function, offers to interrogate contemporary global issues in a variety of contexts: economic, geographical, historical, sociological. It undertakes its program via a mixed route of travel experience, onsite reportage, and wide-ranging textual reference. A tall order; and it is perhaps unfair to pass harsh judgment on Kaplan's book, probably the most ambitious and broadly defined of a clutch of popular "political" travelogues sparked by the end of the Cold War, the dissolution of the U.S.S.R., a growing fear of the Islamic East, and the end of the twentieth century. The Western commentators in these accounts most frequently find their encounters confirming ideological biases and prescripted knowledge, and many of them find it hard to negotiate the spaces between what Kaplan calls Theroux- and Gunther-type travel. It might well seem from Kaplan's nostalgic cultural reverence, his sense of depletion and failure, and his declarations of futile guilt, that a sacrificial rhetoric of exhaustion has overtaken contemporary travel writing, particularly the kind of travel writing that purports to offer political analysis (see discussion of Naipaul's work in chap. 2). But need this be so? Peter Robb's *Midnight in Sicily* (1996), a study of southern Italian Mafia culture, offers an alternative model, demonstrating that the travel book's generic flexibility and hybrid status can be turned to positive effect in contemporary, disaster-tilted documentary writing.

The Australian Robb, who lived in southern Italy for fourteen years from 1978 onward, returned to Sicily in 1995 as the Andreotti trial began. Robb reports a friend's concerns about the possibility of his writing about Sicily and the Mafia: that he would have to trivialize contexts, events, and characters; that he would end up, in short, by turning it all into travel writing. This skeptical friend, the Sicilian Clara, tells of an Italo-American woman, who had come to Trapani (in Sicily) some years before to find out more about her family. This woman had enlisted Clara's help through letters of introduction; but as it turned out, she was also preparing a travel book. When the book was eventually published, Clara discovered to her horror that her local restaurant featured in it as a prime tourist site:

> Ten days ago [Clara explains to Robb], I got a phone call from a travel agent in Palermo. He had a coachload of American ladies and they all wanted to come and eat at Clara's restaurant. I told him it was closed and he said they were coming anyway. They wanted to see me. (247)

But as Clara acknowledges, "you wouldn't be writing anything like that, after all" (247); and it is certainly true that Robb is no Peter Mayle, selling a romance of Mediterranean peasant life (and gourmet cooking) to hundreds of thousands of eager Anglo-American consumers.

Midnight in Sicily is a subtly written and allusively layered travel book. Robb frames each of its twelve chapters with episodes such as visiting a market or a restaurant, catching a bus to some destination, interviewing a political or artistic figure. Several of these episodes derive from the earlier years he spent in Sicily. Political commentary, as well as historical narrative, unfolds from local specificity, with discussions of regional cuisine (say, the ice cream of the Mezzogiorno) opening out into accounts of Mafia revenge killings. The book is alive with movement, from walks through city streets and assorted local car, bus, and ferry rides, to the narrative oscillations between geography and history, aesthetic commentary and urban practice, political analysis and dramatically reconstructed scenes. The effect is at first immediate and artless but, on reflection, heavily mediated, with the sense of careful patterning of a densely woven tapestry. The various transitions, from apparently "free" experiential narratives to more structured histories and commentaries, attune the practice of reading to the recognition of travel as a process close to that of negotiating between disparate orders of life and knowledge.[11]

Robb's specific narrative investigations—into the notorious Andreotti Kiss, the assassinations of the prosecutors Borsellino and Falcone, the kidnapping and killing of Aldo Moro, and a host of violent Mafia murders—gain in complexity and, paradoxically, credibility as they are balanced against other literary accounts: most notably, the Sicilian novelist Sciascia's. Lampedusa's *The Leopard* (1957) also receives careful attention, and other key artists, including Eugenio Montale, Pasolini, Renato Guttuso, Letizia Battaglia, and Lina Wertmüller, heighten the nuanced sense of a rich, fraught culture of exploitation and intimidation. Robb's figuring of the midnight at which the book begins and ends is another heightening device; but it is one that, in spite of its melodramatic symbolism, does not act to reduce the cultural specificity of Sicily's politics of violence by naturalizing it or assimilating it to some overarching "universal" theory. Thus, although Robb quotes Sciascia as having declared that "Sicily is a metaphor for the modern world" (314), he at no point balloons it out into a "cause," instance, or explanation of a millennially exhausted world—as Kaplan might well have done.

But Robb's travel book has more up its sleeve than an informed commentary on the Mafia crisis in postwar Italy. This surplus is connected with Tisdale's gloss (in her previously mentioned essay on travel writing) on Isherwood's remark that "the ideal travel book should be perhaps like a crime story in which you're in search of something" (qtd. in Tisdale 71). Tisdale adds her own observation:

> Part of a search is momentum, and not knowing where you might end up. In the best travel books, the narrator is *looking:* for a person, a building, a view, a rare bird, a certain truth. (71)

In this case, Robb is retracing Sciascia's (the midcentury novelist's) footsteps. Sciascia lived in Racalmuto, a quiet mining town—and Mafia stronghold. Robb takes a bus to the town, which occupies two sides of a hill looking seaward and inland; on this particular afternoon, the town is bleak on both its slopes, "closed and shuttered" with doors "tight shut" and "sightless streets." The atmosphere is one of containment, augmented by a somber funeral procession. Robb seeks a town center and a hotel, but ends up finding neither. Instead, the town offers only a vista of sheep-tracked slopes and lifeless streets. The visitor speculates that

> these horizontal streets weren't in fact parallels, like altitude lines on a map but a single spiral, one immensely long street winding through the deserted town from top to bottom, like the thread in a screw. Then in the shadows I saw another hearse, another glimpse of polished mahogany, dragging me up and down the narrow parallels or

winding round and round Racalmuto on its way to the graveyard. (278)

The description seems to have both writer and reader trapped in a kind of *mise en abyme;* but, as Robb suggests, Sciascia was already familiar with this territory, and it is less that the earlier writer had created this seemingly postmodern moment than that the "town embodied the hidden secrets and the vertiginous symmetries or asymmetries in the architecture of Sciascia's labyrinthine stories" (280). Sciascia, in turn, "owed to his master Borges that sense of an annihilating metaphysics hidden in experience" (280); and before them both come the mazes and winding, redoubled narratives of *The Thousand and One Nights.*

Robb makes the case, if indirectly, that certain literary tropes and techniques situate the writing of southern Italy within the ambience of European postmodernism, with its pastiche of actions and agents replacing "confidently realistic fiction" (280). Yet he ultimately finds "something pinched and limited in the solutions [Borges and Sciascia] found, a withering of promise" (282). Robb shows here how some conventions of contemporary, postmodern travel writing (discontinuous narrative, allusiveness, free allegory; see chap. 4) can be used to produce a defined rendering of culture, rather than—as is more usually the case—freeing the material from such "historical" portraits. If Robb corresponds to a type of Tisdale's searching traveler-writer, he leaves the reader feeling that he has found at least part of what he sought. At the same time, Robb's travel book suggests possibilities for the replenishment of the genre through an intuitive, informed use of some of its most traditional elements: the quest to become an insider without resorting to appropriative arrogance; the deployment of a firm yet flexible repertoire of cultural knowledge; the practice of a lively and nuanced narrative art. Such resources are still available, and their adoption holds more promise than the tactic, more commonly practiced, of falling back on forms of generic imitation (see chap. 2).

At the millennium, the travel writer occupies a compromised, ambivalent position. On the one hand, as we have seen, he or she is likely to be dismissed as a pulp producer, a pawn of crass industry pressures, an overexuberant performer, even a liar: as a participant, in short, in what Jonathan Raban has memorably called "a notoriously raffish house where very different genres are likely to end up in the same bed . . . literature's red-light district" (qtd. in Bourke 46). Raban, who has declared that he "absolutely detest[s] the term 'travel writer,'" recites a familiar catalogue of the genre's stock-in-trade types:

> the classic young person's travel book, which is basically descended from the picaresque novel; the adventures of a rolling stone in foreign territory; the political journey; social history; some very explicit fiction writing, particularly Waugh, Greene and Robert Byron's *The Road to Oxiana;* landscape writing, which is almost the verbal equivalent of landscape painting; and the travel book which belongs in the genre of memoir. (Qtd. in Bourke 46)

Yet Raban, a leading practitioner, still very much believes in the travel *book,* distinguishing between the type of book that is little more than an assemblage of fragments, a promiscuous mixture, and the one that subtly modulates between different literary registers and cultural resources. Raban clearly knows what he believes to be a "superior" travel book; but neither he nor anyone else can provide a prescription—a formula—for it.

Millennial thinking is, by definition, a form of closure; it radically domesticates time and space by turning them into ghosts in the house. Travel, at least potentially, opens up a world of estrangement: one in which the work—the travail—of travel is to engage with others productively, to produce a site or number of sites that resist uniformity, and that gesture instead to difference, "otherness," and a diversity of (cross-)cultural forms. This study has suggested that travel and travel writing are flourishing, and will continue to flourish beyond the millennium. Some of the reasons for this are only too apparent. It is certainly true that selling travel is one of the things that helps to sell travel books, and that these sales pay literal tribute to all the clichés of the moment: a shrinking world, "global culture," the containment of cultural difference through the processes of commodification. Yet it is also true that the travel book, through its negotiation of time, space, and culture, continues to engage large numbers and several different kinds of readers. There is every reason to invite the travel book to reexamine its biases, to realign the boundaries within which travel risks being reified and paradoxically immobilized as a discursive category. There is no reason, though, to announce an obituary on travel or, what would be just as premature, to decree travel writing's end.

NOTES

INTRODUCTION

1. Private conversation with Martin Roberts, 1996; with thanks.

2. Travel writing is, of course, a primary vehicle for the exotic insofar as it registers appreciation of—sometimes revulsion for—peoples and cultures considered "different" or "remote." The exoticist objectification of the cultural "other" is a staple of travel writing, as is the conversion of "other" cultures into a media-friendly spectacle. Victor Segalen's definition of exoticism as the "aesthetics of diversity" is well suited to a genre that frequently depoliticizes (and/or dehistoricizes) the objects of its study, and that seeks to capitalize on aestheticized myths of cultural difference. As an exoticist mode, Euro-American travel writing risks being seen as tacitly imperialist: see, for example, Arac and Ritvo's definition of exoticism as "the aestheticizing means by which the pain of [imperial] expansion is converted to spectacle, to culture in the service of empire" (3). For further discussion of the exoticist project in its historical perspective, see Bongie, the introduction to Rousseau and Porter, and Todorov.

3. See, for example, Eric Newby's and Redmond O'Hanlon's self-mocking attempts to pass themselves off as nineteenth-century travelers (chap. 1), or the ubiquitous distaste for tourists shown in the work of, among many others, Paul Theroux (chap. 2). The rhetoric of nostalgia often accompanies such distinctions—a nostalgia on which, ironically, the modern tourist industry depends. See here Culler's essay "The Semiotics of Tourism"; Frow's "Tourism and the Semiotics of Nostalgia"; MacCannell's *The Tourist;* Krotz's less analytical *Tourists;* and Buzard, esp. chaps. 1 and 2. As Culler says, "[F]erocious denigration of tourism is in part an attempt to convince oneself that one is not a tourist. . . . The desire to distinguish between tourists and real travelers is a part of tourism—integral to it rather than outside it or beyond it" (156). Travel writing, by corollary, remains complicit with the (mass) tourism it denounces; and while it may be given to see itself as an antidote to modern tourism, its more usual effect may be to provide a further incentive for it.

4. For an account of the "reality effect" of contemporary travel writing, see Pratt's discussion of Theroux's work in the final chapter of *Imperial Eyes.* Pratt offers the following reasons for her students' defense of Theroux's "veracity": "The depth-creating powers of the travel writer must compete with the ten-day nine-night air package, tips included, and the glossy, disembodied fantasies of tourist propaganda. In the 1960s and 1970s, exoticist visions of plenitude and paradise were appropriated and commodified on an unprecedented scale by the tourist industry. 'Real' writers took up the task of providing 'realist' (degraded, counter-

219

commodified) versions of postcolonial reality. The 'effect of the real' Theroux had on the class I taught was doubtless constructed in part out of students' own identification with 'real' representation over and against commodified representations through which tourism, quite successfully, markets the world to them" (221).

5. See here also Leed, esp. introduction and epilogue. For Leed, "the history of travel is in crucial ways a history of the west. It recounts the evolution from necessity to freedom, an evolution that gave rise to a new consciousness, the peculiar mentality of the modern traveler" (14). Here as elsewhere in his book (as also in Cocker's), Leed prefers to see freedom in generalized existential terms—thereby eliding the economic distinctions that usually make travel possible.

6. See, for example, the rather weighty introduction to Van den Abbeele's *Travel as Metaphor.* For Van den Abbeele, the metaphor of travel is paradoxical: it necessarily implies a change of place, yet it is predicated on, and restricted by, a certain conception of home (the *oikos*). "Home, the very antithesis of travel, is the concept through which the voyage is 'oikonomized' into a commonplace" (xviii). Hence the contradiction: "Despite its association with the interesting or the innovative, the motif of the voyage counts as among the most manifestly banal in Western letters" (xiii). For a different view of the dialectic between "home" and displacement in the age of postmodernity, see the essays in Robertson et al., and Caren Kaplan's *Questions of Travel.* It is interesting to note the discrepancy between "transgressive" academic approaches to travel and the more traditional, often nostalgic, narratives that are still very common in contemporary travel writing. This discrepancy is discussed further in chapters 3 and 4 of this book.

7. On belatedness in travel writing, see Behdad, *Belated Travelers.* For Behdad, travel writing expresses the "exoticist desire for the disappearing other" (14); "belated orientalists," such as Flaubert in the nineteenth century, are traveler-writers struggling to "come to terms with the loss of the object of [their] desires—the disappearance of the Orient, its dissolution by European colonialism" (66). Flaubert's travel writing inscribes the "impossibility of . . . dreams of restoration" (66); it articulates the desire to preserve a past that has already passed into myth. Twentieth-century travel writing like, say, O'Hanlon's also articulates this desire, but with more than a measure of self-parody. See the discussion of O'Hanlon's work, and of his attitude to belatedness, in chapter 1 of this book.

8. See Frow and also Bongie (e.g., 4–5), for a discussion of the complex relationship between travel writing, exoticism, and nostalgia. Nostalgia, as Frow and Bongie suggest, enacts a dialectic of desire: it seeks a past of its own invention that it knows in advance to be impossible. But while nostalgia offers a spurious panacea for disaffection with a "degraded" present, it is its very falseness, paradoxically, that makes it so appealing. The "inauthenticity" of nostalgia is its own motivating force; tourism and, indirectly, travel writing turn this afflictive desire to their own material advantage, exploiting to commercial ends nostalgia's self-perpetuating anxiety. Hence the elegiac strain in much contemporary travel writing, as it yearns nostalgically for lost visions of "authentic" experience. For an exploration of the ironies implicit in this position, see the discussion of Rosaldo's term "imperialist nostalgia" in chapter 1 of this book.

9. See, for example, Watt's discussion of verisimilitude in the early novel in *The Rise of the Novel,* chapter 1, or the attempt to account for the influence of Defoe's journalism on his fiction in chapters 3 and 4.

10. White's argument applies primarily to Western historiography, whose

tropological nature defies some of its practitioners' claims to recorded "fact." The status of the "factual" in travel writing is further complicated, both by the (often conspicuous) unreliability of the information being presented and by the ambivalent function of the presenter as a reporter/storyteller. While some travel writers claim, or wish to claim, documentary status for their work, it is clear that most travel narratives are infused with the traveler-writer's subjectivity. Also, like certain kinds of investigative journalists, travel writers often withhold their sources—they mediate between the desire to impart verifiable information and the temptation to obfuscate, to present the spectacle of "mystique." Travel writing, in this context, is not just profit-driven or entertainment-oriented, but may be used to chart the limits of knowledge and to test the claims of information. For further discussions of the truth claims of travel writing, see the introductions to Mary Campbell and Nixon; for detailed analysis of the interplay between "fact" and fiction in referential writing, see also Foley, Sauerberg, and the essays in Weber, esp. MacDonald's piece on "parajournalism."

11. See also Pratt's essay "Fieldwork in Common Places." Like Wheeler, Pratt deconstructs the opposition between travelers and ethnographers, commenting for example on the figure of the "castaway" as a popular, strategically mystificatory self-image for the ethnographer. "The authority of the ethnographer over the 'mere traveler' rests chiefly on the idea that the traveler just passes through, whereas the ethnographer lives with the group under study. But of course this is what captives and castaways often do too, living in another culture in every capacity from prince to slave, learning indigenous languages and lifeways with a proficiency an ethnographer would envy, and often producing accounts that are indeed full, rich, and accurate by ethnography's own standards" (38). Like Wheeler, Pratt uses comparisons with travel writing to demystify ethnography's pretension to objectivity, and to draw attention to the investment placed by both travel writing and anthropology in exoticist representations of a designated cultural "other." See here also Keesing's essay "Exotic Readings of Cultural Texts." Like Pratt and Wheeler, Keesing sees ethnographers as "dealers in exotica"; he goes further, however, than either in claiming that the anthropological "predilection for purveying exotica" impels ethnographers "not only to choose the most exotic possible cultural data for [their] texts but to give them the most exotic possible readings—and, in doing so, often distort and mistranslate" (459–60). The difference with travel writing here is that many travel writers willfully mistranslate and distort; they are not constrained by the same rules and regulations governing the presentation of "factual" data, and outlandish interpretations of such data are not only common to, but sometimes desirable in, the genre. For further discussion of the links between travel writing and ethnography, see chapters 2 and 3 (on Varawa's "uncommon anthropology").

12. The notorious diatribe against travel writing at the beginning of *Tristes Tropiques* cannot disguise the fact that Lévi-Strauss goes on to produce, precisely, an ethnographic travel narrative. For a further discussion of the ironic implications of his disclaimer, see the section on Amazon travel in chapter 2. Despite the obvious slippage in Lévi-Strauss's argument, the venom that accompanies his dismissal of travel writing remains memorable (see the excerpt from *Tristes Tropiques* in the preface to this book).

13. See Ignatieff's interview with Chatwin and also Chatwin's posthumous collection *Anatomy of Restlessness* (discussed in chap. 4).

14. The definition is taken from *Chambers Twentieth Century Dictionary* (Edinburgh: Pitman Press, 1981), 818.

15. See Rosaldo, esp. 68–74; see also the discussion of imperialist nostalgia in chapter 1.

16. For Pratt, contemporary travel writing often hearkens back to "lost idioms of discovery and domination" (*Imperial Eyes* 224); in continuing to deploy imperialist tropes such as the "monarch-of-all-I-survey," it replaces the nineteenth-century White Man's Burden with the twentieth-century White Man's Lament (chap. 9, esp. 216–21).

17. See Mary Campbell, *The Witness and the Other World*, esp. chaps. 2 (on the medieval Wonder Book) and 5 (on Columbus's voyages). As Campbell notes acerbically, "[Columbus's] *Journal* and the *Letter* conflate the Earthly Paradise of Mandeville's East with the pastoral *locus amoenus;* the result is a Caribbean that belongs as much to the Other World of medieval geographic fantasy as it does to the map [he] helped realize. . . . [His] literal belief in the fantastic may seem charming to a modern reader, but may well have helped propagate the monstrous stereotypes through which the Spanish Empire perceived—and monstrously abused—its American 'subjects'" (10–11).

18. See Greenblatt, 128–36, and Mary Campbell, chaps. 5 and 6; see also de Certeau, for whom "the discourse that sets off in search of the other with the impossible task of saying the truth returns from afar with the authority to speak in the name of the other and command belief" (69).

19. On voyeurism in anthropology, see Torgovnick's discussion of the work of Malinowski and Mead in chap. 5 of *Gone Primitive,* 225–43; see also Hawthorn's "The Politics of the Exotic" and Lutz and Collins's critical study *Reading National Geographic,* for discussions of the voyeuristic tendencies of dominant cultures in their perception and exploitation of those whom they strategically consider "other." All of these writers detect a link between cultural voyeurism as imperialist practice and the objectification—the "othering"—of the ethnicized/gendered body; for a further discussion of this relationship, see chap. 3 in this book.

20. See Lutz and Collins, esp. chaps. 4 and 7. As they observe, "Nothing defines the *National Geographic* for most older American readers more than its 'naked' women. The widely shared cultural experience of viewing women's bodies in the magazine draws on and acculturates the audience's ideas about race, gender, and sexuality, with the marked subcategory in each case being black, female, and the unrepressed. . . . [T]he magazine's nudity forms a central part of the image of the non-West that it purveys" (115).

21. In exoticism, according to Todorov, "otherness is systematically preferred to likeness" (264). But "otherness," by definition, is also separated from likeness; the effect of exoticist representation is to derealize the represented subject. As Todorov explains in an instructive comparison of the "exotic" and "colonial" novels: "The exotic novel glorifies foreigners while the colonial novel denigrates them. But the contradiction is only apparent. Once the author has declared that he himself is the only subject on board and that the others have been reduced to the role of objects, it is after all of secondary concern whether these objects are loved or despised. The essential point is that they are not full-fledged human beings" (323). The exoticist relationship between "self" and "other" is more complex than Todorov implies; nonetheless, Todorov's argument helps account for the singular

discrepancy in much travel writing between the expressed attraction toward "other" people/cultures and the tacit wish to keep them at a distance.

   22. For a discussion of the further implications of cross-dressing, see chap. 3 of this book.

   23. For a critique of the—explicit or implicit—ethnocentrism of Euro-American travel writing, see the introductions to Porter's *Haunted Journeys* and Pratt's *Imperial Eyes;* see also, in more polemical vein, Sugnet. Chapter 1 of this book deals in some detail with "postcolonial" alternatives to these Eurocentric models.

   24. The work of James Clifford is exemplary here: see, for instance, his essays "Traveling Cultures" and "Diasporas," reprinted in his most recent book *Routes* (1997), and the special edition of the journal *Inscriptions,* ed. Clifford and Dhareshwar (1989). The emergence of transnational and/or postnational studies as an academic discipline is signaled in new journals such as *Diaspora* and *Public Culture,* which focus on complex flows (of information, ideas, money, etc.) that traverse, transcend, and challenge the status of national/cultural boundaries. For expressly transnational approaches to travel writing, see the recent work of Grewal and Caren Kaplan. See also chapters 1 and, especially, 4 of this book.

   25. See, for example, Bhabha's essay "DissemiNation," in his edited *Nation and Narration;* for a more detailed discussion of the "emergence of a postnational order," see also Appadurai, *Modernity at Large.*

   26. The term *transculturation* is usually accredited to the Cuban anthropologist Fernando Ortiz. For its applicability to travel writing, see Pratt, *Imperial Eyes;* also, in this book, the discussion of Iyer's work in chapter 1.

   27. For a discussion of the impact of speed on (post)modern society, see Virilio. For Virilio, speed potentially erases the gaps that separate global spaces—precisely the gaps that travel and travel writing occupy. Virilio's emphasis is on the violence of speed and its deployment in the global arms race; speed consists in "the acceleration of the means of communicating destruction" (138). What speed ultimately gestures toward, according to Virilio, is "the end of the world as distance"; but this "distanceless" world in which "every locality . . . is juxtapos[ed]" creates a "fearsome friction of places and elements that only yesterday were still distinct and separated by a buffer of distances" (136). Virilio's is a paranoid vision akin, to some extent, to Deleuze and Guattari's influential "Treatise on Nomadology." It is a useful counterweight, nonetheless, to contemporary media fantasies of a happy "global village" brought together through "instant" communication, and enjoying the fruits of a single world united in the pursuit of consumer goods. For further discussions of the impact of speed and/or globalization on travel writing, see also chapters 1 and 4 of this book.

   28. The British edition of Fraser's anthology is instructive in its change of title: *Worst Trips,* as if the aggravation merely increased with each retelling.

   29. On the phenomenon of the "theoretical traveler," see the essays in Clifford and Dhareshwar, and also Van den Abbeele's essay "Sightseers: The Tourist as Theorist."

   30. See Feifer, *Going Places,* for an analysis of the implications of "post-tourism." See also Huggan's discussion of Feifer in the essay "Some Recent Australian Fictions." From Huggan's essay: "Post-tourists, according to Feifer, are distanced from the tourist world, yet open to the many delights it offers; theirs is a democracy of taste, as likely to take pleasure in a cheap piece of mass-produced kitsch as in an expensive item of local handicrafts, aware that the one is no more

genuine than the other, and that both are products of a leisure industry designed to convert the trappings of indigenous culture into a profitable supply of consumer goods" (173).

CHAPTER ONE

1. Newby cites directly from Waugh's preface to *A Short Walk* at the end of the introduction to *A Traveller's Life.*

2. For further discussions of imperialist nostalgia in the context of travel and travel writing, see the relevant sections of Grewal (esp. 151) and Caren Kaplan (esp. *Questions of Travel* 70–71).

3. See Nixon's essay on the Naipaul brothers, "Preparations for Travel." Conrad is one of the Naipauls's favorite writers: see, for example, "Conrad's Darkness" in *The Return of Eva Peron.* See also O'Hanlon's critical study of Conrad, *Joseph Conrad and Charles Darwin,* in which he traces the influences of Darwin's evolutionary thought on Conrad's fiction. O'Hanlon's work belongs to a self-consciously primitivist school of travel writing that trades, sometimes ironically, on the "backwardness" and seductiveness of "remote" indigenous peoples. Travel writing is a primary vehicle for the reinvention of the "primitive" in the overdeveloped (Western) world of the late twentieth century. For a useful discussion of primitivist tropes circulating in Western consumer culture, see Torgovnick, particularly the first section "Going Primitive" and the subsection "Traveling with Conrad." Also relevant here is Michael Taussig's work on the figure of the "wild man." The "primitive" and the "wild man," tropes liberally sprinkled throughout O'Hanlon's work, testify both to the exoticist construction of the "other" in travel writing and to the genre's continuing critical role in interrogating a putatively civilized self.

4. Useful background on the Brookes is provided in the chapter on *Lord Jim* in Moses's *The Novel and the Globalization of Culture.*

5. The irony here is that Newby is a full-time professional travel writer who, like other well-known travel writers, is working on commission in a lucrative field. Newby is by no means alone in choosing to downplay this professional aspect. Travel writers rarely let us know about their income, or inform us about the economic circumstances behind their trips. It could be argued, of course, that such information is uninteresting to the reader. But it also suggests that travel writers like to keep their motives hidden, or at least to pretend that their trips, often prepaid and preprogrammed, are generated by nothing more than artless curiosity and spontaneous enthusiasm.

6. Travel writing, of course, has a venerable tradition of artful lying and prankish deceit: see, for example, Percy Adams's *Travelers and Travel Liars,* or the chapter on Mandeville in Mary Campbell's *The Witness and the Other World.* Wilde's recuperation of lying as "the proper aim of art" is expressed with characteristic wit in his seminal essay "The Decay of Lying."

7. On Chatwin's "nomad aesthetic," see the italicized sections of *The Songlines,* which both explore the metaphysics of restlessness and imitate it in literary form. See also Huggan's discussion of *The Songlines* in his essay "Maps, Dreams, and the Presentation of Ethnographic Narrative"; and the treatment of nomadism elsewhere in this book, especially in chapter 4.

8. Malraux describes the museum without walls in *The Voices of Silence;*

Chatwin's profile of Malraux can be found in *What Am I Doing Here* (114–35). The museum is a topos of travel writing, drawing attention to the discrepancy between the mobility of traveler-writers and the curatorial immobilization of the peoples/cultures about which they write. Chatwin, like several of his contemporaries, is an enthusiastic museum visitor; but the museum is equally important as an illustrative metaphor for the process of travel writing itself as it gathers, observes, and reifies its culturally "othered" subjects.

9. See, for example, the dubiously cathartic ending of *The Songlines,* a tongue-in-cheek paean to a "dying" people, obviously camp in sensibility, which turns a pseudomystical appreciation for Aboriginal Australia into another aestheticized cameo of a "wondrous" nomadic race.

10. On the duties and symbolic importance of the squire, see Castronovo, esp. 79–80, 102–4.

11. For an extended discussion of the notion of conspicuous consumption, see Veblen's classic study *The Theory of the Leisure Class.* Veblen's work clearly underscores MacCannell's socioanthropological approach to tourism (see *The Tourist* 11–12). Tourism is of course itself a mode of consumption, both literally (the purchase of goods and services) and metaphorically (the practice of "sightseeing"). The conspicuous consumption of leisure in Mayle's Provence narratives is literalized in the gourmet meal.

12. Continuing in the tradition of the travelogue-as-cookbook are Tom Higgins, *Spotted Dick, S'il Vous Plaît* (1995), a quirky account of the author's first eight years as an English restauranteur in Lyon (including twelve recipes); Peter Biddlecombe, *Travels with My Briefcase* (1994), where the author's business trips provide the pretext for a series of succulent expense-account dinners; and, not least, Mayle himself, whose *Acquired Tastes* (1993) furthers the search undertaken in the Provence books for gentlemanly luxury by taking vicarious pleasure in the extravagant spending—and, particularly, eating—habits of the rich. Finally, see also Peter Robb, *Midnight in Sicily* (1996)—discussed in the postscript to this book—where the author's strongly aestheticized descriptions of traditional Italian cuisine are held in counterpoint to his accounts of Mafia violence.

13. See the chapter on Naipaul, "Originary Displacement and the Writer's Burden," in Porter.

14. For a thoroughgoing critique of Naipaul's travel writing, see Nixon, *London Calling.* As Nixon points out, Naipaul's anti-imperialist stance is inevitably compromised by his ambivalent subject position as the First World's expert on the Third World and as an expatriate cultural critic.

15. For a critique of Naipaul's view of himself as a ubiquitous exile, see Nixon, *London Calling,* esp. chap. 1.

16. On Naipaul's "mimicry thesis," and the (often heated) response to it in the Caribbean, see Huggan, "A Tale of Two Parrots" and, particularly, Walcott.

17. On Naipaul's perception of the dilemma of "historylessness" in the Caribbean region, see his controversial historical study *The Middle Passage,* esp. the introduction.

18. For a sample of recent critiques of the totalizing tendencies of postcolonial theory and criticism, see Ahmad's essay "Postcolonialism: What's in a Name?" and McClintock's and Shohat's essays in a special issue, devoted mainly to Ahmad, of *Social Text* (1992). It has arguably become more fashionable to

attack postcolonialism than to defend it; but in spite (or possibly because?) of this, postcolonial studies prospers.

19. For an exploration of this discrepancy, see Appiah's chapter "The Postmodern and the Postcolonial" in *Africa in the Philosophy of Culture.*

20. See, for example, Bryson, *Neither Here Nor There* (1991); and Theroux, *The Pillars of Hercules: A Grand Tour of the Mediterranean* (1995). See also, on the grand tour, Porter; Leed, 184–85; and Buzard, 97–110.

21. See the title essay of Rushdie's collection *Imaginary Homelands,* where he describes himself as a "literary migrant," a product of cultural transplantation and of the "literary cross-pollination" of an international era (20–21). For a critique of this position, and of the cosmopolitan privileges it disguises, see Brennan, *Salman Rushdie and the Third World;* also Huggan's "The Postcolonial Exotic," which discusses the implications of Rushdie's status as a beleaguered celebrity.

22. See, particularly, *The Satanic Verses* (1988), which is, among many other things, a ludic allegory of the demonization of British immigrants.

23. See, for example, the somewhat naive celebration of "migrancy" in Chambers. As Caren Kaplan points out in *Questions of Travel,* the fashionable theories surrounding the figure of the diasporic migrant may be little more than postmodern updates of earlier, equally uncritical, notions of the modernist exile (140). Such theories, in invoking the universal poststructuralist mantra of "displacement," risk "obfuscating and even erasing the representation of social relations in historically grounded and politically meaningful ways" (140). For further discussions of "migrancy" and/as "displacement," see chapters 3 and, especially, 4 of this book.

24. Said's essay is the (direct or indirect) inspiration behind a whole new school of cultural critics who practice "traveling theory," Georges van den Abbeele, Caren Kaplan, James Clifford, Iain Chambers, and Rey Chow among them. For an overview, see Clifford, *Routes;* Kaplan, *Questions of Travel;* and the essays in Clifford and Dhareshwar.

25. See, particularly, the introduction and "The Scope of Orientalism" in Said's *Orientalism.* Although it has attracted a good deal of negative criticism, this remains one of the foundation texts for contemporary postcolonial studies.

26. See the section on "imaginative geography" in *Orientalism,* 49–72. Imaginative geography, for Said, provides an expansive image-repertoire that legitimates distinctions between the familiar, "inside" spaces of dominant (imperial) cultures and the "outer" reaches of the "barbarians" whose territories they invade and whose cultures they subjugate. As Said suggests, and as his followers (e.g., Behdad) have gone on to demonstrate in more detail, travel writing—particularly European travel writing—has tended to bolster preconceived cultural distinctions: it has served as a vehicle of "imaginative geography" that answers the dominant culture's needs.

27. Several contemporary travel narratives have contributed to popular myths of Asian ascendancy: see, for example, Winchester, *Pacific Rising,* and Viviano.

28. Roberts's work, currently in progress, charts the transition from European "planetary consciousness" (Pratt, *Imperial Eyes* 9–10) to the transnational "global imaginary," seeing the boom in travel writing—and tourism in general—as symptoms of a postmodern condition in which the capitalist world-system produces and manipulates images of a "global culture."

29. Timothy Brennan, in *At Home in the World* (1997), takes this criticism further, seeing Iyer (and other travel writers like him) as endorsing a utopian globalism that fails to acknowledge its own, pointedly Euro-American, frame of cultural reference. For Brennan, Iyer's travel writing fuses a naively "up-to-date" internationalism with a nostalgic "colonial erotics." The result is a refashioned exoticism, more continuous with imperialisms of the past than critical of imperialisms of the present, and wholly complicit with the global process of Americanization it claims to resist. While Brennan's criticisms have some validity, his argument is weakened by his tendency to contrast writers like Iyer, self-serving cosmopolitans, with writers like Rushdie, Dorfman, and Gordimer, whose travelogues take the form of political interventions. As with the example of *The Jaguar Smile,* analyzed earlier in this chapter, such distinctions—presumably based on political stance and degree of perceived commitment—are complicated by a genre that tends (as Brennan recognizes) to aestheticize the dispossessed.

30. The travel "zones" selected for discussion in the following chapter are intended to provide some balance; comprehensive coverage is out of the question, though, so to some extent the "zones" chosen reflect the authors' current interests and preferences. The popularity of particular "zones"—and the narratives attached to them—shifts according to fashion, a recent instance being the spate of travel books (notably Jon Krakauer's) on Mount Everest expeditions.

CHAPTER TWO

1. For a rather different, but influential usage, see also Pratt's invocation of the "contact zone" in *Imperial Eyes.* The contact zone is "an attempt to invoke the spatial and temporal copresence of subjects previously separated by geographical and historical disjunctures, and whose trajectories now intersect. . . . A 'contact' perspective emphasizes how subjects are constituted in and by their relations to each other. It treats the relation among colonizers and colonized, or travelers and 'travelees,' not in terms of separateness or apartheid, but in terms of copresence, interaction, interlocking understandings and practices, often within radically asymmetrical relations of power" (7). Pratt's "zone" emphasizes, to a greater extent than McHale's, the often intricate workings of (imperial) power; like McHale's, however, it is a site of contention, of continual renegotiation: it is shaped and reshaped by a history of social interaction and ideological conflict.

2. The Belgian Congo (1908–60) took the name Zaire in 1971. On May 17, 1997—after a period of instability and internal resistance to Mobutu—it became the Democratic Republic of the Congo.

3. Hyland describes his African journey as "transgressing the hot limit" (21–22), borrowing the phrase the "hot limit" loosely from Camões's *Os Lusiades,* the sixteenth-century Portuguese epic poem. For Camões, what was later to become Conrad's/Marlow's "dark" river had never before been "seen by the ancients"; this conveniently clears the way for Camões to celebrate the "discovery" of the Congo by the Portuguese explorer Giorgio Cão in 1482.

4. On the prevalence of "low," demonized images (strategies of "debasement" and "abjection") in colonial discourses, see Spurr.

5. For a further discussion of the impact of Naipaul's colonial background on his travel writing, see Nixon, *London Calling,* and the section on Naipaul's *The Enigma of Arrival* in the previous chapter of this book.

6. For a more recent chronicle of an East African trip under the sign of AIDS, see Conover.

7. See, particularly, Lévi-Strauss's landmark *Tristes Tropiques*. Drawing on a European tradition of mythicizing the Amazon, *Tristes Tropiques* has itself become a mythical text for a whole new school of environmentally-minded travel writers. For further background on myths of the Amazon, see Slater; see also the discussion of "ecotravel writing" in chapter 4 of this book.

8. See, for example, Cahill's dispatches from the jungle in *Jaguars Ripped My Flesh* (1996) and *A Wolverine Is Eating My Leg* (1994). Like O'Hanlon (and so many others), Cahill takes inspiration from Conrad, accentuating the dangers of the jungle but also its capacity for farce and high jinks. Also like O'Hanlon, Cahill stresses the physicality of travel, favoring a waggish voyeurism and a (dubious) taste for the scatological joke. Unlike O'Hanlon's, however, Cahill's books are not sustained picaresque narratives, but collections of—often irreverent—journalistic reports ranging broadly in time and space.

9. Both *In Trouble Again* and *Into the Heart of Borneo* include fairly extensive bibliographies; O'Hanlon, for all his faults, cannot be accused of not having done his homework.

10. O'Hanlon draws most obviously on the work of Napoleon Chagnon, whose sensationalist account of Yanomami aggression has proven popular with Amazon travel writers. O'Hanlon's unashamedly amateur anthropology also hints, however, at the work of earlier evolutionary anthropologists, such as Edward Tylor, whose influential treatise on "primitive" culture is much invoked but little understood. O'Hanlon's understanding of anthropology is by no means as naive as his narrative implies; he is profiting, here as elsewhere, from the rhetorical stance of the faux naïf (as also suggested in the introduction to this book). See also Porter's comment, in his chapter on Darwin, that "the professional naturalist [often] turns out to be . . . a perceptive amateur ethnographer, who comments on racial or cultural difference as well as on diverse forms of collective behavior or social organization" (148). O'Hanlon is well aware of his limitations as an ethnographer, but, like many other travel writers, he cannot resist an observation or two against his better judgment.

11. On the "scientific traveler-writer," see Porter's chapter on Darwin; chapter 1 of Pratt's *Imperial Eyes;* chapter 7 of Leed's *The Mind of the Traveler;* and Peter Raby's *Bright Paradise*. It is as common for travel writers to disguise their scientific authority as to invoke it—a strategy that supports their advantageous rhetorical position as inquiring amateurs. For a discussion of the rhetorical benefits of (dissimulated) "amateurism," see the introduction to this book and, especially, the section on Eric Newby in chapter 1.

12. On "wildness" in an Amazonian context, see Taussig.

13. There are many image/myth patterns in the Western repertoire of Japan other than that of the eroticized Orient: for example, a masculine Japan of feudal hierarchy and militarism, or a demonized Japan of grotesque monsters (see Buruma). In the case of Western literary representations of Japan, the selection of an erotic paradigm not only reflects a dominant strain in travel writing, but also signals the West's inability to deal with the complexity of a range of nonidentical cultural characteristics.

14. For a discussion of Loti's other erotic narratives, see Bongie, 79–106.

15. See Kaori O'Connor's introduction to Loti, *Madame Chrysanthemum,* esp. 5.

16. Particularly influential among these was Lafcadio Hearn, whose surprisingly full and complex commentaries on Japan were reaching America in the late nineteenth century. The range of these commentaries—along with Hearn's modesty—detracted from their ability to "fix" a singular image of Japan for many Western readers. See Francis King's representative selection of Hearn's work in *Writings from Japan.*

17. Jean-Pierre Lehmann has provided a useful account of the story's transmission, and of its various transformations, in his essay "Images of the Orient," in a special issue of *Opera Guide.* The text of John Luther Long's story "Madame Butterfly" can be found in the same volume. Transferred from Japan to Vietnam, and from the late nineteenth to the late twentieth century, the story of the abandoned Oriental woman continues to hold sway in the popular musical *Miss Saigon.*

18. A popular narrative in this vein is Mark Salzman's *Iron & Silk* (1986). Salzman, a martial-arts expert, taught English in China in the early eighties, then starred in a martial-arts movie before moving back to his native United States.

19. For a comparison of *Empire of Signs* with other Orientalist narratives by French poststructuralist writer-intellectuals, see Lowe, esp. chap. 5.

20. On Cook and the Pacific, see the work of Bernard Smith; see also the often ill-tempered exchange between the anthropologists Marshall Sahlins and Gananath Obeyesekere over the mythical status of Cook.

21. See, for example, the discussion of Joana Varawa's "ethnographic" travel writing, and of its indebtedness to Mead, in chapter 3 of this book. For a critical view, see also Albert Wendt's essay "Toward A New Oceania." Wendt, a native Samoan, complains bitterly about the mythologizing of the "South Seas" as a site for ethnographic voyeurism and commercialized Euro-American fantasy. Several of these myths are critically analyzed in Neil Rennie's *Far-Fetched Facts.*

22. For a fuller, Foucault-inflected discussion of the emergence of a new knowledge-regime in eighteenth-century Europe, focusing particularly on the intersections between geography, anthropology, and travel observation, see Gregory, esp. 16–30.

23. Theroux is one of the most self-reflexive of contemporary travel writers; for an analytical overview of his often self-ironic commentaries, see Glaser, "The Self-Reflexive Traveler," and also Glaser's "Paul Theroux and the Poetry of Departures."

24. See Bongie's *Exotic Memories* for a thorough investigation of (modern) Western exotic myths; see also the introduction to this book for further discussions of exoticism—that ambivalent discourse of the "other" that underpins so much travel writing.

25. It is worth noting here, as in much of Theroux's travel writing, a purgatorial tinge; this becomes more prominent in the writers of Arctic travel discussed later in this chapter.

26. Woodcock performs a similar elegizing act on an old beachcomber in Samoa: "I wondered whether he was really . . . the last of those wandering Melvillean sailors, fetched up at last to die upon some distant strand, or whether he was a Mendelian throwback, grandson or great-grandson of the original beachcomber, his long line taken into the absorbent and infinitely tolerant fabric of fa'a Samoa" (76).

27. On belatedness, see the introduction to this book, which draws on the work of, among others, Ali Behdad.

28. On the symbiotic relationship between exoticism and nostalgia, see Bongie, particularly the chapter on Conrad. The nostalgic impulses of travel writing are discussed several times in this book: see the introduction, for example, or the treatment of Newby's and O'Hanlon's work in chapter 1.

29. The Canadian Ronald Wright, author of the acclaimed *Time among the Maya,* seems obsessed by the protocols surrounding hospitality and the exchange of gifts. See, for example, Wright's travelogue *On Fiji Islands* (1986), where his gift giving, like Theroux's, is perhaps intended to diminish his privilege while attempting to gain insider status. While travel books, despite appearances, rarely communicate Bakhtinian "heteroglossia"—a multiplicity of languages and viewpoints— they can and occasionally do convey a degree of "subaltern resistance" (Guha), as in the unexpected rebuff that so irritated Theroux. For a discussion of the relevance of Bakhtinian concepts to cross-cultural perception and representation, see the introduction to James Clifford's (meta-)anthropological study, *The Predicament of Culture.* Clifford's argument is clearly relevant to travel writers like Wright and Theroux, whose work is obviously influenced by relativist ethnography.

30. The "in search of" trope is a common one among contemporary travel writers, who frequently hark back (sometimes ironically) to their predecessors. See, for example, the discussion of O'Hanlon's work in this chapter and in chapter 1. See also yet another Conradian travel book, very much in the spirit of Bell's: Gavin Young's *In Search of Conrad* (1991).

31. See Hugh Brody, *The People's Land* (1991), esp. chap. 5, "White Attitudes to the Inuit."

32. For further discussion of the distinction between "areal" and "linear," see Leer.

33. The lifeworld—a term derived from the phenomenology of Husserl—is explained by the geographer Anne Buttimer as "the culturally defined spatiotemporal setting or horizon of everyday life" (277). For alternative perspectives on the lifeworld, see the essays in Buttimer and Seamon, and also the "geosophical" essays in Lowenthal and Bowden, especially those by Allen and Tuan. For a critique of Buttimer's and Tuan's phenomenological approach to geography, see Pickles.

34. See Lopez's discussion of the migratory patterns of Arctic birds and animals in chapters 3 and 5 of *Arctic Dreams.* The lives of many of these birds and animals, says Lopez, "are constrained by the schemes of men, but the determination in their lives, the traditional pattern of movement, are a calming reminder of a more fundamental order" (155). Thus, in a gesture characteristic of Lopez's pattern-seeking narrative, the animals' mobility consists in their capacity to repeat their movements according to preestablished codes.

35. All three writers, but most obviously Lopez, are influenced by Yi-Fu Tuan's phenomenological geography: one that emphasizes the effect of human perception on the landscapes that people inhabit and, to some extent, shape according to their fears and desires. "Topophilia" is a perception of the land as benevolent and/or curative; it is based on a special affinity with certain places. For further discussion, see the opening chapter of Tuan's *Topophilia* (1974).

36. Antarctica, that territory at the other polar limit, is now a much-visited travel-writing destination. The ill-fated Scott expedition performs a catalyzing role

similar to that of the third Franklin expedition for the Arctic; the literary monument here is Apsley Cherry-Garrard's *The Worst Journey in the World* (1922). The most recent Antarctic travel narratives, interestingly, are both by women. Jenny Diski's *Skating to Antarctica* (1997) mobilizes the experience of travel to, and in, Antarctica for a kind of psychic archaeology related to the musings of Lopez, Wiebe, and Moss, with the very starkness of the visual images melding imperceptibly with states of isolation and deprivation to produce a story. In contrast, Sara Wheeler, in *Terra Incognita: Travels in Antarctica* (1996), finds that it is male territory, a place where men have imposed their (imagined) mastery upon nature. In several important respects, of course, Antarctica differs from the Arctic—not least in the absence of an indigenous population. Francis Spufford's acclaimed study of the polar regions in the European imaginary, *I May Be Some Time: Ice and the English Imagination* (1996), redresses the imbalance, in travel accounts, of polar discourse. In confirmation of this book's insistence on the close relation between travel writing and the travel industry, a Lonely Planet *Antarctica* is now on the travel guide shelves in bookstores.

37. For a further discussion of the desire to become indigenous, see the opening chapter of Goldie's *Fear and Temptation* (1989). See also Goldie's reading of Wiebe's work (191–214).

CHAPTER THREE

1. In fairness to Porter, he is primarily interested in a psychoanalytic approach to travel writing that explores the "transgressive" relationship between the father and his "errant" son; and in fairness to Leed, he does include a chapter entitled "Space and Gender: Women's Mediations," in which he analyzes what he infelicitously calls "the genderization of travel": the increasing challenge to patriarchal myths of space, belonging, and movement that once designated travel as a "masculinizing activity" set over and against a femininity often seen as "rooted in place" (116). Fussell is probably the worst offender, implying that (interwar British) "literary traveling" is an overwhelmingly male tradition, and thus overlooking the important work of, among several others, Freya Stark. Sara Mills, in her study of women's travel writing, puts it bluntly: "Fussell explicitly refuses to consider women travel writers within his account of literary travel, as he states that they are not sufficiently concerned either with travel or with writing itself" (3).

2. Said's hugely influential work has been challenged by a number of feminist critics for its masculinist and/or heterosexual assumptions about colonial emplacements of power. See, for example, the criticism of Said by Sara Suleri (whose autobiography *Meatless Days* will be analyzed later in this chapter) in *The Rhetoric of English India,* or the rejoinder to Said in Julia Emberley's *Thresholds of Difference* (1993).

3. For a critical analysis of Clifford's work, see Caren Kaplan, *Questions of Travel,* esp. 127–39; see also bell hooks's critique of Clifford's inattention to both gender and racial politics. Clifford addresses some of these criticisms in his most recent book, referring approvingly to the work of Janet Wolff on masculinist biases in theories of travel, and admitting the tendency for "theoretical accounts of diasporas and diasporic cultures to talk of travel and displacement in unmarked ways, thus normalizing male experiences" (*Routes* 258).

4. See, for example, Elaine Showalter's discussion of the "wild zone" as a liberated female space.

5. See, for instance, the final scene in *A Short Walk,* where Newby and Carless meet the celebrated explorer (and travel writer) Wilfred Thesiger. Thesiger, after venting much wrath at the general decline in British standards, turns his scornful attention to his two awestruck British companions. "'Let's turn in,' he said.... The ground was like iron with sharp rocks sticking up out of it. We started to blow up our air-beds. 'God, you must be a couple of pansies,' said Thesiger" (248). See also the next section of this chapter for an examination of homosexual anxiety in contemporary travel writing.

6. See Sarah Hobson, *Through Persia in Disguise* (1973); see also Virago Press's rereleased diary of Isabelle Eberhardt, *The Passionate Nomad* (1987), and the brief but interesting commentary on Eberhardt in Garber, 324–29, 334–36.

7. See Patrick Holland's unpublished essay on Morris, "(Post)imperial Nostalgia and Possession." As Holland suggests, however, Morris's sex change was and is a source of fascination to others—including other travel writers. Jonathan Raban and Paul Theroux, for example, both document their encounters with the post-sex-change Morris. Theroux displays less deference than his younger colleague Raban, although, like Raban, he puts the subject of Morris's sex change at the center. Where Raban finds Morris warmly affable, Theroux detects something "malicious" in her voice. There is also a hint of provocative antagonism in Theroux's allusions to the sex change. In speaking of Welsh nationalism, for instance, Theroux suggests that it was sometimes "like a kind of feminism, very monotonous and one-sided"; when Morris replies that this seems to her a very *male* view of the matter, Theroux snaps back, "Didn't it look that way to you when you were a man?"—spitefully implying that Morris's change has affected her ("male"/"rational") ability to see such issues as nationalism and feminism in their proper perspective (for further details of the encounter, see Theroux, *The Kingdom by the Sea*). Theroux's and Raban's respective encounters indicate the—not always cordial—connections that several contemporary travel writers like to maintain with one another. Theroux is particularly fractious: see also the testiness underlying his collaboration with Chatwin on *Patagonia Revisited.*

8. See, for example, Garber's discussion of Lawrence of Arabia, and of other Orientalized Hollywood icons, in the chapter of *Vested Interests,* "The Chic of Araby." Morris is mentioned in Garber's book, though not in any great detail; but while Garber refrains from treating Morris's case as an overstated transsexual drama, there is no strong evidence to link Morris, as she does, with a "cultural fantasy that played itself out in cross-dressing" (224).

9. See Said, *Orientalism,* esp. "Orientalism Now." Interestingly, with regard to Morris, Said's richly documented study has been criticized for its relative lack of attention to sexual—particularly homosexual—politics (see also note 2 above). Suleri, who tends to blame Said's followers rather than Said himself, draws attention to the "discourse of effeminacy" that traverses Orientalist representation. The "narratives of colonialism . . . assume [a] predominantly homoerotic cast . . . [which] further suggests that the manifold complications that gender poses to the cultural location of the imperial tale" (*Rhetoric of English India* 15–16). For a further discussion of the implications of colonialist homoerotics, see the next section of this chapter, particularly the treatment of Ackerley's *Hindoo Holiday.*

10. See the next section of this chapter for a more extended discussion of some of these "masking" tactics.

11. *Desert Places* is the title of Davidson's latest book (1996).

12. The desert remains a favorite topos of Western travel writers. See Chatwin's *The Songlines,* for instance, and Chatwin and Theroux's Patagonian narratives. Chatwin and Theroux both seem to be attracted to Patagonia for the same reason Borges (whom Theroux meets) hates it. As Borges says, "'[Patagonia] is dreary . . . the gate of the hundred sorrows. . . . There is nothing in Patagonia. It's not the Sahara, but it's as close as you can get to it in Argentina. No, there is nothing there" (qtd. in *Old Patagonian Express* 374, 377). Yet it is precisely the unremitting harshness and absence of features that make the desert so compelling: as Davidson says in *Tracks,* "The self in a desert becomes more and more like the desert. It becomes limitless, with its roots more in the subconscious than the conscious—it gets stripped of non-meaningful habits and becomes concerned with realities related to survival. But as is its nature, it desperately wants to assimilate and make sense of the information it receives, which in a desert is almost always going to be translated into the language of mysticism" (197).

13. See Lutz and Collins's uncompromising study, *Reading National Geographic.* As Lutz and Collins suggest, the magazine is, by any standards, a phenomenal success story, representing for its American—and, increasingly, international—public a sanitized exotic world that confirms American self-worth. See particularly the overview chapters (1 and 2) and the extended analysis of the function of photography in chapters 3, 4, and 7.

14. See here Janice Radway's reading of romance as a potentially liberating form.

15. On the problematic relation between tourism and development, see also MacCannell, *The Tourist,* 170–72, and Krotz, chaps. 3–7.

16. See Bernard Smith, *European Vision and the South Pacific* (1985), for a distinction between "soft primitivism"—the native as Noble Savage—and "hard primitivism"—the native as depraved barbarian. It seems likely that the anthropology courses Varawa (then McIntyre) took in California in the sixties debunked the primitivist myths that are so vigorously reinstalled here. Varawa's "uncommon anthropology," with its glossary and "Notes on Customs" for the layman, provides a reminder of the racist implications of travel writing when it masquerades as (popular) ethnography. But it also draws attention to the exoticist potential that already exists within ethnography, a potential that Varawa seeks, however crudely, to exploit.

17. See, for example, Stevenson's colorfully embroidered novella, "The Beach of Falesá," of which he boasted at the time that he had written "the first realistic South Sea story"! On Stevenson's personal experience of the South Seas, see also Knight. Mead's relevant work includes the classic *Coming of Age in Samoa,* the "meticulousness" of which has been called in question, most notoriously by Derek Freeman. For a "corrective" to what James Clifford has aptly called the "counter-mythologies" of Mead and Freeman, see the literary analyses of Bill Pearson and, particularly, the "counter ethnographic" fictions of Wendt. Elsewhere in his work, the Samoan Wendt has given short shrift to Euro-American travel writing, which he sees as continuing to conspire in imperialist representations of the South Pacific (see, particularly, the essay "Toward a New Oceania"). But the myth of the "island

paradise," however tired and tiresome, is still productive, as has been demonstrated by, among others, Paul Theroux. See the discussion of Theroux's *The Happy Isles of Oceania* in chapter 2 of this book and, most recently, Dea Birkett, whose Serpent in Paradise (1997) provides a useful antidote to the excesses of Irvine and Varawa.

18. On the practice of "othering" in travel writing, see Mills, 88–92. Condensing the work of Said, Lévi-Strauss, Fabian, Pratt, and others, Mills demonstrates that the "othering" process is intrinsic to European travel narratives, which tend to assert, explicitly or implicitly, the supremacy of the traveler-writer's culture, even when that culture (as in Irvine's and Varawa's cases) is subject to critique. On the connection between "othering" and the ethnic body, see also Lutz and Collins, esp. chap. 3; Trinh Minh-ha, esp. 79–118; and the influential work of Spivak.

19. In her work on postcolonial autobiography, Lionnet distinguishes—perhaps too sharply—between the more or less individualistic tradition of white Western autobiography and the more community-oriented autobiographies of "ethnic" (non-Western) writers. For further relevant discussions of autobiography, see Caren Kaplan's and Warley's essays in *A/B,* and the essays in Smith and Watson.

20. The term "countermemory" is derived here from the work of the French historian Michel Foucault. For Foucault, countermemory opposes a progressivist view of history underpinned by notions of identity, continuity, and tradition. Suleri's text also implicitly undercuts this "antiquarian" view of history, replacing it with the dynamic, radically discontinuous microhistories of the body.

21. The question of audience is paramount in any study of travel writing. See the preface of this book for some preliminary observations, which are connected to perceptions of travel and travel writing as popular phenomena. An in-depth study of audience, similar perhaps to Radway's work on the reception of romance, remains to be undertaken—some useful pointers are provided by Mills in chapter 4 of *Discourses of Difference.* The detailed sociological approach that such a study requires is unfortunately beyond the scope of an introductory survey such as this one.

22. Mills's emphasis is on the range of "discursive possibilities" and roles in women's travel writing. This "discursive" approach is valuable in complicating, and sometimes correcting, naive celebrations of women's travel/travel writing that champion female bravery.

23. The list above could obviously be added to; for women's travel writing is in a "boom" phase, for reasons partly explained above, even if women's narratives continue (for reasons also partly explained) to be outnumbered by men's. It is interesting to note that women's travel writing, to a far greater extent than men's, is dominated by the anthology (a representative selection here might include Morris's *Maiden Voyages,* de Teran's *Indiscreet Journeys,* Govier's *Without a Guide: Contemporary Women's Travel Adventures,* and, most recently, Birkett and Wheeler's *Amazonian: The Penguin Book of Women's New Travel Writing*). While this is a sign, as previously suggested, of the current commodification of "women's writing," it might also be taken as an indication that women's travel narratives are seen as occupying a special province of travel writing, and are thus implicitly—falsely—considered as being less wide-ranging than men's. For further thoughts on this issue (among others) in women's travel writing, see Kröller.

24. The issue of terminology—*homosexual, gay,* or *queer*—has recently become particularly tricky. In the discussion that follows in this section, *homosexual* appears as a provisional category marker; *gay* signifies homosexual (self-)presentation where a liberationist inflection seems appropriate; and *queer* is used to

suggest a provocative counterdiscourse. *Queer* is the most problematic of the terms, since until recently it tended to signal the transgression of boundaries; its inexplicitness, however, frequently separates it from contemporary deployment. For a general discussion of the three terms in their historical contexts, see Jagose.

25. A Belgian character in Alan Hollinghurst's novel *The Folding Star* (1994) tells a younger English friend of his earlier sexual attachment to an older, working-class man: "I'm sure there was that class thing, too, which you're supposed to have much worse than us—the place and the event conspired to make me think of him as a, what's the word, a woodlander" (408).

26. Ackerley's male selection contrasts with that of Forster, who "understood Mohammedans as he did not understand Hindus" (Furbank 2:99); in *Hindoo Holiday,* Ackerley's Muslim tutor is the rejected youth, a foil for the attractive young Hindus Sharma and Narayan.

27. Saros Cowasjee provides useful information about Ackerley's book and its reception in his introduction to a reprinting of the second (1952) edition, which was withdrawn before publication.

28. In 1985 John Fuller "found" the manuscript, dated 1929, in the University of Texas library. It remains unclear to what extent *The Temple* (1988) is a rewrite of the originally unpublished work or whether it is virtually a new novel; Spender himself has said that he relied heavily on the earlier manuscript for two sections. But he had already sent an "intermediate version" to Auden and Isherwood, among others; it is even possible that Isherwood drew on it for *Goodbye to Berlin,* although it is equally likely that Spender, in turn, drew on earlier work by Isherwood (the novel that the young Bradshaw is working on as Paul leaves London for Hamburg may well represent a project of Isherwood's). At any rate, there are clear intertextual links between Spender's work and that of his friend, particularly in the figure of Otto, an Isherwood protégé in both *Goodbye to Berlin* and *The Temple.* Also clear is that Spender, revisiting a manuscript piece that had participated in a shared experience of English homosexuality in Germany, heightened the earlier work's quotient of political and moral allegory.

29. Another passage in Hollinghurst's *A Folding Star* (see n. 25) suggests the connection: "Once inside the heavy sound-proofed door with its little wired judas I was in a place so familiar . . . There was the same mad delusion of glamour, the same over-priced tawdriness, the same ditsy parochialism and sullen lardy queenery, and underneath it all the same urgency and defiance" (21).

30. Australian gay writer Robert Dessaix perhaps echoes Busi in his postmodern travel memoir/fiction *Night Letters* (1996). For a discussion of *Night Letters,* see chapter 4 of this book.

31. Mrabet is somewhere on the sidelines, resisting marginalization, in many of the interviews collected in Caponi's *Conversations with Paul Bowles* (1993).

32. In *My Kenya Days* (1994), Wilfred Thesiger also augments and authenticates a homoerotic, quasi-anthropological account of his travels in East Africa with idealizing photographs of attractive native youth.

33. White's book may well be the inspiration behind the emergence of the subgenre of "gay travel guides," a significant category that is related to the gay travelogue, but is not under scrutiny in this study.

34. For an account of queer performativity and its contestations, see Jagose, 72–126. Judith Butler's influential *Gender Trouble* should also be acknowledged, not least for its indirect link to the title chosen for this chapter.

35. Patrick Leigh Fermor arguably merits more than a passing reference. Part of the mandarin tradition of English gentleman-eccentric-stylists that perhaps culminates in Bruce Chatwin, he achieved the status of minor cult figure with the anachronistic *A Time of Gifts* (1977). Mark Cocker's tribute is characteristic: "In a literary age consumed with the literary prize, four of his works have been honoured with six awards. He is the most obvious heir to [Robert] Byron's pre-war mantle as leading philhellene amongst British writers and as the travel book's great stylist" (Cocker 195).

36. This point emerges very clearly from a recent travelogue, in which a highly articulate but temporarily destitute gay man takes to the streets and roads of the American Southwest. In *Travels with Lizbeth* (1993), Lars Eighner makes a virtue of economic powerlessness, apparently refusing to enlist his sexual endowments to produce economic gains. He presents himself as economic, not gay, victim: he can take his sexuality for granted, but not his joblessness or his poverty.

CHAPTER FOUR

1. It is possible to argue, also, that space and place have become increasingly "*de*ontologized"; as Umberto Eco, for example, has it, "the logical distinction between Real Worlds and Possible Worlds has been definitively undermined" (14).

2. See, for example, the recent, characteristically snide accounts by Brook and Amis.

3. See also the discussion of Chatwin's work in chapter 1 of this book.

4. For another, theoretically inflected account of "nomadic" culture, also distinct from Chatwin's enterprise, see Deleuze and Guattari. See also Ascherson's history/travel book *Black Sea* (1996), esp. 55–86, for a layered, historicized discussion of nomadism and nomadology. Ascherson, glancing particularly in Bruce Chatwin's direction, writes pointedly of "Europe's long, unfinished ballad of yearning for noble savages, for hunter-gatherers in touch with themselves and their ecology, for cowboys, cattle-rievers, gypsies and Cossacks, for Bedouin nomads and aboriginals walking their song-lines through the unspoiled wilderness" (83). Ascherson alerts us to the tendency (present in Chambers as well as Chatwin) to abnegate history and context, eliding enforced migrancy with the "freedom" of the nomad.

5. Neither HIV nor AIDS is explicitly named as the condition of Dessaix's traveler. Interestingly, as in a surprising number of contemporary travel fictions, the traveler tells a story about Chatwin that suggests that the "outing" of AIDS, in the context of travel, is transgressive: "Harry started telling the story of Bruce Chatwin's slow decline. . . . It was a long story—the illness in India, the two-hour struggles to get to the bathroom and back unaided, every tiny, ghastly detail. The consensus, of course, was that Chatwin had AIDS, although the moment Harry mentioned the word on the telephone [to Chatwin], the calls ceased. A taboo had been broken. Very English" (Dessaix 104). For a further discussion of the implications of the AIDS epidemic for travel writers, see chapters 2 and 3.

6. Dessaix's traveler believes that "[t]here will always be something about the bisexual and homosexual male which favours a picaresque existence—and something about a picaresque existence which will always have homosexual overtones" (225). See also the discussion of Aldo Busi's work in chapter 3 of this book.

7. For a further discussion of the metafictional and self-reflexive aspects of Theroux's work, see the essays by Glaser.

8. One example is Naipaul's *The Enigma of Arrival,* analyzed in chapter 1 of this book.

9. On millenarianism, see Cohn; see also the essays in Rabkin, Greenberg, and Olander.

10. Lévi-Strauss is a spectral figure hovering behind much of the contemporary environmental literature. *Tristes Tropiques,* in particular, has had a great influence on what James Clifford calls those "salvage narratives" that take it upon themselves to "rescue" endangered peoples, animals, and cultures ("On Ethnographic Allegory"). Lévi-Strauss had seen his famous ethnography of the "deteriorating" indigenous tribes of central Brazil as nothing less than an act of atonement for the "civilization"—his—that corrupted them; this spiritual dimension, and the guilty conscience that inspired it, can also be found in several contemporary travel narratives that popularize Lévi-Strauss's sentiments without imitating his structural methods. Foremost among these are the ethnographic/nature studies of Peter Matthiessen, whose ecological jeremiad *The Cloud Forest* (1961) will be dealt with later in this section.

11. The term is explained more fully in Clifford's "On Ethnographic Allegory."

12. Matthiessen, in keeping with several other post-Lévi-Strauss travel writers, laments the loss of "authenticity" that has come with the incursion of the white man. Encounters with the white man, he implies simplistically, can only have negative consequences: "In South America, with few exceptions, the tribe that permits itself to come into complete contact with the white man, on the white man's terms, has perhaps a half-century of existence left to it" (*The Cloud Forest* 223). For a critique of this romantic view, see the work of MacCannell and Clifford, for whom "authenticity" is a talisman of *white* perceptions of the "native other": it is "something produced, not salvaged" (Clifford, *The Predicament of Culture* 250), and serves the dominant culture's needs. It is striking how often the terminology now considered dated in anthropology is picked up in contemporary travel writing as part of its nostalgic stock-in-trade. See here the treatment of Varawa's "uncommon anthropology" in the previous chapter; also the discussion of Van der Post's work that follows in this section.

13. The work of Ali Behdad is useful here in elucidating the various strategies that travel writers deploy to recuperate—or "conserve"—an "other" under threat of disappearance. Behdad distinguishes between the informational guidebook, with its curatorial retentiveness, and the travelogue, which encourages an illusive identification with the (questing) traveler-writer (44–45). Contemporary travel narratives, balanced between documentation and fabrication, may use both of these recuperative strategies, although—as is the case with Matthiessen's and Van der Post's—what information they provide is often overshadowed by the traveler's mythologized quest. For further attempts to clarify, and complicate, the distinction between travel narratives and guidebooks, see the introduction and the postscript to this book.

14. This is particularly true of New Age travelogues, which are often produced "in conjunction" with Aboriginal shamans, or in which the traveler-writer, acting as an intermediary, "channels" Aboriginal wisdom. See the discussion of Castaneda's and, especially, Morgan's work later in this section.

15. It is one of the ironies of travel writing that its frequent appeals to "time-

less nature" or the "timeless essences" of native cultures effectively rob the very cultures they celebrate of their history—and their agency for change.

16. For further background on the links between travel writing, tourism, and spiritual quest, refer back to chapter 2 (the work of Barry Lopez); see also chapter 5 of Leed; the work of Nelson Graburn; the essays in Bhardwaj, Rinschede, and Sievers; and, particularly, Gita Mehta, *Karma Cola: Marketing the Mystic East* (1979). Mehta's book, an acerbic backlash at the pretensions of the "spiritual tourist," should be required reading for travel writers who see their journeys, uncritically, as "pilgrimages." Among those who should read it is Rudolph Wurlitzer, the screenwriter for Bertolucci's *The Little Buddha,* whose book *Hard Travel to Sacred Places* (1994) is very much grist to Mehta's mill. A much subtler example, and the acknowledged classic of its subgenre, is Peter Matthiessen's *The Snow Leopard* (1987).

17. For an introduction to New Age concerns, see Rhodes; see also the essays in Lewis and Melton and in Hoyt and Yamamoto.

18. Castaneda's "Don Juan" trilogy (*The Teachings of Don Juan,* 1968; *A Separate Reality,* 1971; *Journey to Ixtlan,* 1972) can perhaps only be considered peripherally as travel writing, even though it famously documents a variety of weird and wonderful drug-induced "trips." The record of the hallucinatory "trip," itself a surrogate form of travel, becomes another limit case for travel writing's ontological status: a status that, as previously argued, is not and cannot be rigorously fixed.

19. Harvey (*Condition of Postmodernity,* esp. chap. 1) and Fredric Jameson are the best known of a large group of postmodern theorists who insist on postmodernism's connections with late-capitalist commodity culture. Seen in this context, the New Age emerges as very much a postmodern phenomenon: another sign of the massive reach and scope of Western commodity culture, and of its capacity to ransack the whole range of human experience—material and spiritual—for consumer goods.

20. New Age soul-searching is also a symptom of the postmodern cult of self: see here Dean MacCannell's extraordinary attack on postmodernism in "The Desire to be Postmodern" (*Empty Meeting Grounds* 183–229). "[I]n California," says MacCannell sneeringly, "in precisely those regions that are the most markedly postmodern, we also hear almost constant chatter about 'getting in touch with' one's own 'true,' 'inner' feelings, 'centering' and so on. The predictable result is an aggressive promotion of the ego and individualism" (188).

21. See, by way of comparison, Henry Shukman's *Savage Pilgrims* (1996). Shukman, although equally whimsical in cataloguing New Age eccentricities, is less acerbic than McGrath, and less revealing of the writer's angst.

POSTSCRIPT

1. For other comments on Tisdale's provocative article, see Krotz, 183–84.

2. Variations on this theme include Millman, *Last Places* (1990); Middleton, *The Last Disco in Outer Mongolia* (1992); Winchester, *Outposts* (1985); and Iyer, *Falling Off the Map* (1993).

3. Robert Byron's *The Road to Oxiana,* volume 2 in the series, carries an introduction by Chatwin; the founding volume is Apsley Cherry-Garrard's *The Worst Journey in the World.*

4. The omission of women's texts from Pearson's selection seems to bear out

Tisdale's observation about the classic travel book, that it is "a little bit sacred and masculine. It despises the masses and loves the unbeaten track, the self-imposed but public exile" (67). See chapter 3 of this book for an extended discussion of masculine models and paradigms in travel writing.

5. The phenomenon is so widespread that it seems pointless to provide specific examples.

6. The practice among leading writers of introducing their colleagues or friends, and then staging encounters with them in their travelogues, is surely an elaboration of the courtesies of the blurb.

7. Lonely Planet is apparently expanding in all directions. Another newspaper article observes, "They're on the Internet, of course, and now on our television screens. . . . You can't help but like [the presenter] Ian Wright. He's a great Lonely Planet man. Try anything once. And perfect for Alaska which, as Wright told us, is a wild place. Full of moose, the cause of some rather manufactured anxiety for Wright" (*New Zealand Herald,* February 19, 1997, B10). Even the newspaper plug assumes the flippant Lonely Planet tone.

8. The chapter on Africa makes considerable use of Joseph Conrad and Graham Greene, though not, surprisingly, of V. S. Naipaul. However, it clearly "reads" Africa from within the Conrad-Naipaul tradition (see Nixon, *London Calling;* also chap. 2 of this book).

9. Kaplan protests that "mine would be an unsentimental journey [unlike that of Laurence Sterne]. My impressions might be the 'wrong' ones to have, but they would be based on what I saw" (11); later, he asserts that he is "a time traveler, but not necessarily a romantic one. . . . I chart places where a literary tourist would rarely go" (131). *The Ends of the Earth,* nonetheless, is saturated with literary references; despite his attempts to provide alibis, Kaplan ultimately invites recognition as sentimental traveler, literary tourist, and adventurer—precisely the models of the traveler he wishes to disclaim.

10. For a recent, coruscating critique of Kaplan's work, which sees its "prognoses of disintegration" as possibly "testing conservative waters for the depths of a reemergent positivist racism," see Brennan, *At Home in the World,* 125–27. As Brennan argues, Kaplan's "rhetoric of fear and loathing" is "entirely at odds with mainstream humanities discourse" (126). But as will be clear from this book, it is not at odds with a certain strand of "political" travel writing, which uses the genre to justify—although also, in some cases, to ironize—xenophobic sentiments and cultural myths. Sophisticated examples of this form of political travelogue are the "African" and "Indian" works of V. S. Naipaul (see chaps. 1 and 2).

11. Two other recent narratives successfully negotiating between individual travel experience and the stuff of history, in layered and nuanced fashion, are Neil Ascherson's *Black Sea* (1996; see chap. 4, note 4 above), and Dorothy Carrington's *The Dream-Hunters of Corsica* (1995).

WORKS CITED

Ackerley, J. R. *Hindoo Holiday: An Indian Journal.* 1932. New Delhi: Arnold-Heinemann, 1979.

Ackerman, Diane. *The Rarest of the Rare: Vanishing Animals, Timeless Worlds.* New York: Random House, 1995.

Adams, James Eli. *Dandies and Desert Saints: Styles of Victorian Masculinity.* Ithaca, N.Y.: Cornell University Press, 1995.

Adams, Percy. *Travelers and Travel Liars, 1660–1800.* Berkeley and Los Angeles: University of California Press, 1962.

Ahmad, Aijaz. "Postcolonialism: What's in a Name?" *Late Imperial Culture,* ed. Román de la Campa, E. Ann Kaplan, and Michael Sprinker. New York: Verso, 1995. 11–32.

Alexander, Brian. *Green Cathedrals: A Wayward Traveler in the Rain Forest.* New York: Lyons and Burford, 1995.

Allen, John L. "Lands of Myth, Waters of Wonder: The Place of the Imagination in the History of Geographical Exploration." *Geographies of the Mind,* ed. David Lowenthal and Martyn Bowden. New York: Oxford University Press, 1976. 41–61.

Amirthanayagam, Guy, ed. *Writers in East-West Encounter: New Cultural Bearings.* London: Macmillan, 1981.

Amis, Martin. *The Moronic Inferno and Other Visits to America.* London: Jonathan Cape, 1986.

Appadurai, Arjun. "Disjuncture and Difference in the Global Cultural Economy." *Colonial Discourse and Post-Colonial Theory: A Reader,* ed. Patrick Williams and Laura Chrisman. New York: Columbia University Press, 1994. 324–39.

———. *Modernity at Large: Cultural Dimensions of Globalization.* Minneapolis: University of Minnesota Press, 1996.

Appiah, Kwame Anthony. *In My Father's House: Africa in the Philosophy of Culture.* New York: Oxford University Press, 1992.

Arac, Jonathan, and Harriet Ritvo, eds. *The Macropolitics of Nineteenth-Century Literature: Nationalism, Exoticism, Imperialism.* Philadelphia: University of Pennsylvania Press, 1991.

Ascherson, Neil. *Black Sea: The Birthplace of Civilisation and Barbarism.* London: Vintage, 1996.

Bandy, Joe. "Managing the Other of Nature: Sustainability, Spectacle, and Global Regimes of Capital in Ecotourism." *Public Culture* 8 (1996): 539–66.

Barr, Patricia. *The Memsahibs: The Women of Victorian India.* London: Secker and Warburg, 1976.

Barthes, Roland. *Empire of Signs.* 1970. Trans. Richard Howard. New York: Noonday Press, 1989.

———. *The Grain of the Voice: Interviews, 1962–1980.* 1981. Trans. Linda Coverdale. New York: Hill and Wang, 1985.

———. *Mythologies.* 1957. Trans. Annette Lavers. London: Jonathan Cape, 1972.

———. *The Pleasure of the Text.* Trans. Richard Miller. New York: Noonday Press, 1990.

Baudrillard, Jean. *America.* 1986. Trans. Chris Turner. New York: Verso, 1988.

Behdad, Ali. *Belated Travelers: Orientalism in the Age of Colonial Dissolution.* Durham, N.C.: Duke University Press, 1994.

Bell, Gavin. *In Search of Tusitala: Travels in the Pacific after Robert Louis Stevenson.* London: Picador, 1994.

Bennett, Catherine. "Why the Right People Choose to Stay at Home." *Guardian Weekly,* June 23, 1996, 30.

Bhabha, Homi. "The Other Question: Difference, Discrimination, and the Discourse of Colonialism." *Literature, Politics and Theory: Papers from the Essex Conference,* ed. Francis Barker et al. London: Methuen, 1986. 148–72.

———, ed. *Nation and Narration.* London: Routledge, 1991.

Bhardwaj, S. M., G. Rinschede, and A. Sievers, eds. *Pilgrimage in the Old and New World.* Berlin: Dietrich Riemer Verlag, 1994.

Biddlecombe, Peter. *Travels with My Briefcase: Around the World, on Expenses.* Boston: Little, Brown, 1994.

Birkett, Dea. *Serpent in Paradise.* London: Picador, 1997.

Birkett, Dea, and Sara Wheeler, eds. *Amazonian: The Penguin Book of Women's Travel Writing.* London: Penguin, 1998.

Bongie, Christopher. *Exotic Memories: Literature, Colonialism, and the Fin de Siècle.* Stanford, Calif.: Stanford University Press, 1991.

Bourke, Chris. "Have Imagination, Will Travel. Jonathan Raban: The Studious Englishman Abroad." *New Zealand Listener,* April 12–18, 1997, 46–47.

Bowles, Paul. *The Sheltering Sky.* New York: New Directions, 1949.

———. *Up above the World.* New York: Simon and Schuster, 1966.

Brennan, Timothy. *At Home in the World: Cosmopolitanism Now.* Cambridge, Mass.: Harvard University Press, 1997.

———. *Salman Rushdie and the Third World: Myths of the Nation.* New York: St. Martin's Press, 1989.

Brody, Hugh. *The People's Land: Inuit, Whites, and the Eastern Arctic.* Vancouver: Douglas and McIntyre, 1991.

Brook, Stephen. *Honky Tonk Gelato: Travels through Texas.* London: Hamilton, 1985.

Bryson, Bill. *Neither Here Nor There: Travels in Europe.* London: Secker and Warburg, 1991.

———. *Notes from a Small Island.* New York: Doubleday, 1996.

Buck-Morss, Susan. "Semiotic Boundaries and the Politics of Meaning: Modernity on Tour—a Village in Transition." *New Ways of Knowing: The Sciences, Society, and Reconstructive Knowledge,* ed. M. Raskin and H. Bernstein. Totowa, N.J.: Rowman and Littlefield, 1987. 200–236.

Buhasz, Laszlo. "An Introspective South Pacific Voyage." *Toronto Globe and Mail,* June 27, 1992, n.p.

Burroughs, William. *Naked Lunch.* New York: Grove, 1959.

Buruma, Ian. *Behind the Mask: On Sexual Demons, Sacred Mothers, Transvestites, Gangsters, and Other Japanese Cultural Heroes.* New York: Pantheon, 1984.

Busi, Aldo. *Sodomies in Elevenpoint.* Trans. Stuart Hood. Boston: Faber and Faber, 1992.

Butler, Judith. *Gender Trouble: Feminism and the Subversion of Identity.* New York: Routledge, 1990.

Butor, Michel. "Travel and Writing." *Mosaic* 8, no. 1 (fall 1974): 1–16.

Buttimer, Anne. "Grasping the Dynamism of the Lifeworld." *Annals of the Association of American Geographers* 66, no. 2 (1976): 277–92.

Buttimer, Anne, and David Seamon, eds. *The Human Experience of Space and Place.* London: Croom Helm, 1980.

Buzard, James. *The Beaten Track: European Tourism, Literature, and the Ways to "Culture," 1800–1918.* Oxford: Clarendon Press, 1993.

Byron, Robert. *The Road to Oxiana.* 1937. London: Picador Travel Classics, 1994.

Cahill, Tim. *Jaguars Ripped My Flesh.* New York: Vintage, 1996.

———. *A Wolverine Is Eating My Leg.* London: Fourth Estate, 1994.

Callenbach, Ernest. *Ecotopia: The Notebooks and Reports of William Weston.* Berkeley, Calif.: Banyan Tree Books, 1975.

Calvino, Italo. *Invisible Cities.* 1972. Trans. William Weaver. London: Harcourt Brace Jovanovich, 1974.

Campbell, Alan. *Getting to Know Waiwai: An Amazonian Ethnography.* New York: Routledge, 1995.

Campbell, Mary. *The Witness and the Other World: Exotic European Travel Writing, 400–1600.* Ithaca, N.Y.: Cornell University Press, 1988.

Caponi, Gena. *Conversations with Paul Bowles.* Jackson: University Press of Mississippi, 1993.

Carpenter, Humphrey. *W. H. Auden: A Biography.* London: Allen and Unwin, 1981.

Carrington, Dorothy. *The Dream-Hunters of Corsica.* London: Weidenfeld and Nicolson, 1995.

Carter, Paul. *Living in a New Country: History, Travelling and Language.* London: Faber and Faber, 1992.

Castaneda, Carlos. *Journey to Ixtlan: The Lessons of Don Juan.* New York: Simon and Schuster, 1972.

———. *A Separate Reality: Further Conversations with Don Juan.* New York: Simon and Schuster, 1971.

———. *The Teachings of Don Juan: A Yaqui Way of Knowledge.* New York: Ballantine Books, 1968.

Castronovo, David. *The English Gentleman: Images and Ideals in Literature and Society.* New York: Ungar, 1987.

Caulfield, Annie. *Kingdom of the Film Stars.* Melbourne: Lonely Planet, 1997.

de Certeau, Michel. *Heterologies: Discourse on the Other.* Trans. Brian Massumi. Minneapolis: University of Minnesota Press, 1986.

Chagnon, Napoleon. *Yanomamo, the Fierce People.* New York: Holt, Rinehart and Winston, 1968.

Chahardi, Driss ben Hamed. *A Life Full of Holes.* 1964. Trans. Paul Bowles. New York: Grove Press, 1982.

Chambers, Iain. *Migrancy, Culture, Identity.* London: Routledge, 1994.
Chatwin, Bruce. *Anatomy of Restlessness.* Ed. J. Borm and M. Graves. London: Jonathan Cape, 1996.
———. *In Patagonia.* London: Jonathan Cape, 1977.
———. *On the Black Hill.* London: Jonathan Cape, 1982.
———. *The Songlines.* New York: Viking, 1987.
———. *Utz.* London: Pan, 1988.
———. *The Viceroy of Ouidah.* New York: Summit Books, 1980.
———. *What Am I Doing Here.* London: Jonathan Cape, 1989.
Chatwin, Bruce, and Paul Theroux. *Patagonia Revisited.* Boston: Houghton Mifflin, 1986.
Cherry-Garrard, Apsley. *The Worst Journey in the World.* London: Constable, 1922.
Choukri, Mohamed. *For Bread Alone.* Trans. Paul Bowles. London: P. Owen, 1973.
———. *Jean Genet in Tangier.* Trans. Paul Bowles. New York: Ecco Press, 1974.
———. *Love with a Few Hairs.* Trans. Paul Bowles. London: Owen, 1967.
———. *Tennessee Williams in Tangier.* Trans. Paul Bowles. Santa Barbara, Calif.: Cadmus Editions, 1979.
Clifford, James. "On Ethnographic Allegory." *Writing Culture: The Poetics and Politics of Ethnography,* ed. James Clifford and George Marcus. Berkeley and Los Angeles: University of California Press, 1986. 98–121.
———. *The Predicament of Culture: Twentieth-Century Ethnography, Literature, and Art.* Cambridge, Mass.: Harvard University Press, 1988.
———. *Routes: Travel and Translation in the Late Twentieth Century.* Cambridge, Mass.: Harvard University Press, 1997.
———. "Traveling Cultures." *Cultural Studies,* ed. Lawrence Grossberg, Cary Nelson, and Paula Treichler. New York: Routledge, 1992. 96–116.
Clifford, James, and Vivek Dhareshwar, eds. *Inscriptions* 5 (1989), special issue on travel.
Clifford, James, and George Marcus, eds. *Writing Culture: The Poetics and Politics of Ethnography.* Berkeley and Los Angeles: University of California Press, 1986.
Cocker, Mark. *Loneliness and Time: British Travel Writing in the Twentieth Century.* London: Secker and Warburg, 1992.
Cohn, Norman. *Cosmos, Chaos, and the World to Come.* New Haven, Conn.: Yale University Press, 1993.
Conrad, Joseph. *Heart of Darkness.* 1898. London: Penguin, 1985.
———. *Lord Jim.* 1900. Oxford: Oxford University Press, 1983.
Condon, Sean. *Sean and David's Long Drive.* Melbourne: Lonely Planet, 1996.
Conover, Ted. "Trucking through the AIDS Belt." *The New Yorker,* August 16, 1993, n.p.
Cortazzi, Hugh. *The Japanese Achievement.* New York: St. Martin's Press, 1990.
Cowasjee, Saros. Introduction to *Hindoo Holiday: An Indian Journal,* by J. R. Ackerley. 1952. New Delhi: Arnold-Heinemann, 1979.
Culler, Jonathan. "The Semiotics of Tourism." *Framing the Sign: Criticism and Its Institutions.* Norman: University of Oklahoma Press, 1988. 153–67.
Dante Alighieri. *The Divine Comedy.* Trans. Allen Mandelbaum. London: David Campbell, 1995.

Davidson, Basil. *The Black Man's Burden: Africa and the Curse of the Nation-State.* New York: Times Books, 1992.

Davidson, Robyn. *Desert Places.* New York: Viking, 1996.

———. *Tracks.* New York: Pantheon, 1980.

———. "Walk on the Wild Side." *Guardian Weekly,* August 4, 1996, n.p.

de la Campa, Román, Ann Kaplan, and Michael Sprinker, eds. *Late Imperial Culture.* London: Verso, 1995.

de Lauretis, Teresa, ed. *Feminist Studies, Critical Studies.* Bloomington: Indiana University Press, 1986.

Deleuze, Gilles, and Felix Guattari. "Treatise on Nomadology—the War Machine." *A Thousand Plateaus: Capitalism and Schizophrenia,* trans. William Weaver. Minneapolis: University of Minnesota Press, 1987.

Descola, Philippe. *The Spears of Twilight: Life and Death in the Amazon Jungle.* London: HarperCollins, 1996.

Dessaix, Robert. *Night Letters.* Sydney: Macmillan, 1996.

de Teran, Lisa St. Aubin, ed. *Indiscreet Journeys: Stories of Women on the Road.* Boston: Faber and Faber, 1990.

Diski, Jenny. *Skating to Antarctica.* London: Granta Books, 1997.

During, Simon. "Postcolonialism and Globalization." *Meanjin* 48, no. 2 (1992): 339–53.

Eberhardt, Isabelle. *The Passionate Nomad: The Diary of Isabelle Eberhardt.* Trans. Nina de Voogd. Ed. Rana Kabbani. London: Virago, 1987.

Eco, Umberto. *Travels in Hyperreality.* Trans. William Weaver. San Diego: Harcourt Brace Jovanovich, 1986.

Eighner, Lars. *Travels with Lizbeth.* New York: Fawcett Columbine, 1993.

Emberley, Julia. *Thresholds of Difference: Feminist Critique, Native Women's Writing, Postcolonial Theory.* Toronto: University of Toronto Press, 1993.

Empson, William. *Some Versions of Pastoral.* 1935. London: Hogarth, 1986.

Evans, Julian. *Transit of Venus: Travels in the Pacific.* London: Secker and Warburg, 1992.

Feifer, Maxine. *Going Places: The Ways of the Tourist from Imperial Rome to the Present Day.* London: Macmillan, 1985.

Fermor, Patrick Leigh. *A Time of Gifts.* London: John Murray, 1977.

Fleming, Peter. *Brazilian Adventure.* 1933. London: Penguin, 1957.

Foley, Barbara. *Telling the Truth: The Theory and Practice of Documentary Fiction.* Ithaca, N.Y.: Cornell University Press, 1986.

Forster, E. M. *Maurice.* London: E. Arnold, 1971.

———. *A Passage to India.* 1924. London: E. Arnold, 1978.

Foucault, Michel. "Nietzsche, Genealogy, History." *The Foucault Reader,* trans. D. F. Bouchard and Sherry Simon, ed. Paul Rabinow. New York: Pantheon, 1984.

Fraser, Keath, ed. *Bad Trips.* New York: Vintage, 1991.

Freeman, Derek. *Margaret Mead and Samoa: The Making and Unmaking of an Anthropological Myth.* Cambridge, Mass.: Harvard University Press, 1983.

Frow, John. "Tourism and the Semiotics of Nostalgia." *October* (fall 1990): 127–54.

Fukuyama, Francis. *The End of History and the Last Man.* New York: Free Press, 1992.

Furbank, Philip N. *E. M. Forster: A Life.* 2 vols. London: Secker and Warburg, 1977–78.

Fussell, Paul. *Abroad: British Literary Traveling between the Wars.* Oxford: Oxford University Press, 1980.

Garber, Marjorie. *Vested Interests: Cross-Dressing and Cultural Anxiety.* New York: Routledge, 1992.

Ghosh, Amitav. *In an Antique Land: History in the Guise of a Traveler's Tale.* New York: Vintage, 1992.

Gide, André. *Travels in the Congo.* 1927. Trans. Dorothy Bassy. Harmondsworth: Penguin, 1986.

Glaser, Elton. "The Self-Reflexive Traveler: Paul Theroux on the Art of Travel Writing." *Centennial Review* 33 (summer 1989): 193–206.

———. "Paul Theroux and the Poetry of Departures." *Temperamental Journeys: Essays on the Modern Literature of Travel,* ed. Michael Kowalewski. Athens: University of Georgia Press, 1992. 153–63.

Goldie, Terry. *Fear and Temptation: The Image of the Indigene in Canadian, Australian, and New Zealand Literatures.* Montreal: McGill-Queen's University Press, 1989.

Govier, Katherine, ed. *Without a Guide: Contemporary Women's Travel Adventures.* New York: Hungry Mind, 1996.

Graburn, Nelson. "Tourism: The Sacred Journey." *Hosts and Guests: The Anthropology of Tourism,* ed. Valene Smith. Philadelphia: University of Pennsylvania Press, 1977. 21–36.

Green, Martin. *Dreams of Adventure, Deeds of Empire.* New York: Basic Books, 1979.

Green, Michelle. *The Dream at the End of the World: Paul Bowles and the Renegades of Tangier.* New York: HarperCollins, 1991.

Greenblatt, Stephen. *Marvelous Possessions: The Wonder of the New World.* Chicago: University of Chicago Press, 1991.

Gregory, Derek. *Geographical Imaginations.* Oxford: Blackwell, 1994.

Grewal, Inderpal. *Home and Harem: Nation, Gender, Empire, and the Cultures of Travel.* Durham, N.C.: Duke University Press, 1996.

Grossberg, Lawrence, Cary Nelson, and Paula Treichler, eds. *Cultural Studies.* New York: Routledge, 1992.

Guha, Ranajit, and Gayatri Spivak, eds. *Selected Subaltern Studies.* New York: Oxford University Press, 1988.

Harvey, David. *The Condition of Postmodernity.* Oxford: Blackwell, 1989.

Hawthorne, Susan. "The Politics of the Exotic: The Paradox of Cultural Voyeurism." *Meanjin* 48, no. 2 (1989): 259–68.

Hearn, Lafcadio. *Writings from Japan.* Ed. Francis King. London: Penguin, 1984.

Herdt, Gilbert. *Ritualized Homosexuality in Melanesia.* Berkeley and Los Angeles: University of California Press, 1984.

Higgins, Tom. *Spotted Dick, S'il Vous Plaît: An English Restaurant in France.* New York: Soho Press, 1995.

Hobson, Sarah. *Through Persia in Disguise.* London: J. Murray, 1973.

Holland, Patrick. "Jan Morris: (Post)imperial Nostalgia and Possession." Unpublished essay, 1994.

Hollinghurst, Alan. *The Folding Star.* London: Chatto and Windus, 1994.

hooks, bell. "Representing Whiteness in the Black Imagination." *Cultural Stud-*

ies, ed. Lawrence Grossberg, Cary Nelson, and Paula Treichler. New York: Routledge, 1992. 338–46.

Horwell, Veronica. "Sensibility on a Grand Tour." *Guardian Weekly,* July 14, 1996, 28.

Hoyt, Karen, and J. Yamamoto, eds. *The New Age Rage.* Old Dominion, N.J.: Power Books, 1987.

Huggan, Graham. "Maps, Dreams, and the Presentation of Ethnographic Narrative." *Ariel* 22, no. 1 (1991): 57–69.

———. "The Postcolonial Exotic: Rushdie's 'Booker of Bookers.'" *Transition* 64 (1994): 22–29.

———. "Some Recent Australian Fictions in the Age of Tourism: Murray Bail, Inez Baranay, Gerard Lee." *Australian Literary Studies* 16, no. 2 (1993): 168–78.

———. "A Tale of Two Parrots: Walcott, Rhys, and the Uses of Colonial Mimicry." *Contemporary Literature* 35, no. 4 (1994): 643–60.

Hyland, Paul. *The Black Heart: A Voyage into Central Africa.* New York: Paragon House, 1988.

Ignatieff, Michael. "An Interview with Bruce Chatwin." *Granta* 21 (spring 1987): 23–37.

Irvine, Lucy. *Castaway.* London: Victor Gollancz, 1983.

Isherwood, Christopher. *Goodbye to Berlin.* 1939. London: Triad Panther, 1977.

Iyer, Pico. *Falling Off the Map: Some Lonely Places of the World.* Toronto: Knopf Canada, 1993.

———. *The Lady and the Monk: Four Seasons in Kyoto.* New York: Knopf, 1991.

———. *Video Night in Kathmandu, and Other Reports from the Not-So-Far East.* 1988. New York: Vintage, 1989.

Jagose, Annamarie. *Queer Theory.* Carlton, Victoria: Melbourne University Press, 1996.

Jameson, Fredric. "Postmodernism and Consumer Society." *The Anti-Aesthetic: Essays on Postmodern Culture,* ed. Hal Foster. Seattle: Bay Press, 1983. 111–25.

———. *Postmodernism; or, the Cultural Logic of Late Capitalism.* Durham, N.C.: Duke University Press, 1991.

Kane, Joe. *Running the Amazon.* London: Bodley Head, 1989.

———. *Savages.* Vancouver: Douglas and McIntyre, 1995.

Kaplan, Caren. "Michael Arlen's Fictions of Exile: The Subject of Ethnic Autobiography." *Auto/Biography* 4, no. 2 (1988): 140–49.

———. *Questions of Travel: Postmodern Discourses of Displacement.* Durham, N.C.: Duke University Press, 1996.

Kaplan, Robert D. *Balkan Ghosts: A Journey through History.* New York: St. Martin's Press, 1993.

———. "The Coming Anarchy: How Scarcity, Crime, Overpopulation, Tribalism, and Disease Are Rapidly Destroying the Social Fabric of Our Planet." *Atlantic Monthly,* February 1994, 44–76.

———. *The Ends of the Earth: A Journey at the Dawn of the 20th Century.* New York: Random House, 1996.

Keesing, Roger M. "Exotic Readings of Cultural Texts." *Current Anthropology* 30, no. 4 (1989): 459–79.

Kincaid, Jamaica. *A Small Place.* New York: New American Library, 1988.

Kinglake, Alexander. *Eothen.* 1844. Evanston, Ill.: Marlboro Press, 1996.

Knight, Alanna. *Robert Louis Stevenson in the South Seas.* New York: Paragon House, 1987.

Korn, Eric. "Shelf-Travelling." *Times Literary Supplement,* July 26, 1996, 36.

Kowalewski, Michael, ed. *Temperamental Journeys: Essays on the Modern Literature of Travel.* Athens: University of Georgia Press, 1991.

Krakauer, Jon. *Into Thin Air: A Personal Account of the Mount Everest Disaster.* New York: Villard, 1997.

Kröller, Eva Marie. "First Impressions: Rhetorical Strategies in Travel Writing by Victorian Women." *Ariel* 21, no. 4 (1990): 87–99.

Krotz, Larry. *Tourists: How Our Fastest Growing Industry Is Changing the World.* London: Faber and Faber, 1996.

Lampedusa, Giuseppe. *The Leopard.* 1957. Trans. Archibald Colquhoun. New York: Knopf, 1991.

Lawrence, Karen. *Penelope Voyages: Women and Travel in the British Literary Tradition.* Ithaca, N.Y.: Cornell University Press, 1994.

Leed, Eric. *The Mind of the Traveler: From Gilgamesh to Global Tourism.* New York: Basic Books, 1991.

Leer, Martin. "From Linear to Areal: Suggestions toward a Comparative Literary Geography of Canada and Australia." *Kunapipi* 12, no. 3 (1990): 75–85.

Lehman, Jean-Pierre. "Images of the Orient." *Madam Butterfly: Opera Guide No. 26.* London: John Calder, 1984.

Lévi-Strauss, Claude. *Tristes Tropiques.* Trans. John and Doreen Weightman. New York: Atheneum, 1984.

Lewis, James R., and Gordon Melton, eds. *Perspectives on the New Age.* Albany: State University of New York Press, 1992.

Lionnet, Françoise. *Postcolonial Representations: Women, Literature, Identity.* Ithaca, N.Y.: Cornell University Press, 1996.

Lopez, Barry. *Arctic Dreams: Imagination and Desire in a Northern Landscape.* London: Pan, 1986.

Loti, Pierre. *Madame Chrysanthemum.* Intro. Kaori O'Connor. Trans. Laura Ensor. London: KPI, 1985.

Lowe, Lisa. *Critical Terrains: French and British Orientalisms.* Ithaca, N.Y.: Cornell University Press, 1991.

Lowenthal, David, and Martyn Bowden, eds. *Geographies of the Mind: Essays in Historical Geosophy.* New York: Oxford University Press, 1976.

Lutz, Catherine A., and Jane L. Collins. *Reading National Geographic.* Chicago: University of Chicago Press, 1993.

MacCannell, Dean. *Empty Meeting Grounds: The Tourist Papers.* New York: Routledge, 1992.

———. *The Tourist: A New Theory of the Leisure Class.* 1976. 2d ed. New York: Schocken, 1989.

MacDonald, Dwight. "Parajournalism, or Tom Wolfe and His Magic Writing Machine." *The Reporter as Artist,* ed. Ronald Weber. New York: Hastings House, 1974. 223–33.

Malinowski, Bronislaw. *A Diary in the Strict Sense of the Term.* 1967. New York: Harcourt, Brace and World, 1976.

———. *The Sexual Life of Savages in North-Western Melanesia.* 1929. Boston: Beacon Press, 1987.

Malraux, André. *The Voices of Silence.* 1951. Trans. S. Gilbert. New York: Doubleday, 1953.

Mann, Thomas. *Death in Venice and Other Stories.* 1912. New York: Knopf, 1991.

Mason, Philip. *The English Gentleman: The Rise and Fall of an Ideal.* London: Andre Deutsch, 1982.

Matthiessen, Peter. *The Cloud Forest: A Chronicle of the South American Wilderness.* New York: Viking, 1961; New York: Penguin, 1987.

———. *The Snow Leopard.* New York: Penguin, 1987.

Mayle, Peter. *Acquired Tastes.* New York: Bantam, 1993.

———. *Toujours Provence.* New York: Vintage, 1991.

———. *A Year in Provence.* New York: Vintage, 1989.

McClintock, Anne. "The Angel of Progress: Pitfalls of the Term 'Post-Colonialism.' " *Social Text* 31, no. 2 (1992): 84–98.

McGrath, Melanie. *Motel Nirvana: Dreaming of the New Age in the American Desert.* New York: Picador, 1995.

McHale, Brian. *Postmodernist Fiction.* New York: Methuen, 1987.

McLuhan, Marshall. *Understanding Media.* New York: New American Library, 1964.

Mead, Margaret. *Coming of Age in Samoa.* 1928. New York: Quill and Morrow, 1961.

Mehta, Gita. *Karma Cola: Marketing the Mystic East.* New York: Simon and Schuster, 1979.

Melchett, Sonia. *Passionate Quests: Five Modern Women Travellers.* London: Faber and Faber, 1991.

Melville, Herman. *Typee.* 1846. New York: Oxford University Press, 1996.

Memmi, Albert. *The Colonizer and the Colonized.* Trans. Howard Greenfeld. New York: Orion Press, 1965.

Middleton, Nick. *The Last Disco in Outer Mongolia.* London: Sinclair-Stevenson, 1992.

Millman, Lawrence. *Last Places: A Journey in the North.* Boston: Houghton Mifflin, 1990.

Mills, Sara. *Discourses of Difference: An Analysis of Women's Travel Writing and Colonialism.* London: Routledge, 1991.

Miyoshi, Masao. *Off Center: Power and Culture Relations between Japan and the United States.* Cambridge, Mass.: Harvard University Press, 1991.

Moorhead, Alan. *The Fatal Impact: An Account of the Invasion of the South Pacific, 1767–1840.* New York: Harper and Row, 1966.

Morgan, Marlo. *Mutant Message Down Under.* 1991. New York: HarperCollins, 1994.

Morley, John David. *Pictures from the Water Trade: Adventures of a Westerner in Japan.* Boston: Atlantic Monthly Press, 1985.

Morris, James. *Farewell the Trumpets.* London: Faber and Faber, 1978.

———. *Heaven's Command: An Imperial Progress.* 1973. New York: Harcourt Brace Jovanovich, 1974.

———. *Pax Britannica: The Climax of an Empire.* New York: Harcourt Brace and World, 1968.

Morris, Jan. *Conundrum.* New York: Harcourt Brace Jovanovich, 1974.

———. *Destinations: Essays from Rolling Stone.* New York: Oxford University Press, 1980.

————. *Last Letters from Hav.* New York: Random House, 1985.

Morris, Mary. *Nothing to Declare: Memoirs of a Woman Traveling Alone.* 1988. New York: Penguin, 1989.

————, ed. *Maiden Voyages: Writings of Women Travelers.* New York: Vintage, 1993.

Moses, Michael Valdez. *The Novel and the Globalization of Culture.* New York: Oxford University Press, 1996.

Moss, Robin. *Enduring Dreams: An Exploration of Arctic Landscape.* Concord, Ontario: Anansi Press, 1994.

Mrabet, Mohamed. *Chocolate Creams and Dollars.* Trans. Paul Bowles. New York: Inanout Press, 1992.

————. *Look and Move On.* Trans. Paul Bowles. London: Owen, 1989.

————. *Love with a Few Hairs.* Trans. Paul Bowles. New York: Grove Press, 1967.

Murphy, Dervla. *Full Tilt: Ireland to India with a Bicycle.* 1965. Woodstock, New York: Overlook Press, 1986.

Naipaul, V. S. *An Area of Darkness.* New York: Viking, 1964.

————. *A Bend in the River.* New York: Knopf, 1979.

————. "Conrad's Darkness." *The Return of Eva Peron.* New York: Knopf, 1980. 199–218.

————. *The Enigma of Arrival.* 1987. New York: Knopf, 1991.

————. *India: A Million Mutinies Now.* London: Heinemann, 1990.

————. *India: A Wounded Civilization.* 1976. New York: Knopf, 1977.

————. *The Middle Passage.* London: André Deutsch, 1962.

————. *The Return of Eva Peron.* New York: Knopf, 1980.

Newby, Eric. *The Big Red Train Ride.* London: Penguin, 1978.

————. *A Short Walk in the Hindu Kush.* London: Penguin, 1958.

————. *A Traveller's Life.* London: Pan, 1982.

Nixon, Rob. *London Calling: V. S. Naipaul, Postcolonial Mandarin.* Oxford: Oxford University Press, 1992.

————. "Preparations for Travel: The Naipaul Brothers' Conradian Atavism." *Research in African Literatures* 22 (1991): 177–90.

Obeyesekere, Gananath. *The Apotheosis of Captain Cook: European Mythmaking in the Pacific.* Princeton, N.J.: Princeton University Press, 1992.

O'Hanlon, Redmond. *Congo Journey.* London: Hamish Hamilton, 1996.

————. *Into the Heart of Borneo.* 1984. New York: Vintage, 1987.

————. *In Trouble Again.* New York: Random House, 1988.

————. *Joseph Conrad and Charles Darwin: The Influence of Scientific Thought on Conrad's Fiction.* Edinburgh: Salamander Press, 1984.

Pearson, Bill. *Rifled Sanctuaries: Some Views of the Pacific Islands in Western Literature to 1900.* Oxford: Oxford University Press, 1984.

Pearson, Ian. "Around the World in 6,000 Pages: A Guide to the Ultimate in Armchair Journeys." *Toronto Globe and Mail Destinations,* November 1992, 15–24.

Phillips, Caryl. *The European Tribe.* London: Faber, 1987.

Pickles, John. *Phenomenology, Science and Geography.* Cambridge: Cambridge University Press, 1985.

Porter, Dennis. *Haunted Journeys: Desire and Transgression in European Travel Writing.* Princeton, N.J.: Princeton University Press, 1991.

Pratt, Mary Louise. "Fieldwork in Common Places." *Writing Culture: The Poetics and Politics of Ethnography,* ed. James Clifford and George Marcus. Berkeley and Los Angeles: University of California Press, 1986. 27–50.

———. *Imperial Eyes: Travel Writing and Transculturation.* New York: Routledge, 1992.

Quammen, David. *The Song of the Dodo: Island Biogeography in an Age of Extinctions.* New York: Scribner, 1996.

Quinby, Lee. "The Subject of Memoirs: *The Woman Warrior*'s Technology of Ideographic Selfhood." *De/Colonizing the Subject: The Politics of Gender in Women's Autobiography,* ed. Sidonie Smith and Julia Watson. Minneapolis: University of Minnesota Press, 1992. 297–320.

Raban, Jonathan. *Coasting.* London: Collins Harvill, 1986.

———. *Hunting Mister Heartbreak: A Discovery of America.* London: Collins Harvill, 1990.

Rabkin, Eric, Martin Greenberg, and Joseph Olander, eds. *The End of the World.* Carbondale: Southern Illinois University Press, 1983.

Raby, Peter. *Bright Paradise: Victorian Scientific Travellers.* London: Pimlico, 1996.

Radway, Janice. *Reading the Romance: Women, Patriarchy, and Popular Literature.* Chapel Hill: University of North Carolina Press, 1991.

Raven, Simon. *The English Gentleman: An Essay in Attitudes.* London: Anthony Blond, 1961.

Rennie, Neil. *Far-Fetched Facts: The Literature of Travel and the Idea of the South Pacific.* Oxford: Oxford University Press, 1995.

Rhodes, Ron. *The New Age Movement.* Grand Rapids, Mich.: Zondervan, 1995.

Robb, Peter. *Midnight in Sicily.* Point Potts, New South Wales: Duncan and Snellgrove, 1996.

Robertson, George, Melinda Mash, Lisa Tickner, Jon Bird, Barry Curtis, and Tim Putnam, eds. *Travellers' Tales: Narratives of Home and Displacement.* London: Routledge, 1994.

Rosaldo, Renato. *Culture and Truth: The Remaking of Social Analysis.* 1989. London: Routledge, 1993.

Rose, Gillian. *Feminism and Geography: The Limits of Geographical Knowledge.* Minneapolis: University of Minnesota Press, 1993.

Rouse, Roger. "Mexican Migration and the Social Space of Postmodernism." *Diaspora* 1, no. 1 (1991): 8–23.

Rousseau, G. S., and Roy Porter, eds. *Exoticism in the Enlightenment.* Manchester: Manchester University Press, 1990.

Rushdie, Salman. *Imaginary Homelands: Essays, 1981–1991.* London: Granta Books, 1991.

———. *The Jaguar Smile: A Nicaraguan Journey.* 1987. New York: Penguin, 1988.

———. *The Satanic Verses.* London: Viking, 1988.

Sahlins, Marshall. *How "Natives" Think: About Captain Cook, for Example.* Chicago: University of Chicago Press, 1995.

Said, Edward. *Orientalism.* New York: Vintage, 1978.

———. "Traveling Theory." *The World, the Text, and the Critic.* Cambridge, Mass.: Harvard University Press, 1983. 226–47.

Salzman, Mark. *Iron & Silk.* New York: Random House, 1986.

Sansom, Ian. "Travel's Essential Futility." *Guardian Weekly,* June 16, 1996, 28.

Sauerberg, Lars Ole. *Fact into Fiction: Documentary Realism and the Contemporary Novel.* London: Macmillan, 1991.

Schneebaum, Tobias. *Where the Spirits Dwell: An Odyssey into the New Guinea Jungle.* New York: Grove Press, 1988.

Segalen, Victor. *Essai sur l'exotisme: une esthétique du divers.* Paris: Fata Morgana, 1986.

Serres, Michel. *Hermes: Literature, Science, Philosophy.* Trans. Josué Harari, David Bell, Susan Willey, Suzanne Guerlac, Marilyn Sides, Mark Anderson, and Lawrence Schehr. Ed. Josué Harari and David F. Bell. Baltimore: Johns Hopkins University Press, 1982.

Seth, Vikram. *From Heaven Lake.* 1983. New York: Vintage, 1987.

Shohat, Ella. "Notes on the 'Post-Colonial.'" *Social Text* 31, no. 2 (1992): 99–113.

Shoumatoff, Alex. *African Madness.* New York: Knopf, 1988.

Showalter, Elaine. *A Literature of Their Own: British Women Novelists from Brontë to Lessing.* Princeton, N.J.: Princeton University Press, 1977.

Shukman, Henry. *Savage Pilgrims: On the Road to Santa Fe.* London: Harper-Collins, 1996.

Slater, Candace. *Dance of the Dolphin: Transformation and Disenchantment in the Amazonian Imagination.* Chicago: University of Chicago Press, 1994.

Smith, Adam. *An Inquiry into the Nature and Causes of the Wealth of Nations.* Ed. Edwin Cannan. Chicago: University of Chicago Press, 1976.

Smith, Bernard. *European Vision and the South Pacific.* New Haven, Conn.: Yale University Press, 1985.

Smith, Sidonie, and Julia Watson, eds. *De/Colonizing the Subject: The Politics of Gender in Women's Autobiography.* Minneapolis: University of Minnesota Press, 1992.

Smith, Valene, ed. *Hosts and Guests: The Anthropology of Tourism.* Philadelphia: University of Pennsylvania Press, 1977.

Sontag, Susan. "Notes on Camp." *A Susan Sontag Reader.* New York: Farrar, Straws, Giroux, 1982. 105–20.

Spender, Stephen. *The Temple.* London: Faber and Faber, 1988.

Spivak, Gayatri Chakravorty. *In Other Worlds: Essays in Cultural Politics.* New York: Methuen, 1987.

Spufford, Francis. *I May Be Some Time: Ice and the English Imagination.* London: Faber and Faber, 1996.

Spurr, David. *The Rhetoric of Empire: Colonial Discourse in Journalism, Travel Writing, and Imperial Administration.* Durham, N.C.: Duke University Press, 1993.

Stevenson, Robert Louis. "The Beach of Falesá." *Dr Jekyll and Mr Hyde and Other Stories.* London: Penguin, 1979. 99–170.

———. *Travels with a Donkey.* 1879. New York: Limited Editions, 1957.

Sugnet, Charles. "Vile Bodies, Vile Places: Traveling with *Granta.*" *Transition* 51 (1991): 70–85.

Suleri, Sara. *Meatless Days.* Chicago: University of Chicago Press, 1989.

———. *The Rhetoric of English India.* Chicago: University of Chicago Press, 1992.

Swift, Jonathan. *Gulliver's Travels.* 1726. New York: Signet, 1960.

Taussig, Michael. *Shamanism, Colonialism, and the Wild Man.* Chicago: University of Chicago Press, 1987.

Theroux, Paul. *The Happy Isles of Oceania: Paddling the Pacific.* New York: G. P. Putnam's Sons, 1992.

———. *The Kingdom by the Sea: A Journey around Great Britain.* New York: Washington Square Press, 1983.

———. *My Other Life: A Novel.* London: Hamish Hamilton, 1996.

———. *The Old Patagonian Express: By Train through the Americas.* Boston: Houghton Mifflin, 1979.

———. *The Pillars of Hercules: A Grand Tour of the Mediterranean.* New York: G. P. Putnam's Sons, 1995.

Thesiger, Wilfred. *Arabian Sands.* New York: Dutton, 1959.

———. *My Kenya Days.* London: HarperCollins, 1994.

Tisdale, Sallie. "Never Let the Locals See Your Map: Why Most Travel Writers Should Stay Home." *Harper's,* September 1995, 66–74.

———. *Talk Dirty to Me: An Intimate Philosophy of Sex.* New York: Doubleday, 1994.

Todorov, Tzvetan. *On Human Diversity: Nationalism, Racism, and Exoticism in French Thought.* Trans. Catherine Porter. Cambridge, Mass.: Harvard University Press, 1993.

Torgovnick, Marianna. *Gone Primitive: Savage Intellects, Modern Lives.* Chicago: University of Chicago Press, 1990.

Trinh T. Minh-ha. *Woman, Native, Other: Writing Feminism and Postcoloniality.* Bloomington: Indiana University Press, 1989.

Tuan Yi-Fu. "Geopiety: A Theme in Man's Attachment to Nature and Place." *Geographies of the Mind,* ed. David Lowenthal and Martyn Bowden. New York: Oxford University Press, 1976. 11–39.

———. *Topophilia: A Study of Environmental Perception, Attitudes, and Values.* Englewood Cliffs, N.J.: Prentice-Hall, 1974.

Twain, Mark. *The Innocents Abroad.* 1869. Oxford: Oxford University Press, 1996.

Tylor, Edward. *Primitive Culture.* 1871. New York: Harper, 1958.

Van den Abbeele, Georges. "Sightseers: The Tourist as Theorist." *Diacritics* 10 (winter 1980): 2–14.

———. *Travel as Metaphor: From Montaigne to Rousseau.* Minneapolis: University of Minnesota Press, 1992.

Van der Post, Laurens. *The Lost World of the Kalahari.* New York: Morrow, 1958.

Varawa, Joana McIntyre. *Changes in Latitude: An Uncommon Anthropology.* New York: Harper and Row, 1989.

Veblen, Thorstein. *The Theory of the Leisure Class: An Economic Study of Institutions.* 1899. New York: New American Library, 1953.

Venuti, Lawrence, ed. *Rethinking Translation: Discourse, Subjectivity, Ideology.* New York: Routledge, 1992.

Virilio, Paul. *Speed and Politics: An Essay on Dromology.* Trans. Mark Polizzotti. New York: Columbia University Press, 1986.

Viviano, Frank. *Dispatches from the Pacific Century.* Reading, Mass.: Addison-Wesley, 1993.

Walcott, Derek. "The Caribbean: Culture or Mimicry?" *Journal of Interamerican Studies and World Affairs* 16 (1974): 3–13.

Warley, Linda. "Assembling Ingredients: Subjectivity in *Meatless Days.*" *Auto/Biography* 7, no. 1 (1992): 107–23.

Watt, Ian. *The Rise of the Novel.* 1957. New York: Oxford University Press, 1971.

Waugh, Evelyn. *Brideshead Revisited.* 1946. London: Everyman's Library, 1993.

———. Preface to *A Short Walk in the Hindu Kush,* by Eric Newby. London: Penguin, 1958.

———. *When the Going Was Good.* London: Duckworth, 1946.

Weber, Ronald, ed. *The Reporter as Artist: A Look at the New Journalism Controversy.* New York: Hastings House, 1974.

Welch, Denton. *Maiden Voyage.* London: Routledge and Kegan Paul, 1943.

Wendt, Albert. *Flying-Fox in a Freedom Tree.* Auckland, New Zealand: Longman, 1974.

———. "Toward a New Oceania." *Writers in East-West Encounter,* ed. Guy Amirthanayagam. London: Macmillan, 1982. 202–15.

Wheeler, Sara. *Terra Incognita: Travels in Antarctica.* London: Jonathan Cape, 1996.

Wheeler, Valerie. "Travelers' Tales: Observations on the Travel Book and Ethnography." *Anthropological Quarterly* 59, no. 2 (1986): 52–63.

White, Edmund. *States of Desire: Travels in Gay America.* New York: E. P. Dutton, 1980.

White, Hayden. "Fictions of Factual Representation." *The Literature of Fact,* ed. Angus Fletcher. New York: Columbia University Press, 1976. 21–44.

White, Patrick. *Flaws in the Glass.* London: Jonathan Cape, 1981.

Wiebe, Rudy. *Playing Dead: A Contemplation Concerning the Arctic.* Edmonton: NeWest, 1989.

Wilde, Oscar. "The Decay of Lying." *Complete Works.* London: Collins, 1948. 970–92.

Wills, David. *Prosthesis.* Stanford, Calif.: Stanford University Press, 1995.

Wilson, Alexander. *The Culture of Nature: North American Landscape from Disney to the Exxon Valdez.* 1991. Cambridge, Mass.: Blackwell, 1992.

Winchester, Simon. *Outposts.* London: Hodder and Stoughton, 1985.

———. *Pacific Rising.* London: Hutchinson, 1991.

Woodcock, George. *A South Sea Journey.* London: Faber, 1976.

Wolff, Janet. "On the Road Again: Metaphors of Travel in Cultural Criticism." *Cultural Studies* 7, no. 2 (1993): 224–39.

Wright, Ronald. *On Fiji Islands.* New York: Viking, 1986.

———. *Time among the Maya: Travels in Belize, Guatemala, and Mexico.* New York: Weidenfeld and Nicolson, 1989.

Wurlitzer, Rudolph. *Hard Travel to Sacred Places.* Boston: Shambala, 1994.

Young, Gavin. *In Search of Conrad.* 1991. London: Penguin, 1992.

Youngs, Tim. *Travellers in Africa: British Travelogues, 1850–1900.* Manchester: Manchester University Press, 1994.

INDEX

Calvino, Italo, 158, 161, 163, 166, 169; *Invisible Cities,* 158–60, 177
camp, 34–35, 39, 46, 153
Campbell, Alan, 78
Campbell, Mary, 15
Carless, Hugh, 32–35, 46–47
Carter, Paul, 170
Casablanca, 121
Castronovo, David, 28, 33
Caulfield, Annie, 208
Cavafy, C. P., 211
Chamberlain, Richard, 85
Chambers, Iain, 166–67, 169
Chatwin, Bruce, viii, 6, 9, 10, 13, 17–18, 21, 23, 35–40, 42, 44, 121, 167–70, 177, 200, 205, 211; *The Songlines,* 39, 123, 169
China, 22, 56–57, 59, 62
Choukri, Mohammed, 143
class, x, 4, 43, 49–50, 132, 134, 135, 136, 139, 154
Clifford, James, ix, 2, 111, 181
Cocker, Mark, 1, 4
colonialism, 73–74, 76, 92, 103–4, 130–31, 141, 164; anticolonialism, 114, 115; neo-colonialism, 49, 53, 73, 179; and sexuality, 146, 148–49. *See also* postcolonialism
commodification, 29, 48, 126, 164, 185, 204, 209; cultural, 3, 15–16, 62–64, 128, 143, 178–80, 191, 195, 217; spiritual, 179, 192; of travel writing, 113, 122–24, 132, 187–89, 197–99, 202, 203
Condé Nast Traveler, 1, 206
Condon, Sean, 208–9
Congo. *See* Democratic Republic of Congo
Conrad, Joseph, 30, 69–73, 75, 76, 175, 211
Constantinople. *See* Istanbul
consumption, 40–42, 48, 128, 179–80, 187, 193, 199; conspicuous, 40, 166; cultural, 62, 65; over-, 155
Cook, Captain James, 91, 92, 93, 97
Cortazzi, Hugh, 84
counterculture, 142, 165, 178, 189
counterdiscourse, 41, 45, 54, 64–65, 131; historical, 57; illusionary, 96;

counter-Orientalist, 59, 65; counter-travel, 50, 198–99
counternarrative. *See* counterdiscourse
cross-dressing, 20, 117–18, 135, 136

dandyism, 36–40
Dante, Alighieri, 173, 174
Davidson, Basil, 69–70
Davidson, Robyn, 20, 128, 132, 201; *Tracks,* 121–23
de Chirico, Giorgio, 44
deferral, 100, 105
de Lauretis, Teresa, 112
Democratic Republic of Congo (Congo, Zaire), 69–76
Derrida, Jacques, 89, 170
Desai, Anita, 20
Descola, Philippe, 78
Dessaix, Robert: *Night Letters,* 170–74
destination, 158, 159
displacement, viii, ix, 2, 10, 20, 23, 43, 51, 55, 60, 131; originary, 42
Dodwell,Christina, 132
During, Simon, 64
Durrell, Lawrence, 153

Eberhardt, Isabelle, 20, 118
Eco, Umberto, 24, 160–62, 164
ecological effects of travel (eco-tourism), xii, 76, 78, 101, 105–6, 178–80, 183–89, 191, 193–95, 198
Egypt, 56–60
emancipation. *See* freedom
emigration. *See* migration
Empson, William, 40
England, 43, 44
eroticism, 68, 92, 116–17, 125, 127; of culture, 81, 82, 86–87, 89, 148, 153; homoeroticism, 119, 134–35, 153; textual, 84, 136
essentialism, 38, 70, 75, 113, 149, 154, 161, 163, 167, 192–93, 199; cultural, 72–73, 90, 120, 125
ethnocentrism, viii, 5, 11, 20–21, 33, 43, 51, 88, 109, 129–30, 161, 166, 168, 178, 198
ethnography, 57, 86, 88, 91–92, 111, 127, 169, 185; salvage, 179, 180–81; travel

writing as, 18, 68, 94–95, 97–98, 149–51; vs. travel writing, 11–13, 33, 68

Eurocentrism. *See* ethnocentrism

Europe, 49, 161–63

Evans, Julian, 93, 94–95, 96, 99

exhaustion, 202–6, 213, 215

exoticism, 2, 18–19, 48, 64, 86, 90, 125, 130–32, 138, 146, 187, 200; of cultures, 61, 92; of memory, 94–95, 97; of "Other," viii, 5, 65, 182; of places, 38, 99, 127, 128, 166, 198, 204; sexual, 133

farce, 29–31

feminization, 68, 81–85, 89–90, 112, 124, 133, 138, 141, 144

feminism, xii, 113–14, 122, 123, 132; and geography, 112, 117

Fenton, James, 30, 79

Fleming, Peter, 27, 68; *Brazilian Adventure,* 77–78

Forster, E. M., 138; *A Passage to India,* 136

Foucault, Michel, 173

Franklin, John, 101–4

Fraser, Keath, 23–24

freedom, ix, xiii, 64, 124, 128, 140, 142, 151, 169; sexual, 87, 138, 148, 152–53, 198; textual, 176, 214; of travel, 4, 20–21, 46, 55, 59, 116–17, 133–34, 154, 172; of women, 93, 94, 113, 114, 121, 132

Freud, Sigmund, 138, 139

Frommer, Arthur, 207

Frow, John, 126

Furon, Raymond, 32

Fussell, Paul, vii, 3, 9–10, 12, 14, 27, 48, 109, 111, 197, 203, 205

Gagné, Raymond, 103

Galoa, 124–25

Garber, Marjorie, 118

Gauguin, Paul, 96

gay liberation, 151–53

gay travel, 133–55, 198

gender, x, xii, 4, 37, 39, 47, 50, 88, 110–55, 198

gentlemanliness, xi, 6–7, 22–23, 25, 28–37, 39–47; vs. dandyism, 36–37

Ghosh, Amitav, 22, 65; *In an Antique Land,* 56–60

Gide, André, 69–70

Gilbert Islands, 97

globalization, 2, 8, 64, 97, 161, 178–79, 185, 192, 198, 205, 209, 213; of culture, 22, 62, 164–66, 199, 217

global village, 168, 198

Granta, 1, 5, 206

Greek Islands, 153–54

Green, Martin, 4

Green, Michelle, 143

Greenblatt, Stephen, 15–16

Greene, Graham, 27, 175, 217

Gregory, Derek, 91–92

Grewal, Inderpal, 4, 47, 131

Grizzuti Harrison, Barbara, 132

Guardian Weekly, 200–202

guidebook, 9, 151, 197, 200, 208

Gunther, John, 209–10, 211, 213

Habegger, Larry, 207

Hall, Radclyffe, 138

Hamburg (Germany), 141

Haynes, Jim, 207

Hearst, William Randolph, 161

Herdt, Gilbert, 149, 150

history, 56–60, 70, 74, 102, 157–58, 160, 162, 183, 198, 199, 212; alternative, 129–31; cultural, x, 161, 169, 184; of exploration/travel, 100, 111, 170, 204; imperialist, 46; mythicized, 76, 183

Hobson, Sarah, 118

Homer: *Odyssey,* 112

Hornby, John, 107

Horwell, Veronica, 168–69, 202

Hyland, Noelle, 71

Hyland, Paul, 70, 76; *The Black Heart,* 69–73

hyperreality, 160–62, 177, 198

Ignatieff, Michael, 14

imperialism, ix, x, xi, xii, xiii, 28, 43–48, 57–58, 67, 69, 75, 114, 119–20, 132, 138, 164, 184, 194–95, 199; connection to travel writing, 15–16;

Morley, John David, 18, 21, 82, 89; *Pictures from the Water Trade,* 86–88
Morocco, 142–49
Morris, Jan (James), viii, 6, 20, 118–21; *Conundrum,* 120–21
Morris, Mary, 20, 113, 131; *Nothing to Declare,* 114–18
Moss, John: *Enduring Dreams,* 100–110
Mrabet, Mohammed, 143; *Look and Move On,* 144–46
Murphy, Dervla, 17, 20, 128, 132, 205; *Full Tilt,* 114–18
Mururoa, 96
Myanmar, 200–201
myths, 23, 45, 74, 81, 91, 101, 137, 142, 160, 163, 164, 185, 188, 211; cultural, viii, x, xi, 3, 5–7, 8, 71–72, 123, 144, 184; of gender, 4, 93, 111, 122–24, 127–28; imperialist, 25, 45, 61, 121; New Age, 179, 191; Orientalist, 34; personal, 33, 169; of place, xii, xiii, 3, 65, 67–69; primal, 186; romantic, 181, 194; of travel, 25, 34, 94, 190, 201, 209

Nagasaki, 81–82
Naipaul, V. S., viii, 6, 10, 11, 13, 18–19, 42–45, 51, 55, 57, 70, 72, 73–74, 75, 76, 213; *The Enigma of Arrival,* 44–45; *The Return of Eva Peron,* 73–74
National Geographic, 1, 18, 122–23
Neruda, Pablo, 101
New Age travel, xii, 178–95
Newby, Eric, 6, 13, 15, 18, 23, 27–29, 31–36, 37, 39, 41, 42, 43, 45, 46, 52, 119, 203, 205; *A Short Walk in the Hindu Kush,* 32–35, 46–47, 117; *A Traveller's Life,* 34
Nicaragua, 53–55
Nixon, Rob, 11, 30, 44, 73
nomadism, 38, 167–70, 172, 177–78, 198, 212
Northwest Passage, 101–2
nostalgia, xi, xii, 5, 8, 20, 24–25, 28–29, 40, 45–46, 52, 59, 84, 86, 97, 99, 114, 120, 129–30, 166, 191, 197, 203–4; cultural, 44–45, 48, 131, 213; imperialist,

15, 29, 33–34, 36, 42–43, 199; instant, 161–62, 164; primitivist, 180, 181
Nuristan, 33–35

Occident, 90
O'Hanlon, Redmond, 6, 13, 17–18, 23, 29, 30–32, 34, 35, 36, 37, 39, 42, 43, 45, 46, 52, 68, 77, 78–81, 119, 187, 205, 206, 208; *In Trouble Again,* 79–80
O'Reilly, James, 207
Orient, 81–90
Orientalism, 58–59, 83–86, 90
origins, 13, 44; cultural, xi, xii, 22, 43; of identity, 43

Pakistan, 129–30
Papua New Guinea, 149–51
parody, 33, 38, 77–78, 125, 166, 197, 198
Pearson, Ian, 205
Persia. *See* Iran
Peru, 180, 182
Phillips, Caryl, 21, 53, 54, 55, 65; *The European Tribe,* 48–52
Picador Travel Classics series, 205–6
Porter, Dennis, viii, 2, 5, 42, 89–90, 111
Porter, Roy, 19
postcolonialism, x, xii, 4–5, 22, 43–45, 47–48, 52, 63–65, 73, 131, 164–65, 170, 198
postcoloniality, xi, 48, 64, 129, 202
postmodernism, x, xii, 4, 15, 67–68, 146, 154–55, 157–95, 198, 202, 216
Pratt, Mary Louise, viii, ix, 2, 4, 5, 15, 47, 61, 183–84, 185, 194
Provence, 40–42
Puccini, Giacomo, 81–82

Quammen, David, 195; *The Song of the Dodo: Island Biogeography in an Age of Extinction,* 179, 184–85, 187–89
quest, 17, 83, 94, 95, 114, 128, 172, 199, 204, 216; sexual, 86–87, 135, 136, 145, 150; spiritual, 102, 179, 182, 186, 191–92
Quimby, Lee, 14

Raban, Jonathan, 6, 13, 176–77, 200, 205, 216–17

race (racism), 4, 5, 48–51, 132, 135, 179

Raven, Simon, 29

reminiscence. *See* nostalgia

representation, 58, 63–64, 70, 120, 128, 159, 167; and culture, viii, 64, 81, 164; imperialist, 43; of subject, 134; virtual, 166

Robb, Peter: *Midnight in Sicily,* 213–16

Roberts, Martin, 2, 64

Rogers, Michael, 142

Rosaldo, Renato, 15, 29

Rose, Gillian, 112

Rouse, Roger, 22

Rousseau, G. S., 19

Rushdie, Salman, 62, 65; *The Jaguar's Smile,* 53–55

Sahlins, Marshall, 92

Said, Edward, ix, 2, 58, 111, 119

Samoa, 96

Sansom, Ian, 202

Sarawak, 30–31

Schneebaum, Tobias, 152; *Where the Spirits Dwell,* 149–51

Sciascia, 215–16

Segalen, Victor, 96

self. *See* subject

Sennett, Richard, 152

Serres, Michel, 112

Seth, Vikram, 22, 65, 173; *From Heaven Lake,* 56–57, 59–60

sexuality, 81, 86–87, 89, 131, 134–55, 173–74; ambiguous, 117–19, 121; bisexuality, 142, 174; heterosexuality, xii, 21, 133–34, 142, 144, 198; homosexuality, xii, 121, 133–55; queer, 21, 142; and voyeurism, 18

Shoumatoff, Alex, 21, 70; *African Madness,* 75–76

Sicily, 213–16

simulacra, 45, 128, 160, 162

Smolan, Richard, 122

Solomon Islands, 97

Sontag, Susan, 34–35, 172

South Seas, 91–99

Spender, Stephen: *The Temple,* 138–42

Spurr, David, viii, 4, 47

Stanley, Henry Morton, 71, 72, 74

Stark, Freya, 132

St. Aubin de Teran, Lisa, 113

Stefansson, Vihjalmur, 103

Sterne, Laurence, 175

Stevenson, Robert Louis, 68, 93, 94–95, 96, 98–99, 127, 205

subject (subjectivity), 11, 14–16, 97, 105, 148, 150, 184–85; cultural, 4; and gender, 20, 110, 132, 151, 167; position, 43, 92; queer, 142, 151–53; stability of, 157–59, 167, 174–77, 192, 210; traveling, 151, 167, 202, 210

Sugnet, Charles, 4–5, 46

Suleri, Sara, 20, 43; *Meatless Days,* 128–32

Swift, Johnathan, vii

Taaffe, Philip, 143

Tahiti, 96

Tangier, 42–149

Tehran, 46–47

Theroux, Paul, viii, 1, 6, 13, 23, 50, 91, 92, 93, 94, 97, 98, 99, 121, 202, 205, 206, 209–11, 213; *My Other Life,* 175–77

Thesiger, Wilfred, 6, 28, 29, 205

Tibet, 22, 59, 62

Time, 165

Tisdale, Sallie, 203–5, 215, 216

Todorov, Tzvetan, 19

Tokyo, 88

Torres Strait Islands, 126

tourism, viii, xiii, 8, 42, 49, 50, 62–63, 99, 116, 126, 131, 164, 172, 179, 197, 205; post-tourism, 24, 202, 208; sexual tourist, 148; vs. travel, viii, xi, xiii, 2–3, 8, 27–28, 31, 52, 115, 124, 153, 162, 167, 184, 194, 198, 200–201, 203–4, 206–7, 211

transculturation, xii, 61

transgression, x, xii, 4, 5, 110, 132, 137, 173; sexual, 118, 121, 133, 147, 151; travel as, 70, 134, 158

transnational space, 22, 129

travel: armchair, 202, 205; political obstacles to, 59–60; technologies of, 23–24, 103, 163–64, 197

traveling theory, ix, 198